CQ GUIDE TO

CURRENT AMERICAN GOVERNMENT

Spring 2003

CQ PRESS

A Division of Congressional Quarterly Inc.

Washington, D.C.

Congressional Quarterly Inc.

Congressional Quarterly Inc., an editorial research service and publishing company, serves clients in the fields of news, education, business and government. It combines the specific coverage of Congress, government and politics contained in the *CQ Weekly* with the more general subject range of an affiliated service, the *CQ Researcher*.

Under the CQ Press imprint, Congressional Quarterly also publishes college political science textbooks and public affairs paperbacks on developing issues and events, information directories and reference books on the federal government, national elections and politics. Titles include the *Guide to the Presidency*, the *Guide to Congress*, the *Guide to the U.S. Supreme Court*, the *Guide to U.S. Elections* and *Politics in America*. CQ's A-Z collection is a reference series that provides essential information about American government and the electoral process. The *CQ Almanac*, a compendium of legislation for one session of Congress, is published each year. *Congress and the Nation*, a record of government for a presidential term, is published every four years.

CQ publishes the *Daily Monitor*, a report on the current and future activities of congressional committees. An online information system, CQ.com on Congress, provides immediate access to CQ's databases of legislative action, votes, schedules, profiles and analyses. Visit www.cq.com for more information.

CQ Press
1255 22nd St. N.W., Suite 400
Washington, D.C. 20037
202-729-1900; toll free, 1-866-4CQ-PRESS (1-866-427-7737)

www.cqpress.com

ISBN 1-56802-730-3
ISSN 0196-612-X

Contents

Contents

Introduction

Guide to Current American Government is a collection of articles selected from the CQ Weekly, a trusted source for in-depth, nonpartisan reporting and analyses of congressional action, presidential activities, policy debates and other news and developments in Washington. The articles, selected to complement introductory American government texts with up-to-date examinations of current issues and controversies, are divided into four sections: Foundations of American Government, Political Participation, Government Institutions and Politics and Public Policy.

Foundations of American Government. This section examines issues and events that involve interpretation of the U.S. Constitution. The *Guide* explores the changing face of Congress after the Sept. 11, 2001, terrorist attacks; the war-making powers of the president versus those of Congress; the intergovernmental problems surrounding the Patriot Act, the anti-terrorism law; and the role of the military in civilian law enforcement.

Political Participation. The articles in this section examine current issues in electoral and party politics, including changes in congressional leadership and the balance of power after the 2002 midterm elections. Writers investigate how these changes will affect Congress's attention to such issues as the economy and war with Iraq.

Government Institutions. This section explores the inner workings of the major institutions of American government. Congress, the presidency and the judiciary are examined in light of recent events at home and abroad. The articles examine partisanship and cooperation in Congress, the terrorism insurance bill, the investigation of management practices at investment banks, election machinery upgrades, the proposed Department of Homeland Security, costs of war with Iraq and the judicial nomination process.

Politics and Public Policy. These articles focus on major social policy issues, specifically energy, the environment and international trade. This section also looks at what lies ahead for House and Senate committees and their role in policy development.

The *Guide to Current American Government* reprints articles largely unchanged from their original appearance in the *CQ Weekly*. The date of original publication is provided with each article to give readers a time frame for the events described. Page number references to related and background articles in the *CQ Weekly* and the *CQ Almanac* facilitate additional research. Both publications are available in many school and public libraries.

Foundations of American Government

This section covers issues that go to the heart of American democracy, including the balance of federal power and the composition of Congress. The articles focus on the political landscape of Congress and the changing use of military forces one year after the Sept. 11, 2001, terrorist attacks.

The first article discusses how the war on terrorism has affected the way Congress functions, comparing Congress's dealings in foreign policy and defense issues with its handling of domestic legislation. The year following Sept. 11 saw dramatic changes in the organization of the federal government, most noticeably the restructuring to create a Department of Homeland Security. The president received bipartisan support for his war on terrorism, and congressional leaders from both sides worked together on the homeland security bill and related issues, pushing them through a united Congress. (The bill passed despite controversy over labor rules, which nearly caused its defeat.) At the same time, however, domestic issues languished, and as the midterm elections of 2002 approached, divisiveness returned, along with a desire by both parties to control Congress.

The second article examines the roles of the president and Congress in decisions on the use of military forces. The 1973 War Powers Act dictates that, when possible, the president must consult Congress before using U.S. military forces. In the past several administrations, this controversial law was thwarted by presidents who made executive decisions on troop deployment and weapons development. As commander in chief the president has the authority to respond to imminent attacks; however, some legislators worry that President George W. Bush will decide to strike first against Iraq without consulting Congress.

The third article addresses the relationships among Congress, the Justice Department and the courts in light of the Patriot Act, the anti-terrorism law, which has been used for investigative and prosecutorial purposes. The Patriot Act was passed in 2001 with bipartisan support, but many civil libertarians from both parties questioned the law as problems arose. Although counterintelligence requires a certain level of secrecy, good governance requires cooperation. The Justice Department's actions conflicted with the courts (on nondisclosure of detainee names and closed deportation hearings) and with Congress (on oversight of the Patriot Act). Controversy also surrounded the use of the 1978 Foreign Intelligence Surveillance Act (FISA) in tandem with the Patriot Act in terrorist investigations and prosecutions. Attorney General John Ashcroft and the FISA courts argued over the use of FISA warrants in criminal investigations and over the rights of defendants. Congress may need to bridge the gap by setting standards for using FISA in terrorism investigations.

The final article explores the role of the U.S. armed forces in civilian law enforcement. When Washington, D.C.–area police investigated a series of sniper shootings in October 2002, the Defense Department's new Northern Command offered the use of reconnaissance aircraft. But did this action violate the 1878 Posse Comitatus Act, which prohibits using armed forces in domestic law enforcement? The Northern Command's purpose is to aid civilian federal agencies in dealing with terrorist incidents. Although some legal scholars considered the Northern Command's actions a violation of the act, the Pentagon insisted it had complied with the law. Some members of Congress want to revise the law to address terrorist attacks on U.S. territory.

For Congress, a New World — And Business as Usual

Lawmakers seek their way in shifting political landscape left by Sept. 11

There are moments in time so horrifying that one can almost feel history skidding to a halt, then slowly, painfully, limping in another direction. For Congress, like the rest of the country, the sight of nearly 3,000 lives being wiped out on live television one year ago this week was that unmistakable moment when nothing that came before it seemed to matter at all.

Everything will be different after this, lawmakers said, and nobody disagreed. After Sept. 11, 2001, the war on terrorism was not just the most important issue before Congress. It was the only issue. Domestic issues that had been vitally important just days before — education, tax cuts, the disappearing budget surplus, health care, energy policy — seemed irrelevant. For a while, Congress itself was in danger of being lost in the shadows, as a newly strengthened President Bush set most of the agenda for the only issue that mattered.

And the war on terrorism showed every sign of dominating the rest of the 107th Congress, diminishing every divisive domestic issue that came before it and transforming the entire political environment. Congress would treat foreign policy, defense and the nation's security differently, of course, but the fate of domestic legislation that had nothing to do with terrorism also would be changed. Ultimately, the course of the 2002 elections, and therefore the balance of power in Congress, might be altered too.

One year later, everything is not different after all. The landscape of Congress has certainly changed. But it is not the completely new landscape that everyone had expected.

Instead, Congress now faces two worlds, both battling for dominance over Washington's political future. One is the new world that was jolted into being by Sept. 11: the war on terrorism abroad, the powerful new anti-terrorism tools at home, and the biggest reorganization of government since World War II to create a new department of homeland security. The other is the old world that existed before Sept. 11 and now has returned with full force: divisive domestic issues such as health care and energy, bitter partisan brawls, and a narrowly divided House and Senate in which every move by congressional leaders is driven by the desire to win control of both chambers in the fall elections. *(2002 CQ Weekly, p. 2294)*

They are both very real, and they operate under completely different rules. One world is a product of Sept. 11; the other hardly has changed at all. At any moment, one can eclipse the other. If, for example, Congress is asked to vote in October on a resolution authorizing an invasion of Iraq, the new world could eclipse the old at a critical moment — right before a congressional election so close that control of both the Senate and the House could swing either way. *(2002 CQ Weekly, p. 2313)*

That is why the political environment for Congress in the aftermath of Sept. 11 may be unstable for years to come.

"Everyone is less secure about what the hell they're doing," said former Rep. Leon E. Panetta (1977-93), a California Democrat who served as White House chief of staff under President Bill Clinton. "They're basically playing the

CQ Weekly Sept. 7, 2002

THE YEAR AFTER 9/11

In the anguish and anger over terrorist attacks, Congress increased police powers and airline protection. Broader bills still are pending.

 SEPT. A bright day that began with the season's first crisp hints of autumn had darkened by noon into the opening of a disorienting era of anxiety and anguish. The jetliner bombings on Sept. 11 of both World Trade Center towers and the Pentagon — and the wreckage of a fourth hijacked airliner that plowed into the Pennsylvania countryside as passengers tried to reclaim it — stirred in Congress a wartime unity and resolve.

Before the end of that week, the House and Senate cleared legislation that appropriated $40 billion in emergency funds for the cleanup and the military response. The shock of the attack left Congress little appetite for disagreement on spending matters and swept members of both parties into line behind President Bush and the agenda he declared.

❝There was a strong feeling that we needed to be at this Capitol tonight.❞

Sen. Jeff Sessions, R-Ala.

LAWS ENACTED
Use of force (S J Res 23) — A joint resolution authorizing the president to use "all necessary and appropriate force" against those involved in the Sept. 11 attacks.
Airline bailout (PL 107-42) — A $15 billion package of loans and guarantees to help airlines recover.
Supplemental spending (PL 107-38) — $40 billion to help recover from and respond to the attacks.
Public safety benefits (PL 107-37) — Accelerated benefit payments for families of public safety officers killed or injured.

REUTERS PHOTO / SEAN ADAIR

politics and issues on a day-to-day basis."

So far, the politics of the new world have not decisively changed the direction of the issues and events in the old world. Domestic concerns about the economy, corporate misbehavior and health care still are as powerful as they used to be, and they still divide the public as much as they used to. If the new world had truly taken over the political landscape, Republicans would be looking forward to a sweep in the upcoming congressional elections. Instead, it is expected to be just as much of a cliffhanger as the last one.

Nobody, however, is betting any life savings that the public's priorities will not change again in the next two months — and with them, the future of Congress.

Members of Congress and visitors must negotiate a labyrinth of new security barricades and checkpoints around the Capitol, stark reminders of democracy's vulnerability to terrorism.

"We really don't have any models for this," said Michael L. Mezey, a professor of political science and dean of the College of Liberal Arts at DePaul University in Chicago. "We just don't know what's going to occur."

The Two Worlds

In the new world, Republicans and Democrats work together with unusual speed and unity to handle threats to American security. Long after the initial rush of post-Sept. 11 legislation, they are still moving quicker to establish a department of homeland security than they would have moved on any other government reorganization of a similar scale. Even the current flare-ups over civil service rules and the degree of congressional oversight have not changed that.

And for one morning in New York on Sept. 6, as lawmakers gathered to pay tribute to the victims of the attacks, their partisan differences were set aside as thoroughly as they were for those terrifying first few months. (*2002 CQ Weekly, p. 2282*)

"This was the kind of landmark event that really did change people's approaches toward their jobs," said Rep. Rob Portman, R-Ohio, a member of the select committee that drafted the House version of the homeland security bill (HR 5005). "It was a horrible tragedy that made all of us rethink how we do business."

In the old world, meanwhile, the parties are so deadlocked that they are unable to address important domestic issues such as the lack of prescription drug coverage for Medicare beneficiaries and the problems some Americans have faced under managed health care. Energy and trade bills take

---

Members of Congress joined in near-total solidarity after the attacks.

Heightened security was quickly and permanently in place across Capitol Hill.

OCT. Order had only begun returning to Capitol Hill when an aide in the Hart Senate Office Building sliced open an envelope Oct. 15 that was addressed to Majority Leader Tom Daschle, D-S.D. As she pushed the blade through, a cloud of fine white dust escaped from the envelope and bloomed over her desk. In that instant, Capitol Hill was infected with anthrax.

While biohazard teams scoured the area, all congressional offices were evacuated for at least a week. Anthrax spores were found in a House mailroom. Senators doubled up in those offices that were declared safe first, while most House members relocated to temporary space several blocks away. After the Capitol Building was found to be clear, negotiations resumed on an economic stimulus bill, an insurance industry bailout and the breadth and depth of new spending.

Innocent-looking letter contained the nation's second terror attack in two months.

LAWS ENACTED
Anti-terrorism (PL 107-56) — Broad new authority for law enforcement agencies to tap telephones, conduct searches and monitor Internet communications in pursuit of suspected terrorists. The law also includes money laundering provisions. It expires in 2005.
Help for Pakistan (PL 107-57) — To reward a key ally in the campaign against terrorism, allows President Bush to waive sanctions against Pakistan through fiscal 2003.

weeks to get through the Senate. A simple extension of unemployment benefits to laid-off workers takes months.

"I think the whole range of issues related to terrorism has been more bipartisan and consensual," House Minority Leader Richard A. Gephardt, D-Mo., said. "I don't sense more of a collaborative approach on anything else."

As Republican Sen. Orrin G. Hatch of Utah put it: "We're back to where we were."

And there is another important difference. In the new world, Bush is practically invulnerable, so much so that many Democrats waited to raise questions about his Iraq plans until prominent Republicans already had done so.

But he has turned out to be just as vulnerable on domestic issues as he was before Sept. 11. Bush was far outpaced by Congress in addressing the recent wave of corporate scandals, ultimately signing an accounting overhaul bill (PL 107-204) that was strengthened at the hands of Senate Democrats. And he has been struggling to rebuild the nation's confidence in its faltering economy. (2002 *CQ Weekly*, pp. 2115, 2301)

The new legislative agenda certainly has overshadowed the old one, consuming valuable time and distracting congressional leaders who might otherwise have gotten more involved in solving the deadlocks on domestic issues. But it is hard to make the case that Sept. 11 alone will be responsible for any domestic legislation that does not get done by the end of the 107th Congress.

The political forces are stacked so badly against the most troubled cases — prescription drug coverage, patients' rights, an increase in the minimum wage, election overhaul and Bush's "faith-based initiative" — that even their supporters say they would be struggling just as much if Sept. 11 had never happened.

What has happened is that rather than replacing the old world, the new world has simply dumped a thick new agenda on Congress' doorstep. The fact that both worlds are relevant to the voters, political consultants say, means neither party can turn its full attention to one agenda at the expense of the other.

"Americans didn't suddenly say, 'Oh, I'm not interested in education anymore. Now I'm interested in terrorism.' They're thinking about education and terrorism," said Republican pollster David Winston. "This isn't where one issue wiped out the other. People did what they don't usually do, which is that they added a whole lot of new issues to their plate."

Democratic consultants agree. "The easiest thing to do in the wake of a huge event is to predict massive change, and massive change rarely happens," said Democratic pollster Mark Mellman.

The Signs

But the changes have been big enough, and it is impossible for members of Congress to ignore them.

Physically, there are reminders everywhere — the barricaded streets around the Capitol, the new screening booths outside the building and the torn-up East Front grounds, where construction on a visitors' center has been accelerated to allow tourists to be screened before they get close to the Capitol itself.

After all, Sept. 11 also was the day when members of Congress were frantically evacuated amid fear that a plane was heading for the Capitol.

"I remember so vividly racing through this hallway, actually, as we departed the building as quickly as we could, having been told that we may be under attack," said Senate Majority Leader Tom Daschle, D-S.D. It would not be Daschle's last brush with danger: A month later, his staff opened a letter filled with anthrax spores. (2001 *Almanac*, p. 1-12)

For many lawmakers, the new sense of vulnerability already has turned from frightening to annoying. "To get to Point A from Point B, you've got to go through 10 obstacles, and it makes me wonder if it hasn't been overdone a bit," said Sen. Charles E. Grassley, R-Iowa. But, he added, "I think it's something that we're all going to have to live with as long as we're in public life."

Still, the security crackdown at the Capitol is only the most visible sign of a different world.

Some of the political changes are seen as welcome improvements. Hatch and other Republicans say they have

---

NOV. Though half the senators remained in temporary offices, issues returned to center stage on Capitol Hill. Ideology and partisan disagreement, which had been driven to the periphery in the aftermath of the attacks, resurfaced as Congress again became a place of give and take. Democrats laid claim to the view, opposed by the White House, that Homeland Security Director Tom Ridge needed authority conferred by Congress to have the clout necessary to effectively manage his multi-agency job.

Completion of the aviation security law was delayed because Democrats and Republicans could not agree on whether baggage screeners should be federal employees or private contractors. President Bush broke the impasse by agreeing to Democratic demands that the screeners work directly for the federal government, but he won the authority to exempt them from civil service rules.

LAWS ENACTED
Aviation security (PL 107-71) — The federal government takes over airport security with a new Transportation Security Administration (TSA) within the Transportation Department.
Transportation spending (PL 107-87) — The fiscal 2002 appropriations law includes more money for the Coast Guard, the Federal Aviation Administration and the new TSA.
Recruiting spies (PL 107-77) — Bill allowed the recruitment of intelligence sources on terrorism despite past human rights violations.

❝ We needed to have somebody in charge with the responsibility to carry out the transportation and aviation security requirements. ❞

Rep. John L. Mica, R-Fla.

DEC. The congressional agenda had boiled down to a single concern: helping the American economy overcome the jolt of an attack that crippled the aviation industry and laid waste to several square blocks in the heart of the nation's financial district. The intangibles of consumer unease about future attacks and the concrete reality that the sudden disappearance of the World Trade Center's twin towers had thrown tens of thousands of people out of jobs conspired to shake the overall economy.

But Republicans and Democrats again could not agree on what to do. Republicans held fast to the conservative view that accelerating the tax cuts of the previous spring would ignite business and consumer spending and launch a recovery.

" *This was the kind of landmark event that really did change people's approaches toward their jobs.* **"**

— Rep. Rob Portman, R-Ohio

won more support from Democrats for strengthening the military. And even though senators from both parties raise doubts about the wisdom of invading Iraq, Senate Minority Leader Trent Lott, R-Miss., said he still sees a greater willingness by Democrats to work with Republicans if military action is required.

When congressional leaders met with Bush on Sept. 4 to discuss his plans on Iraq, Lott said, Daschle and Gephardt went out of their way to tell Bush that while they had disagreements, they would work through them.

"I told the president the same thing I told him on Sept. 12: 'We're in this together; this is too important for politics,' " Gephardt said.

By contrast, Lott said, when the United States prepared to go to war with Iraq in 1991, the Senate resolution authorizing military action was barely adopted, 52-47. (*1991 Almanac, p. 437*)

"I think the events of 9/11 have changed that. I hope it's permanent," Lott said in an interview.

Said Daschle: "I'd like to think that it's made us more sober about our responsibilities and about how we do a better job of protecting this country in the future."

Other changes have raised grave concerns. The crackdown against possible terrorism at home has prompted warnings that civil liberties are being undermined. Congress grappled with the issue when it wrote the sweeping new anti-terrorism law (PL 107-56) last year, but it has not ended the debate. (*2002 CQ Weekly, p. 2284*)

Even though Congress rejected Attorney General John Ashcroft's request for authority to detain non-citizens indefinitely if they were considered risks to national security, people are being detained anyway. As of June, 74 immigrants rounded up after Sept. 11 were still being held by the Immigration and Naturalization Service for alleged immigration violations, according to court filings by the Justice Department.

In addition, 73 others had been detained on federal criminal charges since the attacks, and an undisclosed number were being held as material witnesses.

"People are intimidated by the talk of the new world after 9/11," said Sen. Russell D. Feingold, D-Wis., who voted against the anti-terrorism bill because he viewed it as an assault on civil liberties. "They think it means we can have a kind of Democracy Lite. I don't buy that, and I don't think members of Congress should buy that."

The Legislative Impact

In practical terms, Sept. 11 shifted lawmakers into legislative overdrive.

In the first few months, Congress signed off on an avalanche of new legislation with a speed unimaginable just weeks earlier: emergency spending, the anti-terrorism bill, an ambitious federalization of airport security and a resolution authorizing the president to strike back at the terrorists.

But it also moved ahead on issues unrelated to the war on terrorism. The corporate accounting overhaul, an education bill heavily promoted by Bush, a campaign finance overhaul and fast-track trade authority all moved through a narrowly divided Congress and became law after the attacks. "I don't think you're going to compare this to past years and say we're getting fewer things done," said a Daschle aide.

Democrats focused on spending more, emphasizing the need to lengthen unemployment benefits and extend help to other industries as Congress had done for airlines. With Christmas closing in and the stakes seemingly high, but not quite clear, Congress adjourned without doing anything on economic stimulus.

LAWS ENACTED
Intelligence (PL 107-108) — The annual intelligence agency authorization included significantly more money for spy agencies, but Congress rejected the idea of a special commission on intelligence lapses before Sept. 11.
Health funding (PL 107-116) — Fiscal 2002 spending for Labor, Health and Human Services, and Education included increased spending for bio-terrorism and the Centers for Disease Control.
New York tax breaks (PL 107-134) — Provided tax relief for businesses affected by the Trade Center attacks.
Patriot Day (PL 107-89) — Designates Sept. 11 as Patriot Day, though not a federal holiday.

" It is far more important to be right than quick. **"**

Alan Greenspan, Federal Reserve chairman

JAN.

After this White House breakfast meeting, Bush and Daschle had few agreements.

LAWS ENACTED
Income taxes (PL 107-134) — An income tax exemption for 2001 for those killed in the World Trade Center and Pentagon attacks.

It had become clear by the end of the year that the powerful impulses of unity and patriotism that so dominated Washington after Sept. 11 had limits. Democrats would not agree with President Bush on everything; in fact, on airport security and economic stimulus, Democrats staked out positions in willful opposition. In both cases, they argued for their political base of labor unions and middle-income workers, and in both cases Senate Majority Leader Tom Daschle led the charge.

Daschle and Bush opened the year at odds on nearly everything. Rumors persisted that Daschle would challenge Bush for the presidency in 2004, but at the very least he was positioning his party to oppose Republicans in the midterm election of 2002.

A critical issue, however, is whether even more important legislation is not getting done because of the attacks — and, if so, whether the delays could kill the bills' chances in future Congresses.

At a time when health care concerns still rank high among voters' priorities, the divided Senate was unable to pass any of its proposals for a prescription drug benefit. Patients' rights legislation appears dead, once again stuck over the right to sue managed-care plans for damages. (*2002 CQ Weekly, pp. 2111, 2114*)

Bush still may get a trimmed-down version of his faith-based initiative, but it will bear little resemblance to his original proposal to get religious groups more involved in social services, and he has had little time to spend lobbying for it. (*2002 CQ Weekly, p. 1662*)

Democrats are becoming more reluctant to push for an increase in the minimum wage, which has not been raised in six years. An energy bill (HR 4) is stuck in negotiations between the House and Senate, slowed by divisive issues and lack of attention from other lawmakers. Even an election overhaul bill (HR 3295) that both parties say they want, in an effort to avoid another debacle like the 2000 election, has become hung up in negotiations, and virtually no progress on it was made over the August recess. (*2002 CQ Weekly, pp. 2034, 2308*)

All of these issues have gotten less attention than they might have before Sept. 11, when the congressional leaders may have had more time to get involved and push lawmakers to settle their disputes. Some believe that lack of attention has been fatal.

"It does mean that a number of issues have been relegated to second-tier status," said Sen. Christopher J. Dodd, D-Conn. "It was decisive in that it allowed the Congress' attention to be diverted from issues at a time when the administration wasn't too interested in having attention focused on them."

Beset by Problems

Gephardt, however, said he does not believe Sept. 11 is the reason the prescription drug bill and other domestic legislation are not getting done. And Democratic aides say that in all of these cases, the bills have run into so much political trouble along the way that Sept. 11 cannot be seen as a decisive factor in any of them.

The prescription drug bill, they point out, was crippled by a lack of money and a fundamental divide between Democrats and Republicans over how the coverage should be provided. Bush's faith-based initiative never had much chance in the Senate even before Sept. 11, they say, because of concerns that religious groups would be able to practice discrimination with federal funds.

The drive to increase the minimum wage is losing steam because of the economy, the aides say, which was troubled even before the terrorist attacks. And the election overhaul bill, they believe, has lost momentum because potential supporters are too unhappy with the emerging conference agreement to lobby for it, not because Sept. 11 knocked it out of the spotlight.

Even with legislation on which Sept. 11 may have had an indirect impact — such as overcrowding the congressional schedule — the delays are not likely to have a practical effect.

Senate GOP leadership aides now say the reauthorization of the 1996 welfare overhaul (PL 104-193), which had been a high priority for Republicans, may not come before the Senate this year because there will not be enough time to address it. But low-income recipients would not face any loss of benefits, they say, because appropriators simply would provide an extra year of funding under current rules, and the reauthorization would come back before Congress next year. (*2002 CQ Weekly, p. 2249*)

The one case where a failure this year might truly be fatal is the patients' rights bill.

In the legislative process, DePaul's Mezey said, there are "windows of opportunity" when a controversial bill builds up enough momentum to overcome its difficulties and get through Congress. Although Mezey said the prescription drug bill may have missed a critical window this year, most other lawmakers and analysts say the need for prescription drug coverage for seniors is so great that there will be other chances.

But this is the third Congress that has attempted to pass a patients' rights bill. If the current versions (HR 2563,

---

FEB. Before Sept. 11, maintaining fiscal discipline was a driving force in all that Congress debated. The first budget surpluses in three decades were only three years old and neither Republicans nor Democrats wanted to be seen as having spent the extra money. The terrorist attacks, and the military campaign in response, eliminated virtually all political obstacles to spending too much and Congress and the White House agreed on $40 billion in emergency spending three days after the attacks. Tens of billions of dollars more would follow.

But the introduction of Bush's fiscal 2003 budget, which proposed a deficit of $80 billion, triggered a swift return of deficit politics. Conservatives within the GOP vowed to insist on a balanced budget and Democrats charged the White House with fiscal imprudence for the tax cut enacted the previous summer.

MARCH Bush's hand had been strengthened in dealing with Congress, and not until spring did lawmakers from both parties begin to chafe at what they considered an overly autocratic White House.

The White House rebuffed requests to have Homeland Security Director Tom Ridge testify before Congress on the administration's budget request, and it kept Congress in the dark on security issues citing a fear of leaks. These episodes were set against the backdrop of a suit filed by Congress' investigative arm to review documents from a White House task force on energy policy. After five months of haggling, and just as Federal Reserve Chairman Alan Greenspan declares that an economic recovery is already "well under way," Congress cuts a deal on an economic stimulus package.

LAWS ENACTED
Economic stimulus (PL 107-147) — Extends federal unemployment insurance coverage, creates tax incentives for rebuilding on lower Manhattan and provides business tax relief at a cost of $94.6 billion through fiscal 2007.
Radio-Free Afghanistan (PL 107-148) — To help the campaign against al-Qaida, establishes a government-sponsored broadcaster akin to Radio Free Europe.

❝I think the whole range of issues related to terrorism has been more bipartisan and consensual. I don't sense more of a collaborative approach on anything else.❞

— House Minority Leader Richard A. Gephardt, D-Mo.

S 1052) remain stuck in negotiations, proponents may face an impossible task getting Congress to try a fourth time. Some of the bill's strongest supporters in the lobbying community, many of whom have been working on the issue for more than six years, privately admit they are tired of it.

For Rep. Charlie Norwood, R-Ga., who struck a deal with Bush that substantially reshaped the House bill, the interruption came at a crucial time, right after the House and Senate had passed versions of the legislation. "There's no question at all that 9/11 took the momentum away from the patients' bill of rights," said Norwood, although "as important as patient protections are, 9/11 is more important."

However, aides to Edward M. Kennedy, D-Mass., a sponsor of the Senate bill, say the window of opportunity more likely closed when Norwood struck a deal with Bush that was unac-

ceptable to Senate Democrats — not when Sept. 11 took the attention away.

The Political Impact

Lawmakers from both parties agree on one thing: There is a clear distinction between the new political dynamics surrounding the war on terrorism — with its impact on foreign policy, defense and homeland security — and the politics of everything else.

"Where it's related to 9/11, it's definitely been easier to work together," Portman said. "Where it's not related, I haven't seen much of a change."

At a time when a shift of just a few seats could determine control of the House and Senate and therefore determine the course of legislation in the 108th Congress, the question is which of the two political worlds will dominate voters' minds right before the November elections.

Republicans are confident that Bush's leadership gives them the upper hand in the new-world issues. But since spring, the debate has been shifting decisively back toward the old world. The scandals at Enron Corp. and WorldCom Inc. led Congress to crack down on corporate fraud more aggressively than Bush had proposed. The plummeting stock markets have made Americans worry about their retirement savings, and Bush has been looking for ways to calm their fears.

"The problems that existed on Sept. 10 still exist, and we're turning back to them," said Senate Democratic Policy Committee Chairman Byron L. Dorgan of North Dakota.

Democratic pollster Mellman said of Bush, "The reason he was in desperate trouble before Sept. 11 was that the economy was weak. Well, guess what? It's still weak. He was seen as being on the wrong side of business issues . . . and now it's a different set of issues, but he's still seen as being on the wrong side."

But since Sept. 11, Bush has proven his ability to change the agenda almost any time he wants. After months of resisting calls for a homeland security department, Bush issued his own proposal in June, ensuring that Congress would have to take up the issue on his terms.

Now, he is forcing Congress to turn its attention to a possible invasion of Iraq to oust Saddam Hussein — an idea that was not on the national agenda before Sept. 11 raised fears that nuclear, chemical or biological weapons could someday be used against Americans.

❝ Everybody is a little taken aback that Congress wasn't included in White House plans for a secret shadow bureaucracy.❞

Sen. Lincoln Chafee, R-R.I.

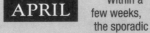

APRIL Within a few weeks, the sporadic violence of the Middle East escalated into one of the worst exchanges between Israelis and Palestinians in a decade. The swift rise to crisis of the conflict between Israel and Palestine put the Bush administration, which had been untouchable on foreign policy issues, in a bad light as it maintained a hands-off approach to the matter. Congressional pressure, and the realization that continued bloodshed was crowding out all other foreign policy issues, pressed the administration into an active role in seeking an end to the immediate violence and in finding a long-term solution.

MAY Early efforts to take up an examination of how the attacks of Sept. 11 could have caught America's extensive intelligence operation by surprise were scuttled in the name of patriotic unity. But ultimately, pointed questions were raised and details were revealed about internal briefings within the White House on possible attacks by Osama bin Laden.

But Congress, whose intelligence committees long have been criticized for being too closely associated with the agencies they oversee — chiefly the CIA — struggled openly and inconclusively with the question of whether a review should focus on the failures of the past or cures for the future.

LAWS ENACTED
Border security (PL 107-173) — Increased border security and closer monitoring of foreign students.
Bio-terrorism (PL 107-188) — A $4.2 billion authorization for fiscal 2003 to fight bio-terrorism.

❝ I don't think this is about what the president knew. I think this is about what didn't the president know and why didn't he know it?❞

Sen. Joseph R. Biden Jr., D-Del.

7

"The important thing is that this is a part of a threat around the world that we cannot ignore," Lott told reporters Sept. 4. "To me, I think it is a part of the overall war on terror. This is a man and a military that has used terror against its own people and against its neighbors."

If the debate is held shortly before the elections, it could shift the spotlight at a crucial moment to the foreign policy and defense issues of the new world that typically favor Republicans. In a CNN/USA Today/Gallup poll of 801 adults conducted Aug. 19-21, 41 percent said they had more confidence in congressional Republicans to make the right decision on Iraq, while 30 percent had more confidence in the Democrats.

The debate also could remind Americans of their own fears for their personal safety.

"Never have people considered themselves in clear and present danger as they do now," said Winston, the Republican pollster. "The one thing that people are more afraid of than anything else is that someone will walk into a mall and blow themselves up."

Still, Democratic leaders insist voters are sophisticated enough to follow both an Iraq debate and a campaign on domestic issues — and that they ultimately care more about whether Congress improves their lives by addressing pocketbook issues such as the economy and prescription drugs.

"If you're a senior citizen, or you have a senior citizen in your family, you're looking for a prescription drug program," said Gephardt. "Yeah, you're concerned about terrorism, and you want it dealt with, but that's not the issue for you."

Besides, he said, it will be impossible to separate the Iraq debate from its effect on domestic issues, because the economy could suffer if Iraq is attacked.

"The president knows this, but there will be necessary economic side effects to whatever we do in Iraq. There will be side effects just by our talking about it," Gephardt said. "I'm not saying we should base our decision on that . . . [but] anything we do there has an impact on other things."

Taking the Lead

However, Democrats privately concede that it is hard to challenge Bush on Iraq because his approval ratings, while dropping slightly overall, are still high when Americans are asked specifically about his handling of the war on terrorism. That could explain why some of the earliest questions about the wisdom of an unprovoked strike against Iraq came not from Democrats, but from House Majority Leader Dick Armey, R-Texas, who is retiring this year.

"It's not a question of disagreeing with him as much as recognizing that he has the confidence of the public," a Democratic leadership aide said of Bush. "And that's where it's difficult for people from either party to challenge him."

There are plenty of other reasons for members of Congress to be uncertain about how the election will play out.

Winston said this election will be full of unprecedented dynamics. Obviously, it will be the first election since Sept. 11, he said, and therefore the first chance to see how the public reconciles all the new issues.

But it also will be the first time an election is held when the president's approval rating is substantially higher than the public's approval of the country's direction. At the moment, Winston said, Bush's approval ratings are 65 percent to 70 percent, while only 40 percent to 45 percent of the country approve of the direction in which the nation is headed.

In addition, Winston said, it will be the first time the performance of the stock market, as opposed to jobs and the economy, has become a political issue. And it may be the first time that Congress has been so closely divided for so long. "Normally, by this point, they've made a decision" and given one party or another a strong majority, he said.

All of the uncertainty is taking a toll on the confidence of members of Congress — and, some say, on the quality of their leadership.

Lawmakers have been thrown off their stride, Panetta said, by a political environment where each party's core issues may no longer be relevant. Republicans can no longer get much mileage out of talking about tax cuts and smaller government, he said. And as much as Democrats count on "pocketbook issues" such as the economy and health care to capture the public's attention, he said, they cannot be sure they will.

JUNE With pressure increasing in Congress for homeland security legislation and congressional committees delving into intelligence lapses before the attacks, the Bush administration unveiled an ambitious plan to merge 22 federal agencies into a new homeland security department. Lawmakers liked the concept — many had been urging much the same thing for months — but some in each party worried about merging multipurpose agencies that have duties beyond countert-errorism, such as the Coast Guard, and about Bush's demand for management "flexibility," including an exemption from civil service rules and the power to shift agency budgets around. In less than two weeks, the administration released a homeland security strategy document, which raised the possibility of a security role for the armed forces, and sent Congress proposed homeland security legislation that would compete with a bill by Sen. Joseph I. Lieberman, D-Conn.

Intelligence gathering would not be part of either proposal: Lawmakers thought the issue should be worked on with later.

Lieberman chats with Ridge after hearings.

JULY The House moved quickly to pass Bush's homeland security legislation. Eleven standing committees were given two weeks to consider Bush's plan and make recommendations to a select leadership committee that wrote the final bill in less than seven days. The House passed the bill July 26, the same day the Senate Governmental Affairs Committee approved its own, significantly different, version. With debate growing over the management and budget authority Bush was demanding over the new department, hopes faded that Congress would be able to complete the legislation by the first anniversary of the terrorist attacks.

Select Committee on Homeland Security hears from cabinet members.

In aviation security, the president removed the former Secret Service agent running the struggling new Transportation Security Administration and the administration said it would reconsider its opposition to some policies, including allowing airline pilots to carry guns. Congress was on the verge of permitting the practice anyway.

Hearings in the Senate on Middle East policy showed growing congressional unease with Bush's threats to overthrow Iraqi leader Saddam Hussein.

> **"** *The problems that existed on Sept. 10 still exist, and we're turning back to them.* **"**
>
> — Sen. Byron L. Dorgan, D-N.D.

"Both sides are so caught up with who's going to win in November that it's questionable as to whether anyone's thinking about the big picture," Panetta said. "What they're failing to do is to tell America exactly where we're heading in the long run."

The Institution

For all of the turmoil, the way Congress works has remained remarkably unchanged.

With its legislative blitz in the first three months after the attacks, Congress did show that it can respond quickly when Americans' safety is threatened. In general, however, the House still moves fast on bills under tightly controlled rules, and the Senate still acts as if it had no rules.

And although the House created a select committee to oversee the homeland security bill, there has yet to be a permanent reorganization to give one panel oversight authority over the proposed new department, rather than the 61 committees and subcommittees that would have jurisdiction now. (*2002 CQ Weekly, p. 2226*)

If that happened in the next Congress, "you'd have major and lasting shifts of power among committees. I think over the long run, that will happen," said Rep. David E. Price, D-N.C.

What has changed is more subtle. At a personal level, lawmakers say they just get along better.

It may not always have a tangible effect, they say, but it could over the long run. "I think some members are just closer personally, and that will have a lasting impact," said Portman.

For example, Portman said, he worked closely with Rep. Ellen O. Tauscher, D-Calif., in an informal group that tried to smooth the homeland security bill's path to passage in the House. They developed a good relationship, he said, and that may have helped Tauscher persuade other Democrats to put aside their concerns about personnel rules, making the final vote — 295-132 — more lopsided than it would have been otherwise. (*2002 CQ Weekly, p. 2028*)

Other lawmakers are not convinced the personal relationships have really changed.

"For three to four months, you had more bipartisan cooperation, but now it's gone back to the way it was," Grassley said. "And as we get closer to the election, the war is going to become more partisan."

Still, some analysts say that even when the parties are deadlocked, most lawmakers do not waste as much time on meaningless, point-scoring legislative maneuvers as they used to.

"It doesn't affect the number of bills, and it may not change the final vote, but it affects the way issues are positioned, and so in very subtle ways, it does affect the institution," said Michael J. Malbin, professor of political science at the State University of New York at Albany.

Lawmakers will always be driven by the political need to win control of Congress. Now, however, they have shared an experience none of them will ever forget. It still packs an emotional punch. For many, not knowing the fate of Osama bin Laden, the man believed to have started the whole thing, may be the most galling part of all.

"There's a lack of completeness," Dorgan said. "We don't have [Osama] bin Laden, don't know where he is. We don't have [Taliban leader Mullah Mohammed] Omar. We don't have the anthrax perpetrator. So a lot of this seems very unfinished."

For Congress as well as the rest of the country, it probably always will. ◆

> **"** If ever there was a need for the Senate to throw a bucket of cold water on an overheated legislative process . . . it is now.**"**
>
> Sen. Robert C. Byrd, D-W.Va.,

AUG. As Congress took its summer break, debate in the Senate on homeland security had come down to personnel policy: Bush said that for the homeland security department to be effective, its managers should be able to hire, transfer and fire employees without the strictures of civil service or unions; Democrats said the workers had to be protected from capricious managers and political pressure. Senate Appropriations Committee Chairman Robert C. Byrd, D-W.Va., threatened to filibuster the legislation but backed down after the recess.

LAW ENACTED
Military spending (PL 107-206) — Supplemental fiscal 2002 appropriations includes $14.5 billion to pay for the campaign in Afghanistan.

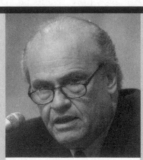

> **"** I guess there are ways of compromising on all of those [personnel] issues but . . . it will be difficult.**"**
>
> Sen. Fred Thompson, R-Tenn.

SEPT. Just before leaving for its commemorative special meeting in New York, the Senate amended its homeland security bill to allow airline pilots to carry guns in the cockpit. The House passed a similar measure in July. The two bills likely will be resolved if the homeland security bill moves from the Senate to a conference committee this fall.

Pilots lobby Sen. Kay Bailey Hutchison, R-Texas, on security issues.

CQ PHOTO / SCOTT J. FERRELL

Pre-Emptive Policy Has Congress Fretting Over Loss of Influence

President says new enemies pose need for rapid decisions, less consensus

Quick Contents

Some lawmakers fear President Bush's readiness to strike first with his high-tech military may weaken their war powers.

President Bush's new doctrine that the United States would strike first at terrorists and rogue states that wield weapons of mass destruction is raising concerns that Congress could lose what little power it has on making decisions about the use of military power abroad.

In the past, Congress based its authority on the controversial 1973 War Powers act (PL 93-148), which limits the president's power to commit U.S. forces overseas without congressional approval. (*1973 Almanac, p. 905*)

But successive presidents have never recognized the law, and after contentious congressional debates about various deployments over the past three decades, the power of the law has eroded and Congress has been largely unable to block presidential decisions to send troops into harm's way.

Indeed, Bush's father, George Bush, once remarked he was prepared to launch his war against Iraq in 1991 without congressional approval, even if it meant risking impeachment. (*1991 Almanac, p.437*)

Now, the younger Bush appears to be challenging Congress with his muscular strategy of pre-emption, using a high-tech military capable of striking swiftly and without warning.

"If we wait for threats to fully materialize, we will have waited too long," Bush declared June 1 in a major policy speech to graduating officers at West Point. "The war on terror will not be won on the defensive. We must take the battle to the enemy, disrupt his plans and confront the worst threats before they emerge."

The president specifically stressed the imperative for an American military that can "strike at a moment's notice in any dark corner of the world," using "pre-emptive action, when necessary, to defend our liberty and to defend our lives."

On one hand, lawmakers from both parties have been quick to embrace the broad outlines of Bush's strike-first doctrine, especially against the backdrop of the war against terror.

"Obviously, when you're dealing with an insidious enemy like terrorists who might be armed with weapons of mass destruction, you

At West Point on June 1, President Bush stressed pre-emptive strikes as U.S. strategic policy.

want to interdict them before they strike you," said House Armed Services Committee member John M. Spratt Jr., D-S.C.

And even some of the most prominent foreign affairs specialists in Congress seem reconciled to the legislative branch's diminished role in decisions about the use of force.

"Generally, the Congress has recognized that, given the trends of technology, when you have to make rapid decisions, the executive has to have a certain amount of discretion," Sen. Richard G. Lugar, R-Ind., said June 12. "We crossed that bridge, technologically, some time back."

But Spratt and other Democrats are troubled by indications that Bush intends to apply the doctrine much more widely. In his West Point speech, Bush seemed to allude to the rogue nations that make up what he calls the "axis of evil" — Iraq, North Korea and Iran. "Containment is not possible when unbalanced dictators with weapons of mass destruction can deliver those weapons on missiles or secretly provide them to terrorist allies," Bush said.

"It could imply that they're going after targets that aren't a present and immediate danger, but have the potential of [becoming] one, like Iraq," Spratt said.

Congressional critics insist that, unlike a terrorist cell with no territory or population to protect, any national government — no matter how radical — will value its own survival enough that it can be deterred from attack by the threat of devastating retaliation.

"[Its] interest is one thing: regime survival," said Senate Armed Services Committee member Max Cleland, D-Ga. "You can apply sanctions and, at some point, [it] hollers uncle."

Going Nuclear

Some lawmakers also are concerned that, in addition to being willing to strike first, Bush may be more willing than his predecessors to use nuclear weapons to eliminate an adversary's nuclear, chemical or biological arms.

They point to an administration request for $15 million to study development of a low-yield nuclear "bunker-buster" bomb, designed to eliminate deeply buried weapons caches. Senate Armed Services eliminated the project from its version of the fiscal 2003 defense authorization bill (S 2514). (2002 CQ Weekly, p. 1567)

"We should not talk about the first use of nuclear weapons," Senate Armed Services Committee Chairman Carl Levin, D-Mich., told reporters during a June 10 breakfast.

Critics contend that a professed U.S. willingness to treat nuclear explosives as usable weapons would erode the nearly 60-year-old taboo against the use of nuclear arms. Levin noted that restraint already is eroding on the subcontinent, where a nuclear-armed Pakistan and India are mobilized for possible war over Kashmir, and in Japan, where politicians are debating openly whether to develop nuclear arms.

"The world is moving in an incredibly dangerous direction," Levin said.

But the notion of acting first to neutralize an adversary who has weapons of mass destruction did not originate with the Bush administration.

In December 1993, after the Gulf War revealed Iraq had more extensive programs to develop mass destruction weapons than U.S. intelligence agencies had believed, Defense Secretary Les Aspin launched a "counterproliferation" initiative to equip U.S. forces for the likelihood that they would be facing mass destruction weapons. Some critics objected that this was a step to-

ward unilateral military action to disarm potential adversaries.

Ashton B. Carter, a former assistant Defense secretary in charge of the counterproliferation initiative, insists the primary focus was defensive. "We thought the one thing we needed to do was better prepare our forces for the near certainty that the major regional contingencies would include at least chemical and possibly biological [weapons]," he said. But he acknowledged those preparations included efforts to develop preemptive weapons designed specifically to punch into underground bunkers and incinerate chemical and biological weapons.

Michael O'Hanlon, a defense policy analyst for the Brookings Institution, says the Clinton administration took an even more dramatic step toward pre-emption when Aspin's successor, Defense Secretary William J. Perry, issued a veiled but unmistakable threat in 1994 to eliminate North Korea's emerging nuclear capability.

"He didn't have to fill in the blanks," O'Hanlon said. "Perry pushed the administration further than the White House or the State Department wanted to go. But once Perry uttered it, no one contradicted him."

Too Much Clarity

Another concern raised by Bush's speech at West Point is the wisdom of making explicit what has been, until now, an implicit willingness to attack first.

"Pre-emption has been an implicit part of our doctrine for a long time," O'Hanlon said. "They are willing to make this a little more explicit, largely to prepare the international leadership so, if they decide to pre-empt, nobody's quite as surprised."

But Senate Foreign Relations Committee Chairman Joseph R. Biden Jr., D-Del., warned that the speech might reinforce foreign leaders' view of Bush as too willing to go it alone, thus making it harder to win their support for other initiatives.

"For him to make the declaration reinforces in the minds of Europeans, 'Oh my God, where's he going?'" Biden said. "That impacts our ability to get other things done."

Biden also argued that how the administration fleshes out the new doctrine would affect Congress' acceptance of it. The administration is expected to elaborate in a formal state-

ment of national strategy this fall.

"There's no doubt that the president has the authority, from a constitutional standpoint, to respond to an imminent attack," Biden said. But it would be a different thing, he said, if the administration, without consulting Congress, attacked North Korea or Iraq simply on the grounds that those regimes could not be trusted to possess nuclear, chemical or biological weapons.

"The founding fathers did not yield to the executive the ability to make the sole judgment as to whether or not we would be in jeopardy as a result of a capability," Biden insisted.

More of a Say

Significantly, some lawmakers contend that Bush's pre-emptive doctrine could give Congress increased leverage on decisions to use force, at least in some cases.

Doug Bereuter, R-Neb., vice chairman of the House Select Committee on Intelligence, speculates that pre-emptive strikes aimed at the threats Bush highlighted — terrorist cells and stockpiles of nuclear, chemical or biological weapons — typically would be undercover operations rather than major military campaigns.

"It would likely be covert action and thus likely to come before the [House and Senate] Intelligence committees," Bereuter said June 11.

Over the past 25 years, those two panels and administrations of both parties developed a working relationship in which officials brief the panels on presidential "findings" to justify any particular covert operation.

"The administration has not gone forward, if there were substantial doubts by the intelligence committees," Bereuter said.

Ultimately, lawmakers say, the debate over Bush's pre-emption doctrine comes down to the dilemma Congress has wrestled with for decades: how to preserve its role in decisions to make war when technology enables small groups to pose crippling threats with little or no notice.

"Technology drives the pace of events and the potential for damage," said House Armed Services Committee member William M. "Mac" Thornberry, R-Texas. "How does that fit in with the Constitution written in 1787? That's a problem we have not come to grips with. . . . But we expect the president to protect us." ◆

Lawmakers Struggle to Keep An Eye on Patriot Act

Congress squirms as Justice takes law into its own hands

For several weeks this summer, three senators — Vermont Democrat Patrick J. Leahy and Republicans Charles E. Grassley of Iowa and Arlen Specter of Pennsylvania — had been meeting privately in a secure room in the Capitol to discuss problems that had cropped up in top-secret terrorism investigations. During one session, a Justice Department official let slip that the Bush administration had drafted new rules for conducting sophisticated electronic surveillance of people suspected of terrorist ties.

Interesting, replied the senators. Let's see them.

The response from the Justice Department was all too typical in the view of an increasing number of lawmakers: Sorry, even the rules for doing secret surveillance are secret.

It has been 10 months since Congress passed an anti-terrorism law (PL 107-56) commonly known as the USA Patriot Act, which granted the government broad new powers to root out terrorists in the United States. Lawmakers who supported and opposed the law alike say it has generated at least as many problems as it has fixed. *(2001 Almanac, p. 14-3)*

It has made for more effective use of intelligence data against suspected terrorists and has allowed federal authorities to hold them for questioning more easily. But in the process, the law and a series of related policies issued by Attorney General John Ashcroft have blurred historic legal differences in the way the government treats suspected terrorists and handles ordinary citizens.

Adding to the concern are complaints from members of both parties that Congress has been stymied in its effort to conduct effective oversight of the new law. Monitoring the effects of the anti-terrorism law would be hard under any circumstances because of the secretive nature of counterterrorism investigations. But the Justice Department has aggravated the problem by refusing to share with Congress even general information about how the law is being used.

The courts are just as displeased with some aspects of the administration's terrorism-fighting efforts. In a series of recent rulings, lower court judges have ordered the government to release the names of hundreds of people detained during its investigation and directed the Justice Department to open secret deportation hearings.

In a rare move, the special federal court that oversees spy-

"The oversight committees are largely flying blind," said Leahy, second from left, with Sen. Richard J. Durbin, D-Ill., left, FBI Director Robert S. Mueller III, center, and Grassley.

ing on suspected terrorists ruled that Justice's proposed expansion of surveillance procedures went too far. The typically secret court, which approves wiretaps and searches in spying and terrorism cases, does not make its rulings public. But it did so in this instance at the urging of Grassley, Leahy and Specter, who were frustrated by Justice's refusal to tell them about the new surveillance rules.

Still, the anti-terrorism law retains a bipartisan legion of backers. Democrats such as Dianne Feinstein of California are defying party typecasting by overlooking the law's individual-liberty weaknesses in favor of its national-security strengths. "The American people first and foremost want their government to protect them," Feinstein said.

The drafters of the anti-terrorism law say its best feature may be that it is nonrenewable. When the bill was speeding through Congress in the emotion-charged weeks following the attacks on the World Trade Center and the Pentagon, even some of its supporters insisted that the most controversial elements expire in 2005. Their concern was the potential fallout for privacy and other civil liberties as the government hurriedly and aggressively sought out terrorists.

"Number one, we did sunset the Patriot Act, so we'll have a chance to review it in four years," said Grassley, a member of the Senate Judiciary Committee. "That's good because I'm sure we'll want to do that."

Justice Department spokesman Mark Corallo said Ashcroft wants to cooperate with Congress, but that the volume of requests has taxed the department while investigators and support staff are focused on the massive terrorism investigation.

"Under the circumstances, we're doing the best we can," Corallo said. "We have the largest investigation in the history of our country underway, and an unprecedented effort to change our focus from prosecuting terrorism to preventing future terrorist attacks. It's a monumental task."

So far, he said, Justice has provided the special joint intelligence committee with "thousands of pages of evidence," including interviews with hundreds of witnesses and agents with knowledge of the Sept. 11 events.

The White House is keeping tabs on the mood on Capitol Hill. The anti-terrorism law has skeptics among civil libertarians in both political parties. If they joined forces, they would be capable of fatally weakening the law.

"The left meets the right on those issues, so you always have to be concerned about them," said Nicholas Calio, the White House liaison to Congress.

For now, the law seems destined to play a major role in the titanic struggle involving the three branches of government. As it has in other policy arenas, the administration has pushed hard for dominance in the war on terrorism. But after a year in which they have deferred to the executive branch, Congress and the courts are ready to push back.

"At the time the Patriot Act was passed, the message from the administration was, 'If you don't give us what we want, the next terrorist act will be on your head,'" said Morton H. Halperin, senior fellow at the Council on Foreign Relations and a leader in the coalition of public interest groups that opposed the law.

"Congress doesn't stand up very well to that kind of demagoguery," he said. "Now they are starting to raise questions."

Expanded Snooping Powers

The anti-terrorism law's expansion of intrusive surveillance techniques such as wiretaps and unannounced searches has proved to be one of its most nettlesome elements. It gives investigators more leeway to invoke the 1978 Foreign Intelligence Surveillance Act (FISA) (PL 95-511), which gave the government far greater snooping powers in cases involving national security than it had in routine criminal cases. (*1978 Almanac, p. 186*)

These include powers to keep a person under watch for long periods with the most sophisticated Tom Clancy-worthy eavesdropping technology. Suspects do not have to be notified that they are being watched, listened to or tapped unless they are charged with a crime.

A natural conflict arises when those techniques turn up evidence of a crime. How does the government then use the evidence gathered under the far more liberal rules of a foreign intelligence investigation in a subsequent criminal trial, where a defendant is entitled to the full gamut of constitutional protections?

In notable instances, the special court that oversees the use of FISA has let such information be used at trial. For example, bank records and other evidence used to convict CIA mole Aldrich H. Ames originally was gathered with a FISA warrant, not a criminal warrant. (*1994 Almanac, p. 458*)

The special court has tried to enforce what it calls "walls" between the two kinds of evidence-gathering so that prosecutors do not abuse the law by using it as a backdoor way to wiretap and conduct searches when they cannot summon the facts to meet the higher threshold of a criminal warrant.

In some cases, the court itself has acted as arbiter, examining the evidence gathered in an intelligence probe and deciding what could be provided to prosecutors and what could not. Another important barrier has been a ban on criminal prosecutors directing the work of intelligence agents.

The anti-terrorism law is making the court's balancing act a lot tougher. In March, Ashcroft issued a set of rules that interpreted FISA to mean that prosecutors could now direct intelligence probes.

Not so, said the FISA court in a May 17 opinion that was made public in late August, at the three senators' request. That would mean prosecutors could direct intelligence investigations toward the goal of obtaining evidence to convict individuals rather than the probes' intended purpose of gathering foreign intelligence.

"These procedures cannot be used by the government to amend the act in ways Congress has not," the court said.

The opinion, in which all seven FISA judges concurred, noted that the FBI, during the Clinton administration, misrepresented facts in 75 separate requests for warrants to hide the overlapping work of prosecutors and intelligence agents.

"In virtually every instance, the government's misstatements and omissions in FISA applications . . . involved information-sharing and unauthorized disseminations to criminal investigators and prosecutors," the judges wrote.

The Justice Department is appealing the ruling, the first ever appeal of a FISA court ruling. A special appellate court would have to be convened to hear the case.

But the muddle ultimately may have to be clarified by Congress. Lawmakers were aiming for more productive communication between criminal investigators and intelligence agents when they liberalized the evidence-gathering rules in the anti-terrorism law. But how far did they intend to go?

"The problem here is we have two extremes" between the FISA court's view and Ashcroft's, said a Senate aide working on the issue.

"If prosecutors are running it, at the very least it gives the appearance of cheating, of 'Let's get this guy with a FISA warrant,'" the aide said. "But prosecution is also a legitimate way to disrupt an operation, just like deportation, detention and using double agents."

Specter, for example, is pressing for adoption of a standard that would signal when FISA warrants are allowable in terrorism probes and when they are not, a spokesman said.

Detention and Deportation

A second major area of concern on Capitol Hill is the government's secretive detention of more than 1,000 people in the course of the terrorism probe, as well as Justice's decision to close deportation hearings for "special interest" cases.

Many of the people arrested — 751 — were foreigners picked up for possible immigration violations. Another 129 were charged with crimes, and an unknown number were detained as material witnesses. Just one individual out of the total arrests was charged with a crime in connection with the attacks.

While the anti-terrorism law gave the government more authority to detain suspects in terrorism cases, critics charge that the Justice Department has gone far beyond the law.

The act says non-citizens can be detained for up to seven days without charges if the attorney general "certifies" them as terrorism risks. But many of the people swept up in the probe were held for weeks or even months, and in most cases, had no involvement with terrorism though some were charged with other kinds of crimes, according to Human Rights Watch. The organization documented a number of the cases in an Aug. 15 report titled, "Presumption of Guilt:

Ashcroft Drawing Criticism From Both Sides of the Aisle

One committee chairman has threatened to subpoena Attorney General John Ashcroft. A senator from his own party rebuked him publicly for being unresponsive, and the leading opponent of his new citizens' informant proposal is the second-ranking Republican in the House.

Ashcroft's critics include a number of House Republicans, who are among the president's strongest supporters on Capitol Hill and his political counterbalance to the Democratically controlled Senate.

At a time when President Bush is pushing for passage of a bill to create a department of homeland security, his top emissary on counterterrorism efforts has done little to engender goodwill on Capitol Hill.

The main grievance among lawmakers is a lack of cooperation from the Justice Department as they attempt to conduct oversight of counterterrorism efforts. In response, department spokesman Mark Corallo says Ashcroft wants to work with Congress, but the requests severely test a department involved in a major terrorism inquiry. The Bush administration in general has had a tendency to go its own way, but Ashcroft is the victim of higher expectations. Because he is a former senator from Missouri, his erstwhile colleagues think he should know better.

"It's been disappointing," said Darrell Issa, a California Republican on the House Judiciary Committee, which has been rebuffed by Justice repeatedly in its requests for information. "He came out of the Senate and has been a leader in the Republican Party at every conceivable level. I would have expected more."

Lawmakers also grumble privately about what they consider Ashcroft's minor-league political fumbles. There was his strange public announcement — broadcast from Moscow, where he was visiting in June — that his investigators had disrupted a plot by former Chicago street gang member Jose Padilla, also known as Abdullah al Muhajir, to detonate a radioactive "dirty" bomb

Expectations were high for Ashcroft, but his former colleagues have been dismayed by his lack of cooperation.

in the United States. Then there was the decision early in the year to cover with drapery two semi-nude statues in the Justice Department's Great Hall. The story supplied late-night comics with material for months.

Frustration on the Hill

During the August recess, House Judiciary Chairman F. James Sensenbrenner Jr., R-Wis., publicly threatened to subpoena Ashcroft for information if he continues to dodge the committee's request for a detailed accounting of how the department has implemented the anti-terrorism law,

Human Rights Abuses of Post-September 11 Detainees."

Ahmed Alenany, an Egyptian physician, was typical of these, the group says. Alenany was arrested Sept. 21 and held for five months after he stopped to check a map in New York City and was approached by a police officer. The officer found Alenany's visa had expired and discovered he had two pictures of the World Trade Center in his car.

Alenany was held despite the fact that he had applied to renew his visa, and therefore, had legal status, the group reported. He later agreed to be deported rather than face several more weeks in jail as he waited to renew his visa, the organization said.

"The Patriot Act has been almost a complete sideshow to what has happened administratively," said Timothy Edgar, who specializes in immigration for the Washington office of the American Civil Liberties Union. "What they've ended up accomplishing is what they wanted in the Patriot Act originally and which Congress refused to give them."

The ACLU, Human Rights Watch and 20 other public interest groups sued last December under the Freedom of Information Act to force the release of the detainees' names, circumstances of their arrests and their attorneys' names.

"We just want these people to have their day in court, and a fair and open hearing and trial," said Jason Erb, director of governmental affairs for the Council on American Islamic Relations, a plaintiff. "If the government has evidence against them, then charge them with something. If not, let them go."

The Justice Department has argued that identifying the detainees would hamper its terrorism probe. Witnesses would be less likely to cooperate, government lawyers say, and terrorist leaders would be able to map the progress of the investigation.

In August, the U.S. District Court for the District of Columbia ordered the Justice Department to release the names of the detainees and to identify their lawyers. But the department could legitimately withhold the dates the administration's centerpiece in the war against terrorism.

The lack of a response is especially irritating to members such as Sensenbrenner who voted for the bill, although his Judiciary Committee's version was scrapped at the eleventh hour in favor of a version negotiated by House leaders with the White House. The Senate Judiciary Committee also never endorsed the final bill; it instead was brought straight to the Senate floor.

At a hearing in July, where Ashcroft appeared to answer questions about how the law is working, Sen. Arlen Specter, R-Pa., complained that he and Ashcroft worked side by side on the Judiciary Committee when Ashcroft was a senator, but that now he cannot get his letters answered. Specter had written the attorney general for clarification about the government's criteria for detaining more than 1,000 suspects in the terrorism investigation.

"Number one is, how do we communicate with you?" Specter asked Ashcroft. "And are you really too busy to respond?"

A bipartisan group of three senators — the Democratic chairman of the Senate Judiciary Committee, Patrick J. Leahy of Vermont, and committee Republicans Specter and Charles E. Grassley of Iowa — took the unusual step during the summer of writing to a special federal court that oversees electronic surveillance of terrorists to ask it to publish its views of Justice's proposed regulations implementing portions of the law. That is because Ashcroft and the Justice Department refused to show them the rules, though they were drafted in March.

Only after the court released its opinion last month did lawmakers get to see what Ashcroft was proposing, rankling even the Republicans who want to support him and the anti-terrorism law.

"There is nothing in there that gives away the keys to the kingdom for a terrorist or a spy," said one GOP Senate aide close to the issue.

Rubbing the Wrong Way

Liberals have long disdained Ashcroft. They vigorously opposed his Senate confirmation as attorney general and have used him to their convenience to portray Republicans as extremists.

Conservatives, especially social and religious conservatives who share Ashcroft's views, remain his biggest fans. But even they have been going public with their second thoughts, filling op-ed newspaper columns with condemnations of his campaign to expand government's powers at the risk of individual privacy and freedom.

"I don't know anyone on the right who is saying Ashcroft is bad, we should get rid of him. But I don't know anyone on the right who says there's no problem with his approach to civil liberties either," said Grover Norquist, an anti-tax and spend conservative who is close to House Republicans.

It was not a Democrat, but a conservative Republican who put a halt to Ashcroft's proposal to create Operation TIPS, a nationwide program to let people who work in a community, such as postal workers and utility repairmen, report suspicious activity to a central hotline. House Majority Leader Dick Armey, R-Texas, killed the program as a condition of letting Bush's homeland security bill move through committee in the House.

The bill, which could create a new Cabinet-level department to fight terrorism, is one of the administration's highest priorities for the relatively short time left before Congress leaves for the November midterm elections. The Senate has been considering its version. (*2002 CQ Weekly, p. 2294*)

Conservative activist David Keene, in a newspaper opinion piece in late July, wrote of Ashcroft: "Conservatives liked him before Sept. 11 and most like him still, but they are wary of what his department has done and wish that in striking a balance between the need for security and the need to preserve our liberties he would be a bit more careful."

and locations of the arrests to protect its investigation, the court said.

As for material witnesses, the judge ruled that their identities could remain confidential while the court reviews the circumstances for holding them.

"Secret arrests are a 'concept odious to a democratic society,' and profoundly antithetical to the bedrock values that characterize a free and open one such as ours," wrote U.S. Judge Gladys Kessler. The Justice Department is appealing.

The department also has lost a couple of legal rounds in its battle to keep terrorism-related deportation hearings closed.

Last month, a federal appeals court affirmed the U.S. Court of Appeals for the Sixth Circuit's order opening deportation hearings of a suspect in Michigan. Four Michigan newspapers, including the Detroit Free Press, and John Conyers Jr. of Michigan, the ranking Democrat on the House Judiciary Committee, sued after they were barred from attending a hearing for Rabih Haddad, a Muslim cleric in Ann Arbor. Investigators say Haddad may have been financing terrorism in the United States though a charity called Global Relief. The Justice Department had sought to deport him.

A federal appeals court in Philadelphia is expected to rule soon on a lower court's order that deportation hearings nationwide must be conducted in public. Closed deportation proceedings, like secret detentions exceeding a week, were not provided for by Congress in the anti-terrorism law. Rather, Justice has used its rulemaking authority over immigration policy to come up with new procedures for terrorism cases. Legal experts say the Supreme Court ultimately will have to decide whether it acted properly.

For instance, with the issue of closed hearings, Immigration and Naturalization Service Chief Judge Michael J. Creppy issued a directive saying all cases deemed "special interest" would be closed — "no visitors, no family and no press."

In two cases, the department has declared suspects beyond the reach of most constitutional protections, including the right to consult a lawyer. They fall into a new category called "enemy combatants," Justice says, which are like prisoners of war. One case involves Jose Padilla, a former Chicago street gang member who also goes by the name Abdullah al-Muhajir. He has been detained as part of what investigators say was a plot to detonate a radioactive bomb in the United States.

At a Senate hearing July 25 to discuss the anti-terrorism law, Sen. Charles E. Schumer, D-N.Y., told Ashcroft, "I think where the Justice Department goes awry . . . is not in the values they come up with. We can argue those. But there's virtually no discussion when the boundaries of privacy change. A program, a new foray is issued with very few guidelines, with very little elaboration.

"Everyone scratches their head and says, 'How far are they going to go?' "

Justifying Broader Powers

Some lawmakers contend that the terrorist threat to the United States justifies extraordinary steps and that Ashcroft has followed the spirit, if not the letter, of the law.

"The constitutional implications of the Bush administration's anti-terrorism efforts are modest," said Jeff Sessions, R-Ala., a member of the Senate Judiciary Committee. "The administration has not suspended the writ of habeas corpus. It has not required a person to be tried, on this date, in a commission without a jury. It has not authorized the internment of citizens based on race or without individualized determinations that they are threats to national security."

Darrell Issa, R-Calif., a member of the House Judiciary Committee, said, "We intended to give the president broad and sweeping authority, with proper safeguards, and thus far there doesn't seem to be abuse."

Public sentiment also tilts in favor of the administration's aggressive counterterrorism investigation, according to several polls over the summer. Like other points in history when Americans felt a national security threat, concern about immigrants' rights is secondary.

Last month, a Gallup Poll showed that Americans continue to be more negative about immigration now than they were before the Sept. 11 attacks.

Sensenbrenner has threatened to subpoena the attorney general if he continues to rebuff panel requests.

And a majority of the public believes there are "too many" immigrants from Arab countries, the survey found.

Although the administration's critics have raised comparisons to the internment of Japanese Americans during World War II, there are some significant differences in today's terrorism cases. Many of the detainees who have been publicly identified are non-citizens, mostly Arab and Muslim men, without proper visas.

"If the administration gets rid of people who have broken our laws, and our procedures for immigration and residency, whether or not they fall under the intent of the Patriot Act, there isn't a lot of sympathy among the American people," Issa said.

Erb, of the Islamic council, acknowledged that it is politically a bigger challenge to defend a group with questionable legal status. "That's always a hard argument to make, but it's what differentiates us from a lot of other countries," he said.

Secrecy vs. Oversight

The administration's desire to control the flow of information may have met its match in Congress' determination to exercise its oversight powers over the anti-terrorism law. Prominent members from both parties are demanding better cooperation from the Justice Department as they try to gauge the effects of the law.

Before the August recess, the judiciary panels submitted long lists of questions about how the law is working, but got either no answer or only vague or partial answers from Ashcroft.

House Judiciary Chairman F. James Sensenbrenner Jr., R-Wis., normally an

administration ally, has threatened to subpoena Ashcroft if he keeps rebuffing the committee this fall.

Said Leahy: "The oversight committees are largely flying blind. The Justice Department hasn't held up its end of the feedback loop for meaningful oversight. Letter after letter from the oversight committees goes unanswered."

For instance, the House panel asked Justice for figures on the number of times and the circumstances under which usually confidential grand jury information has been shared with intelligence agencies as a result of the law.

A provision that allows confidential grand jury information to be used in terrorism investigations was one of the more sensitive additions to the bill. As a protection, lawmakers added a clause that supervising grand jury judges have to be notified of the disclosures within "a reasonable time."

In a July 26 response, Assistant Attorney General Daniel J. Bryant said grand jury information has been disclosed 40 times in the course of the terrorism investigation. But he said the agency has not kept records on the time lapse between the disclosures and the notices to the judges. In many instances, Justice has responded to congressional demands about the most sensitive provisions by saying the information is "classified" and can be shared only with the House and Senate Intelligence committees, though those panels haven't asked for the information.

For example, it refused to say how many U.S. citizens or legal residents have been targets of the wiretaps and other new FISA surveillance techniques. Likewise, Justice said facts about whether or not the law has been used to obtain library, bookstore or newspaper records to analyze a target's reading habits are "classified."

Lawmakers on the oversight panels say they do not buy that argument, noting that they employ staff with top security clearances for the very purpose of handling classified information.

Sensenbrenner was incensed at the rebuff of a 50-question letter to Ashcroft that also was signed by Conyers.

"The way the Justice Department has been behaving on this is going to ensure that Congress is not going to extend the Patriot Act," Sensenbrenner said in a Sept. 5 interview. ◆

Northern Command Stirs Issue Of Military's Role in Security

Some lawmakers say 124-year-old 'posse' law must change to reflect new reality

When the Washington, D.C., area was terrorized by a sniper in October, the Pentagon contributed a high-tech Army reconnaissance plane to the manhunt by local law enforcement. That gesture, along with the inauguration of a new domestic military command, then sparked a debate in Congress and the administration over the role of the armed forces in protecting the homeland against terrorist attacks.

The issue was whether the use of the military for domestic purposes violated the 1878 Posse Comitatus Act, which generally bars the armed forces from domestic law enforcement. Officials say that because the plane's crew reported to an FBI agent on board, it did not violate the law. Some legal scholars are dubious, but amid the relief over the snipers' capture, no one is challenging the government.

But that may not always be the case in the future. On Oct. 1, the Defense Department inaugurated the new Northern Command, which is charged with defending U.S. territory against external attack and commanding the forces that would support civilian federal agencies if they needed to cope with a terrorist incident.

Details of Northern Command's relationship with support agencies and the forces it would command have not yet been nailed down. But at every opportunity, Defense Secretary Donald H. Rumsfeld and other administration officials emphasize that whatever is done will comply with Posse Comitatus.

That sensitivity was evident in Pentagon statements about their assistance in the sniper hunt. "Everything that the Department of Defense assets will do . . . will be under the direction and the supervision of the FBI," Joint Chiefs of Staff Chairman Gen. Richard B. Myers told reporters Oct. 17.

In the end, the aircraft — a turboprop packed with infrared detection gear — played no role in the arrest of two sniper suspects, who were nabbed Oct. 24 as a result of civilian tips.

Still, Eugene R. Fidell, a Washington specialist on military law, questions the mission's legality, noting that the plane was flown for the express purpose of finding criminal suspects. He said the deployment of the aircraft amounted to using an "emergency power, simply because they had a case they couldn't crack."

But in a taste of what may be heard more often, a number of analysts say that despite Posse Comitatus' general prohibitions of domestic use of the military, the law allows the Pentagon to provide many kinds of assistance to civilian law enforcement agencies.

"Posse Comitatus is only an obstacle if they want it to be one," said Phil Anderson, a homeland security specialist at the Center for Strategic and International Studies, a Washington think tank.

In July, Rumsfeld said no change in the law was needed. "I don't think anyone should hold his breath waiting for changes in Posse Comitatus," he said at the time.

Revisiting the Law

But prominent members of Congress have challenged that view, contending that the law must be revised to give the military a freer hand in acting against terrorists on U.S. territory.

"It served the nation these 100-plus years," John W. Warner, R-Va., said during a Senate Armed Services Committee hearing last October. "But it seems to me it's time to re-examine that doctrine."

The declared scope of the new command's mission hardly suggests that any new authority is needed. From its inception, Northern Command has not been assigned any missions that other Pentagon agencies did not previously

Quick Contents

The inauguration of the Northern Command raises legal questions about the role of the military in domestic law enforcement. But there is more room for the military than many think.

The Army contributed a Northrup Grumman RC-7 reconnaissance aircraft to the Washington, D.C., sniper hunt — a sign of more military involvement in police work.

perform. Its purpose, top officials insist, is to bring greater efficiency to the ways in which the armed services currently operate in domestic emergencies.

Air Force Gen. Ralph E. Eberhardt, Northern Command's first chief, emphasizes that domestic operations almost always would be conducted under the direction of a civilian federal agency, as was the case previously. For example, the Federal Emergency Management Agency would be in charge if federal troops were deployed to deal with the aftermath of a terrorist attack on a city.

"It's not like the movies that we grew up seeing, where the [military] shows up and says, 'We're in charge,' " Eberhardt said last month. "We're going to come in and take [orders] from the lead federal agency. We'll command and control the . . . forces that we bring, but we'll take orders from whoever is in charge."

The posse in hundreds of Western movies got its name from the law, which means "the force of the county" in Latin and refers to the common-law principle that permits a sheriff to call on all able-bodied men to help keep the peace and arrest criminals. After 1854, that included the use of Army units, as well as civilians, to enforce the law, including the Fugitive Slave Act, which required the return of escaped slaves to their owners.

After the Civil War, Army troops preserved law and order in the South, and protected newly emancipated slaves from the depredations of the Ku Klux Klan.

But the deadlocked presidential election of 1876 produced the law in its current form. In a deal that broke the deadlock, Southern Democrats gave the White House to Republican Rutherford B. Hayes, and the Republicans gave the South to the Democrats, abandoning the policy of Reconstruction. Enactment of the Posse Comitatus Act in 1878 ruled out any law enforcement role for the military, leaving Southern blacks to the mercy of their state governments.

Though amended since in minor ways, the basic statute is unchanged. Currently, it prohibits any person from using "any part of the Army or Air Force as a posse comitatus, or otherwise to execute the laws." The law has been extended to cover the Navy and Marine Corps.

"In general, the law has been inter-

preted to forbid the military from directly participating in front-line law enforcement activities, such as arrest, search, seizure, surveillance or pursuit or to serve as informants, undercover agents or investigators," according to a Defense Department paper summarizing the law's effect.

Exceptions to the Rule

From the outset, however, the law has permitted exceptions under which the use of armed forces could be authorized by the Constitution or by amendment.

Federal courts have held that the military can assist civilian law enforcement agencies, so long as the troops play a "passive" role. Thus, the military has lent specialized equipment to local police forces, such as night-vision equipment and the reconnaissance plane used in the Washington sniper case. The military can also provide training on the use of equipment and tactical advice. *(2002 CQ Weekly, p. 2869)*

Moreover, Congress has mandated a military role to manage some politically charged problems. In the 1980s, lawmakers gradually expanded the military role against drug smuggling and illegal immigration.

"It started with drug interdiction," says Craig T. Trebilcock, a lawyer in the Army Reserve. "Then people said, 'Well, maybe we can dual-hat these folks, while they're in the neighborhood, to look for illegal aliens, too.' "

Indeed, Christopher H. Pyle, a constitutional law professor at Mt. Holyoke College, argues that the act often has been cited by military leaders anxious to keep the military out of such domestic missions, concerned that they would erode the forces' combat-readiness.

"The people who have been most eager to cross that boundary are civilian politicians," Pyle said.

Moreover, there are U.S. armed services that are exempt from the 1878 law, at least under some circumstances.

The Coast Guard is a federal law enforcement agency. When a Navy ship on a counter-drug patrol stops a ship at sea, a Coast Guard contingent is sent to board the vessel and, if necessary, make arrests.

Similarly, National Guard units are allowed to perform law enforcement missions when they are acting under the authority of their state governors.

When Guard units are called into federal service, they are bound by the same restrictions as active-duty forces.

The National Guard's exemption from the Posse Comitatus Act is particularly important because in most cases, Guard units would be the nearest military forces to the scene of a terrorist-caused disaster. Moreover, Guard officials and the National Governors' Association contend that, except in the case of a sweeping catastrophe that outstrips a state's ability to handle the problem, Guard units should address such crises in their state role, rather than under Defense Department control.

Northern Command

Before Oct. 1, responsibility for defense of U.S. territory was split among four of the Pentagon's major commands: The Pacific Command looked after Hawaii and the Pacific Coast; the Southern Command defended the Mexican border and Gulf Coast; Joint Forces Command commanded U.S.-based units, and Space Command managed defenses against aerial attack.

Other Pentagon organizations coordinated military assistance to state and federal agencies in case of emergencies.

In mid-April, President Bush approved a plan to reshuffle the command structure to create a single organization responsible for the defense of U.S. territory, except Hawaii, and adjacent waters.

But even at its planned full strength, the new Northern Command will have fewer than 1,000 military and civilian personnel regularly assigned. Forces needed to carry out the command's mission would have to be shifted to its control from other commands. The command's annual budget is expected to be about $70 million.

The new organization would step in to cope with a terrorist incident only if the president decided that the crisis was greater than a state could handle.

The headquarters has established official liaisons with the homeland security directors of each state and has begun establishing working ties with related federal and state agencies. It also has begun a program of regular training exercises to iron out those relationships.

"We have to train and exercise with the local responders," Eberhardt said in his Sept. 7 speech. "This should not be a sandlot pickup game."

A major challenge for the Pentagon's approach to domestic defense may be getting the National Guard focused on that issue.

"The National Guard is the Army's combat reserve," says Anderson of CSIS. "It is an organization that is trained, equipped and manned for the heavy fight," with emphasis on tank and mechanized infantry units.

"What [the Guard] does have is a pre-existing relationship with the state and local level [agencies], which has great value," Anderson says.

A Council on Foreign Relations panel chaired by former Sens. Gary Hart, D-Colo. (1975-87), and Warren B. Rudman, R-N.H. (1980-93), argues the same point.

Specifically, the panel said in a report released in October, the Guard should concentrate more on operating in heavily built-up urban areas and training to support civilian agencies in the aftermath of a catastrophically large terrorist attack.

A particularly sensitive area for the new command is efforts to monitor potential domestic terrorist threats that might require a military response. "The underpinning of all this . . . will be shared intelligence," Eberhardt said.

In an interview broadcast Sept. 27 on PBS' "NewsHour with Jim Lehrer," Eberhardt said the command would have as many as 150 people analyzing intelligence. But he emphasized that they would be collating information gathered by authorized civilian agencies.

"They're, in fact, going to be trying to put the information together so that it's useful for us, and then also trying to decide who we should share this with," Eberhardt said. "We're not going to be out there spying on people." ◆

Political Participation

The articles in this section cover the midterm elections of 2002. On November 5 the Republican Party gained control of the Senate and retained control of the House. What will these developments mean for the 108th Congress?

The first four articles cover the post-election situation in Congress and explore what it means for Republicans and Democrats. With increased numbers in the House, Republicans seem poised to push through the Bush administration's agenda, particularly legislation on the economy and the nation's relationship with Iraq. Another article considers what the elections mean for the Democratic minority, which will need to act as a unified opposition party in Congress and prepare for the 2004 elections.

The next five articles focus individually on the House and Senate, especially party leadership. Stories look at Senate leader Trent Lott, R-Miss., and House Majority Leader Tom DeLay, R-Texas, and their plans for the future. Another article examines the decision of Richard Gephardt, D-Mo., not to run for another term as House minority leader and how this leadership change will affect the House. On November 14 Nancy Pelosi of California was elected as the Democratic party leader—the first woman to hold a top partisan leadership position in Congress. Throughout this section, articles examine the effects on election results of redistricting, upcoming tax and spending legislation and relations with Iraq, as well as what is to come in the next term.

The final article in this series looks at gubernatorial races across the nation. As newly elected governors prepare to take office, how will they accomplish their agendas with inherited budgets? To fund programs, some governors will be forced to consider raising revenues through taxes on cigarettes and alcohol or through legalized gambling.

Still-Thin Edge Leaves GOP With a Cautious Mandate

Pressure is on to move the Bush agenda as bruised Democrats struggle to regroup

So much for the status quo election many people had expected. For that matter, so much for the idea that Americans prefer divided government. They may or may not have voted with the big picture in mind, but either way, the end result of the Nov. 5 midterm election was the same: Republicans once again have been given the chance to lead all three elected branches of government.

Now, President Bush and the Republican leaders of the House and Senate have a second chance to show what they can do with them. The most likely answer: more than they could two years ago — before Bush became a commander in chief with record-shattering popularity levels — but less than the public might expect of a party that has been handed such an opportunity.

It was not the tidal wave that swept Republicans into majorities in the House and Senate in 1994. But then, it did not have to be. With a shift of just two Senate seats, Bush regained what he lost in June 2001: a Republican majority in the Senate to work with the Republican majority in the House. Senate GOP leader Trent Lott of Mississippi is now preparing to reclaim the majority leader office he so famously lost last year when James M. Jeffords of Vermont left the Republican Party. (*Senate, p. 35*)

And House Speaker J. Dennis Hastert of Illinois is looking forward to more breathing room with at least a 228 Republican seats to the Democrats' 202, pending the results of three races still undecided. House Republicans picked up five seats, defying the conventional wisdom that the president's party is supposed to lose seats in midterm elections. (*House, p. 41*)

They are now drawing up an agenda for next year that includes market-based prescription drug coverage for seniors, a supply-focused energy policy, an overhaul of pension laws, and regulatory relief for businesses. But the main message of the election, most Republicans and analysts agree, was one of support for Bush and for getting things done. To be successful, Republicans must prove they can deliver on the biggest issue where Congress can make a difference: the economy. The future of the war on terrorism and a possible war with Iraq is largely in Bush's hands now, but if Congress can pass measures to revive the economy, Republicans can make a difference in people's lives — and help Bush get reelected in 2004.

For Democratic leaders, the fallout was instant and painful. House Minority Leader Richard A. Gephardt of Missouri, a four-time loser in his efforts to regain a majority for his party in the House, stepped down as the leader of House Democrats, setting off a chaotic race to replace him. Senate Democratic leader Tom Daschle of South Dakota, who has more loyalty and sympathy from his caucus, appeared safe from a challenge. But Democrats must decide now how to change their approach after an election in which many in their own party charged that they had nothing to say. (*Democrats, p. 33*)

Bush, by contrast, emerged from the elections with even greater political power. He put his prestige on the line by launching an all-out campaign blitz for Republican candidates, asking voters to help him enact his agenda by giving him a Republican Senate, and it appeared to have worked. Republican voters turned out more heavily than Democratic voters, following a last-minute shift in voter sentiment that, according to a Gallup Poll analysis, coincided with the timing of Bush's campaign trips.

The reality, though, is that the Senate will be almost as narrowly divided as it was in the 107th Congress. So far, Republicans can claim only 51 seats. The South Dakota Senate race has not been decided officially, but incumbent Democrat Tim Johnson appeared to have won a narrow victory over Republican John Thune, and Thune indicated he will not seek a recount if that lead is confirmed in the official vote count the week of Nov. 11. Democratic Sen. Mary L. Landrieu of Louisiana is headed for a Dec. 7 runoff against Republican Suzanne Haik Terrell.

Even if Landrieu is defeated in the runoff, that will still leave Republicans far short of the 60 votes needed to end filibusters in the Senate. That means Bush and Lott will have to build some kind of relationship with Senate Democrats to avoid such holdups.

"Some people say, you know, 'Full steam ahead, just get it done.' That's easier said than done in the Senate," Lott said.

Daschle, who has proven he knows how to use every maneuver in the minority leader's playbook to force votes and block legislation, said Bush was effective in campaigning for his agenda. But he said Senate Democrats would keep fighting for their priorities, and he held out the possibility of playing legislative offense by amending GOP bills and filibustering conservative judicial nominees.

Still, Republicans and analysts said the election proved that voters responded to Bush's agenda — and that Democrats may have to take what they can get on many issues to build a record of accomplishments.

Although Bush was careful not to claim a broad mandate from the voters, lawmakers and analysts say the Republican victories will strengthen his case for key proposals such as finishing the homeland security bill (HR 5005), getting his judicial nominees confirmed by the Senate and making last year's tax cuts (PL 107-16) permanent.

Bush is also asking Congress to finish its work on a terrorism insurance bill (HR 3210) and energy legislation (HR 4). Next year, he said, lawmakers should renew their efforts to provide prescription drug coverage to seniors.

The window of opportunity for dealmaking in the 108th Congress will be narrowed by the politics of a presidential election year and, perhaps, a war with Iraq. But Lott said the Senate also will

The Republicans who will run the government, Hastert, Bush and Lott, are devising their 2003 agenda, and they are being warned not to overreach if they want to win again in 2004.

focus on passing pension overhaul and welfare legislation that stalled in the 107th — as well as adopting a budget resolution, an effort that failed in 2002 because Senate Democrats were so divided that Daschle never brought their resolution (S Con Res 100) to the floor.

"I believe if there is a mandate in any election, at least in this one, it's the people [who] want something to get done," Bush said at a Nov. 7 news conference. "They want people to work together in Washington, D.C. to pass meaningful legislation which will improve their lives."

Said Hastert: "I think people are tired of this gridlock that they've seen in the Congress, with the Senate holding up all legislation or a lot of the legislation that we've passed. And I think they want to see a good, positive movement in the Congress."

The Challenges of Narrow Majorities

Right away, GOP strategists and leading Democrats were warning Bush and Republican leaders not to overplay their hand by trying to force divisive issues through Congress, and they gave assurances that they will not. But with the White House, the House and the Senate in Republican hands, they may face just as much pressure not to play it too safe, either.

The day after the election, Lott promised not to overreach in pushing Republican proposals through a narrowly divided Senate. "This president did receive an incredible, historical endorsement of support by the American people. They have expressed their trust in him and in us. And we will not abuse it," he said.

But then again, how would they know? The very nature of overreaching is that the political parties do not realize when they are doing it. Democrats did not believe they were overreaching when they tried to pass President Bill Clinton's sweeping health care overhaul plan in 1993 and 1994, when Democrats controlled the White House and Congress. They learned differently when they lost the House and Senate in the 1994 elections. *(1994 Almanac, p. 319)*

And Republicans did not believe they were overreaching in 1995 when, after gaining the House and Senate majori-

ties, they tried to muscle through a budget-reconciliation package that would have fundamentally restructured Medicare and Medicaid. They figured it out when Clinton's veto led to a government shutdown — and the public overwhelmingly sided with Clinton. *(1995 Almanac, p. 2-3)*

Already, Democrats are warning Republicans not to try to advance proposals such as abortion restrictions or Bush's plan to add private savings accounts to Social Security. And they have promised to keep opposing judicial nominees they view as too conservative. "If they are going to continue to nominate right-wing ideologues, that will cause a battle on the Senate floor," said Sen. Edward M. Kennedy, D-Mass.

Some Republicans, however, say there will be no point in having control of Congress and the White House if they shy away from everything that might be controversial.

Sen. Chuck Hagel, R-Neb., who has been a voice of caution in his party on issues such as Iraq, nevertheless said Congress should at least begin debates over restructuring Social Security to improve its long-term solvency and Medicare to make it more efficient.

"I know, it's the third rail and it's a politically sensitive issue," Hagel said of Social Security. "But my goodness, why are we here? . . . If we're not going to take on the tough issues, we're useless."

Sen. Jon Kyl of Arizona, who is expected to be elected the next chairman of the Senate Republican Policy Committee, said the GOP needs to strengthen and expand its base by producing a bold and unified agenda, as it did in 1994. Neither party had a clear agenda to offer voters in the midterm elections, Kyl said: "If we didn't have George W. Bush and the strength of his popularity, we might have lost this one."

GOP leaders say their agenda was clear enough to draw some lessons from the voters. One of the biggest, they said, was that homeland security and the war on terrorism are important to voters, and their urgency should not be minimized.

"You cannot ignore the fact that America did change on 9/11 . . . and I think that did have an effect on this election," Lott said. The message to Congress, he said, is to "sup-

GOP Won Midterm War by Winning Series of Small Battles

From the instant that the 2002 election results became clear, Washington buzzed with talk about a new voter mandate for Republicans to carry out an ambitious legislative agenda.

But in reality, the 2002 elections did not reflect a sea change in the political preferences of the American electorate. The partisan pendulum swung only a few degrees off center.

The Republicans held just less than 51 percent of the seats in Congress going into the elections, and will come out with just less than 53 percent when all the votes are counted. By comparison, in the big partisan swing election of 1994, Republicans jumped from less than 42 percent of Congress to 53 percent.

Of the 34 states that held Senate elections this year, only four involuntarily retired their incumbents — pending a recanvass in South Dakota and a Dec. 7 runoff in Louisiana.

Even more striking is the fact that no more than four of the 390 House incumbents standing for re-election Nov. 5 were defeated by non-incumbent challengers. The Republicans' net gain of seats will end up in the low single digits in the Senate and only a few seats higher in the House.

It is often the case in politics that the interpretation of the results is more pronounced than the results themselves. But in this case it seems more so. Why?

First, the Senate shift was historic. For the first time since the direct election of senators was ratified in 1913, the president's party took control of the Senate from the opposition in a midterm election. And that victory will give Republicans complete control of the policymaking branches of the federal government.

Second, the Nov. 5 outcome represented a personal victory for Bush.

To an unusual degree, he put his presidential prestige on the line by staging an energetic cross-country push to boost his party's candidates.

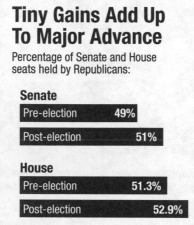

Tiny Gains Add Up To Major Advance
Percentage of Senate and House seats held by Republicans:

Senate
Pre-election 49%
Post-election 51%

House
Pre-election 51.3%
Post-election 52.9%

This was a risky strategy for an incumbent who must turn to his own prospects for re-election in two years. But it paid off famously: The blitz was a major, and perhaps, a determining factor in several key victories.

The third factor is the gravity of the two major issues of the day: national security and the economy. The winning party can and will claim a mandate to protect the homeland and fix the economy.

Bush already has demanded that Congress approve legislation creating a Department of Homeland Security. And Republicans are preparing an economic stimulus plan that is based on tax cuts.

Caution Flags

Here is where the dangers of overreaching are most apparent. Should the economy rebound, the 2002 elections may be remembered as the beginning of a great Republican era in American history.

But if the economy remains troubled, Washington's ruling Republicans will have a harder time than they did this year in sharing the blame with their Democratic foes.

A close look at this year's Senate results raises a caution for Republicans tempted to play the mandate card.

The battle for Senate control was fought on turf that was highly favorable to the Republicans. The Democrats' seven strongest bids to take over Republican-held seats all were in states that Bush carried in the 2000 presidential contest. But four of the six most vulnerable seats that the Democrats had to defend also were in states won by Bush. The exceptions, Minnesota and Iowa, were taken only narrowly by Democratic presidential nominee Al Gore.

But even with that edge, the Republicans' recapture of the Senate hinged on GOP Rep. Saxby Chambliss' upset, by 7 percentage points, of Georgia Democratic Sen. Max Cleland, and two cliffhanger wins.

The latter were a 1 percentage-point win by GOP former Rep. Jim Talent over Democratic Sen. Jean Carnahan in Missouri, and a 2-point win in Minnesota by former St. Paul Mayor Norm Coleman over former Vice President Walter F. Mondale, who stepped in after incumbent Paul Wellstone was killed in a plane crash.

In the House, virtually all of the GOP gains were the results of redistricting overhauls that resulted from reapportionment, which shifted seats mainly to fast-growing, GOP-friendly states in the South and West from slower-growing northern and eastern states more amenable to Democrats.

And the contests for control of both chambers boiled down to a handful of hotly contested races. This played into the hands of the Republicans who — as has been the case for years — enjoyed a large fundraising advantage over the Democrats. The GOP thus was able to concentrate torrents of money in that relatively small number of "battleground" states and districts.

Hence, a series of small wins at the margins of partisan politics became a victory of major, historic consequence.

Before and After

The closeness in the party divide over the last two years meant that a comparatively small number of Republican gains on Nov. 5 will have a big impact.

Pre-election

1 **Independent**
3 vacancies

House Democrats 208
House Republicans 223

1 **Independent**
1 vacancy**

Senate Democrats 49
Senate Republicans 49

**Sen. Paul Wellstone, D-Minn., died in a plane crash Oct. 25.

January line-up

1 **Independent**
1 runoff
1 too close to call

House Democrats 204*
House Republicans 228

1 **Independent**
1 runoff

Senate Democrats 47
Senate Republican 51

*Rep. Patsy T. Mink, D-Hawaii, died Sept. 28 but won her election. A special election will decide her replacement for the 108th Congress on Jan. 4.

port and work with our president as the commander in chief."

Experts warn that Bush can jeopardize that support by pushing divisive initiatives. "If he interprets this election as an across-the-board mandate, he's nuts," said Richard F. Fenno Jr., a professor of political science at the University of Rochester in New York.

On the other hand, much of Bush's presidency has been about proving wrong the conventional wisdom on the danger of acting too boldly. When he took office in 2001, facing a divided Congress after losing the popular vote, lawmakers advised him to start cautiously; he responded by pushing through the biggest tax cut in two decades.

Bush's popularity — his approval ratings are still hovering above 60 percent more than a year after the Sept. 11 attacks — is one big factor that has changed since the last time the GOP held all three elected branches of government. Along with the success of the first election held since he took office, that could make it easier for him to work with a narrowly divided Senate than it was the last time.

It certainly will help him fend off disagreements with congressional Republicans. "There is nobody on Capitol Hill who doesn't recognize that the

majority in both houses of Congress is a factor of the president putting his prestige on the line," said former Rep. Robert S. Walker, R-Pa. (1977-97), who served in the House GOP leadership under Speaker Newt Gingrich, R-Ga. (1979-99).

Still, Bush can overreach just as easily by pushing congressional Republicans too far as he can by antagonizing Democrats. During a Nov. 7 news conference, when he asked lawmakers to finish the homeland security bill before the 107th Congress ends, he threw a wrench into Lott's plans; Lott had wanted to keep the upcoming lame-duck session short and return to the homeland security bill next year. (*2002 CQ Weekly, p. 2901*)

"We have a wonderful operating team, and we are all part of the same team," said one former Republican leadership aide. "If that team turns out to be one guy with a megaphone who doesn't think that the rest of the team players are allowed on the field, then there's going to be a problem."

Regaining the majority in the Senate, with control of the floor schedule and the committees, does give Republicans considerable power to break the Democratic logjam that has stopped much of the White House agenda.

The significance of holding the ma-

jority in the Senate is that "you get to schedule what legislation comes to the floor," said former Sen. Connie Mack, R-Fla. (1989-2001), who was chairman of the Senate Republican Conference under Lott and is now a senior policy adviser at Shaw Pittman, a lobbying firm in Washington. That means Bush priorities can move to the full Senate and either succeed or fail there, rather than being bottled up in committee.

Getting nominees or bills to the floor does not guarantee success. But "you have a better chance of winning the game if you can start it," Mack said.

The Opportunities

Among the bills whose chances will be instantly improved is the president's "faith-based initiative," which would allow religious groups to compete for federal money to provide social services. A compromise version of that legislation (S 1924) has been stalled since last summer, opposed by many Democrats. (*2002 CQ Weekly, p. 1796*)

The shift in control also breathes new life into a "tripartisan" plan (S 2) for adding prescription drug coverage to Medicare, backed by Republican Charles E. Grassley of Iowa, Democrat John B. Breaux of Louisiana and Jeffords. That plan, like a House-passed bill that Bush favors (HR 4954), would look to private insurers to design and offer a benefit. Democrats have fought to make any drug benefit a part of the government-run Medicare program.

Proponents of the tripartisan bill said that Daschle kept it from coming before the Finance Committee, where they said they had the votes to prevail. Daschle instead took the debate straight to the floor, where none of the competing drug plans got enough votes to overcome procedural hurdles. (*2002 CQ Weekly, p. 2111*)

Lott has said passing a Medicare drug plan is one of his top priorities for the 108th Congress, and a GOP aide said Republican leaders favor the tripartisan bill. Back in the majority, Republicans have considerable power to push such a bill through the Finance Committee and see that it hits the floor with plenty of momentum.

Or they could wedge the measure into the protective framework of a budget "reconciliation" bill, which cannot be filibustered.

Most immediately, the new GOP majority gives Bush a better chance of seeing his nominees to the federal

Georgia Republicans Energized By 'Friend to Friend' Campaigns

Georgia Republicans won big last week using a strategy that sounds almost quaint by today's standards: knock on every door, lean on friends of friends, then load up the vans on Election Day. This return to traditional politicking was enough to knock state Democrats for a loop — and knock their U.S. senator, governor and leaders of both statehouse chambers out of office.

Big money and television ads did not win the race for the Georgia GOP. Freshman Democratic Sen. Max Cleland and Gov. Roy Barnes far outspent their Republican rivals and still lost.

What the GOP had was a meticulous organizational plan, including computer analysis, a training program for volunteers and a voter registration drive that included Hispanics, a growing minority in the state, followed by a massive mailing, telephone and neighborhood canvass in the closing days of the campaign. The glitz was a Nov. 2 visit by President Bush to energize the ranks.

Democrats never saw what hit them. "For all the focus on bells and whistles and tactical ingenuity, in the end you still win elections now as a century ago: friend to friend," said Ralph Reed, chairman of the Georgia Republican Party.

When he was director of the Christian Coalition, Reed pioneered what opponents came to call the stealth campaign — organize and energize your base but stay out of the limelight and below the media radar.

In Georgia, Reed helped put together a "72-hour task force" of volunteers to strike before Democrats had time to respond.

Blaise Hazelwood, political director of the National Republican Committee, calls the Georgia strategy a "back to the future" approach. "The only thing that's new is the technology we were able to use, like the Palm Pilots we were using," she said.

Rep. John Linder of Georgia, a former chairman of the National Republican Campaign Committee that

tries to elect House members, said the idea of a last-minute intensive voter drive had proven its worth.

"Grass-roots work at that point will be key for the Bush re-election campaign and for congressional races" in 2004, Linder said.

Sweeping the South

Cleland, Barnes and other Georgia Democrats had a number of other things going against them, of course, not least Bush's popularity and a trend toward the GOP across the South. Georgia, in fact, is the last Southern state to elect a Republican governor since Reconstruction, though races have been close since 1990.

"The state has been trending Republican for a decade," said Georgia Sen. Zell Miller, a Democrat. Miller, a former governor, was elected to the Senate following the death of Republican Sen. Paul Coverdell in 2000, and he seemed to see the handwriting on the wall, frequently siding with Bush and the Republicans in Washington.

bench confirmed. For months, Republicans have accused Judiciary Committee Chairman Patrick J. Leahy of Vermont of slow-walking conservative nominees and working to undercut Bush's power to shape the federal judiciary. (2002 CQ Weekly, p. 2722)

The Judiciary Committee's incoming chairman, Republican Orrin G. Hatch of Utah, will see to it that nominees move quickly to the Senate floor.

Lott has said he will move to the floor two nominees to the 5th U.S. Circuit Court of Appeals blocked earlier this year by Democrats on the Judiciary Committee: Priscilla Owen of Texas and Charles W. Pickering Sr. of Mississippi, a friend of Lott's.

But one Judiciary Democrat, Charles E. Schumer of New York, says it would be a mistake for Bush and Republicans to push those two nominees again. "Democrats in the Senate have opposed only those nominees with the most ex-

treme views," he said. "Given the fact that moving the Senate forward takes 60 votes, we believe [we] will be able to continue our efforts to bring moderation to the federal bench."

If Bush does have a mandate from this election, it came from the enthusiasm of his own political base — and from the lackluster support Democrats received from their voters.

For the last few months before the election, it was unclear whether the election would turn on the war on terrorism or the debate over possible military action in Iraq — both issues that would favor Republicans — or the nation's lackluster economy, an issue that might favor the Democrats.

Why It Happened

From all signs, the factor that overshadowed everything else was the same one that determined the 1994 midterm elections: Republicans were motivated

to vote and Democrats were not.

While overall turnout was up slightly from the 1998 midterm elections — approximately 39.3 percent of eligible voters went to the polls this year — Democratic turnout was down 1.3 percentage points from 1998, while Republican turnout increased by half a percentage point, according to an analysis by the Committee for the Study of the American Electorate, a nonpartisan research organization.

And among those who showed up, pollsters say, the war on terrorism drew votes for Republicans much more strongly than the economy drew votes for Democrats. A post-election survey of 1,600 voters by GOP pollster Bill McInturff found that Republicans only narrowly lost the votes of people whose top priority was the economy, while those whose top concerns were the war on terrorism and Iraq voted for Republicans so decisively that their votes

"The Republican Party is never going to dominate the South the way Democrats once did," said GOP pollster Whit Ayres, who is based in Atlanta. "But all things being even, there's now a general preference for Republicans to various degrees throughout the South, and it means that Bush is very likely to once again sweep every Southern state in 2004."

The Nov. 5 results shook the state's establishment. State Rep. Tom Murphy, the imperious, cigar smoking House speaker since 1974 who made no secret of his distaste for all Republicans, was turned out of office.

State Senate Majority Leader Charles W. Walker lost his seat. His son, Charles Walker Jr., lost his race in a district his father helped design for him. In fact, of the three House seats the state legislature framed expressly to elect Democrats, two were captured by Republicans.

Cleland, a triple-amputee from the Vietnam War, had campaigned for the Senate in 1997 as a moderate Democrat in the mold of former Sen. Sam Nunn (1972-97). His opponent this year, Rep. Saxby Chambliss, portrayed him as too liberal for the state and soft on defense.

Barnes, the governor, had his own problems the GOP could exploit.

GOP Sweeps Through Georgia

Republicans used organization rather than big money to unseat top Democrats in the state. Victims of the election-day sweep:

- **Gov. Roy Barnes**, right, lost to Sonny Perdue.

- **U.S. Sen. Max Cleland** was defeated by Rep. Saxby Chambliss

- **State House Speaker Tom Murphy** of Bremen and **State Senate Majority Leader Charles W. Walker** of Augusta lost their re-election bids.

Teachers were angry with his education plans. Southern traditionalists were furious that he changed the state flag to shrink the size of the confederate emblem. Even gambling interests went after him for banning video poker machines.

The GOP was able to knit much of this discontent into its grass-roots organization and expand its reach. The party says it registered 50,000 new Hispanic voters in the state.

During the weekend before the election and on the heels of Bush's visit, party officials arranged calls to

170,000 voters who had voiced interest in a dozen specific issues. The party sent out millions of flyers; volunteers knocked on thousands of doors in Republican neighborhoods.

From now on, Republicans say, such grassroots drives will be critical.

"Georgia is a good example to use in the next campaign, as was Colorado," Hazelwood said. "We've proven this time that it's a success, and next time we'll be able to do it even better. . . . It started in 2000 and we're getting stronger every time."

more than made up the difference.

Much of the credit for the Republican turnout has to go to Bush's decision to campaign so vigorously for GOP candidates, analysts said. But they added that Republicans improved their get-out-the-vote operations and overcame the advantage Democrats displayed in 1998 and 2000.

For example, Hastert personally made a pitch for a "72-Hour Task Force" the Illinois Republican Party put together to turn out the vote. In a message on the party's Web site, Hastert warned that Democratic presidential nominee Al Gore almost defeated Bush in 2000 because "the Democrats did a much better job marshaling their supporters with an intense voter-turnout program in the last 72 hours of the election. We can't afford to let that happen again, because there is too much at stake in this election."

The other factor, some analysts say,

is that Republicans were no longer the ones with the angry, negative message, as they were seen in the 1990s while Clinton delivered an optimistic Democratic agenda. While both sides launched their share of attacks, the analysts say, it was the Republicans who had a positive agenda this time — led by Bush — while Democrats delivered a negative message that criticized Bush's policies without offering alternatives.

In 1994, "Republicans were motivated primarily out of anger," said Thomas E. Patterson, a professor of government at Harvard University's Kennedy School of Government and author of "The Vanishing Voter." "This time, I think it's more of a positive reaction to Bush and the Republicans and what's happened since 2000."

By contrast, while Daschle said Democrats could not get their message out about the economy because of the Iraq debate, the party's critics said the

bigger problem was that Democrats did not have a coherent alternative to offer voters. That failure, along with their reluctance to challenge Bush on Iraq, meant this election never had the true debate voters need to make an informed choice, some analysts say.

"What you want is a conversation where an argument is made and a counterargument is made," said James Fishkin, a professor of government at the University of Texas at Austin who organizes discussion forums to help voters become better informed on election issues. "The Democrats had ducked too many issues, and to the extent that there was a dialogue, it was a dialogue of attack ads."

It is a safe bet that the Democrats will spend much of the next two years trying to make that counterargument — which means Bush and the Republicans will have to move on their agenda sooner rather than later. ◆

Economy Crucial for GOP

Tax and spending legislation loom large in the 108th

President Bush and Republican congressional leaders will have little time for post-election euphoria.

While the troubled national economy did not appear to hurt the Republicans significantly in the midterm elections, the GOP will try to neutralize the issue before the voters are heard from again, when the stakes will be even higher.

Once GOP control of the 108th Congress was assured on election night, Republicans knew that providing remedies for sagging consumer confidence, investors' loss of faith in the stock market and sputtering economic growth would be their responsibility during the next two years. There would be no Democratically controlled Senate to blame the next time the stock market took a dive or millions of Americans were frightened by 401(k) statements.

"Republicans say all they want to do is stimulate the economy, create jobs and put money in people's pockets. They have an ambitious agenda. And they have two years to do whatever they want to do. But now they have to deliver," said William G. Gale, a Brookings Institution economist. "If they don't deliver, they will have no one to blame but themselves."

A centerpiece of the GOP's strategy will be an extension of last year's $1.35 trillion 10-year tax cuts (PL 107-16), possibly packaged with new tax breaks for business and investors.

House Ways and Means Committee Chairman Bill Thomas, R-Calif., promised on Nov. 6 that in order to spur the economy, House and Senate Republicans will provide tax relief for families and small-business owners, as well as affordable health care for all and "much-needed reforms" in Medicare and retirement programs.

The Federal Reserve Board quickly reinforced the message that Republicans are on their own. The day after the elections, its governors cut interest rates

Economic Stimulus Torch Is Passed

THE FED IS FINISHED:
Federal Reserve Board Chairman Alan Greenspan and his colleagues went beyond the expected on Nov. 6, dropping interest rates by half a point. With the federal funds rate down to 1.25 percent, Greenspan signaled that further rate cuts are unlikely, leaving the Bush administration and Congress to figure out what to do next.

CONGRESSIONAL LEADERS TAKE OVER:
House Ways and Means Committee Chairman Bill Thomas, R-Calif., left, and incoming Senate Finance Committee Chairman Charles E. Grassley, R-Iowa, will be key players when the administration and congressional leaders make their expected bid to stimulate the economy with additional tax cuts. The business community is particularly interested in tax breaks that will encourage investment, while President Bush and Republicans in Congress yearn to make last year's tax cuts permanent.

Greenspan

Thomas

Grassley

by a healthy half a percentage point and signaled that no more stimulative reductions are likely any time soon.

With the monetary policy option exhausted for now, tax and spending legislation driven by the Republican majorities in the House and Senate and signed by Bush now appears to be the only available lever to pump up the economy and prevent a new recession.

"What this means is that any further stimulus will have to come from Congress," said Peter J. Wallison, a resident fellow at the American Enterprise Institute and a former Treasury general counsel. "I'm sure there will be pressure for Congress to stimulate the economy, whether or not it is needed."

For congressional Republicans,

stimulating the economy has recently meant essentially one thing: tax cuts. But the GOP majority and Democratic minority will collide head-on over tax fairness and fiscal responsibility.

The 2001 package will cost the government $1.35 trillion in lost revenue by the time it expires at the end of 2010. Making those cuts permanent — a goal for Bush regardless of economic performance — would increase the budget deficit, though only after 2010.

Deficit increases will be more immediate — and likely would turn into a main issue in the tax cut debate — if Bush proposes further cuts or asks Congress to accelerate those that are being phased in under the 2001 law.

Lobbyists and lawmakers say increasing the deficit likely would give pause to members of both parties, and could be an obstacle to House and Senate passage of proposals that are being readied to stimulate the economy next year with tax breaks for business and investors.

Ron Utt, a senior research fellow at the Heritage Foundation, said the deficit will be a major hurdle for Republicans because the red ink is already likely to increase in the event of a war with Iraq and as a result of increased spending demands for homeland security and transportation.

"A lot of things are going to get locked up by big deficits and competing demands," Utt said. "Deficit politics is probably going to return. It's going to be hard for lawmakers in both parties to vote for measures that increase the deficit."

Republican leaders are searching for ways to deflect Democratic accusations that tax cut proposals that would increase deficit spending amount to a raid on the Treasury for the benefit of the wealthy. Republicans will argue that the impact of tax cuts on deficits is overstated because the estimates Congress works with do not reflect tax cuts' beneficial economic impact.

The GOP is preparing to have the Joint Committee on Taxation and the Congressional Budget Office use so-called dynamic scoring that could considerably reduce the projected cost of tax cuts.

"Efforts will be accelerated to move toward new scoring methods," said House Republican Policy Committee Chairman Christopher Cox of California. "The old methods are like putting a thumb on the scale."

Dynamic scoring involves broader analysis of the economic impacts of tax and spending proposals. Proponents, including Thomas, say that since tax cuts result in business expansion and increased economic activity, cost estimates should include offsetting revenue increases.

Opponents of dynamic scoring, including Congressional Budget Office Director Dan L. Crippen, say there is no consensus in the economic community about how it should be done, and that dynamic scoring would politicize budget forecasts.

Democrats say dynamic scoring would distort the budget debate and make it more difficult to compare the impact of tax bills against enacted tax

Tax Cut Becomes Top Priority

President Bush's proposal to extend last year's tax cut has moved quickly to the top of the priority list for the 108th Congress and will be the centerpiece of an ambitious fiscal agenda.

The permanent extension of the tax cut (PL 107-16), which will reduce revenues by $1.35 trillion before it expires in 2010, is expected to move as a stand-alone bill early next year. Budget rules and Democratic opposition had blocked Republicans from making the tax cuts permanent. (*2001 Almanac, p. 18-3*)

The GOP also is expected to promote measures aimed at simplifying the tax code and cutting taxes for businesses and investors. (*2002 CQ Weekly, p. 2811*)

Democrats blame last year's tax cut for the return of deficit spending over the short term, and for wiping out much of the $5.6 trillion 10-year surplus projected just two years ago. They argue that a permanent extension would add trillions of dollars to the deficit. The Joint Committee on Taxation has estimated that the extension would cost $354 billion just for the first two years, 2011 and 2012.

Despite their party's setbacks in the Nov. 5 elections, most Democrats, including Senate Democratic Leader Tom Daschle of South Dakota, will continue to oppose efforts to extend the tax cuts. "He feels it would be devastating to the economy, the national budget and the outlook of American families," said Ranit Schmelzer, a Daschle spokeswoman.

And the Republican gains in the Senate were offset by the loss of some Democratic allies. Two of the 12 Senate Democrats who voted for the 2001 tax cut — Max Cleland of Georgia and Jean Carnahan of Mis-

souri — were defeated Nov. 5. And Robert G. Torricelli of New Jersey is retiring at the end of the year.

The campaign for an extension is likely to begin in the House. "There will be a push quickly for the extension of the tax cut," said Stuart Roy, a spokesman for House Majority Whip Tom DeLay, R-Texas.

In the Senate, Republican Leader Trent Lott of Mississippi called for quick action on legislation that would "target some tax cuts that would help the economy." He echoed arguments by House GOP leaders last month.

Key Democrats say they are open to a compromise similar to a stimulus law (PL 107-147) enacted earlier this year that paired cuts for businesses and investors with jobless benefits. (*2002 CQ Weekly, p. 633*)

An extension of jobless aid could be paired with GOP tax cut measures similar to those that stalled last month, including a proposal to increase from $3,000 to $8,250 the amount of capital losses investors can deduct each year on their tax returns. Business lobbyists are pressing for another House GOP proposal to increase from $25,000 to $50,000 the amount of capital investment expenses that small businesses can deduct on their tax returns.

Republicans also are expecting White House proposals to simplify the tax code. "I think that the administration is going to be advancing fundamental tax reform," said Christopher Cox, R-Calif., chairman of the House Republican Policy Committee. However, Cox said he doubted that a substantial restructuring of the tax code could be enacted in the 108th Congress. "Fundamental reform will require a referendum in a national election," Cox said.

cuts. John M. Spratt Jr. of South Carolina, ranking Democrat on the House Budget Committee, calls dynamic scoring "a discredited supply-side notion that tax cuts pay for themselves."

Another change that could affect next year's debate on taxes and

deficits is the Bush administration's expected move toward five-year budget projections, like those already used by the House.

Supporters of the change argue that abandoning the current 10-year projections would recognize the difficulty of predicting the course of the economy so far into the future. But those opposed to the change contend that a five-year perspective understates the long-range cost of tax and spending initiatives.

The Business Agenda

If the administration and congressional Republicans need further inspiration to stimulate the economy, the business community is ready to provide it. Corporate lobbyists, eager for their support of GOP congressional candidates to pay dividends, will push for their own priorities including new tax cuts, a pre-emption of data privacy regulation by the states, energy production incentives and limits on liability claims related to asbestos and medical malpractice.

After seeing their proposals gather dust in a closely divided Congress during most of 2002, business groups are practically giddy about the outlook for the new Congress.

"There is a sense of euphoria on K Street. There is a sense that pro-business legislation will be moving," said Jim Albertine, president of the American League of Lobbyists.

Business lobbyists are pushing for a new package of tax breaks for corporations — including more generous write-offs for the cost of equipment.

They also expect Republicans to try, as part of a larger stimulus package, to make modest changes in pension and retirement savings regulations, such as raising the ceiling on individual tax-free contributions.

More immediately, lobbyists are intent on seeing final action during the lame-duck session of the 107th Congress on the conference reports on bankruptcy overhaul (HR 333) and a federal backstop for insurers offering terrorism insurance (HR 3210).

The business community wants much more from the GOP-controlled 108th Congress than tax breaks.

Data privacy regulation will be a prominent issue because of an expiring provision of the Fair Credit Reporting Act (PL 91-508) that pre-empts some state privacy rules. Financial services companies and direct marketers want Congress to extend the pre-emption or, better still, make it permanent.

Corporations also want Congress to write a national energy policy that handles tax and environmental issues in a way that encourages domestic oil

production. But Democrats and even some Republicans are sure to continue to oppose opening any of Alaska's Arctic National Wildlife Refuge to oil and gas explorations.

Also high on the business shopping list is an overhaul of laws governing lawsuits seeking compensation and damages for asbestos exposure and medical malpractice. And if Congress finally clears legislation to help the elderly with the cost of prescription drugs, business wants private insurers to play a leading role in the new coverage.

Machinery and technology exporters want the administration to complete trade agreements with Chile and Singapore. The exporters hope it will be easier now to win congressional approval of those agreements.

Lobbyists predict that the weak economy and sagging stock market are likely to cause lawmakers and the administration to postpone until 2004 a debate on how to shore up Social Security. Bush is expected to begin making his case next year for allowing younger workers to put some of their contributions into private investment accounts, but no legislative proposal is likely until after the upcoming tax-cut debates.

Building Confidence

In its bid to restore investor confidence, the White House needs to combat a perception encouraged by Democrats during the recent campaigns that the administration's economic team is ineffective and that it has little interest in tightening corporate accountability.

A first step will be nominating a new chairman of the Securities and Exchange Commission (SEC).

Harvey L. Pitt, who became an inviting Democratic target during his 15-month tenure as a result of political missteps and his previous ties to major accounting firms, resigned from the SEC post on Election Day. He ultimately was undone by bipartisan congressional criticism of his handling of the appointment of a five-member accounting industry oversight board created by the corporate fraud law (PL 107-204) enacted in July with the aim of restoring investor confidence. (2002 CQ Weekly, p. 2018)

Democrats accused Pitt of abandoning a qualified candidate to head the oversight board, John H. Biggs, at the behest of the accounting industry and House Financial Services Committee Chairman Michael G. Oxley, R-Ohio.

Pitt's departure appeared inevitable after The New York Times reported that he chose not to tell the four other SEC commissioners that his choice for the chairman's job, former CIA and FBI director William H. Webster, had headed the audit committee of a financially troubled company. That disclosure prompted two internal SEC investigations and a General Accounting Office probe.

"The last thing investors need is the kind of turmoil we're seeing at the SEC," said Bruce Josten, executive vice president of government affairs at the U.S. Chamber of Commerce, before Pitt stepped down.

Pitt's exit might be only the first departure from Bush's team as the administration attempts to hone its message on the economy and produce results before the president and congressional Republicans stand for re-election in 2004.

Bush irritably brushed aside questions about his economic team during his Nov. 7 press conference, telling reporters that the group "developed the [2001] tax cut package, sold the tax cut package, is implementing the tax cut package, and for that they deserve a lot of credit."

Speculation on additional departures has focused on Lawrence Lindsey, director of the National Economic Council. Some congressional aides call Lindsey politically inept and unable to sell his ideas for reviving the economy on Capitol Hill. The Bush adviser is scheduled to speak Nov. 13 to a U.S. Chamber of Commerce forum on the outlook for the economy.

Treasury Secretary Paul H. O'Neill, long perceived as out of step with the rest of the administration, is said to remain in Bush's favor as he leads the White House effort to prepare a broad tax code overhaul proposal as early as next year.

R. Glenn Hubbard, chairman of the Council of Economic Advisers, often is reported to be thinking of returning to academia, but may stay on and handle an expanded portfolio.

Now that Bush no longer can blame a Democratically controlled Senate for thwarting his economic revival efforts, the president and his team will have to show nervous investors, anxious business lobbyists and ultimately voters that they can obtain results with the cooperation of a Republican-controlled Congress. ◆

Questions Remain on Iraq

GOP majorities mean conflicts will take new form

President Bush faces tough questions from his own party and renewed opposition from Democrats about the conduct of war and its aftermath in Iraq, notwithstanding last week's Republican electoral victories and U.N. Security Council approval of a resolution insisting that Iraq disarm its nuclear, chemical and biological weapons programs.

"The debate about whether we're going to deal with Saddam Hussein is over," Bush declared in his Nov. 7 news conference, referring to the Iraqi leader. "Now the question is how do we deal with him."

That is still a big question, even after the Nov. 8 unanimous Security Council vote and last month's congressional vote to approve the Iraq war resolution (H J Res 114 — PL 107-243). The issue of how the administration deals with Saddam and Iraq raises a number of unanswered questions that Bush has yet to address in detail. With respected GOP foreign policy moderates already demanding answers, the result could be constraints on Bush's freedom to maneuver, imposed by his own party.

Among the most urgent questions for these moderates is the administration's plans for a post-war Iraq. The incoming chairman of the Senate Foreign Relations Committee, Richard G. Lugar of Indiana, already is pressing Bush to spell out his plans, saying the administration has yet to articulate its vision for how the postwar Iraq will be governed. He says lawmakers and the American public have yet to grapple with the potential military and financial costs of a postwar U.S. occupation.

"We're going to have to have a lot of discussion of this," Lugar said. "This is a big issue for many of us because of the vast expense and potential doctrinal differences" over nation-building that divide the Republican Party.

Meanwhile, Democrats, newly shorn of much political responsibility,

Lugar, left, who will replace Helms, right, as top Republican on the Senate Foreign Relations Committee, is pressing the Bush administration for its plans for a postwar Iraq.

may now feel free to raise the volume of their opposition to war with Iraq. That could affect opinion polls, which show that public support for the issue is fragile.

A key moment in determining whether the nation's nascent anti-war movement coalesces into a more serious political phenomenon could come when House Democrats choose a replacement for outgoing minority leader Richard A. Gephardt of Missouri.

One candidate, Harold E. Ford Jr. of Tennessee, supported a war authorization backed by Bush and Gephardt. The other, Minority Whip Nancy Pelosi of California, opposed it. (*House Democrats, p. 43*)

Shaping the Debate

In any event, partisan tensions can be expected to resurface as the 2004 presidential campaign begins in earnest. Likely Democratic presidential contenders such as Sen. John Kerry of Massachusetts and Sen. John Edwards of North Carolina will need to distinguish themselves from Bush in the national security arena.

So rather than eliminate conflicts

over Iraq between the president and Congress, the GOP takeover of the Senate may merely reshape them along new lines.

"Below the surface there are still a lot of differences on Iraq," a senior Democratic aide said. "The election doesn't have an impact on that."

Many analysts say that as long as Bush hews to his current Iraq policy — giving Saddam one last chance to disarm before turning to war — those differences will remain muted. Bush's basic policy on Iraq continues to receive strong backing on Capitol Hill.

And with Republican control of the Senate, Bush will gain some subtle but important advantages.

He no longer has to fear politically motivated hearings about U.S. policy toward Baghdad. Incoming Senate Majority Leader Trent Lott, R-Miss., will have full control over the legislative calendar, allowing him to advance spending bills to pay for the costs of fighting or rebuilding Iraq.

And full GOP control of Congress is likely to help Bush diplomatically, by reassuring foreign leaders that he can carry through on his commitments, much like parliamentary democracies.

"It will take the president's already strong hand and make it stronger," said Randy Scheunemann, a former foreign policy adviser to Lott and a leader of a new public campaign to build public support for "liberating" Iraq.

But GOP lawmakers say if the president were to significantly alter course he would face a firestorm of criticism, both domestically and overseas.

"I think it would be disastrous to veer off in a different direction," said Sen. Chuck Hagel of Nebraska, the second-ranking Republican on the Foreign Relations Committee.

Even if Bush sticks to his current game plan, he still has many more important decisions to make on how the war and its aftermath will be conducted. With his own administration still divided on many of these concerns, Bush is likely to face continued pressure from Capitol Hill despite the election outcome.

Iraqi Opposition Role

One crucial decision could involve the role of Iraqi opposition forces. Defense Secretary Donald H. Rumsfeld and some conservatives, including Lott and Sen. John McCain of Arizona, a senior Republican member of the Armed Services Committee, say Iraqi exile groups can play a crucial role in providing ground support and governing a postwar Iraq. Relying on groups such as the Iraqi National Congress could limit the need for U.S. ground forces during and after a conflict, they maintain.

But Lugar, Hagel and Secretary of State Colin L. Powell are convinced the exile groups are incapable of governing Iraq or helping in the war. They argue that a large-scale U.S. force will be needed to attack and occupy Iraq.

These Republicans have joined with some Democrats, such as current Foreign Relations Chairman Joseph R. Biden Jr. of Delaware, in a determination to avoid a repeat of what they view as Bush's flawed policy following the recent war in Afghanistan. They claim that his policy there, based on his determination to limit involvement and danger to U.S. troops, has left a security vacuum.

And they fear that without a strong and sustained U.S. commitment, a similar scenario could unfold in Iraq, destabilizing the region. In one of their worst-case scenarios, Iraq — the creation of post-World War I British colo-

nialism — could fracture into its historic Shia, Sunni, and Kurdish-dominated regions, prompting neighboring Turkey and Iran to intervene. In another, Iraq's unconventional weapons could be hidden, be whisked out of the country, or fall under the control of a new and no less dangerous dictator.

These Republican skeptics also are concerned that a tentative U.S. commitment to the reconstruction of Iraq could harm broader U.S. interests in the Middle East. If Arabs and Muslims conclude that the United States was interested only in waging war — and not in improving their lives — the war on terrorism could become more difficult, they say.

Such administration officials as Deputy Defense Secretary Paul D. Wolfowitz agree, warning that any invasion of Iraq must be accompanied by massive international investment to rebuild the country as a democratic bulwark in the Middle East.

But many Republicans, including Bush, have been uncomfortable with the idea of nation-building, after the debacles encountered by United Nations forces in Bosnia and U.S. forces in Somalia in the 1990s.

They also shudder when they hear Powell liken a potential U.S. postwar occupation of Iraq to the extensive post-World War II occupations of Germany and Japan. Such an occupation could require the deployment of tens of thousands of U.S. troops and the expenditure of hundreds of billions of dollars — all at a time when the federal government already is running large budget deficits and U.S. forces are stretched around the globe fighting the war on terrorism.

To address these questions, Lugar says that over the next few months he will press the administration in hearings and private discussions to lay out its strategy for governing Iraq if Saddam is toppled. Lugar adds that Congress may have to draft authorizing legislation for those activities, given the financial and military resources required.

These discussions will take place against the backdrop of the successful White House effort to win Security Council support for confronting Iraq. The Security Council vote came after nearly two months of arduous negotiations.

The U.N. resolution provides Iraq with a "final opportunity" to comply with its disarmament obligation; requires Iraq to declare within 30 days all

of its programs for weapons of mass destruction; insists that U.N. weapons inspectors have unconditional and unrestricted access to any suspected weapons site; and warns Iraq that it will face "serious consequences" for failing to comply with these requirements.

North Korea Battles

The Iraq issue is only the most pressing of the concerns that are likely to pit Republicans on Capitol Hill and in the administration against each other.

Powell, Hagel, and Lugar also are fighting with administration and GOP hard-liners over U.S. policy toward North Korea after Pyongyang recently disclosed its secret uranium-based nuclear program. (*2002 CQ Weekly, p. 2753*)

Senior administration officials insist that no talks with North Korea will take place until that country dismantles the program. That posture has the backing of conservatives such as McCain and Senate Intelligence Committee member Jon Kyl of Arizona, who are urging Bush to initiate a new strategy aimed at what they call the "liberation" of North Korea.

Lugar and Hagel, on the other hand, have urged the White House to continue working with South Korea and Japan to seek a diplomatic solution to the crisis.

Recalling the vast North Korean military arsenal he saw on a visit to Korea's demilitarized zone a few years ago, Lugar said a confrontational stance toward Pyongyang makes little sense.

"Negotiations with North Korea have to continue, whether or not we have formal talks," Lugar said. "We have to keep going here."

With North Korea, as with Iraq, Bush is likely to find that the political victory he fought for has hardly granted him a free ride. Instead, it has produced something resembling a family fight among Republicans. More specifically, some say, it has become a struggle between Bush's hard-edged policy and the more measured policies of his father.

"One of the problems we are going to confront is different Republican perspectives on America's role in the world," said Danielle Pletka, a former aide to Sen. Jesse Helms, R-N.C., and now the head of foreign policy studies at the American Enterprise Institute. "It's really the policy of Bush I vs. Bush II." ◆

A Party Asks: Who Are We?

Democrats begin the search for a unifying theme and a voice to proclaim it

Until this year, the worst election night for Democrats in recent history was on Nov. 8, 1994, when the Republicans took control of both the House and the Senate. But as dispirited as the Democrats were after that election — five House Democrats bolted to the GOP in the months afterward — they took comfort in knowing that the White House remained in the hands of Democrat Bill Clinton. And in the next three elections, their party picked up seats in Congress.

In assessing the election of Nov. 5, 2002, in which their party lost its tenuous control of the Senate and lost at least five House seats to the Republicans, most Democrats quickly concluded that they knew what went wrong: They failed to develop a bold, clear plan on domestic issues that could energize voters, while a popular wartime president with a huge fundraising effort rallied the electorate on issues such as national security and tax cuts.

Now they are searching for a new message and a new messenger to deliver it, and at the moment many say they are hard-pressed to find either one.

In the midst of finger-pointing and outright anger over their election losses, Democrats are asking themselves who they are and what they stand for. Do they want to be true to their liberal base — one that has a history of defending the middle class and civil rights, for example? Or do they want to be more like the party's centrists, the lawmakers who signed on to President Bush's $1.3 trillion tax cut (PL 107-16), which included large breaks for the wealthy?

The answer to that question will start to form Nov. 14, when House Democrats pick a successor to Minority Leader Richard A. Gephardt of Missouri, who is stepping down from his leadership post to consider a race for the White House in 2004. (*House Democrats, p. 43*)

A rancorous fight over ideology in the near term may have been averted when Martin Frost, a Texan who was

Among those mulling changes in the Democratic Party's direction are, from left: Rep. Nita M. Lowey, the head of the House campaign arm; national Chairman Terry McAuliffe; Gov. Howard L. Dean of Vermont; and Sen. Patty Murray, head of the Senate campaign committee.

CQ PHOTO / SCOTT J. FERRELL

courting the caucus' moderates, announced Nov. 8 that he would not oppose California liberal Nancy Pelosi, who was elected party whip a year ago.

Pelosi still faces opposition from Harold E. Ford Jr. of Tennessee, a moderate who is closely aligned with former Vice President Al Gore and who was the first to call for a change in House Democratic leadership after the election. Ford said he entered the race because Pelosi represents an old leadership structure that voters rejected in the election. "The American people don't trust us to govern. If they did, they would have given [the House] back to us by now," he said.

If Pelosi becomes minority leader, her ascension will complicate matters for those such as Frost and Ford who believe the party must take on a more centrist tone if it ever wants to regain control of the House. Frost said that while he endorsed Pelosi, his view has not changed.

"No matter how eloquent our rhetoric or how sound our positions, we must have a realistic strategy to win a major-

ity," Frost said in a letter to his colleagues in the House Democratic Caucus. "To do that, we must ensure that the public sees our party as the mainstream, aggressive advocate for the American people that it is."

The challenge for Democrats is to find a formula that accommodates all of the party's factions.

"Democrats can only be successful by appealing to their base as well as to centrists attracted to the party by other issues and leaders," said Thomas E. Mann, a senior fellow at the Brookings Institution. "Clinton handled this brilliantly."

After Clinton

The question is whether they can find another one like him, especially with the next presidential race only two years away. Majority Leader Tom Daschle of South Dakota will remain as the party's leader in the Senate, but this year's election record has diminished the likelihood he will run for president.

So Democrats must wait to see whose

political star begins to rise. Right now, "every Democrat is a leader," said Rep. John D. Dingell of Michigan.

Sen. John Edwards of North Carolina, who has been considering a presidential run, is seen as the freshest among the potential candidates, who include Gore, the 2000 nominee, and his running mate, Sen. Joseph I. Lieberman of Connecticut. Gov. Howard Dean of Vermont also is presenting himself as an alternative. As a committee chairman of the Democratic Governors' Association, he is the only one who can claim success on Election Day, given Democrats' valuable gains in gubernatorial races.

Democrats had trouble finding a unified theme in this election because they were split on issues that dominated the campaigns. They acknowledge that their message has lacked sharp focus since the days when Clinton could mobilize the party's liberal base while preaching the pro-economic growth message of the centrist Democratic Leadership Council, which he helped to start 18 years ago.

In the weeks after Gore's loss to Bush, moderates and liberals traded blame for the defeat, although they generally agreed that as Gore moved to the left, he failed to embrace the economic successes and principles of the Clinton-Gore administration. But with Gore winning more popular votes than Bush, Democrats maintained that the voters approved of their core principles of middle-class tax cuts, education spending and better health care.

The ideological split grew more pronounced in the Senate, particularly after Democrats gained their one-vote majority in June 2001, when James M. Jeffords of Vermont switched from Republican to independent. Under pressure to produce results, Daschle instead struggled to find compromises within his own party.

During consideration of Bush's tax cut, for example, the Democrats' argument that it benefited the wealthy was undercut by moderates who were anticipating tight election contests and embraced the plan. Then, after the 2001 terrorist attacks, the Democratic domestic agenda was drowned out by national security issues. In October, as Congress debated the Iraq war resolution (PL 107-243), liberals and moderates split over whether to support Bush. Meanwhile, the party's campaign on economic issues was muted.

"The people knew the economy was in trouble, but they did not know who to blame it on, and they did not see that the Democrats have a way out of this no-growth economy," said Robert T. Matsui, a California Democrat.

Senate Democrats do not blame Daschle directly for their election losses. "They know how difficult it is to have a unified message, because many times, they are the reason he can't have a unified message," said Joel Johnson, a Democratic lobbyist and former aide to both Daschle and Clinton.

"It was difficult for our leadership because of the way the votes turned out on tax cuts and foreign policy," said Rep. Sander M. Levin of Michigan. "I don't fault them. I think the circumstances were very difficult for us."

But some in the House questioned whether Gephardt should remain as party leader while also considering a run for president. Friction was evident during the debate over the Iraq resolution. While Gephardt had long supported a regime change in Iraq, his deal-cutting with the White House on the wording of the resolution angered liberals. (*2002 CQ Weekly*, p. 2671)

As Gephardt opted out of the leadership post, he expressed some relief at no longer being responsible for representing the views of a disparate caucus.

"I'm looking forward to the freedom to speak for myself and talk about my vision for America's future," he said.

How to Come Back

Such speaking in an uncompromising fashion is what many Democrats say was missing from the recent election debate. They said they sacrificed their core values for a muddled message and failed to rally their base.

James P. Moran of Virginia, a founder of the centrist New Democrat Coalition in the House, said retrospectively that the party should have clearly distinguished itself from Republicans on the tax cut and Iraqi war resolution.

"We would have lost if we had taken a clear position on taxes, on foreign policy and a number of issues, but we would have lost for the right reasons. I think this week, we lost for the wrong reasons," Moran said.

Looking ahead, Sen. John Kerry of Massachusetts urged a "contest of ideas" with Republicans.

"Cynical strategies that would have Democrats avoid talking about foreign policy and national security or efforts to simply blame the president for the economy without offering an alternative vision defeat the best traditions of our party," said Kerry, who also is considering a presidential run.

Moderates argued that if Democrats want to avoid being a permanent minority, they must appeal to the center of the electorate with workable solutions.

"After four straight election cycles of campaigning on an agenda pretty much limited to promising the moon on prescription drugs and attacking Republicans on Social Security, it's time for the congressional wing of the party, and the political consultants who have relentlessly promoted this message as an electoral silver bullet, to bury it once and for all," said the Democratic Leadership Council in a post-election statement.

Party strategists noted that all but one of the 10 tightest Senate races on Nov. 5 were in states carried by Bush in 2000. In 16 of the 22 districts with the most competitive House races for open or new seats, Gore got less than 50 percent of the vote in 2000.

"Almost without exception, our candidates lost in tight races because they were perceived as being too liberal, and that perception was primarily the result of the leadership and the priorities of the Democratic Party," said Cal Dooley of California, a leader of the House's Democratic moderates. "Democrats have to offer a vision in terms of how we get our economy growing, how do we enhance productivity, and how do we really respond to the challenges that are facing us."

Tim Roemer, a retiring moderate whose seat in Indiana was claimed by a Republican on Nov. 5, worried aloud that the party's soul-searching will get rough. "It could get worse, and it could get even more frustrating," he said.

For now, the Democrats' short-term strategy will center on putting pressure on Republicans to produce solutions for the economy and other domestic issues.

"The Republicans now have nobody to blame for their failures but themselves," Dingell said. "It's going to be great fun watching them gyrate about and avoid responsibility for what has to be done."

Daschle, who seemed to have better success at keeping his caucus united when it was in the minority, will be returning to familiar ground. "We stay relevant by staying cohesive," he said. ◆

The Chamber of Tactics

Senate leader Lott is keenly aware that there is no free ride for Republican legislation

Majority leader of the United States Senate is probably the most difficult, and arguably the most powerful, job in Congress. Given another lease on life in that position, Trent Lott is vowing to curb his authoritarian legislative style and refrain from making every Senate debate a staging ground for the Republican political platform of the moment.

"I'm getting a second chance to do this job," the Mississippian said Nov. 6, a day after the electorate returned control of the Senate to the Republicans for the 108th Congress. "I hope I will, you know, do it better than last time and learn from those experiences. And one of them is, you don't take off down the trail saying what you're going to do without a lot of consultation."

The first and most frequent consultations for Lott will be with President Bush, who will take the lead in setting the agenda for the new, all-Republican Congress. With the House GOP leadership generally capable of passing whatever the president wants, it will be up to Lott to assess which of Bush's wishes are realistically achievable in a Senate where 60 votes are needed to overcome filibusters on most matters — from energy and regulatory policy to judicial nominations and limits on damages in civil litigation.

Republicans will hold 51 seats in the Senate, or perhaps 52, if they can win the Dec. 7 runoff in Louisiana. That means the White House, which has been working more closely with the House Republican leadership during much of the 107th Congress, will now look to the Senate for strategic and tactical guidance from the outset.

Democrats will regroup as the loyal opposition, with emphasis on "opposition." They are being advised on all sides to underscore their differences with the party back in power — not to blur them.

"I don't think they should just cave in to the Bush administration," said American University historian Alan Lichtman. "You can't make a come-

Jubilant over the GOP's return to power in the Senate, Lott vowed at a Nov. 6 news conference to adopt a more collegial, collaborative style in his second tenure as majority leader.

back without standing for something."

Democrat Tom Daschle, thrust back into the minority leadership role he has held for all but the past 17 months of the past eight years, will no longer be held accountable for the Senate's progress — or lack thereof.

"The one consolation about being in the minority is that it's so liberating," the South Dakotan said. "It's easier to keep your caucus together."

Lott's first stint as majority leader, from June 1996, when Republican Bob Dole of Kansas (1969-96) departed to run for president, until June 2001, gave him only a brief taste of the power and problems that come with unified one-party control of Congress and the White House. Last year's decision by James M. Jeffords of Vermont to bolt the GOP and become an independent aligned with Democrats robbed Lott of his authority to set the Senate agenda.

For most of his earlier tenure in charge, he was forced to play the foil to President Bill Clinton, a position of con-

stant defense. He fought to keep the legislative trains "running at any cost," in the words of one GOP leadership aide — a reflection in his public life of Lott's well-noted desire for regular order and precision in his personal life and appearance. The single-minded focus on forcing Republican bills toward passage on the Senate floor exacerbated internal strife in his own caucus — where rifts exist among conservatives, pragmatists and moderates — and created a wellspring of anger among Democrats who resented being shut out of the process.

This time, Lott said, he plans to tap the wisdom of the most senior senators in his caucus, who will chair the most important committees, consult more regularly with his own lieutenants and keep open better lines of communication with the Democrats.

When the 108th Congress convenes in January, Lott will have to walk a fine line between pleasing his staunchly conservative colleagues in both chambers and winning over enough Democrats to reach the 60 votes necessary to overcome a filibuster, the principal parliamentary weapon at the minority's disposal. Many of Bush's top domestic priorities, such as additional tax cuts and the creation of a Medicare prescription drug benefit, probably can be tucked under the protective procedural framework of a budget "reconciliation" bill, which has a special immunity from filibusters. But other objectives, which have no direct impact on the federal budget deficit, will be vulnerable to delaying tactics. Lott will need to pick up eight or nine Democrats and hold all of his own troops in line to advance those.

GOP aides predict that Lott will adopt a more moderate leadership style going forward, which could drain off some of the partisan vitriol of the past two years. "There's going to be more middle-of-the-road governing," said a conservative Republican aide.

The GOP is losing some conservative icons, such as Phil Gramm of Texas, Jesse Helms of North Carolina and Strom Thurmond of South Carolina. A few incoming freshmen have more moderate reputations, including Norm Coleman of Minnesota, Elizabeth Dole of North Carolina, Lamar Alexander of Tennessee and John E. Sununu of New Hampshire.

Lincoln Chafee of Rhode Island, the Republicans' most liberal senator, predicts the GOP agenda will not be so "aggressively conservative" as it has been, in light of upcoming fights in 2004 to hold on to seats in swing states — such as Pennsylvania, Colorado, Missouri and Ohio — that also will be critical to Bush's re-election effort.

Sarah Chamberlain Resnick, executive director of the Republican Main Street Partnership, a GOP moderates' advocacy group, said the moderate freshmen eventually will strike a balance between supporting the president and defining their own role in the Senate. But Chafee, who often splits with his party, expects those members to toe the line for a while. "They're going to owe the president a huge debt of gratitude in all the help he gave," Chafee said.

Signs of Conservatism

Though Lott has promised a more conciliatory tone, he and his deputies will not abandon their conservative principles. That's especially true of two new lieutenants expected to add consistency and reliability to Lott's team.

Kentucky Republican Mitch Mc-

The 108th: Senate Leadership

REPUBLICANS

MAJORITY LEADER
Floor leader since Bob Dole left for his presidential bid in 1996, **Trent Lott** of Mississippi is getting "a second chance" to do the job with a majority on his side. His accommodation of conservatives the last time was blamed for the Jeffords defection that cost the GOP 18 months of Senate control, and he is promising to be a better consensus-builder with Democrats and less dictatorial to his GOP colleagues.

MAJORITY WHIP
Several others tested the waters, but **Mitch McConnell** secured the votes for the job, and no one else ever formally joined the race. A pragmatist who also has the patience for protracted legislative combat, the Kentuckian is expected to focus on the traditional whip roles: counting votes and serving as the floor leader's principal lieutenant. Don Nickles of Oklahoma, who is stepping down because of GOP term limits, sometimes clashed with Lott and liked to focus on policy development.

POLICY COMMITTEE CHAIRMAN
Larry E. Craig of Idaho was compelled to step down by term limits as well, and no one stepped in to challenge **Jon Kyl** of Arizona's bid to be the successor. An emerging conservative leader, Kyl is known for operating energetically and studiously, though often out of the limelight, on a wide range of domestic and international issues.

DEMOCRATS

MINORITY LEADER
Some grumble that his legislative tactics for combating the Bush agenda while he was majority leader fueled the party's loss of control. But no one is challenging South Dakota's **Tom Daschle** for a fifth term as party leader. Some potential rivals want to focus on presidential bids; others say Daschle's style is better suited to running a minority caucus, which he also did from 1995 until June 2001. His motto for the revived role: "We stay relevant by staying cohesive."

MINORITY WHIP
A loyal and trusted lieutenant of Daschle's, **Harry Reid** of Nevada is unchallenged to remain in the job he has held since 1999. Reid's low-key style allows him to cultivate amicable relations with the GOP even when he is pulling the legislative levers of partisan conflict. He is seen as a legislative pragmatist.

Connell, who is running unopposed to become the new majority whip, and Arizonan Jon Kyl, who has no opponent in his bid to become the next chairman of the GOP Policy Committee, are both steadfast conservatives. McConnell enjoys a very close personal relationship with Lott. He raised millions for Republican candidates as chairman of the National Republican Senatorial Committee (NRSC) in the runups to the 1998 and 2000 elections. He led the long GOP effort to derail campaign finance legislation, which finally came to an end when a law was enacted last year (PL 107-155), and he is spearheading the legal battle to kill

the new statute in the courts.

Equally willing to fight for his objectives is Kyl, a dogged conservative who was tapped to defend the record of close friend John Ashcroft when Bush picked Ashcroft to become attorney general soon after he lost re-election to the Senate from Missouri in 2000. Kyl, a member of the Judiciary Committee, also argued strongly for Clinton's conviction in the 1999 impeachment trial.

Their senior aides say that Lott, McConnell and Kyl have remarkably similar personalities and know how to take good measure of their opponents. Both McConnell and Kyl were near-constant fixtures on the Senate floor while Democrats ran the chamber. For the most part, aides say, they took it upon themselves to play GOP defense — a hands-on style they are certain to continue.

That is a change from the current setup, which teamed Lott with two articulate policy strategists, Don Nickles of Oklahoma as whip and Larry E. Craig of Idaho as chairman of the Policy Committee. Nickles showed little interest in floor duty, and Lott held him at arms length because of suspicions that the Oklahoman craved his job. Craig generally focused more on message than on legislating.

Lott can expect continued support from GOP Conference Chairman Rick Santorum of Pennsylvania, who unlike Nickles and Craig is not term-limited this year. Santorum began his Senate career as a conservative purist who was chastised for breaching protocol with his upbraids of Clinton from the Senate floor. But since becoming the leadership's message man, he has softened his tone somewhat, if not his ideology.

Tempering the conservatism of Lott's inner circle is Tennessee's Bill Frist, who is stepping down as chairman of the NRSC to focus on health care policy, his specialty given his background as a surgeon. Lott has relied heavily on Frist to take the lead on social issues that have proved sticky for Republicans in the past. George F. Allen of Virginia is interested in chairing the GOP Senate campaign arm in the runup to 2004, when the party will defend 15 seats and the Democrats will defend 19.

Democrats Holding the Line

While Republican term limits are forcing leadership changes in the GOP, discontent with the Nov. 5 results has not translated into any bid to replace Daschle and Whip Harry Reid of Nevada as the top leaders of the Democratic caucus. However, their strategy is likely to change given their new minority status and pressure from inside the party to redefine their message.

"It's important to ask the question, 'How can we communicate our message more effectively?'" Daschle said. "I'm sure we'll be giving that very careful and extraordinary consideration."

Daschle said that with Republicans controlling the government, it is more important than ever for Democrats to stand up for those who do not have a voice in Washington. "We're going to stand up for our principles and fight when we think the president is wrong," he said. "We're going to do that on economic questions, we're going to do that on domestic issues, we're going to do that on foreign policy issues."

Because Daschle has spent most of his time as leader in the minority, he knows well how to use the power of obstruction to foil GOP initiatives. But Bush's early 2001 success in using the budget reconciliation process to move his top priority — the 10-year tax cut (PL 107-16) — also demonstrated the limits of that power when a filibuster is not an option.

Reid, a close friend as well as a leadership ally, will continue to be Daschle's eyes and ears on the floor. He probably will spend much of his time in the 108th negotiating floor schedules with McConnell and Lott.

And he will have unofficial lieutenants in a pair of Democratic elders — Robert C. Byrd of West Virginia and Edward M. Kennedy of Massachusetts — who will be on the front lines seeking to block proposals the minority dislikes. The pair, who rank No. 1 and 2 in overall Democratic seniority, are masters of parliamentary procedure.

Kennedy will be especially alert for GOP attempts to weaken organized labor, a spokesman said. And Byrd, who has slowed passage of several Bush priorities, including a new Department of Homeland Security, is certain to cause problems for the new majority.

Charles E. Schumer of New York is expected to take a lead role in fighting efforts to fill the federal judiciary with conservatives. Floridian Bob Graham, who led the Intelligence Committee's investigation into the events leading to the Sept. 11 attacks, probably will continue to be the spokesman for Senate Democrats on the war on terrorism.

Moderates who have sometimes been Bush's allies, such as John B. Breaux of Louisiana and Ben Nelson of Nebraska, may hold some resentment against the president for his broad-brush attacks against their party on the stump this year. "The president campaigning so aggressively in some states might have caused some Democrats to try to sharpen their knives," Chafee said.

Life in Opposition

Daschle's mentor and predecessor as Democratic leader, George J. Mitchell of Maine (1980-95), said Democrats need to clarify their message and hammer on it consistently and repeatedly to overcome the advantage Republicans hold with their grip on the White House and Congress.

"The first thing is to define your objective and what it is you stand for," Mitchell advised. "I would reduce it to a pretty simple and direct position: economic growth and prosperity."

Robert B. Dove, a former Senate parliamentarian now at George Washington University, warned that if Democrats oppose every item on the Republican agenda, they run the risk of proving the GOP's charges of the just-completed election cycle. Voters in 2004 will say, "Bush was right, they're just obstructionist," Dove said.

But others said GOP budget priorities may provide some tempting ammunition. Elaine Kamarck, a founder of the New Democrat movement, said a winning strategy for the 108th Congress would be to force Republicans into a discussion of deficit reduction.

Democrats already are salivating at the prospect of attacking an overhaul of the federal tax code that is being talked about by White House economic advisers, although the president has not yet embraced it as an objective for the next Congress. They see tax policy changes as a renewed opportunity to accuse Republicans of favoring the wealthy over the working poor.

Kamarck said that Democrats need to establish a consistent message on defense and foreign policy in the 108th, especially as those issues appear poised to dominate the agenda. Their strategy of going along on Iraq was "a recipe for political irrelevance," she said. "Democrats win when they have ideas. . . . Ideas does not equal left-wing ideas."

While both parties figure out where to position themselves, political strategists warn Republicans not to let electoral euphoria cause them to believe their mandate is broader than it is. "This is not a mandate to push the country to the right," historian Lichtman said.

Additionally, Lott must be careful not to write off Democrats now that the GOP has power to set the agenda. "If they overreach, they are setting themselves up for absolute failure," said Harvard University congressional expert David C. King.

Democrats, likewise, will have to walk a fine line as the minority. To draw distinctions with Republicans that voters can understand, they will have to "move away from the more centrist positions they were taking," said one Senate Democratic aide. "But you've got to be sure you don't go too overboard." ◆

Senate Changes Hands Again

Consistent campaign strategies, Bush influence pay off for Republicans

It is widely accepted that President Bush's vigorous cross-country campaign effort was critical to the Republican Party's retaking of the Senate. But less discussed is the skill that the president showed earlier in this election cycle as a candidate recruiter — a factor that may have been as crucial to the GOP's success as his last-minute barnstorming.

The pre-eminent success for Bush and the White House political strategy unit headed by top aide Karl Rove came in Minnesota on Nov. 5.

Norm Coleman, a former Democrat who had a successful run as mayor of St. Paul, appeared headed for a second consecutive bid for governor this year, hoping for vindication for his 1998 loss to Independence Party winner Jesse Ventura. But Bush administration strategists viewed Coleman as a stronger challenger to the vulnerable Senate incumbent, Democrat Paul Wellstone, than the putative GOP front-runner, state House Majority Leader Tim Pawlenty.

So the president engineered a switch, with Vice President Dick Cheney telephoning to tell Pawlenty that he needed to make way for Coleman to run for the Senate.

The intervention worked. Coleman pulled out a 2 percentage point victory even though the dynamics of the contest changed drastically days before the election, when Wellstone was killed in a plane crash and was replaced on the ballot by former Vice President Walter F. Mondale. Pawlenty, whose consolation prize was the GOP gubernatorial nomination, won his race as well.

Bush and his proxies also nurtured the senatorial ambitions of the two other Republicans — former Rep. Jim Talent of Missouri and Rep. Saxby Chambliss of Georgia — whose Nov. 5 victories took

Georgia's Chambliss was among the candidates the White House recruited who went on to win a seat in the Senate.

seats from incumbent Democrats and clinched the party's Senate takeover.

And Bush personally persuaded South Dakota Rep. John Thune to switch from a planned bid for governor to challenge Democrat Tim Johnson's bid for a second term. Though Thune appears to have fallen short of winning, pending a final canvass, his upset bid forced the Senate's Democratic leader, Tom Daschle, to spend much of his campaign effort defending the seat held by his home-state colleague.

The Republicans succeeded by running consistent campaigns that rarely strayed from a few key issues — and by associating themselves with a president who brought high public approval ratings into the midterm elections.

Talent defeated Democrat Jean Carnahan, who was appointed to the Senate in 2000 after her husband — Gov. Mel Carnahan, who died in a plane

crash three weeks before the election — posthumously defeated Republican Sen. John Ashcroft.

Talent, who narrowly lost for governor in 2000, stayed relentlessly "on message," focusing on his experience as a House member from 1993 to 2001 and on his work on health care and education issues. He also portrayed the Democratically controlled Senate as an obstacle to Bush's agenda.

A turnout strategy of mobilizing conservative rural voters in record numbers while conceding the state's largest city, St. Louis, to the Democrats helped his campaign. He ended up winning by 1 percentage point.

A constituency of conservative voters in rural Georgia, often underestimated because of metropolitan Atlanta's rapid growth, aided Chambliss in blocking Democrat Max Cleland's quest for a second term by a surprisingly wide margin of 8 points.

Like Talent, Chambliss also doggedly stuck to his campaign themes. He focused on a few of Cleland's Senate votes — most notably his opposition to Bush's version of legislation to create a new homeland security department, which contained provisions opposed by the Democrats' allies in organized labor.

Though he received criticism for using defense issues to target Cleland — who was badly wounded during his service in Vietnam — Chambliss persisted and persuaded Georgia voters that he would better serve them on those issues.

Coleman faced a trickier challenge in pursuing the final days of his campaign without violating state voters' grief over Wellstone's tragic death. Wellstone's family and allies from the liberal wing of the Democratic Party unintentionally eased Coleman's way when they turned a memorial service for the senator into a political rally. A

AP PHOTO / ERIK S. LESSER

Senate Is Center of Congressional Competition

The Founding Fathers conceived of the House as the chamber that would reflect the passions of the times, and the Senate as less volatile. But that formula has been reversed in recent election cycles, with the Senate showing higher rates of turn- over and close election contests. Nearly a third of the sena- tors in the 108th Congress will have been elected in competi- tive races (having won with less than 55 percent of the vote), as opposed to barely more than a tenth of the House.

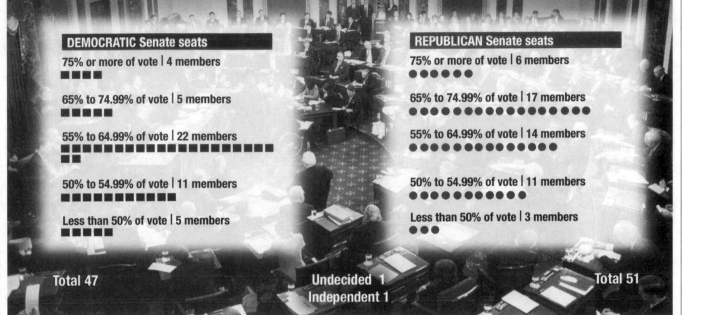

DEMOCRATIC Senate seats

75% or more of vote | 4 members

65% to 74.99% of vote | 5 members

55% to 64.99% of vote | 22 members

50% to 54.99% of vote | 11 members

Less than 50% of vote | 5 members

Total 47

REPUBLICAN Senate seats

75% or more of vote | 6 members

65% to 74.99% of vote | 17 members

55% to 64.99% of vote | 14 members

50% to 54.99% of vote | 11 members

Less than 50% of vote | 3 members

Total 51

Undecided 1
Independent 1

backlash helped Republicans mobilize their base to turn out for Coleman.

Ground Game

Those turnout efforts benefited from planning by national Republi- can operatives seeking to prevent the party from being outdone by Demo- crats in their get-out-the-vote quest — which political operatives refer to by the acronym GOTV — as oc- curred in some key 1998 and 2000 races. The Republicans did this with a national effort called 72-Hour Task Force, organized by the Republican National Committee.

"After 2000, the decision in the par- ty was made that we can't win on mes- sage and then lose at the end in these close races," said Glen Bolger of the Republican polling firm Public Opin- ion Strategies.

Bush's airport-stop tour of states with competitive races at the end of the campaign cemented this effort.

Bush's rallying of the troops not only helped secure the three GOP takeovers, but it also bolstered the party's successful efforts to prevent Democratic takeaways in half a dozen states: Colorado, New Hampshire and the four Southern states where incum-

bent Republicans are retiring: Texas, North Carolina, South Carolina and Tennessee.

In Bush's home state, Republican state Attorney General John Cornyn won 55 percent of the vote to defeat for- mer Dallas Mayor Ron Kirk — who is black — and a slate of Democratic can- didates specifically designed to turn out minority voters, who make up a large segment of the party's voting base. Cornyn did so by campaigning hard in the state's mainly white, rural areas and spending enough time in urban areas to keep Kirk busy trying to shore up his own base.

Returning home to run in her native North Carolina, Republican Elizabeth Dole — a 30-year veteran of national politics and government service — spent her summer touring every county, mobilizing small-town voters enamored with her celebrity. The payoff was a 9- point victory over Erskine Bowles, who was one of the White House chiefs of staff in the Clinton administration.

Wayne Allard, considered one of the most vulnerable Republican in- cumbents, won by 6 points over Demo- crat Tom Strickland. Allard's campaign organized a huge grass-roots push in the last 96 hours of the campaign,

sending volunteers to wave signs on street corners, make phone calls and knock on doors. His margin of victory was about the same as when the pair met six years ago.

The Republicans prevailed in anoth- er tossup race when New Hampshire Re- publican Rep. John E. Sununu defeated Democratic Gov. Jeanne Shaheen.

Republican officials worried that Sununu, though solidly conservative, might face a backlash from GOP voters loyal to the incumbent he defeated in the Sept. 10 primary, ideological fire- brand Robert C. Smith. But Sununu was co-beneficiary of Republican turnout energized by opposition to a Democratic gubernatorial nominee who had proposed a state income tax. Sununu won with 51 percent.

Middle Ground

In addition to Republicans' tactical and strategic victories, Democrats ad- mit they campaigned without a solid is- sue agenda this year.

They faced difficulty in running on two of their main issues: prescription drug benefits under Medicare and ed- ucation. Republicans touted an educa- tion policy overhaul (PL 107-110) Bush signed in January and a GOP-

Voting Upgrades Paid Off on Nov. 5

Jan 1, 2000 and Nov. 5, 2002, have something in common: They both are dates associated with disasters that never happened. The "Y2K" catastrophe of a worldwide computer meltdown did not occur at midnight on New Year's eve, and the multitude of voting problems predicted for the Nov. 5 elections never materialized.

Just two out of the hundreds of congressional and gubernatorial races waged across the country may be challenged. The South Dakota Senate race, decided by 528 votes, may go to a recount, and the Alabama gubernatorial contest looks likely to linger, with both candidates claiming victory.

In South Dakota, incumbent Democrat Tim Johnson claimed victory on Nov. 6. Republican challenger John Thune, who was the state's only House member, signaled he probably would not request a recount unless the state's official vote canvass Nov. 12 changed the tally or discovered irregularities.

In Alabama, both incumbent Democrat Donald Siegelman and his GOP challenger, Bob Riley, have claimed victory in the tight race. The debate centers on votes out of Baldwin County, which first listed 19,070 votes for Siegelman and then changed that tally to 12,736. The first tally would give the race to Siegelman, the second to Riley.

The state canvassing board will certify the results on Nov. 20. Seigelman has asked for a recount.

Those contests were the excep-

In Florida, epicenter of the disputed 2000 presidential race, balloting on Election Day went smoothly, in part because of voting system upgrades and voter education efforts.

REUTERS PHOTO / DAVID FRIEDMAN

tion, not the rule on Election Day. "Generally speaking, it went well," said Ralph Neas, president of People for the American Way, who was an observer in South Florida on Election Day. His group was part of a coalition of liberal interest groups that joined to educate voters about their rights after the chaotic 2000 election. Neas said problems were "more episodic than systemic."

The midterm elections drew unprecedented scrutiny, as volunteers from civil rights groups flocked to sights where voter intimidation had been charged in the past. Democratic and Republican lawyers also closely

monitored the contests for any irregularities that could serve as the basis for challenges in the courts. (*2002 CQ Weekly, p. 2854*)

Doug Chapin, director of electionline.org, a nonprofit organization that has tracked state election law changes, credited the significant investments many states made to update voting systems and teach voters how to use them after Florida's seemingly never-ending presidential contest in 2000. Florida was one of the states that upgraded.

Elections this time were "close because they were close, not because of election problems," Chapin said.

drafted prescription drug bill (HR 4954) pushed through the Republican-controlled House in June. Democratic pollster Mark Mellman says his party could have been more aggressive in laying out differences between the parties on those issues. "In a lot of cases we didn't go out there and say, 'Here is what is wrong with their plan,' " he said.

Carnahan conceded after her defeat that she did not do enough to differentiate

herself from Republican challenger Talent. "Maybe we didn't define those issues as clearly as we should have," she said.

In the many competitive races played out in states Bush carried in 2000, Democratic candidates ran to the center-right, blurring differences and leaving them without a defined message.

In the end, Republicans lost just one of the 20 seats they were defending, in Arkansas. And that appeared less of a political statement than a personal vic-

tory for Democratic state Attorney General Mark Pryor, who is popular in his own right and is the son of a Democratic icon in the state, former Sen. David Pryor (1979-97). The younger Pryor won with 54 percent.

It was a personal as well as political defeat for Hutchinson, who had won the seat in 1996 on a "family values" platform but was politically wounded three years later after divorcing his wife of 29 years and marrying a Senate aide. ◆

Nurturing the GOP Agenda

House Majority Leader DeLay will champion conservative goals with a firm hand

For the past year and a half, the House has been the Republican Party's front line, dutifully drafting, refining and passing President Bush's bills, knowing full well that the most sweeping measures — energy policy, taxes, pensions and prescription drugs — would go nowhere in the Senate. Bush and Republican leaders could then blame Senate Democrats for holding them up.

Now, the House must compete with the Senate for Bush's attention as he tries to enact many of those bills with a newly won but slender Senate majority. *(Senate, p. 35)*

The dynamics will be much the same as in the early months of Bush's term in 2001, when the White House was preoccupied with a bitter struggle for working control of the Senate.

The House will continue to be the incubator of the GOP's conservative legislative agenda, as it has for the past eight years. Tom DeLay of Texas, who will be the new majority leader, promises strict party discipline and a controlled message. Speaker J. Dennis Hastert of Illinois will have at least 228 seats in hand, close to the 230 that Republicans had after taking control of the House in 1995 and passing much of their "Contract With America."

"He's got a little easier job than he had before," said Rep. Johnny Isakson, R-Ga., who spoke to Hastert on election night.

House Democrats, who will have spent a decade in the minority by the next election, are reassessing their own strategy and message. Minority Leader Richard A. Gephardt, D-Mo., who took some of the blame for the latest losses, has decided to relinquish his leadership post. *(Democrats, p. 43)*

While the GOP picked up seats, it also begins the next Congress without three of its leading moderates: Rep. Constance A. Morella of Maryland, who was defeated by Democrat Chris Van Hollen, and retiring Reps. Benjamin A. Gilman of New York and

DeLay, shown here at an Oct. 31 Republican rally in Houston, will be named House Majority leader the week of Nov. 11. He promises tighter control of legislation and the GOP message.

Marge Roukema of New Jersey.

Although those departures will not obviate the need for Hastert to listen to his party's moderates, they do reduce the numbers of those willing to buck the party on some issues.

The cushion of a handful of extra votes — the exact number will not be determined until after a Dec. 7 runoff in Louisiana — is tempered by the knowledge that House Republicans will have to produce results they can campaign on.

"As a party, we have to deliver," said Stuart Roy, a spokesman for DeLay, who is now the party whip. "What we passed last year in the House were things that we want to become law."

'From Cradle to Grave'

DeLay will figure even more prominently in the workings of the House. He is expected to be named majority leader the week of Nov. 11, succeeding the retiring Dick Armey, R-Texas.

DeLay's current job requires him to find the 218 votes necessary to pass legislation among the 223 Republicans in the House. That involves regular meetings with deputy whips, who then fan out to gauge support among the rank and file.

In his new posting, which will begin in January, DeLay is expected to play a more hands-on role in shaping the structure of floor debates and managing the flow of bills to the floor.

DeLay aims to bring committee chairmen into leadership discussions more often so that the progression of legislation can be managed "from cradle to grave" by top leaders, Roy said.

As leader, DeLay plans to be more visible as a spokesman for the party, but he does not see that as his primary role, aides said. He probably will continue Armey's tradition of holding weekly news conferences, but he is more reticent and will bring along committee chairmen and other key lawmakers to speak about each week's topics.

Control of the party's message would fall to the conference chairman, but that task has been a matter of some contention among Republican leaders since 1995.

Outgoing conference Chairman J.C. Watts Jr. of Oklahoma, who is retiring from Congress this year, had expressed frustration that other leaders — DeLay in particular — encroached on his turf.

But Roy said DeLay would seek to delegate communication responsibilities to the conference chairman, while maintaining a role through a "fully integrated" leadership structure.

"What he wants is a true division of labor between the people who are elected by the conference," Roy said.

Three candidates are vying for the conference chairman's post, but none are explicitly backed by the current leadership. Three others are vying for the vice chairman's post, while John T. Doolittle, R-Calif., appears to be unchallenged for the conference secretary job.

Staying the Course

The GOP's legislative priorities will not change much, Republicans said. One of their biggest challenges will be an intraparty dispute over spending levels, with fiscal conservatives bent on curtailing domestic spending as Bush has demanded. The dispute held up action on most bills this fall.

The party's new seats may make it possible to proceed on new legislative fronts. If Senate Republicans decide not to move House-passed measures on welfare reform (HR 4737) and pension protection (HR 3762) in the lame-duck session, they will be near the top of the agenda for the 108th Congress. Making permanent the $1.35 trillion, 10-year package of tax cuts (PL 107-16) signed by Bush last year is another goal. (2002 *CQ Weekly*, pp.2377, 2811, 2817)

Chief Deputy Whip Roy Blunt, R-Mo., the sole announced candidate for DeLay's current job, said that having more Republicans means that "some new things are possible," and he specifically mentioned liability reform and a broader swath of tax cuts.

Blunt is likely to continue DeLay's style of trying to ensure enough Republican support for passage of GOP legislation without relying on Democrats. Asked about reaching out to Democratic leaders, Blunt said that was Hastert's area, not his.

Blunt, who had been trying to stitch together a deal on appropriations, is well-suited for his job of rounding up votes, Republicans say. As DeLay's top deputy, he played a key role in getting the necessary support for last fall's $15 billion airline bailout (PL 107-42). (2001 *Almanac*, p. 20-3)

Blunt told reporters Nov. 7 that he will not select his own top assistant "for a while." Republican Reps. Kay Granger of Texas, Mike Rogers of Michigan and Todd Tiahrt of Kansas are among the leading candidates. ◆

The 108th: House Leadership

REPUBLICANS

SPEAKER OF THE HOUSE
Unopposed for a third term as the highest congressional officer under the Constitution, **J. Dennis Hastert** of Illinois is on course to become the longest serving GOP Speaker since Ohio's Nicholas Longworth, who held the job from 1925-31. Hastert's style is to delegate authority and work behind the scenes, then make decisions and settle disputes with self-assurance.

MAJORITY LEADER
The day Dick Armey announced his retirement 11 months ago, fellow Texan **Tom DeLay** claimed the votes to succeed him as floor leader. Nicknamed "The Hammer" for his vote-counting style as whip since 1995, DeLay's new job is more about legislative agenda-setting, a job to which he is not accustomed.

MAJORITY WHIP

At the start of his second term, in 1999, Missouri's **Roy Blunt** was tapped by DeLay as chief deputy whip when Hastert stepped up to Speaker. Backed by his mentor again, Blunt is unchallenged for the No. 3 leadership spot. Seen as a skilled communicator, he was liaison between the 2000 Bush presidential campaign and the House GOP.

CONFERENCE CHAIRMAN

Three want to succeed retiring J.C. Watts Jr. of Oklahoma. **Deborah Pryce** of Ohio, the current vice-chairman, portrays herself as an experienced leader who would bring diversity to an all-male leadership. Former broadcaster **J.D. Hayworth** of Arizona (center) says would be the most effective salesman of the party message. **Jim Ryun** of Kansas has the backing of some prominent conservatives.

DEMOCRATS

MINORITY LEADER
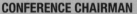
By relinquishing the Democratic leader's job he has held since 1989, Richard A. Gephardt of Missouri set up a succession battle that foreshadows the debate about the party's post-election direction. The frontrunner is California's **Nancy Pelosi**. Elected whip just 13 months ago in part on the strength of her fundraising, she represents the liberal wing and is among the most prominent Democratic women in the country. Late entrant **Harold E. Ford Jr.** of Tennessee wants to steer the party toward the center. A member of the "Blue Dog" coalition, he would be the first African-American in the leadership. Martin Frost of Texas, a policy maven and political pragmatist, abandoned his campaign Nov. 8, concluding he could not defeat Pelosi.

MINORITY WHIP
Maryland's **Steny H. Hoyer** is unopposed to win the post — on his third try. He lost to Pelosi last year and in 1991 he lost to Pelosi's predecessor, David E. Bonior of Michigan. Hoyer wants to use the job to improve communication between the rank-and-file and leaders as legislative strategies are developed.

CAUCUS CHAIRMAN

Connecticut's **Rosa DeLauro** is the candidate of the most liberal, confrontational wing. She lost this job to Frost in 1998 and since has been an appointed Gephardt deputy. Similarly brash and ambitious, current Vice Chairman **Robert Menendez** opted for this race rather than standing in when Robert G. Torricelli gave upon his New Jersey Senate campaign this fall. He would be the first Hispanic ever in the party leadership.

House Democrats Begin 'Anew'

Gephardt steps down; leadership torch likely to pass to Pelosi

Like President Harry S Truman, another famous Democrat from Missouri, Richard A. Gephardt has used a simple desktop sign to remind himself that some of the responsibilities of power simply cannot be delegated. The blunt declaration: "The Buck Stops Here."

While mulling his future on Nov. 6, the day after his party failed to reclaim the House majority in its fourth consecutive attempt, Gephardt said he took those words to heart. His conclusion was that it was time for him to step down from the job of House Democratic leader after more than a dozen years, first in the majority and for the past eight years in the minority.

As head of the team, Gephardt said, he bears special responsibility for the results of the past four elections, and it was necessary to step aside so the party can begin "anew."

By week's end, the House Democrats were on the verge of doing so, as Nancy Pelosi of San Francisco emerged as the solid, perhaps prohibitive, favorite to win election as minority leader.

Gephardt, the congressman for St. Louis, has long been considering a candidacy for the 2004 Democratic presidential nomination, and in a series of conversations the morning after the election he had been advised by some senior members of the caucus that he should not both run for president and maintain his leadership position into the 108th Congress.

A few House Democrats said that Gephardt would have faced a challenge for the top job had he tried to keep it, and some wanted to make him the party's sacrificial offering for its unexpected electoral setback in the midterm

Rep. Martin Frost, D-Texas, and Rep. Nancy Pelosi, D-Calif., both hope to replace House Democratic leader Richard Gephardt, D-Mo. At a Nov. 8 news conference, Pelosi declared that she had more than enough commitments to become the next House minority leader.

election. But others said that most members of the caucus hoped that Gephardt would remain their leader and serve as a continued unifying force as the party sought to redefine itself.

"By no means was he pushed out," said Rep. James L. Oberstar of Minnesota. "I think if he had decided to run again for leader he would have been elected."

Gephardt's desire to make a second bid for the presidency — his first was in 1988 — has been far from secret, even if he had the opportunity to be Speaker instead next year. And so well before the election, two Democratic leaders were seeking support for elevation to the top spot: Pelosi, the highest-ranking woman in congressional history since she became whip earlier this year, and Democratic Caucus Chairman Martin Frost of Dallas. (*2002 CQ Weekly, p. 2734*)

Their behind-the-scenes wooing of colleagues already had compelled the Democrats to take sides in a fundamental question: Should the party steer itself

back to its liberal roots, which Pelosi represents, or should it modify but maintain its appeal to moderates and swing voters, the approach Frost advocated?

By the afternoon on Nov. 8, just two days after their campaigns came into the open, Frost dropped out of the race and pledged his support to Pelosi. Just a day earlier, he had declared that Pelosi's liberalism would make her a polarizing figure in American politics and that the Democrats might go many years more without winning back the House as a result.

By that time, however, Harold E. Ford Jr. of Memphis had made a last-minute entry into the race, having been tipped off by Frost that the Texan had concluded he could not win and was dropping out.

Still, Pelosi said she had in hand a list of 105 members willing to say publicly that they would support her, and that she knew of many others whose vote she could count on. "This race is over," she declared.

The secret ballot will be taken Nov. 14, and to win Pelosi will need a majority of the people who will belong to the Democratic Caucus in the 108th Congress: at least 202 House members — plus potentially one more still locked in a too-close-to-call race in New York — and three congressional delegates from outside the 50 states.

"I don't think they chose me as an outspoken San Francisco liberal," Pelosi said in explaining her candidacy. "I think they chose me as a person who can lead the caucus to victory, as a person who can build coalitions among the various segments of our caucus and as a person who represents various points of views within the caucus. The next leader had to come from some segment of the party, and I'm the one who got the votes."

A member of the "Blue Dog" coalition of the most conservative Democrats, Ford offered himself as a moderate who would also bring generational and ethnic diversity to the leadership. He was just elected to his fourth term at age 32; she was first elected in 1987 and is 62. And he would be the first African-American top congressional leader ever.

Intraparty Angst

The intensity of the campaign between Pelosi and Frost, and the last-minute entry of Ford, highlighted antagonisms within the party that have simmered near the surface for years but that bubbled over again as the election returns poured in Nov. 5.

The more moderate and conservative members of the party, such as the Blue Dogs and the New Democrat Coalition, have long complained they are being ignored, and now they are clamoring even more loudly for change.

"I feel like the Democratic Caucus needs to realize the growth of the party, that we have to reach out to other political persuasions, particularly in the South and West," said Gene Green of Texas, who had been backing Frost.

But Pelosi fought back hard, offering a hint of the aggressiveness she would use to combat the agenda of President Bush and his GOP allies in the two years until the next election.

Asked Nov. 8 whether Ford was accurately characterizing himself as the leading edge of the party's future and Pelosi as part of its past, she did not miss a beat. "Well, I've only been in office for eight months," Pelosi said,

pointing to the length of her tenure as whip. "I guess when you're very young, eight months seems like a long time."

She conceded, however, that for the party "some self-criticism is in order — and then we move on."

Ford said he would keep his eleventh-hour campaign going until the end because "the Democratic Caucus needs a change," and "I don't think Ms. Pelosi represents that change."

But Pelosi's claim that she has the race sewn up is credible; last fall, she predicted within two votes the number of colleagues who would support her elevation to the whip's job over Steny H. Hoyer of Maryland. He is now unopposed for election as whip with Pelosi's bid to move up the ladder. (*Background, 2001 CQ Weekly, p. 2397*)

And it is not likely members will go back on their word if they pledge support to one candidate, said former Rep. Vic Fazio, D-Calif. (1981-99), who won the race for caucus chairman in 1994. "If you are careful, you come away with a fairly accurate portrayal," Fazio said. "There are very few ways members can avoid the image of being duplicitous if they actually are."

Pelosi is known for her hard work and ability to gather allies and for her diligence in rewarding them by raising money for their campaigns. She also showed that she can give as good as she gets and has aggressively helped the campaigns of members who have supported her.

Working the phones from California, Pelosi methodically reached out to liberals, moderates, pro-business "New Democrats" and every other faction of the party. In her one-on-one appeals she asked colleagues to give her a chance despite Frost's efforts to depict her as too liberal to lead without alienating the moderates.

Frost failed to get much traction out of highlighting a major policy disagreement he had with Pelosi. She voted last month against the resolution (PL 107-243) giving Bush the authority to use force against Iraq. Frost supported it and argued that had more Democrats done likewise, the party could have picked up seats Nov. 5.

Style Setter

If Pelosi wins, she will become the first woman to hold a top partisan congressional leadership post, and Democrats can expect a different leadership style. While both Pelosi and Gephardt

are prolific fundraisers, they take different approaches on several issues.

On trade, Gephardt struggled to find a consensus in his caucus that could please free-traders, who come from exporting states such as Washington and Texas, without violating his own belief in the need for stricter environmental and labor standards. Pelosi, however, approached the trade debate from the standpoint of protecting human and worker rights — issues that have become some of her specialties while serving as top Democrat on the Intelligence Committee.

As Gephardt announced the end of his time in the leadership, Democrats complained about his "top-down" leadership style that increasingly omitted them from deliberations on key issues. For example, they said, a tax cut plan that he offered in the campaign was his own idea and not a product of the caucus.

Despite that criticism, there is little doubt that Gephardt will be missed.

After the election reduced the Democratic strength in the House by at least seven seats, it did not take Gephardt long to figure out his next step. By Nov. 7, he had arranged a conference call with his colleagues to announce his decision. About 100 participated in a discussion that lasted about an hour. James P. Moran of Virginia described Gephardt as sounding "disappointed, saddened, very affectionate. It was like family. He kept telling everybody, 'I love you' so and so."

It was Gephardt, after all, who pulled the caucus up by its political and emotional bootstraps after they lost House control in 1994. And when Democrats were in electoral trouble, Gephardt rallied the troops to new levels. He inspired them to raise record sums of money to support candidates in 2002 elections, telling them that this was the year Democrats would finally regain the majority.

Gephardt told colleagues he plans to keep serving in the 3rd District seat he has held since 1976 — he won a 14th term with 59 percent Nov. 5 — but the caucus would have to look to someone new to lead it. Moran said that when his turn came to speak during the conference call, he said, "Dick, it's sad because we spend more time with our colleagues than anybody, and because of your leadership, we feel as if we are family. The head of the household, the person who sits at the head of the table, that seat is empty." ◆

Redistricting Helped GOP

Most of the newly drawn congressional districts went to Republicans

By actually picking up more seats for the 108th Congress, House Republicans and the White House bucked a historical political trend — and surprised hardly anyone.

President Bush's sustained popularity was a big reason, to be sure. But the most significant factor in the way the GOP expanded its majority may well have been the long-anticipated rewards of redistricting.

Republican strategists contended throughout the year that they would benefit from the once-in-a-decade process of reapportioning House membership among the states. And they were right. Twelve seats were awarded to other states, most in Republican-friendly parts of the South and West, at the expense of the more Democratic-friendly North and East.

Republicans won both new seats that were awarded to Texas, both new seats in Florida and the new seat in Nevada. The two parties split the two new seats in Arizona, with the GOP capturing the only competitive one.

And the Republicans implemented highly partisan plans to near-perfection in Pennsylvania and Michigan, which elected six fewer Democrats to the 108th Congress than are currently in those combined delegations.

While the Democrats' best-laid plans worked in Maryland, they did not in other states where the party was in charge of the remapping. In Georgia, Alabama and Indiana, for example, Republicans won just as many seats Nov. 5 as they currently hold.

In most other states, Republicans were able to broker incumbent protection plans with Democrats that sharply limited the number of competitive districts in play: Only 45 seats were ranked

After almost ousting a Democratic incumbent in 2000, Indiana Republican Chris Chocola won a key open-seat race this year.

by Congressional Quarterly as highly competitive just before the election.

The narrower field gave Democrats fewer seats to target and made surmounting the GOP's six-seat advantage that much more difficult.

"The field is truncated, and we're playing on their end of the field," Howard Wolfson, executive director of the Democratic Congressional Campaign Committee, said after the election.

The result was that, for only the third time since the Civil War, the president's party gained strength in the House in a midterm election. The other times were 1998, when President Bill Clinton faced a politically unpopular impeachment process and picked up five Democratic seats in November, and 1934, when Franklin D. Roosevelt gained nine Democratic seats to help him press the New Deal.

Securing the Vulnerable

Republicans particularly wanted to boost the political security of members who won only narrowly in 2000.

Two years ago, Mike Rogers of Michigan, Mark Kennedy of Minnesota and E. Clay Shaw Jr. of Florida each prevailed by fewer than 600 votes. All ran this year in districts made strongly Republican by redistricting; their victory margins were 37, 22 and 21 percentage points, respectively.

"Redistricting did inure to our benefit, not just in pickups, but in stabilizing and solidifying Republican incumbents who, previous to this, had been vulnerable," said Rep. Thomas M. Davis III of Virginia, chairman of the National Republican Congressional Committee (NRCC).

Republican and Democratic strategists agreed that Bush's nationwide popularity, established by his performance following the September 2001 terrorist attacks, was another major factor in the GOP's precedent-breaking gain.

Matthew Dowd, a senior adviser to the Republican National Committee, said Bush's approval rating on Election Day was 96 percent among Republicans and 67 percent among all Americans.

The president — who barnstormed 15 states in the campaign's final week — parlayed his popularity in a way that spread his coattails and "created a political atmospheric in which Republican candidates could prosper," said the NRCC's Davis.

Top Democrats tended to emphasize what they said was an unprecedented — and, they implied, excessive — partisan political effort by the president. "This year he became the fundraiser-in-chief and the campaigner-in-chief for the Republican candidates," said Terry McAuliffe, chairman of the Democratic National Committee.

Still, Democrats recognized Bush's popularity and the historical tendency of voters to rally behind the president in times of perceived crisis. "This election was a referendum on a popular wartime president and the wind was in our face," said Rep. Nita M. Lowey of New York, chairwoman of the Democratic Congressional Campaign Committee.

Wolfson said Democratic polling showed the party and its candidates slipping in mid-October, when Congress authorized the president to use force against Iraq.

With their House gains, Republicans met three top goals: They extended their margin of control to double digits; ended the series of incremental but steady gains the Democrats had made since their 1994 electoral debacle; and gave Bush a larger legislative cushion for advancing his priorities.

Republicans are assured of at least 228 House seats at the start of the 108th Congress, five more than they hold now.

And the total could grow, depending on the outcomes of two races undecided by the end of the week of Nov. 4: In the new 7th District in Colorado, Republican Bob Beauprez held a tiny lead over Democrat Mike Feeley, while in Louisiana's 5th District, Republican Lee Fletcher appears favored over Democrat Rodney Alexander in a Dec. 7 runoff.

If the Republicans end up with 230 seats, they would be back to their strength at the start of the 104th Congress, when they took control of the House for the first time in 40 years.

Democrats will caucus with 204 members if Tim Bishop's apparent narrow upset of Republican Rep. Felix J. Grucci Jr. in New York's 1st District holds up after absentee ballots are counted.

The Democratic total includes liberal independent Bernard Sanders, who holds Vermont's sole seat. But it excludes the vacant seat in Hawaii's strongly Democratic 2nd District, where the late Patsy T. Mink was re-elected posthumously Nov. 5.

Mink — whose remaining time in the 107th Congress will be filled in a Nov. 30 special election — will be re-placed in the 108th Congress by the winner of another election Jan. 4.

Republican Takeaways

The following is a sampler of contests in which Republicans took control of Democratic-held districts:

● **Indiana 2nd.** With his 50 percent to 46 percent victory over Clinton administration Agriculture Department official and former Democratic Rep. Jill Long Thompson (1989-95), Republican businessman Chris Chocola will succeed Tim Roemer — a Democrat whom Chocola nearly defeated two years ago. The district backed Bush in 2000 by a 9 percentage-point margin, and few Republican candidates were as vocal as Chocola in support of the president and his policies.

Social Security was a major issue. Thompson maintained that Chocola appeared to advocate an eventual privatization of the national pension program. But Chocola sought the offensive on the issue, accusing Thompson of voting as a House member for federal budgets that "raided" the Social Security trust fund.

● **Florida 5th.** A Republican-drawn redistricting plan and the coattails from the landslide re-election of Republican Gov. Jeb Bush — one of the president's brothers — combined to help Republican state Sen. Ginny Brown-Waite defeat Democratic Rep. Karen L. Thurman, who was seeking a sixth term, by 4,200 votes, or about 2 percentage points.

● **Minnesota 2nd.** After losing close challenges to Democrat Bill Luther in 1998 and 2000, Republican John Kline prevailed by 11 percentage points in a suburban district with a constituency that was mostly new to Luther under the new congressional map, which was drawn by a judicial panel.

● **Ohio 3rd.** The GOP took over a Dayton-based district that was vacated in September when veteran Democrat Tony P. Hall was named U.S. Ambassador to the United Nations Agencies for Food and Agriculture. Aided by a GOP-drawn remap, Republican Mike Turner — a former mayor of Dayton — defeated Democrat Rick Carne, Hall's longtime former chief of staff, with 59 percent of the vote.

Democrats' Ups . . .

Democrats did manage to win a few Republican-held districts that were altered in redistricting to give decided edges to Democratic candidates.

● **Maryland 2nd.** Democrat C.A. Dutch Ruppersberger, the Baltimore County executive, defeated Republican former Rep. Helen Delich Bentley (1985-95) by 9 percentage points in a district that was altered to the Democrats' advantage after incumbent Republican Robert L. Ehrlich Jr. launched his ultimately successful bid to become the first Republican elected governor in the state since the 1960s.

● **Maryland 8th.** In part because so many political operatives and journalists live in Montgomery County, for two years the battle for this seat was labeled as one of the marquee races for the battle to control the 108th Congress. But the result was not the harbinger it was predicted to be: Democratic state Sen. Chris Van Hollen took 52 percent to defeat Republican Rep. Constance A. Morella, a leading GOP moderate. Morella had held an otherwise strongly Democratic district for eight terms, but the Democratic redistricters in the state added even more members of the party to her constituency this time.

● **Tennessee 4th.** Democratic state Sen. Lincoln Davis defeated Republican Janice Bowling, a former aide to Rep. Van Hilleary, by 5 points. With Hilleary pursuing a gubernatorial bid that failed, the Democrats who controlled the redistricting process made the 4th more favorable to Davis' candidacy.

. . . and Downs

Democratic candidates put in surprisingly poor performances in some other important open-seat races.

● **Nevada 3rd.** Located mainly in the suburbs of Las Vegas, this new district was drawn to be politically competitive. Democratic officials early on promoted Dario Herrera, a Clark County commissioner, as a strong contender. But news reports of ethics allegations lodged against Herrera helped his Republican opponent, state Sen. Jon Porter, prevail by a 19 percentage-point margin.

● **West Virginia 2nd.** The estimated $7 million that Democratic lawyer Jim Humphreys spent in his rematch with freshman Republican Shelley Moore Capito was wasted. In 2000, he lost by 3 percentage points; Capito defeated him this year by 20 points.

● **Georgia 12th.** Democratic mapmakers drew a seat to accommodate Charles Walker Jr., the son of the state Senate majority leader whose election

True Competition a Rarity in House Races

As was expected, and as has been the case in recent election cycles, the battle for partisan control of the House came down to just a few dozen highly competitive races. The winner received less than 55 percent of the vote — the tradi- tional threshold for "competitive" — in barely more than 10 percent of all 2002 House contests. Most of the candidates elected to the 108th Congress won by landslide margins, with 30 facing no opposition.

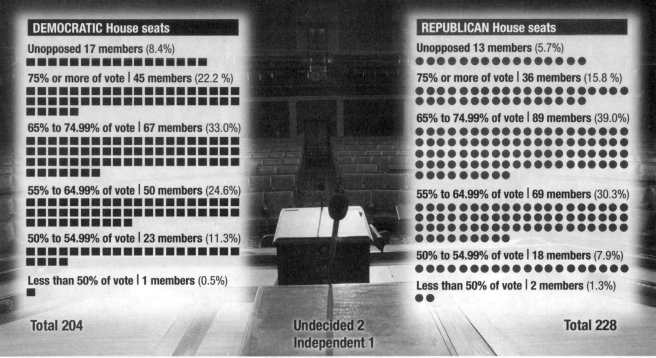

DEMOCRATIC House seats

Unopposed 17 members (8.4%)

75% or more of vote | 45 members (22.2 %)

65% to 74.99% of vote | 67 members (33.0%)

55% to 64.99% of vote | 50 members (24.6%)

50% to 54.99% of vote | 23 members (11.3%)

Less than 50% of vote | 1 members (0.5%)

Total 204

REPUBLICAN House seats

Unopposed 13 members (5.7%)

75% or more of vote | 36 members (15.8 %)

65% to 74.99% of vote | 89 members (39.0%)

55% to 64.99% of vote | 69 members (30.3%)

50% to 54.99% of vote | 18 members (7.9%)

Less than 50% of vote | 2 members (1.3%)

Total 228

Undecided 2
Independent 1

---

would have given Georgia five black House members, a first for any state. But Walker's alleged ethical lapses led to the election by 10 points of Republican professor Max Burns.

Incumbents Stay In

Thanks in large part to redistricting, Democrats and Republicans alike had great success defending their incumbents. In the end, 96 percent of the House members who ran for re-election won. That was only 2 percentage points less than in the previous two elections.

Only 15 incumbents have gone down to sure defeat — Grucci would be the 16th — and eight of those were defeated by one of their House colleagues, half in primaries and half in the general election. Only four members, all Democrats, were denied renomination otherwise. And on Election Day only Morella, Thurman and Luther were defeated by a non-member; Grucci would be a fourth.

Republicans won three of the general election matchups between incumbents. The most lopsided was in Mississippi's 3rd District, where Charles W. "Chip" Pickering Jr. defeated Democrat Ronnie

Shows by nearly 30 percentage points. Republican John Shimkus beat Democratic David Phelps by 10 percentage points in Illinois' 19th District. In Connecticut's 5th District, 10-term Republican Nancy L. Johnson parlayed her seniority and superior fundraising into a 11-point victory over Democrat Jim Maloney.

The one incumbent matchup won by a Democrat was in Pennsylvania's 17th District, where Tim Holden edged Republican George W. Gekas by 51 percent to 49 percent.

So few incumbent losses is unusual for a first election after redistricting — underscoring the status quo tendency of the process this time around. In the 1992 post-redistricting election, 43 House incumbents lost. In 1982, the number was 39. The 96 percent re-election rate this time compares with 88 percent a decade ago and 90 percent two decades ago.

Democrats fell short in their bids to oust Republicans Anne M. Northup of Kentucky and Jim Leach of Iowa, who prevailed in the closest re-election campaigns of their careers.

In Texas' 23rd District, Democrat

Henry Cuellar, a former Texas secretary of state, came close to surprising Henry Bonilla, one of only three Hispanic Republicans in the House. Cuellar benefited from a strong turnout of Hispanic Democrats in Laredo, hometown of both Cuellar and Democratic businessman Tony Sanchez, who lost his bid to become the state's first Hispanic governor. Texas' 23rd was one of the few districts where Democratic turnout was higher than expected. But Bonilla held on by 6,500 votes.

Though they staved off defeat, seven Democratic incumbents from conservative-leaning districts that backed Bush in 2000 were re-elected with 52 percent of the vote or less: Jim Matheson won by just 2,000 votes to hold Utah's 2nd District. Ken Lucas of Kentucky won a third term with 51 percent. Charles W. Stenholm won a 13th term in Texas with 51 percent. Chet Edwards, another Texan, was held to 52 percent. Baron P. Hill, won his third term in Indiana with 51 percent. Dennis Moore of Kansas won his third term by 7,000 votes. And North Dakota's lone congressman, Earl Pomeroy, won a sixth term with 52 percent. ◆

Departing Members of 107th Congress

SENATORS DEFEATED IN GENERAL ELECTION (2 D, 1 R)*

Name	Age	Began Service	Winner
Jean Carnahan, D-Mo.	68	2001	Former Rep. Jim Talent, R-Mo. (1993-2001)
Max Cleland, D-Ga.	60	1997	Rep. Saxby Chambliss, R-Ga.
Tim Hutchinson, R-Ark.	53	1997	State Atty. Gen. Mark Pryor

HOUSE MEMBERS DEFEATED IN GENERAL ELECTION (5 D, 2 R)**

Name	Age	Began Service	Winner
George W. Gekas, R-Pa.	72	1983	Rep. Tim Holden, D-Pa.
Bill Luther, D-Minn.	57	1995	John Kline
Jim Maloney, D-Conn.	54	1997	Rep. Nancy Johnson, R-Conn.
Constance A. Morella, R-Md.	71	1987	Chris Van Hollen
David Phelps, D-Ill.	55	1999	Rep. John Shimkus, R-Ill.
Ronnie Shows, D-Miss.	55	1999	Rep. Charles W. "Chip" Pickering Jr., R-Miss.
Karen L. Thurman, D-Fla.	51	1993	Ginny Brown-Waite

DEFEATED IN PRIMARY (6 D, 3 R)

Name	Winner
Rep. Bob Barr, R-Ga.	Rep. John Linder, R-Ga.
Rep. Gary A. Condit, D-Calif.	Dennis Cardoza
Rep. Earl F. Hilliard, D-Ala.	Artur Davis
Rep. Brian Kerns, R-Ind.	Rep. Steve Buyer, R-Ind.
Rep. Frank R. Mascara, D-Pa.	Rep. John P. Murtha, D-Pa.
Rep. Cynthia A. McKinney, D-Ga.	Denise L. Majette
Rep. Lynn Rivers, D-Mich.	Rep. John D. Dingell, D-Mich.
Rep. Tom Sawyer, D-Ohio	Timothy J. Ryan
Sen. Robert C. Smith, R-N.H.	Rep. John E. Sununu

RESIGNED (4 R, 1D)

Name	Effective Date
Rep. Bud Shuster, R-Pa.	Feb. 2, 2001
Rep. Asa Hutchinson, R-Ark.	Aug. 6, 2001
Rep. Joe Scarborough, R-Fla.	Sept. 6, 2001
Rep. Steve Largent, R-Okla.	Feb. 15, 2002
Rep. Tony P. Hall, D-Ohio	Sept. 9, 2002

RETIRING HOUSE MEMBERS (12 R, 6D)

Name	Age	Began Service
Dick Armey, R-Texas	62	1985
Robert A. Borski, D-Pa.	54	1983
Sonny Callahan, R-Ala.	70	1985
Eva Clayton, D-N.C.	68	1992
William J. Coyne, D-Pa.	66	1981
Benjamin A. Gilman, R-N.Y.	79	1973
James V. Hansen, R-Utah	70	1981
Steve Horn, R-Calif.	71	1993
John J. LaFalce, D-N.Y.	63	1975
Carrie P. Meek, D-Fla.	76	1993
Dan Miller, R-Fla.	60	1993
Tim Roemer, D-Ind.	46	1991
Marge Roukema, R-N.J.	73	1981
Bob Schaffer, R-Colo.	40	1997
Joe Skeen, R-N.M.	75	1980
Bob Stump, R-Ariz.	75	1977
Wes Watkins, R-Okla.	63	1997
J.C. Watts Jr., R-Okla.	44	1995

DIED (6)

Name	Date
Sen. Paul Wellstone, D-Minn.	Oct. 25, 2002
Rep. Julian C. Dixon, D-Calif.	Dec. 8, 2000
Rep. Patsy T. Mink, D-Hawaii	Sept. 28, 2002
Rep. Joe Moakley, D-Mass.	May 28, 2001
Rep. Norman Sisisky, D-Va.	March 29, 2001
Rep. Floyd D. Spence, R-S.C.	Aug. 16, 2001

EXPELLED (1)

Name	Date
Rep. James A. Traficant Jr., D-Ohio	July 24, 2002

RETIRING SENATORS (4 R, 1D)

Name	Age	Began Service
Phil Gramm, R-Texas	60	1985
Jesse Helms, R-N.C.	81	1973
Robert G. Torricelli, D-N.J.	51	1997
Fred Thompson, R-Tenn.	60	1994
Strom Thurmond, R-S.C.	99	1954

SOUGHT OTHER OFFICE (19)

Name	Age	Goal/Outcome
Rep. John Baldacci, D-Maine	47	Governor/won
Rep. James A. Barcia, D-Mich	50	State Senate/won
Rep. Thomas M. Barrett, D-Wis.	48	Governor/lost
Rep. Ken Bentsen, D-Texas	43	Senate/lost
Rep. Rod R. Blagojevich, D-Ill.	45	Governor/won
Rep. David E. Bonior, D-Mich.	57	Governor/lost
Rep. Ed Bryant, R-Tenn.	54	Senate/lost
Rep. Saxby Chambliss, R-Ga.	58	Senate/won
Rep. Bob Clement, D-Tenn.	59	Senate/lost
Rep. John Cooksey, R-La.	61	Senate/lost
Rep. Robert L. Ehrlich Jr., R-Md.	44	Governor/won
Rep. Greg Ganske, R-Iowa	53	Senate/lost
Rep. Lindsey Graham, R-S.C.	47	Senate/won
Rep. Van Hilleary, R-Tenn.	43	Governor/lost
Sen. Frank H. Murkowski, R-Alaska	69	Governor/won
Rep. Bob Riley, R-Ala.	58	Governor***
Rep. John E. Sununu, R-N.H.	38	Senate/won
Rep. John Thune, R-S.D.	41	Senate/lost
Del. Robert A. Underwood, D-Guam	54	Governor/lost

*Mary L. Landrieu, D-La., in Dec. 7 runoff

**Race between Rep. Felix J. Grucci Jr., R-N.Y., and Democrat Tim Bishop too close to call

***Race between Riley and Democratic Gov. Donald Siegelman too close to call

States' Priorities Vs. Funds

New governors with their own agendas must work with inherited budget constraints

Maryland Republican Robert L. Ehrlich Jr. already knows one side of the federalist principles espoused by his party's leadership: During his four terms in the House, he has supported efforts to push responsibility for policymaking to the states.

Beginning in January, Ehrlich will get a close-up view of the other side as Maryland's new governor — at a time when economic difficulties will force him to make tough choices.

The first Republican to be elected governor in heavily Democratic Maryland since 1966, Ehrlich will be one of about two dozen new state chief executives.

Charged with the usual responsibilities of providing services and balancing the books, these governors will be uniquely challenged in a time of economic stress. And they take office after an election that gave full control of the federal government to the Republican Party, with its philosophical commitment to moving more responsibilities to the states and localities.

During his campaign this year against Democratic Lt. Gov. Kathleen Kennedy Townsend, Ehrlich joked that he would spend as much time lobbying for money in the nation's capital as he would spend in the state capital of Annapolis. He contended, though, that he could do a better job of finding cash for the state than the outgoing governor, term-limited Democrat Parris N. Glendening.

"Given Maryland's budget mess right now, I'll be leveraging as much federal funding as possible," Ehrlich said. "Transportation projects and health and education programs will be direct beneficiaries of my relationship with the president and congressional leadership."

But some experts say Ehrlich and his counterparts in other states may be left to marshal their own budget solutions, as a wartime federal government is dealing with its own fiscal crunch. Congress may, in fact, ask more of the states — through changes to welfare, health care and education policy —

Ehrlich, who accused Maryland's incumbent Democratic administration of failing to fix state problems, must now compete for limited federal resources as he seeks his own solutions.

without giving them extra money.

"Some of them will respond to that by making serious cuts, some of them will respond by raising taxes and still others will respond with some mixture of the two," said James Gimpel, a political scientist at the University of Maryland. "That will clearly be the case with this war effort soaking up discretionary spending."

But Rep. Michael N. Castle, R-Del., a former governor himself, said there has not been as much of a shift toward federalism as some might think and that money is still available.

"The federal largess is not exactly dried up at this point," Castle said.

The nation's governors faced a collective $49.1 billion budget shortfall this year, according to the National Conference of State Legislatures (NCSL). Some new governors may call their legislatures into special sessions just to focus on budgeting.

"It's the worst fiscal crisis that states have had since the Second World War," said Ray Scheppach, executive director of the National Governors Association (NGA). "We're going to see some pretty draconian cuts."

While such medicine may be bitter-tasting, at least most of the governors elected Nov. 5 have four years before they have to face voters.

"Those just elected are probably in better shape than those that have to do it in two years," said University of Georgia political scientist Charles Bullock.

Election Results

Voters expressed their worries over state fiscal woes, but in an indirect sort of way. No more than four of the 16 incumbents who sought re-election were defeated. But seats changed hands in 16 of the 20 states in which no incumbent ran.

Democrats had predicted big gains in governorships, if for no other reason than because the Republicans had so much more exposure. Of 36 seats up this year, 23 were held by Republicans, 11 by

Democrats and two by independents.

But the backlash against incumbent administrations dashed the Democrats' hopes. Trailing the Republicans 27-21 going into the elections, the best the Democrats will be able to do is break even at 25 — and that's only if Alabama Gov. Don Siegelman is able to reverse the tiny lead held by his Republican challenger, Rep. Bob Riley, in a recount of the disputed Election Night canvass.

Democrats did win in big industrial swing states, grabbing the governorship for the first time in eight years in Pennsylvania, 12 years in Michigan, 16 years in Wisconsin and 26 years in Illinois.

They also succeeded in some Western states that typically are Republican strongholds, such as Arizona, Oklahoma, Kansas and Wyoming, and took over the governor's seat in politically competitive New Mexico, where former Energy Secretary Bill Richardson ended an eight-year Republican run.

But Republicans offset some of these reversals by flexing their muscles in what increasingly has become their strongest region: the South.

The GOP scored the biggest upset in Georgia, where former state Sen. Sonny Perdue ousted Democratic Gov. Roy Barnes to become the state's first Republican governor since the Reconstruction era.

Democratic Gov. Jim Hodges in South Carolina also lost, and Siegelman is on the razor's edge in Alabama. Democrats pushed back a little, with former Nashville Mayor Phil Bredesen taking over the open seat in Tennessee.

Overall, Republicans did a much better job defending their own seats, going 13-10 in states where they held power, than did the Democrats, who successfully defended California, Iowa and Oregon while losing at least seven races.

GOP incumbents held on to big states such as Texas, New York, Florida and Ohio, and smaller states such as Connecticut, Idaho and Arkansas.

The election was notable for the number of competitive women candidates. Four women were elected to governors' offices, breaking the previous single-year record of three set in 1990. And when they take office, they will bring the number of sitting women governors to an all-time record of six. (*Women gubernatorial winners, this page*)

As they embark on their difficult efforts to set state priorities in a time of fiscal stress, the nation's fresh-faced governors will be joined by many new state lawmakers. More than 2,000 of the

Women Break Election Record

It was a record-setting year for women running for governor — though it was not as big a step forward as some had anticipated.

Winning governors' seats on Nov. 5 were two Democratic women serving as their states' attorneys general, Jennifer Granholm of Michigan and Janet Napolitano of Arizona; a Kansas Democrat, state Insurance Commissioner Kathleen Sebelius; and Hawaii's Linda Lingle, a former mayor of Maui who was the only Republican woman nominated for governor this year.

These four victories broke the previous single-year record of three, set in 1990. When they take office, they will bring the number of women serving as governors to a record six.

The total could have been higher, though. Kathleen Kennedy Townsend of Maryland and Shannon P. O'Brien of Massachusetts lost close races, while women in Alaska, Arkansas and Rhode Island also lost. All were Democrats.

Hawaii was the only state to field two women candidates; the Democrat was Mazie Hirono.

Ellen R. Malcolm, president of EMILY's List, a group that supports Democratic women candidates who favor abortion rights, said the "new women governors won . . . because they had impressive records in office, built strong coalitions, and attracted independents and a large outpouring of support from women voters."

7,382 state legislators elected Nov. 5 are new to the job, political analysts say.

Every state except Vermont requires a balanced budget each year. Some new governors may be forced to turn to "sin" taxes on products such as cigarettes or alcohol to bridge fiscal gaps.

In many states, gubernatorial candidates proposed raising revenues by introducing various forms of gambling, such as slot machines and state lotteries.

Most said they would eliminate wasteful spending in state budgets, though many were short on specifics.

There is little doubt the new governors will ask Washington for more cash and less interference. "They'll probably have their hands out. They'll want fewer regulations on how they use the money — especially if there's a new welfare reform law," Gimpel said.

Places to Watch

Brookings Institution scholar Thomas E. Mann predicted that the three main issues to watch are: funding to implement the education law (PL 107-110) enacted last year, federal aid to states for rising Medicaid costs, and funds to strengthen homeland defenses.

"Medicaid is a huge fiscal problem for states, and it's an open question: Will the administration be open in the new Congress to increased revenue-sharing through Medicaid as part of a one-time

stimulus package? I'm a bit skeptical, but it will certainly be discussed," he said.

How well governors use the money they do get, and how successful they are at using their states as incubators for policy, could determine whether any ultimately become serious contenders for the White House.

The Senate once was the preferred launching pad for presidential bids, but voters have favored candidates with executive experience in recent elections. Four of the past five presidents — George W. Bush, Bill Clinton, Ronald Reagan and Jimmy Carter — came from the gubernatorial ranks.

Democratic losses in the South, particularly, diminish that party's numbers in a region that produced four of the last five presidents.

Beyond acting as a proving ground for presidential contenders, governors play an important role in national campaigns. They can rally the party troops by lending fundraising and organizational support to a presidential candidate in crucial states.

Thus, Democratic California Gov. Gray Davis' re-election and wins by Democrats in battleground states such as Michigan (state Attorney General Jennifer Granholm), Illinois (Rep. Rod R. Blagojevich) and Pennsylvania (former Philadelphia Mayor Ed Rendell) could be the silver lining for a party that had a cloudier Election Day than expected. ◆

Government Institutions

The articles in this section provide insight into the inner workings of the major institutions of American government, focusing in turn on Congress, the presidency and the judiciary. The articles examine partisanship, defense, homeland security and judicial nominations.

The section on Congress begins with a look at partisanship. The first article addresses Congress's bipartisan solidarity against terrorism in the year following the Sept. 11, 2001, terrorist attacks and covers Congress's Sept. 6, 2002, meeting in Federal Hall in New York City—the first meeting of Congress in New York since 1790. The second story focuses on House Speaker Dennis Hastert, R-Ill., and how he manages that chamber. The third article describes the terrorism insurance bill's year in Congress and the impact industry lobbyists had on its progress. The House passed a bill in November 2001, but the Senate version stagnated. Finally, one year later, the legislation passed.

The next article in the Congress section examines the House Financial Services Committee's investigation into investment bank management of initial public offerings (IPOs)—just one of several congressional investigations of corporate America in the past year. The article focuses not only on the IPO investigation but also on Congress's oversight powers in business and government.

The section ends with an article explaining the planned overhaul of voting machinery and databases and the costs of the upgrades. In October 2002 Congress reached an agreement that would set national standards for elections and provide aid to help the states meet these standards. The article also examines the bill's voter identification provisions designed to prevent fraud. The goal is to have an improved system in place before the 2004 elections to avoid a repeat of voting problems that occurred in 2000.

The articles on the presidency cover homeland security and the possible war with Iraq. The first and last articles examine the political and financial ramifications of war. One story considers how war will affect U.S. foreign policy and the roles of the president and Congress in placing sanctions on Iraq; the other article examines how the costs of war will affect the federal budget, which has already returned to deficit spending. The costs of war are also outlined in an article that compares U.S. defense spending with that of other nations. How does this spending affect the United States' standing in the world?

The other two articles on the presidency focus on homeland security. The first discusses the disputes between the Senate and White House over the president's power in personnel decisions involving the proposed department. The second piece examines the relationship between President George W. Bush and congressional Democrats in the creation of the department and the passage of related legislation.

The final government institution examined is the judiciary. This article looks at the Senate confirmation process for judicial nominees and the relations between Senate leaders and the president, as well as the influence of the voting public. Senate Democrats and Republicans are bitterly divided over judicial nominations. Politicians on both sides use nominations to please their constituents, removing the president's authority to shape the judiciary and leaving many courts understaffed and some judgeships vacant. Experts caution that as the appointment and confirmation process becomes more political, the courts could appear to have political leanings. Judges may be perceived as favoring the political philosophies of those who appointed them, particularly on hot-button issues such as abortion and gun control. The article examines how this process has deteriorated and what it means for both parties, as well as the nominees.

A Road Show of Solidarity

Partisanship gets a day off as Congress reconvenes at its original meeting place

NEW YORK

Sometimes it takes a tragedy to call even a temporary halt to sibling rivalry. And New York and Washington — the former the country's financial capital, the latter its political center — long have competed for the nation's attention. But to commemorate the first anniversary of the deadliest attack ever on the United States, the leaders of both places brushed aside regional rivalries, and members of Congress put away their partisanship, to join for a day of solemn ceremonies designed to show their solidarity against terrorism.

The principal symbol employed by the 107th Congress was its own presence in New York. For only the second time in history, the federal legislature convened in a place away from the seat of government.

"For all our differences, how remarkably one we are all today," House Minority Leader Richard A. Gephardt, D-Mo., told the 48 senators and 253 House members who convened Sept. 6 in Federal Hall, the place where the 1st Congress met in 1789 and 1790 and just around the corner from where the Twin Towers of the World Trade Center stood until last Sept. 11.

Many of the lawmakers on hand — most had come to New York aboard a special train early in the morning from Union Station on Capitol Hill — said they had not expected to be so moved by the day's events. In addition to the session of Congress, which was formally designated a "special meeting," there was a lunch for the lawmakers and an afternoon wreath-laying at Ground Zero, the sprawling hole where the towers had been.

"I thought it would be ceremonial

and kind of formal," said New York's senior senator, Democrat Charles E. Schumer, "but it was touching to me."

Added Rep. David E. Price D-N.C.: "More than I would have anticipated, things came rushing back."

More than most Americans, members of Congress had reason to fear for their lives after hijacked jetliners crashed into the trade center and Pentagon on Sept. 11. They had nervously if defiantly huddled on the steps of the Capitol that evening in an attempt to project confidence to their constituents, but many recalled their fear as they rushed through the congressional office building hallways, scurried across the Capitol grounds and desperately tried to telephone loved ones across the country.

On the steps that day, members had simultaneously burst into an a cappella chorus of "God Bless America," and some could not contain their emotions when the Stuyvesant High School Chamber Choir sang the song during the special meeting. Democratic Sen. Barbara A. Mikulski of Maryland wept, and Rep. Anthony Weiner put his arm around fellow New York Democrat

Nita M. Lowey as she wiped away tears as well.

"We are here to remember and to continue to mourn," Senate Minority Leader Trent Lott, R-Miss., told the members. "We're also here to express our recommitment. . . . We will continue our efforts to help you to rebuild physically and spiritually, and to recommit ourselves to do everything in our power to make sure that America is secure against this horrible event or anything like it ever happening again."

Focus on Defense

With the meeting coming just two days after President Bush promised to seek a formal authorization from Congress before moving to end Saddam Hussein's regime in Iraq, many of those on hand signaled their desire for a continued focus on a vigorous defense against future attack. (*2002 CQ Weekly, p. 2313*)

"Since the hour of those attacks, we've been a nation at war, called once again to defend our liberty and our lives and to save humanity from the worst of horrors," said Vice President Dick Cheney, who was on the dais in Federal

After their special meeting, most lawmakers went to the site of the World Trade Center towers to lay a wreath and leave American flags nearby. Mayor Bloomberg and Gov. Pataki, in red ties, looked on.

Hall in his capacity as the president of the Senate. "As a nation born in revolution, we know that our freedom came at a very high price. We have no intention now of letting it slip away."

In his address to the meeting, Gephardt offered this message to the world: "On the fundamental issues, let there be no doubt. In this great and fateful struggle, there are no Democrats, there are no Republicans. There are only Americans."

Although House Speaker J. Dennis Hastert, R-Ill., early on had expressed some reservations about convening such a ceremonial meeting, he eventually concluded that it was an appropriate gesture "to symbolize the nation's solidarity with New Yorkers."

Charles B. Rangel, the senior New York Democrat in the House, who had been one of the promoters of such an event since last year, said it was important to "give us in New York an opportunity to say thank you for the way" Congress has responded, principally with the delivery of an assortment of appropriations and tax breaks, worth about $20 billion, to help in the recovery of New York.

At the ceremonial session, Rangel and other New York lawmakers read the text of the resolution (H Con Res 448), adopted by voice votes in the House and Senate in July, that called for the special meeting "in remembrance of the victims and the heroes of Sept. 11, 2001, and in recognition of the courage and spirit of the City of New York." Rangel was joined by Benjamin A. Gilman, the senior Republican in the New York congressional delegation, and the state's senators — Schumer and fellow Democrat Hillary Rodham Clinton.

Federal Hall, reconstructed in the 1840s into its present form, was New York's city hall when it was lent to the federal government as the first meeting place for Congress after the Constitution's ratification. George Washington was inaugurated as the first president in the building in 1789, the Bill of Rights

In Federal Hall on Sept. 6, New York's senators and most senior House members, left, read the resolution calling for the first meeting of Congress in New York since 1790. More than half the membership attended; some stood for a better view, above.

was agreed upon there — and so was the decision to move the nation's capital to the shores of the Potomac.

Congress last met in New York on Aug. 12, 1790. The only other time Congress has convened away from Washington since moving there permanently was in 1987, when it spent a day in Philadelphia commemorating the bicentennial of the Constitution.

The Sept. 6 session was not without its critics. Senate President Pro Tempore Robert C. Byrd, D-W.Va., pointedly stayed away, saying that Congress had far more important legislative business to attend to in Washington and that he also was worried that terrorists might pierce the extraordinarily tight security in lower Manhattan.

But there were lighthearted moments, too. When a version of the concurrent resolution was presented to Republican Gov. George E. Pataki of New York and GOP Mayor Michael Bloomberg of New York City, Democratic Rep. Gary L. Ackerman of Queens leaned on the shoulder of Senate Majority Leader Tom Daschle, D-S.D., to get a better angle for his photograph. Returning to his seat, Ackerman made a show of giving a high-five to Rep. Christopher Shays, R-Conn.

Disposable cameras were in abundance before the session began as members lined up at the dais to have their pictures taken with the Bible used for the Washington inauguration. Many lawmakers wore matching ties and scarves that had been given to them for the occasion.

When the hourlong session had ended, members joined Bloomberg and other New York dignitaries at a Wall Street hotel for chateaubriand on a bundle of truffled green and white asparagus. Most costs for the ceremonies were paid through a $1 million grant to New York City by the Annenberg Foundation.

At the luncheon, Bloomberg joked that the city was honored to be the nation's capital again for the day but was happy to be reclaiming its self-anointed "capital of the free world" moniker for all time.

Hastert and Daschle gave Bloomberg a flag that had flown over the Capitol last Sept. 11 and expressed hope that it would someday be displayed in a memorial to the attack's victims. Members completed their day by walking single-file through the former World Trade Center site, placing small American flags beside a wreath. Many members said they felt the trip had been worthwhile, for the residents of New York and for themselves.

"There is a certain sense of closeness that this type of event brings to Congress that I think is good," said Sen. John B. Breaux, D-La. But, he added, the "day-to-day partisan politics" had returned in Congress.

Breaux termed that a benefit of "getting back to normal." ◆

The Seasoned Speaker: Still Hastert, but Harder

Fractious caucus, struggle to keep his majority test Speaker's famed collegiality

When a Speaker of the House appears before his caucus, unvarnished political talk and unambiguous partisan marching orders are often in store. But not on the midsummer morning when the House Republicans met behind the closed doors of their low-ceilinged conference room in the Capitol basement.

Rather than insisting that conservatives bend to the political will and embrace strict new federal regulations of corporate behavior, J. Dennis Hastert tried to cajole his troops in that direction by reciting Robert Frost's "The Road Not Taken" from memory. But he bungled the well-known poem badly from the outset, prompting a wave of chuckles — and at least one lawmaker to call out the words of the opening stanza correctly.

Hastert neither took umbrage nor pressed on with his recitation until he could deliver the literary payoff pitch: "Two roads diverged in a wood, and I / I took the one less traveled by, / And that has made all the difference." Instead, he joined in the laughter at his own expense, then exhorted his audience to compromise so as to prevent the Democrats from winning the upper hand on one of the most politically potent consumer issues of this election year.

That small moment is a window into the management style that Hastert has employed since he was propelled into the speakership almost four years ago — an approach that will be put to one of its most arduous tests yet this fall.

"Denny is not a screamer, but Denny is not afraid to be in the room," says GOP Rep. Fred Upton of Michigan.

A "regular order" type of lawmaker since his days in the Illinois legislature, Hastert prefers to let chairmen and others in the leadership work with minimal intrusion, and to force them to settle their intraparty differences with as little preemption or pressure as possible. To make that approach work, he cultivates a regular-guy image and seeks to form a personal bond with almost every House Republican.

Someone who never planned to become the highest congressional officer under the Constitution, he remains con-

"I need to make the House work," Hastert said in a July 26 interview in his office. **"I need to be able to deliver."**

CQ PHOTO / SCOTT J. FERRELL

tent to leave the flash and the fancy rhetoric to others in the egocentric Capitol and present himself as an ordinary man, shaping legislation out of public view much as he has since he arrived in Congress in 1987. But his non-threatening style, those close to him say, is coupled with a self-assurance and resolve that should not be underestimated.

For as he has matured in the job, Hastert has grown steadily bolder, occasionally railing against Republicans in the Senate as well as the Bush administration for choosing pragmatic compromises with Democrats instead of standing behind the more conservative GOP principles embedded in the House's legislative work.

In the eight weeks until his first midterm election as the 51st Speaker, Hastert will be under pressure to trade more frequently on the loyalties he has developed. If he cannot find a consensus within the Republican Conference, he will be pressed to dictate House GOP positions on domestic issues ranging from bankruptcy regulation to terrorism insurance — largest among them, the fight over social spending and the overall growth in appropriations for the coming year.

Hastert not only wants to keep peace within his caucus, he wants to help protect President Bush's legislative agenda from being undermined by the Democratic Senate and develop a record of accomplishments before Nov. 5 — even if a lame-duck session comes after. Further complicating matters is the question for lawmakers over which the GOP whip organization is unlikely to exercise control: Should Bush be given authority to send troops to Iraq? (*2002 CQ Weekly, p. 2352*)

The Speaker acknowledges that the political stakes could not be higher for him. "It's my job that we keep the majority," he said in assessing his style during a recent interview.

Thomas M. Davis III of Virginia, chairman of the House GOP campaign organization, said in order to do that Hastert must leave voters with the impression that the Republican House is a productive place. "You can't put lipstick on a pig. If Congress does not produce, it doesn't help us," he said.

Some of the most politically important debates, especially those over spending, pit allies of the GOP's conservative political base — the voters most likely to cast ballots in non-presidential elections — against Republican moderates in districts that could elect a Democrat if the incumbent is viewed as not taking care of voter priorities.

But House Republicans maintain that in such politically unsettled times, Hastert's steady eye on legislation and his aversion to headline-making is precisely the kind of leadership they need. It is essentially the same way Hastert was viewed by his colleagues four years ago, when he was catapulted from chief deputy whip to Speaker. His unexpected elevation came after GOP setbacks in the last midterm election forced the resignation of the polarizing Newt Gingrich of Georgia (1979-99) and the revelations of personal indiscretions forced Gingrich's anointed successor, Robert L. Livingston of Louisiana (1977-99), to announce his departure on the very day the House impeached President Bill Clinton. (*1998 Almanac, p. 7-4*)

Back then, J.C. Watts Jr. of Oklahoma had just been elected to the leadership as chairman of the House Republican Conference, and he remembers the advice Gingrich imparted.

"You are going to have to have a Speaker who's going to have the ability, every day, to sit down and listen to members, every day, and understand the problems, every day. And that man is Denny Hastert," Watts quoted Gingrich as saying.

Hastert's Balancing Act

As a partisan leader, Hastert's room to maneuver is severely limited: He has only 223 Republican votes at his disposal — just five more than a House majority, the narrowest margin of control since 1954. But throughout the 107th Congress, he has tried to inoculate the House GOP against criticism by moving legislation that blends his troops' desires with those of the president. (*2002 CQ Weekly, p. 1923*)

Democrats have felt marginalized along the way, complaining loudly that Hastert's partisan approach too often has prevented them from even offering alternatives to top-tier legislation, such as the economic recovery package enacted early this year (PL 107-147) or this summer's bill (HR 4954) to create a Medicare prescription drug benefit. (*2002 CQ Weekly, pp. 633, 1737*)

In urging Hastert to change his ways, Minority Leader Richard A. Gephardt, D-Mo., says maintaining party loyalty for an exclusively Republican measure does not produce enacted law — which is what the electorate is looking for, in Gephardt's view.

"The test is, 'What have you done to take care of my problems? What's the performance of government? Is there a prescription drug program? Is the economy working well? Do I have a job? Are my investments safe? Do I have retirement?' I think they are failing on that," Gephardt said of House Republicans.

Engineering a Success

A sense of how Hastert operates as legislative driver and arbiter was evident during one peripatetic 20-hour workday: Friday, July 26. That was the day before the House recessed for its summer break — a time when months of inconclusive negotiation traditionally collides with lawmakers' desires to have more accomplishments to boast about when they arrive back home.

Hastert arrived at work that day with a nagging cough born of fatigue. The heavy workload had left time for no more than four hours of sleep most nights that week. But already he could claim one accomplishment. The day before, he had helped persuade Republican leaders to set aside their initial resistance and embrace on the floor the most sweeping package of regulations governing corporate behavior since the 1930s — Congress' main response to the business scandals of the past year. The measure (PL 107-204) was cleared on a nearly unanimous vote. (*2002 CQ Weekly, p. 2018*)

Scheduled for debate that day was the bill (HR 5005) embodying Bush's request to combine 22 federal agencies into a Cabinet-level homeland security department. But more work had come in overnight. House and Senate negotiators unexpectedly had announced deals on two stalled measures — one (HR 333) to help retailers, credit card companies and banks collect more from those who declare bankruptcy; the other (HR 3009) to enhance the president's trade negotiating authority.

While buoyed by those agreements, Hastert remained uncertain

whether either could muster a House majority that day. Factions in his own caucus were wavering on each, meaning that Democratic votes would be necessary to guarantee their success — a dicey prospect in that polarized climate.

Before Hastert could manage those challenges, however, he had another problem that morning as he took his seat at a conference table in a room adjacent to his office near the Capitol Rotunda. Arrayed before him were more than two dozen GOP moderates bent on giving their leader a political reality check.

Unless more money was added to the fiscal spending bill that funds aid to local schools, health research, winter heating subsidies for the poor and other social programs, the moderates warned, their support would fade, and the bill likely would falter on the House floor, where Democrats were sure to unite against it. And if that happened, work on the must-pass fiscal 2003 appropriations bills would come to a screeching halt.

But the Speaker already had promised conservatives that the package (HR 5320) — governing spending by the Labor, Health and Human Services, and Education departments — would move in the House at the 5 percent increase level Bush had requested.

Rather than reversing field at his meeting with the moderates, Hastert explained the constraints with what he termed "third-grade economics." The appropriations process, he said, is akin to trying to sell 13 different-sized bowls of ice cream to a hungry crowd. In this case, no additional ice cream is in the freezer, so the only argument is over how much of the available supply to put in each dish.

Hastert told the moderates to go haggle over serving sizes with the conservatives — an argument that, seven weeks later, continued to yield nothing but an impasse the week of Sept. 9. As a result, the Labor-HHS bill, and with it the rest of the appropriations agenda, remains in limbo. (*2002 CQ Weekly, p. 2372*)

"The moderates feel very comfortable with Denny," Michael N. Castle of Delaware said after hearing the ice cream analogy and Hastert's inconclusive decision. "We view him as being a true conservative, but we believe he listens."

Others would not be so easily mollified as the day wore on.

Suburban Maryland's Constance A. Morella, one of the most vulnerable House Republicans this fall, failed to persuade the leadership to distance itself from the weakening of civil service protections Bush wants in the homeland security bill — but which her federal worker constituency cannot abide. (*2002 CQ Weekly, p. 2368*)

On the trade bill, last-minute opposition came from Appropriations Committee Chairman C. W. Bill Young, R-Fla., who said the package's increase in spending on displaced worker benefits should have been considered by his panel. When Hastert and his chief of staff, Scott Palmer, could not persuade Young to drop his objection, they arranged for the president to telephone him. Several hours later, Young voted "yes" as the trade package cleared — by three votes. (*2002 CQ Weekly, p. 2127*)

The bankruptcy deal never made it to the floor. In another reminder of how few GOP defections can doom a Republican priority, abortion opponents gave notice they would not support the package — stalling its progress ever since. (*2002 CQ Weekly, p. 2380*)

In the end, Hastert's day had been filled with the sounds of disgruntlement from fellow Republicans, and his compromises had strayed a bit further from his conservative instincts than he normally would allow. But Hastert could hit the campaign trail four days later and boast to voters that the House had passed bills involving corporate misbehavior, trade and a new homeland security department to protect the nation against terrorists.

The Coach

From the start of his tenure in the Speaker's chair, Hastert has defined himself by what he is and by what he is not.

He is a former high school wrestling coach who says the members of his team, not he, should be the "stars."

He is not Gingrich, the party visionary who toiled for years on the elaborate strategy for returning the House to the first GOP control in 40 years. (*1994 Almanac, p. 3*)

Gingrich was the face of the party while serving as Speaker. Hastert is still barely recognized by tourists when he walks through the Capitol, even though he has held the office almost as long as his predecessor.

Television talk shows, the favored venues for the politicians whom Hastert derides as the "prancing ponies running for president," are almost anathema to him. "I'm not running for president, and I don't have to be out there every day," Hastert said.

Gingrich was the Republican whom Democrats loved to hate, but Hastert's approach to conservatism has never been seen as polarizing — which has made him welcome at the side of dozens of House incumbents and challengers in the 2000 and 2002 elections.

"The high profile brings up the negatives. You bring Tom Daschle in a district and that loses votes," Davis said, referring to the Senate majority leader from South Dakota. "Denny Hastert does not lose any votes when he comes into a district."

And in those travels, Hastert now has raised more money for House candidates than any previous Speaker — of either party, according to the National Republican Congressional Committee. He devoted 26 days to the task during this summer's recess, raising an estimated $1.5 million in a series of low-key fundraisers from coast to coast. (*2002 CQ Weekly, p. 2359*)

By this time in his tenure as Speaker, Gingrich had survived a coup attempted by GOP conservatives and had been formally reprimanded by the House and fined $300,000 for ethical lapses. (*1997 Almanac, p. 1-11*)

Hastert, at a similar point in his speakership, can boast that loyalty is his greatest political calling card.

"Newt could give you that staredown" if a member stepped out of line or was not thinking "big enough," recalls Rep. Mark Foley of Florida. Hastert wraps his thick arm around the wavering member. "Denny does not try to bawl you out. He says, 'Let's see how we can work that out.'. . . I don't want to disappoint him," Foley said.

Hastert drew on that loyalty July 23 when the House voted for a second time on a proposed $6.6 billion expansion of Chicago's O'Hare International Airport (HR 3479), legislation defeated a week earlier. The number of Republican "no" votes dropped to 51 from from 96 on the second ballot, and the bill passed.

The DeLay Factor

He manages by coordinating with — rather than dictating to — members of his leadership team, including the

two Texans who participated in the failed Gingrich putsch: Majority Leader Dick Armey and Majority Whip Tom DeLay.

The latter's forceful personality and more polarizing approach to politics has many lawmakers wondering how the Speaker will control DeLay in the 108th Congress, when he is positioned to move up to floor leader upon Armey's retirement.

That is a recurring theme in the discussion of the relationship between the two. Hastert is a DeLay protégé — his previous post was chief deputy in the DeLay vote-counting operation — and in his early months as Speaker he was viewed as a handmaiden of DeLay, who moved quickly to fill a power vacuum on many issues in the 106th Congress.

Today, there is a widespread view that if the GOP loses its majority in November, Hastert will be forced out of the leadership, in part to atone for the defeat but also because DeLay's style would be better suited to the combative role a minority leader is expected to play.

But Hastert has nurtured a working relationship with DeLay that eluded Gingrich, whom Republicans say viewed DeLay as a competitor. Instead of marginalizing his former mentor, Hastert has given DeLay an important role — that of "bad cop" in enforcing party discipline and conservative ideologies to Hastert's more ameliorative and moderate "good cop."

Asked how Hastert "handles" him, DeLay laughed and then thought for several seconds. "By constantly making sure we are on the same wavelength," he finally replied. "He has to spend a lot of his time listening to me."

Hastert's way of doing business often draws comparisons to Thomas S. Foley of Washington (1965-95), the most recent Democratic Speaker.

Like Foley, Hastert "is not a guy who angers easily; he's a real preacher of the House — he grew up in the body, he has a reverence for the body, he understands the legislative process, and he gets along with everybody," said Norman J. Ornstein, resident scholar at the American Enterprise Institute.

The "do-nothing Congress" label that dogged Gingrich's later years has failed to stick with Hastert.

While Gingrich was widely praised in 1995 for getting the House to endorse the main tenets of the 10-point "Contract With America" GOP campaign manifesto of the preceding year, Hastert has advanced a more limited agenda designed to respond directly to the political and policy desires of his party and the voters.

In Hastert's first term as Speaker, for example, Clinton vetoed a $792 billion Republican tax package. Rather than give up, Hastert came up with the idea of breaking up the package into smaller components. None became law either, but the proposals to cut taxes for married couples and on estates garnered Democratic votes — and helped set the stage for the Bush tax cut law (PL 107-16) enacted last year. (*2001 Almanac, p. 18-3*)

"He was more or less the accidental Speaker," Marshall Wittmann, a political analyst for the conservative Hudson Institute, said of Hastert. "Now he's become someone who will leave more of a legislative mark than his predecessor, who was celebrated as the master of the universe."

Strict Party Adherence

In some ways, having only a six-vote majority has helped Hastert impress upon his rank and file the need to stick together, Ornstein said.

"He's been able to keep almost perfect party unanimity and get a lot of legislation through the House," Ornstein said. "Gingrich would not have worked in a hand-in-glove fashion with the White House because he would have been seen as a rival."

An unusually large bloc of Republicans did go against Hastert's will once this year, when 41 of them joined most Democrats to pass the campaign finance legislation that became law (PL 107-155) in March. It was one of the few times that a Speaker has lost so completely a vigorous quest to bury a popular bill. (*2002 CQ Weekly, p. 799*)

"He did everything he could to prevent us from having a vote. He forced us to get 218 signatures on a discharge petition," said Martin T. Meehan of Massachusetts, the bill's main House Democratic sponsor. "I would say that was playing hardball."

Few things irritate Democrats more than to hear House Republicans take credit for passing legislation on issues high on voters' priority lists. Democrats say the proposals are so partisan-tinged or friendly to Republicans' corporate allies that they have little chance of becoming law.

Hastert and his leadership team have successfully instilled strict party discipline on key votes, Gephardt reluctantly conceded, but to the point that "they are able to get their people to often do things that I know they don't want to do."

Only legislation connected to the new war on terrorism has reflected bipartisan negotiations, Gephardt said. But at least Hastert talks to him, the Democratic leader said; Gingrich rarely did. (*2002 CQ Weekly, p. 2360*)

Though it is not often publicized, Hastert occasionally discusses matters with Daschle, as well, and the Senate leader describes the Speaker as a political adversary but legislative partner.

"I don't apologize for not taking up some of the crazy things that these guys have passed," Daschle said of the House. "But he's clearly not a polarizing figure, and I think that serves him well. He has a job to do, and to whatever extent he feels he has to take his caucus's message, I think he does it, and I think he does it reasonably well."

Hastert does not have many public political rivals, though a couple of spats are well known.

The proposed expansion of Chicago's major airport tops the list of disagreements between him and the second most-powerful Illinois Republican in Congress, Sen. Peter G. Fitzgerald.

The Speaker also broke with one of his closest friends in the House, Thomas W. Ewing (1991-2001), by endorsing someone other than Sam Ewing as his father's successor in a neighboring Illinois district two years ago. The seat was won by a third Republican, Timothy V. Johnson.

Bulldog Resilience

Those incidents reflect Hastert's unshakable tenacity in doing what he thinks is right for his caucus, his party and his constituents back home. Sometimes that has led him purposefully down legislative dry holes.

After the terrorist attacks, Republicans twice pushed through the House versions of an economic stimulus package, both with generous business tax cuts, that were dead letters in the Senate. It took three more months for the final, more modest bill to get to Bush.

The Hastert-blessed bill that would create a Medicare prescription drug benefit also has passed the House twice — and its market-based approach has clearly insufficient Senate support.

Democrats say more legislation would become law if House Republicans would compromise sooner. And when compromises have been agreed to by the White House and Senate Republicans without the House's input, Hastert has shown his frustration.

"We try to help the White House achieve its ends," Hastert said. "We pass the legislation in the beginning, it ends up in the Senate, and the White House, because they want a deal so much, ends up cutting the deal. And not necessarily working with us or dealing with us, but a deal at all costs. And sometimes we have to end up eating that."

He also holds Senate Republicans responsible for not driving harder deals with the Democrats. During a recent meeting of the House and Senate GOP leadership, Hastert complained to Senate Minority Leader Trent Lott of Mississippi that the breakdown in the appropriations process was because the Senate has never adopted its budget resolution (S Con Res 1000) for fiscal 2003.

"I said, 'Wait just a minute, Mr. Speaker,'" Lott recalled. "You do understand, of course, that it was the Democrats who didn't do a budget."

The Senate GOP leader said he admires the work Hastert has done but does get "a little agitated" by the criticism of fellow Republicans on the House side. "I told the Speaker, 'Look, Mr. Speaker. Don't waste your time focusing on the Senate. You do what you have to do, we'll do what we have to do. We'll do the best we can.'"

The testiness is another sign of how Hastert has become more aggressive in his drive to accomplish his legislative goals. "He's hardened as a leader, which was inevitable," Wittmann said.

Hastert is working toward an election that will take place in what many political observers say is an uncertain climate. The Speaker, however, does not even entertain the notion that Republicans will lose control of the House. He said the improved prospects for the GOP in some swing seats because of redistricting, combined with the roster of House-passed GOP bills will be sufficient to keep Republicans in power in 2003.

"I made up my mind a long time ago that, following Newt Gingrich . . . what I needed to do was be able to run the House. I need to make the House work. I need to be able to deliver," he said. ◆

57

How the Real Estate Industry Rescued Terrorism Insurance Bill

White House insider helps tip the scales for legislation

Quick Contents

Congress is expected to send President Bush legislation that would help pay for damages if there are more catastrophic terror attacks. While the evidence is mixed on the need for legislation, the real estate industry took the lead in showing how to successfully retool a congressional lobbying campaign.

Shortly before the second session of the 107th Congress began, lobbyists from the real estate industry organized a conference call with White House senior adviser Karl Rove.

The mood was bleak among the lobbyists who dialed into the Jan. 7 call. Congress had adjourned in December without clearing a bill that would install a federal backstop for commercial property and casualty insurers in case of future terrorist attacks. This was in spite of a dogged campaign by insurers and others who had warned of dire economic consequences if Congress failed to act by Jan. 1, when many reinsurance policies — taken out by insurance companies to lay off some of their risk with other insurers — were set to expire.

The House had passed a bill in November, but the more fractious Senate moved nothing, largely because it could not resolve how, or whether, to ban punitive damages awards in civil suits arising from terrorist acts. The fight went into the final hours of the Senate session, to no avail.

Samuel Zell, chairman of Equity Office

CQ Weekly Aug. 31, 2002

Properties Trust, the nation's largest public owner of office buildings, and other real estate industry executives met for 40 minutes in early January with Rove and other officials in the Roosevelt Room to urge the White House to take a larger role in the campaign.

On the conference call that followed, Rove said previous warnings of a tidal wave of cancellations of insurance policies turned out to be a false alarm. The economy had not ground to a halt. "We're still around," he said. The core argument for immediate federal action had imploded.

That's why lobbyists for owners and investors in commercial real estate concluded that buyers of insurance — not the insurance industry, which had already raised rates and taken other steps to lower their risks — had to take the lead.

Rove assured the battalion of lobbyists they still had White House backing for a bill. But he said the success or failure of the measure was up to them. Rove urged the lobbyists to provide a stronger argument, especially to the Senate, about the potential economic damages they might suffer.

The show of support from such a high-level White House official invigorated the demoralized lobbyists. In short order, the imperative for the legislation shifted from a bailout for insurers to the need to protect the overall economy by boosting commercial construction and limiting potentially huge losses for property owners.

That helped turn the bill from a dim prospect to must-pass legislation touted by President Bush almost every time he stepped before a microphone. Such a transformation amounts to a case study for the retooling of a congressional lobbying campaign — especially since passage of the legislation is now likely, according to Republicans and Democrats.

"We will get it done," said Richard H. Baker, R-La., chairman of the House Financial Services subcommittee that oversees capital market and insurance issues, and one of the architects of the House bill. "If we don't, people will point fingers and ask why we didn't do it."

By capping losses for insurers, the legislation is designed to encourage them to roll back premium increases and coverage limits imposed after the Sept. 11 attacks. A provision in the Senate bill would require insurers to offer

Rove, left, shown walking with Bush earlier this year, suggested changes in the lobbying approach that helped generate support for the terrorism insurance bill.

REUTERS PHOTO / LARRY DOWNING

More Profit Than Loss For Property/Casualty Insurers

Only twice in the past 10 years has the U.S. property and casualty insurance industry suffered net losses — that is, when the net underwriting loss, the difference between premiums collected and payments on claims, more than offset investment gains.

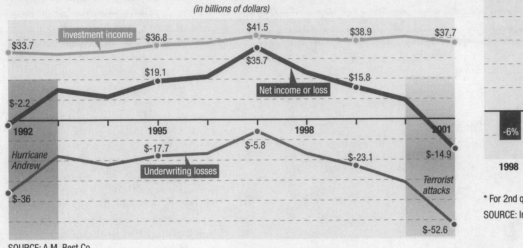

(in billions of dollars)

SOURCE: A.M. Best Co.

Changes in Rates For Commercial Property Insurance

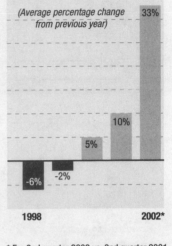

(Average percentage change from previous year)

* For 2nd quarter 2002 vs. 2nd quarter 2001

SOURCE: Insurance Information Institute

---

terrorism insurance on terms comparable to other types of property insurance.

In mobilizing the lobbyists, Rove appeared as interested in turning up the political heat on Senate Majority Leader Tom Daschle, D-S.D., as he was in getting the measure to the president's desk. The Bush administration had been laboring to cast Daschle as obstructionist.

And win or lose, the Republicans knew they could use the issue in the November midterm elections. If legislation passed, Bush could claim credit. If it did not, Rove and other Republican tacticians would blame a "do nothing" Democratic-controlled Senate.

A Gamble to Regret

For real estate industry lobbyists, though, Rove's request for more evidence also was a wake-up call. It underscored growing doubts on Capitol Hill about whether legislation really was necessary, and whether President Bush and allies in Congress could save it.

The new Coalition to Insure Against Terrorism also knew they faced a new handicap: pushing legislation through a Congress that had grown deeply skeptical about real or perceived handouts to big business.

Insurance industry lobbyists, eager to seize the momentum of the chaotic weeks following the Sept. 11 attacks, had bet Congress would move to van-

quish the specter of economic paralysis, based on the swift clearance of emergency aid for the airlines industry. It was a gamble they would regret. *(PL 107-42, 2001 Almanac, p. 20-3)*

Since the January conference call, the skepticism of Senate Minority Leader Trent Lott, R-Miss., and other lawmakers about whether a backstop is actually needed has gradually faded. So has the distracting argument over so-called tort reform provisions. This can be attributed to patient, steady lobbying by the coalition that includes not only real estate interests but other diverse groups, including the Association of Art Museum Directors and the National Football League.

"Our job was to stay on the Hill every day and make sure people understood the need for this," said Andy Barbour, a lobbyist for the Financial Services Roundtable, a coalition member.

The expenditure of all of that shoe leather appears to be paying off. An 84-14 vote on the Senate version (S 2600) on June 18, combined with Bush's repeated calls for congressional action, tipped the scales decisively. *(2002 CQ Weekly, pp. 1671.)*

The support of Rove, Bush's chief domestic policy adviser, "was an insulin shot to all of us who wanted a bill," said one insurance lobbyist.

A House-Senate conference on the legislation, likely to be chaired by Sen-

ate Banking Committee Chairman Paul S. Sarbanes, D-Md., is set to kick into gear the week of Sept. 2.

To be sure, lawmakers could deadlock over several significant differences between the two bills. But lobbyists and congressional aides predict that a compromise will be struck before the end of the session.

"There is substantial consensus and support in the Congress," said one of the conferees, Sen. Richard C. Shelby, R-Ala. "I see no reason why the conference should not be able to work out the differences between the House and Senate versions and send a bill to the president early this fall."

The Insurance Information Institute, an industry group, estimates that the Sept. 11 terrorist attacks could require payouts of $40 billion or more in insured claims. Immediately after the attacks, commercial property and casualty insurers converged on Capitol Hill to promise they would honor all claims arising from the attacks.

But they also warned that the reinsurers who backed them would stop offering coverage against the risk of future terrorist attacks as of Jan. 1.

David B. Mathis, chief executive of the Kemper Insurance Companies Inc., testified Oct. 24 before the House Financial Services Capital Markets subcommittee. He called for the "immediate enactment of legislation to create a

Most States Cap Terrorism Claims

Just five states have so far refused to put caps, typically of $25 million, on terrorism insurance claims. Those states, however, include nearly 35 percent of the nation's population and its two largest cities — New York and Los Angeles.

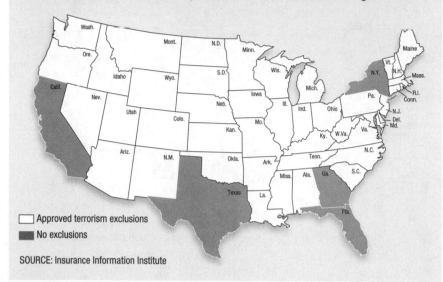

☐ Approved terrorism exclusions

■ No exclusions

SOURCE: Insurance Information Institute

federal financial backstop," saying it "must be enacted before Congress recesses for the year."

On Nov. 29, Financial Services Committee Chairman Michael G. Oxley, R-Ohio, and Baker pushed a bill (HR 3210) through the House on a 227-193 vote. (*2001 Almanac, p. H-158.*)

The House bill would require the federal government to pay most of the cost of terrorist attacks that result in more than $1 billion but less than $100 billion in insured claims. Assistance to individual insurers would be available below the $1 billion threshold, subject to certain conditions.

In any case, insurance companies — and possibly commercial policyholders — eventually would be required to repay the government. Punitive damages awards in civil lawsuits arising from terrorist attacks would be banned, except against the terrorists themselves.

Tort Reform Fight

The compromise reached within the Senate Banking Committee, which was blessed by the White House, also contained a punitive damages ban. That was anathema to Daschle, who feared it would establish a wedge for the "tort reform" movement, led by lawmakers such as Sen. Mitch McConnell, R-Ky., who for years has crusaded to impose such curbs on jury awards.

Daschle took direct control of the legislation, squelching a brief jurisdic-

tional flare-up between the Banking and Commerce committees. He also embarked on a months-long dance with Senate Republicans such as McConnell and Phil Gramm of Texas, in which each side made a great show of blocking the other's attempts to bring their version of the bill to the floor. Meanwhile, frustrated insurance industry lobbyists darkly joked they would be out of jobs if the bill did not pass.

After Congress did not act last year, the chances for survival of the legislation in the second session hung on the deep concerns of the nation's landlords and real estate investors. Stung by their failure to shepherd a bill to enactment, insurance lobbyists realized they had to let the new broad coalition take the lead in the continuing battle in order to quiet critics who charged that the bill was little more than a bailout for insurance companies.

Indeed, a White House visit by a group of top executives and lobbyists for major insurance companies 10 days after the terrorist attacks had been viewed unfavorably by key lawmakers.

"It wasn't a smart idea for a bunch of high-paid insurance executives to go to the White House and then to come out and say, 'we don't want anything; we're just here for good public policy.' That didn't work. It looked like they were asking for money. It looked like a bailout," Baker said.

For their part, real estate lobbyists

feared in early 2002 that the momentum for legislation was waning because of sweeping changes in the insurance industry after the September attacks.

Insurers turn profits in most years because money received from premiums and investment income usually exceeds administrative costs and the amount paid out in claims. But insurance is a cyclical business: In bad years, investment gains can be more than overwhelmed by outlays for damage from hurricanes, floods and other disasters. (*Chart, p. 59*)

In 2001, property/casualty insurers had their first industry-wide loss in nine years: $14.9 billion. In addition to rising claims related to the attacks, insurers suffered along with other investors as stocks tanked. The red ink dwarfed the $2.2 billion in losses absorbed by the industry in 1992, when Hurricane Andrew devastated Florida.

Insurers responded to last year's loss much as they had historically after other catastrophes. They raised rates and put limits on coverage.

Premiums Soar

Property/casualty rates in this year's second quarter were about 33 percent higher on average than a year earlier, according to the Insurance Information Institute. In contrast, rates actually fell in 1998 and 1999, when insurers were scrambling to book more business — and boost the amount of money they could invest — in anticipation of hefty gains on their investments.

In the case of Berkshire Hathaway Inc., one of the reinsurance companies it owns charged premiums that turned out to be too low and assumed too much aggregate risk, according to Chairman Warren E. Buffett's letter to shareholders Feb. 28. The letter showed that Berkshire's reinsurance operations posted a $4.3 billion pretax loss in 2001. At the same time, Buffett noted that another reinsurer owned by Berkshire Hathaway wrote policies after Sept. 11 for the Sears Tower in Chicago, the World Cup soccer tournament in Japan and South Korea, and the winter Olympics in Salt Lake City — presumably at rates designed to avoid big losses.

Insurers also made sure they would cut any future losses by insisting on restrictions on coverage. They won exemptions from regulators in 45 states allowing them to either restrict or refuse coverage for terrorist attacks. The coverage limits sharply reduced the chances that insurers would have to absorb huge losses similar to those resulting from the attack on the World Trade Center.

The policies written by insurers in many states capped terrorism coverage for many businesses at $25 million. That was ample for a small- or medium-sized business that might be damaged by a terrorist attack. But limits written into policies for more valuable properties — such as skyscrapers, shopping malls, power plants and assembly lines — would shift liability for huge losses from insurers to landlords and real estate investors.

In the view of the real estate industry, the caps protected insurers but left policyholders with big risks.

"We felt the sense of urgency in the insurance industry had dissipated," said Deborah B. Beck, vice president of the Realty Board of New York. "They had raised rates and gotten exclusions. We had a lot more risk. They had dropped the banner. We wanted to pick it up and start waving it."

Lobbying 101

The coalition that was formally announced Feb. 13 was designed to reduce policyholder risk. It was the brainchild of a handful of lobbyists led by Martin DePoy, vice president of the National Association of Real Estate Investment Trusts; his boss, company president Steven A. Wechsler; and Jeffrey D. De-Boer, and Clifton E. Rodgers Jr., president and senior vice president, respectively, of the Real Estate Roundtable, a group representing the nation's biggest owners of commercial property.

The coalition unified owners of commercial property and reached out to some natural allies, including construction unions and pension fund managers.

The new campaign emphasized that the legislation was not intended to protect insurers, but their customers.

"The problem did not lend itself to easy, quantitative evidence," DeBoer said. "It was like rolling fog. It was hard to see, but it was there." He and his allies, including Beck, sought to persuade lawmakers that the bill was needed by a much broader constituency than just insurers.

Their efforts, like those of the insurance industry before them, were hampered by a lack of insurance expertise on Capitol Hill. Because the insurance industry is state-regulated, few lawmakers are experts in the subject.

Lobbyists also had to struggle to per-

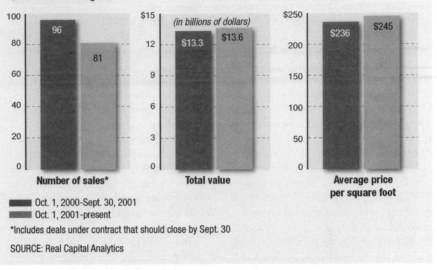

No Real Estate Slowdown

Sales of major office buildings in the United States have continued at a strong pace in the wake of the Sept. 11 attacks. Transactions with price tags of $50 million or higher:

Number of sales*: 96 (Oct. 1, 2000-Sept. 30, 2001), 81 (Oct. 1, 2001-present)

Total value (in billions of dollars): $13.3, $13.6

Average price per square foot: $236, $245

■ Oct. 1, 2000-Sept. 30, 2001
■ Oct. 1, 2001-present

*Includes deals under contract that should close by Sept. 30

SOURCE: Real Capital Analytics

suade reluctant developers and property owners to come forward with their individual stories. Most, if not all, are still unwilling to discuss problems publicly. "Nobody wants to put a bull's-eye on their building," DePoy said.

The lobbyists pointed to statistics such as those released by the Mortgage Bankers Association, which said more than $8 billion in commercial property financing has been killed or delayed because of the terrorism insurance issue. As evidence that financing for development could dry up in the absence of terrorism insurance, they pointed to loan covenants requiring properties to be fully insured and to decisions by ratings agencies to downgrade some commercial mortgage-backed securities because of terrorism concerns.

Furthering the case for legislation, association lobbyists have urged their member companies to write letters and send e-mail to lawmakers. They also crafted a new marketing blitz of print advertisements emphasizing the plight of working people — not insurance executives — who could lose their jobs if construction projects were delayed or if buildings without adequate insurance were destroyed by terrorists.

Critics said the legislation seemed to provide a subsidy to owners of big buildings in big cities. But members of the coalition — such as the National Rural Electric Cooperative Association — countered that a terrorist attack on a power plant or a dam could

bankrupt the operators and turn lights off in the heartland.

Even though he made no mention of the issue in his State of the Union address Jan. 29, within a matter of weeks the terrorism insurance legislation became one of President Bush's top domestic priorities. Standing near union workers in hard hats at an April 8 news conference, Bush said a slowdown in construction was worrisome and that terrorism insurance was vital to the nation's economic growth.

Questionable Examples

Bush cited two examples of the economic dangers of congressional inaction. The president described a Nevada casino that he said was not getting built because developers could not obtain terrorism insurance coverage. He also said the Hyatt Hotels Corp. could not break ground on a new 1.5-million square-foot office building in downtown Chicago because of a lack of terrorism coverage.

But both projects now appear to be moving forward.

The Pritzker family, developer of the 47-story Hyatt project, broke ground in August with a target completion date of late 2004. The developer is negotiating with several other potential tenants, including a law firm and Goldman Sachs Group Inc.

Wynn Resorts Ltd., a Nevada casino developer headed by Steve Wynn, filed a plan with the Securities and Exchange Commission this summer for an initial offering of stock to help fund the $2.4 billion Le Rêve casino hotel on the site of the former Desert Inn resort. In addition to equity investments by a Japanese pachinko gaming machine company, Wynn has the backing of Deutsche Bank Securities; Bear, Stearns & Co. Inc.; and Banc of America Securities LLC.

Wynn's SEC filing says ground will be broken for the resort in September even though "we do not have insurance coverage for occurrences of terrorist acts."

Despite some anecdotal evidence that commercial insurance coverage against terrorist acts has become more difficult and more expensive to obtain, the Federal Reserve in May released a survey of domestic banks that showed little or no change in demand for commercial real estate loans.

In a study of the issue last February, the General Accounting Office said commercial property owners could incur uninsured losses that "threaten their ability to survive," but that the effect a dearth of terrorism insurance would have on the overall economy was "uncertain at this time."

Other data suggests that investors, developers and property owners have adjusted to higher insurance premiums and other changed circumstances. Commercial property sales, even of large, expensive properties in New York and other cities, have accelerated as nervous investors pull funds out of seesawing stock markets in favor of safer real estate investments. *(Chart, p. 61)*

Billion-Dollar Sale

That point was underscored on Aug. 29 when Boston Properties Inc., headed by magazine publisher Mort Zuckerman, announced that it was paying $1.06 billion to acquire the Park Avenue headquarters of Citigroup Inc.

"There are still a significant number of trophy assets selling," said Robert M. White Jr., president of Real Capital Analytics Inc., a real estate research firm. "I don't see that [the lack of legislation] has had that material of an impact."

But the administration, along with lobbyists such as DePoy, say such assessments are not a true representation of market conditions. "A lot of those deals have been able to go through in anticipation of a federal program being in place," DePoy said.

"Projects are getting done, but at a higher cost," said Peter Fisher, under-

secretary of Treasury for domestic finance. "If there is another incident, there could be serious problems."

While the marketplace went through its adjustments, the Senate remained hamstrung over the punitive damages issue.

Sen. Christopher J. Dodd, D-Conn., and other lawmakers who usually take the lead on insurance-related legislation were distracted by major legislation dealing with corporate accountability and election reform.

A June 10 letter from Bush's top economic advisers, including Treasury Secretary Paul H. O'Neill and Lawrence Lindsey, chairman of the National Economic Council, was widely regarded as a signal to Senate Republicans such as Lott, Gramm and McConnell that the White House would stand by them during conference negotiations.

The Senate bill passed in June would require the government to pay 90 percent of claims after insured losses exceeded $10 billion, with assistance available sooner to individual insurers.

Both chambers named their conferees on the legislation shortly before leaving for the August recess. Meanwhile, Bush has cited the issue whenever he talks about the nation's economic woes.

Lobbyists and congressional staffers say little progress was made on conference negotiations at the staff level during the August recess. That makes it unlikely a conference report could be completed by the anniversary of the Sept. 11 attacks, as the coalition lately has been urging.

Nevertheless, some observers say the differences between the bills can be resolved quickly. "This is a two-day conference," one insurance lobbyist said.

The main difference between the two bills is that while the House bill requires payback to the federal government, the Senate bill does not.

But after having seen much of the Senate language adopted in the July conference on corporate accountability legislation (PL 107-204), Oxley and Baker are likely to insist that some provision for reimbursement remain in the bill. "It's a philosophic problem between the House and Senate. We don't want to be viewed as having opened the public's checkbook to industry," Baker said.

The conferees could decide to require insurance companies to pay back the

government for some assistance, such as that rendered above the individual company's deductible but below the industry-wide trigger for government aid.

While the Senate bill does not contain a punitive damages ban, it does specify that court-ordered punitive damages would not count as insured losses. One potential compromise: retaining the Senate language, and adding a provision requiring approval of out-of-court settlements by the Treasury Secretary.

Possible Complications

To be sure, the conference could become complicated by lobbyists' efforts to expand the scope of the bill. For example, some life insurers are pushing for language extending the terms of the bill to group life insurance. And there is talk within the commercial insurance industry of pushing to make the program permanent after Bush signs the bill into law.

But provided that lawmakers are not distracted by such new issues, the White House support for the bill — evidenced so strikingly in January by Rove and echoed many times since by Bush — and the lack of any substantial opposition in Congress should spur the conferees to finish a report before adjourning for the year.

"I think (lawmakers) are fully convinced now that there is a problem," DePoy said. "We've gotten beyond the skepticism that was present early in the year."

Dodd said he was "optimistic that common ground can be found."

Opponents of the bill still are hoping to derail negotiations. Using actuarial predictions developed by the insurance industry, they are questioning whether any legislation is needed at all.

"We are worried that Congress will do something stupid in the rush to finish at the end of the session, and just adopt what industry wants," said J. Robert Hunter, a spokesman for the Consumer Federation of America.

Though passage of the bill now seems likely, lobbyists are mindful they cannot take the outcome for granted, no matter how much Bush and his lieutenants, such as Rove, push the measure.

"There has been this huge coalition all saying the same thing — 'pass it, pass it now,' " said David Liddle, a Financial Services Roundtable spokesman. "Confidence is high. But we're not going to let up until the president puts down the pen." ◆

Hearings May Be as Mighty As the Legislative Pen

Oxley probe of IPO management moves business and government

On the same day in July that House and Senate conferees struck an agreement on legislation targeting the accounting profession and corporate governance, House Financial Services Committee Chairman Michael G. Oxley, R-Ohio, announced that he was launching a separate probe into how investment banks manage initial public offerings (IPOs).

While the implicit message was that Congress is not yet done with corporate America, Oxley now says the goal of the inquiry is limited. With the Sarbanes-Oxley Act of 2002 (PL 107-204) barely on the books, more legislation aimed at Wall Street is unlikely either this year or next.

But lawmaking is not the only tool Congress has at its disposal. Oxley's IPO investigation and other congressional hearings this year demonstrate that Congress' oversight role can quickly lead to profound changes at federal agencies and companies in the private sector.

Oxley's hearings about IPOs provided an eye-opening look at how loose the rules are on Wall Street — including the amount of leeway investment banks have under existing rules to divvy up IPO shares.

What the Financial Services Committee now wants to find out is whether investment banks allocated shares in hot IPOs to corporate executives such as former WorldCom Inc. Chief Executive Bernard J. Ebbers in exchange for getting and keeping their firms' investment banking business.

The IPO probe already has led to an executive shake-up at Citigroup Inc., the parent company of the Salomon Smith Barney brokerage firm. It also could spur regulatory changes by the Securities and Exchange Commission (SEC) and self-regulatory bodies such as the National Association of Securities Dealers (NASD) and the New York Stock Exchange (NYSE).

"It's another opportunity for Congress to shine a glaring light on a profession that probably deserves some closer scrutiny," said Patrick McGurn, vice president of Institutional Shareholder Services. "I always felt there was going to be a Chapter Two. I think that's what we're seeing now."

Oxley is not the only lawmaker looking for results. House Energy and Commerce Committee Chairman Billy Tauzin, R-La., who held a series of oversight hearings on the Enron Corp. collapse, says his investigation of biotechnology firm ImClone Systems Inc. led to a consolidation of review procedures within the Food and Drug Administration (FDA) announced Sept. 6. Tauzin even passed an opportunity to put lifestyle publishing executive Martha Stewart at the witness table to answer questions about her controversial sale of ImClone stock, calling Stewart's possible false statements to Congress a peripheral matter in the larger effort to enact change at the FDA and in the pharmaceutical industry.

IPO Mania

Since 1980, almost 10,000 companies have gone public in the United States, raising $551.3 billion through initial sales of stock and another $933.8 billion in follow-on sales of additional shares, figures from Thomson Financial show. This bonanza slowed along with the plunge of stock prices in 2000. *(Chart, p. 64)*

Oxley said that when Congress was assembling what would become the Sarbanes-Oxley Act, the IPO issue "didn't seem to be as big a deal." He added that once his com-

Quick Contents

While more legislative attempts to crack down on business practices appear unlikely this year or next, congressional committees are having an impact by using their oversight powers to spur companies and regulatory bodies to act on their own.

Grubman's July 8 testimony widened the House Financial Services Committee's interest in how initial public offerings are handled by Wall Street firms.

REUTERS PHOTO / HYUNGWON KANG

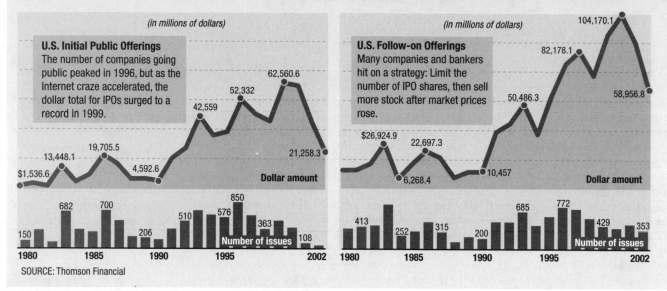

$1.5 Trillion in U.S. Stock Sales Since 1980

Almost 10,000 companies have gone public in the last two decades, providing a bonanza of business for investment banks.

U.S. Initial Public Offerings (in millions of dollars)
The number of companies going public peaked in 1996, but as the Internet craze accelerated, the dollar total for IPOs surged to a record in 1999.

Dollar amount: $1,536.6 · 13,448.1 · 19,705.5 · 4,592.6 · 42,559 · 52,332 · 62,560.6 · 21,258.3

Number of issues: 150 · 682 · 700 · 206 · 510 · 850 · 576 · 363 · 108

U.S. Follow-on Offerings (in millions of dollars)
Many companies and bankers hit on a strategy: Limit the number of IPO shares, then sell more stock after market prices rose.

Dollar amount: $26,924.9 · 6,268.4 · 22,697.3 · 10,457 · 50,486.3 · 82,178.1 · 104,170.1 · 58,956.8

Number of issues: 413 · 252 · 315 · 200 · 685 · 772 · 429 · 353

SOURCE: Thomson Financial

---

mittee, which has had jurisdiction over securities regulation since January 2001, started "connecting all the dots," potential problems became more readily apparent.

Then, too, Congress historically has been reluctant to meddle in the business of Wall Street — especially when times are good. "In the go-go days, nobody wanted to mess with a roaring market," said Scott Cleland, chief executive officer of The Precursor Group, an investor research firm. "No one wanted to rain on that parade."

The committee's curiosity was piqued during a July 8 hearing into the WorldCom collapse in which Salomon Smith Barney Inc. analyst Jack Grubman said he could not recall whether WorldCom executives were provided any special access to IPO shares.

More Records Sought

Two weeks after that hearing, the committee sent requests for records to WorldCom, Citigroup and a former accountant for Arthur Andersen LLP. Among other things, Citigroup was asked to document which current and former WorldCom executives acquired shares in IPOs underwritten by Salomon Smith Barney since 1996.

Eventually, Citigroup submitted records showing that Salomon Smith Barney had funneled shares that generated millions of dollars in profits to Ebbers and other corporate executives. The company has denied that it used

IPO shares as a quid pro quo to win investment banking business.

Citigroup's revelation spurred the committee to make further requests. It asked for details of IPOs underwritten by Credit Suisse First Boston Corp. and the Goldman Sachs Group Inc. The committee also sought details of any investment banking services provided to a list of companies that included bankrupt Global Crossing Ltd. and Enron.

Oxley set a Sept. 19 deadline for responses to those requests. But he already has declared that he will not write another bill because he prefers instead to work with the SEC and self-regulatory organizations such as stock exchanges and the NASD to curb whatever abuses he might uncover.

"It would be very difficult for Congress to legislate the IPO issue," Oxley said. "We're not competent to do it, and anybody who says we are is crazy."

That sentiment is shared by many in the private sector, who fear that Congress again might be tempted to use the blunt instrument of legislation, potentially choking the free market.

Michael Holland, chairman of the Holland and Co. investment firm, says he is "not necessarily a fan of Congress micromanaging" business regulation.

But neither is Oxley, whose own version of the corporate accountability law was regarded as more hands-off than that produced by Senate Banking panel Chairman Paul S. Sarbanes, D-Md. Oxley intends to follow the model

he used for his committee's earlier investigation into possible conflicts of interest among securities analysts. That inquiry led to the development of new industry rules on analyst conduct by the NASD and the NYSE.

"Hopefully, we can get a different regime," Oxley said.

Oxley broached the subject of IPO allocations with NYSE Chairman Richard Grasso during a visit to New York City the week of Sept. 2. He said he also planned to discuss the issue with SEC Chairman Harvey L. Pitt at a Sept. 12 meeting.

Frank Reserves His Option

Rep. Barney Frank of Massachusetts, who is in line to become the top Democrat on the Financial Services Committee in the 108th Congress — and its chairman if Democrats recapture the House in the midterm election — shares Oxley's interest in exploring the IPO practices at investment banks. But where Oxley flatly ruled out more legislation, Frank said it is far too early to decide on a congressional course of action.

"That's what you decide at the end of the process, not the beginning," Frank said.

The House Financial Services Committee investigation already is getting results. Grubman left Salomon Smith Barney in August; on Sept. 8, Citigroup announced it had shuffled Michael A. Carpenter, chairman of its global corporate and investment bank, to a new assignment, replacing him with chief operating officer Charles Prince.

The company also announced it was forming a business practices committee. "There are certain industry practices that we should all be concerned about, and although we have found nothing illegal, looking back, we can see that certain of our activities do not reflect the way we believe business should be done," Citigroup Chairman Sanford I. Weill said in a statement.

On Aug. 22, the SEC asked the NYSE and the NASD to study the issue of IPO allocations and develop recommendations. The NASD already has proposed a new rule that would forbid members and their associates from giving IPO shares to executives or directors in exchange for their companies' investment banking business.

Justice Department Referral

Like Oxley, Tauzin appears to be emphasizing his committee's oversight role. At a Sept. 10 news conference, he argued that subpoenaing Stewart would not contribute to his committee's larger goal of prompting changes in the regulation of new drugs. That is why the Louisiana Republican said his panel had decided instead to refer the case to the Justice Department.

Stewart sold nearly 4,000 shares of ImClone stock the day before the share price plummeted on an announcement that the FDA had refused to accept the company's application for the colon cancer drug Erbitux. The committee wanted to know whether Stewart got inside information from her broker at Merrill Lynch & Co.

While refusing to meet voluntarily with the committee, Stewart provided them with her account of her phone conversations with the broker on the day of the sale. Tauzin said Stewart's account conflicted with other evidence, leading them to believe she had lied to the committee.

Justice Department spokesman Bryan Sierra said Sept. 11 that department officials would not decide whether to act on Tauzin's recommendation until they review the case.

Robert Morvillo, one of Stewart's attorneys, said he is "glad that the political aspects of this matter will now terminate and [I] am confident that the

Tauzin, left, and Greenwood say they are more interested in FDA practices than in Stewart's stock sale.

CQ PHOTO / SCOTT J. FERRELL

investigation will lead to Ms. Stewart's exoneration."

Oversight and Investigations Subcommittee Chairman James C. Greenwood, R-Pa., and Tauzin said lawyers for Stewart had made clear that if she was subpoenaed by the committee, she would invoke her Fifth Amendment right to not testify.

This type of strategy had never stopped Tauzin and other zealous committee chairmen from subpoenaing various fallen corporate executives throughout the past year. But with no less than 13 cameras focused on him Sept. 10, Greenwood claimed that a he-said, she-said examination of Stewart's actions was but a small part of the larger ImClone inquiry.

"We didn't want to make a media circus of this," Greenwood said. "This is a sideshow in this investigation."

Tauzin — whose high-profile investigation of Enron arguably contributed to the downfall of accounting giant Arthur Andersen — also sees oversight itself as an adequate weapon in Congress' arsenal for affecting change in the marketplace.

In the midst of Tauzin's committee's investigation, the FDA decided to change its approval process so that the pharmaceutical side of the agency will now review biological products — a change the FDA said was not related to

the congressional probe.

"Whether FDA will ever admit the hearings produced this change is irrelevant," Tauzin said. "The fact is that this is a good change, and if our hearings helped produce that change so much the better."

Back-Burner Inquiries

Besides the Financial Services Committee probe, however, the congressional appetite for investigations into corporate wrongdoing seems to have waned, crowded out by issues such as the creation of a new Cabinet department for homeland security and whether to launch an invasion of Iraq.

The Senate Governmental Affairs Committee, chaired by Joseph I. Lieberman, D-Conn., is expected to put out a report in the coming weeks on corporate watchdogs, including the SEC and credit raters, but otherwise has ratcheted down its focus on corporate misbehavior. The Governmental Affairs Permanent Subcommittee on Investigations, chaired by Carl Levin, D-Mich., is slogging through an extensive probe of Enron Corp. but has not widened its investigation.

All that is unlikely to change as long as Lieberman continues his prominent role in the homeland security debate, and Levin, who also chairs the Senate Armed Services Committee, is focused on the question of whether the United States should go to war with Iraq.

Byron L. Dorgan, D-N.D., chairman of the Senate Commerce panel's Consumer Affairs, Foreign Commerce and Tourism Subcommittee, still is trying to obtain information from Enron about its secret partnerships, to no avail. While further hearings this year are possible, no action seems imminent.

Sarbanes, who held 10 exhaustive hearings earlier this year on corporate governance and accounting practices, is showing little interest in mounting his own probe of IPOs.

"The House is looking at that," Sarbanes said. "They seem to be doing a pretty good job of it."

Indeed, even though no new legislative partnership of Sarbanes and Oxley is in the offing, Oxley's IPO probe suggests that Wall Street will continue to draw uncomfortable attention from Capitol Hill for months to come. ◆

Election Upgrades Could Prove Expensive For States Seeking Federal Help

Under the overhaul bill, localities would start the process of modernizing machinery and centralizing voter databases before they could tap into a $3.9 billion grant pool

The beleaguered election officials of Florida's Miami-Dade and Broward counties are ready for federal help in avoiding a repeat of voting troubles that occurred in 2000 and again this year.

While the federal government has pledged to provide money to replace outdated voting equipment and has moved to establish rules to prevent voter fraud, those same state and local election officials who have overseen manual recounts, confusing butterfly ballots and hanging chads will be responsible for fixing things.

That prospect, and the potential difficulties of finding enough money when the federal budget will run a deficit, could take some of the promise out of what supporters called "the first civil rights legislation of the 21st Century."

After months of talks, House and Senate negotiators reached agreement Oct. 4 on an election overhaul measure (HR 3295) that would set nationwide election standards for the first time and authorize nearly $3.9 billion in aid to the states over the next three years to help them meet those standards. *(2002 CQ Weekly, p. 2585)*

The House adopted the conference report, 357-48, on Oct. 10. The Senate is expected to debate the measure Oct. 15 and clear it for President Bush's signature Oct. 16. *(2002 CQ Weekly, p. 2694)*

To qualify for the billions in federal grants that would be made available under the bill, states will have to develop a plan for updating their machinery and have specific procedures, such as a centralized and computerized statewide voter registration database, already in place. *(Highlights, p. 67)*

To do so, they will have to commit to extensive training of poll workers, voter education projects and technological upgrades. They also will be asked to enforce new voter identification requirements that voting rights

" *We'll have a grant proposal for our [election] supervisors immediately.* **"**

— Rep. Alcee L. Hastings, D-Fla., on what officials in Miami-Dade and Broward counties will do when funds from an election overhaul bill are available. Hastings represents portions of those counties.

groups opposed.

The measure would authorize about $850 million in grants that would be available as soon as the money is approved — not a moment too soon for supporters who want to begin the process of modernization.

"We'll have a grant proposal for our [election] supervisors immediately," said Rep. Alcee L. Hastings, D-Fla., who represents portions of Miami-Dade and Broward, where problems during the state's September primary echoed those during the disputed presidential election in November 2000.

But a delay in getting money to localities could occur because of the snarled appropriations process, and because of reservations about the election bill among lawmakers who control the cash flow.

House and Senate appropriators put

$400 million in the fiscal 2002 supplemental appropriations law (PL 107-206) and $200 million in the House version of the fiscal 2003 Treasury-Postal spending bill (HR 5120). *(2002 CQ Weekly, p. 2038)*

But the supplemental money was rescinded earlier this year by the administration, and the Treasury-Postal bill is caught in a deadlock between the House and Senate over spending. *(2002 CQ Weekly, p. 2647)*

Hastings, like other members of the Congressional Black Caucus (CBC), is concerned about the potential effects of anti-fraud provisions of the legislation and also about getting the money to fully fund the measure.

"I want stronger commitments for the money," said Rep. Eddie Bernice Johnson, D-Texas, the CBC's chairwoman. "I want them to show me the money."

Backers of the bill said the financing will not be a problem, although they have failed thus far to provide details on exactly how, or when, the money would be approved. In the Senate, the task of securing the funds will fall to Majority Leader Tom Daschle, D-S.D., and Rules and Administration Committee Chairman Christopher J. Dodd, D-Conn.

House Administration Committee Chairman Bob Ney, R-Ohio, a key negotiator on the bill, said if Congress is slow in providing funds, "tens of thousands of local election officials will make their views known. This is serious business."

States' 'To-Do List'

Most of the money would be allocated in the Treasury-Postal spending bills, but in the House that could be complicated by Rep. Ernest Istook, R-Okla., chairman of the appropriations subcommittee that drafts that bill.

Oklahoma is one of several states that spent millions in the past few years to upgrade its voting equipment, installing optical scanner machines in each precinct. Under the conference agreement, those states would not be eligible for reimbursements through federal grants provided by the measure.

"I've got a problem with the bill," Istook said, calling the reimbursement policy unfair to states such as his.

Prospects in the Democratically controlled Senate seem better, although the appropriations process remains in limbo.

Under the bill, the federal government would provide the grant money to states only when certain voting standards have been established.

"Everybody sees the money for new machines, but there are things that have to be done before that," said Doug Chapin, director of electionline.org, a nonprofit that studies election issues. The project is funded by The Pew Charitable Trusts.

States "now have something approaching a to-do list," he said.

Successful implementation of the measure's provisions, Chapin and other advocates said, would depend in large part on the ability of state and local officials to coordinate their efforts.

"We hope that states take seriously the larger role they now have in administering federal elections," said Kay J. Maxwell, president of the League of Women Voters of the United States. "They must step up to their constitutional responsibility to run elections effectively."

Identifying Voters

After the 2000 elections, several states moved ahead to change their election systems, spending millions to update equipment and change procedures. Some of those states, such as New York, adopted provisional voting for individuals who cannot provide identification, an idea that the conference report incorporates.

"We expect states like New York are going to do just great" under a new system, said Hilary O. Shelton, director of the NAACP's Washington bureau. "It's states like Missouri, Texas and Florida that we're worried about."

Under the measure, if a voter's registration cannot be validated immediately, that voter can still cast a provisional ballot that can be verified later. That provision was cheered by voting rights supporters as an important step.

But voting rights advocates decried provisions that would require that voters certify their citizenship, and Maxwell predicted that the new identifica-

Highlights of the Bill

The House adopted an election overhaul conference report (HR 3295) on Oct. 10 that would set nationwide election standards and authorize $3.9 billion in aid to states over the next three years to help them meet those standards. The Senate plans to clear the measure Oct. 16. The following are highlights of the legislation:

ISSUE	DESCRIPTION
Election standards	Each state must certify that it has implemented certain standards. They include provisions: • To give voters a chance to check for and correct errors in casting their votes privately and independently. This would take effect in 2004, but states could get a waiver that would delay the requirement until 2006. • To provide at least one voting machine in each precinct for a disabled voter. This would take effect in 2004, but states could obtain waivers to delay implementation until 2006. • To provide a provisional ballot if there is doubt about a voter's eligibility. A provisional ballot is one cast but not counted until the individual demonstrates his or her eligibility. The requirement must be in place by 2004. • To define what is a legal vote for each type of voting machine used in the state. This requirement must be in place by 2004, but a waiver could delay it until 2006. • To limit the error rate for the voting system, which must not exceed the rate established by the Federal Election Commission Office of Election Administration. This must be met by 2004, but a waiver could delay applicability until 2006. • To establish a centralized and computerized statewide voter registration database to ensure accurate voter lists. This must be done by 2004, but a waiver could be granted until 2006. • To continue to provide ballots in other languages pursuant to the 1965 Voting Rights Act (PL 89-110).
Election Assistance Commission	The bill creates a four-member, presidentially appointed Election Assistance Commission that would provide funds through the grant programs and oversee work on creating voluntary election standards. The appointees would be subject to Senate confirmation.
Federal grants to states	The bill would authorize $1.4 billion in fiscal 2003, $1 billion in fiscal 2004 and $600 million in fiscal 2005 — a total of $3 billion over three years. In addition, the bill would authorize $50 million in fiscal 2003 and $25 million in each of fiscal years 2004 and 2005 to increase access to polling places for those with disabilities. An additional $20 million in fiscal 2003 would be spent on improving voting technology, and $10 million for a pilot program to test new voting machines and other equipment. In each of the fiscal years 2003 through 2006, $10 million would be authorized for state protection and advocacy programs.
Voting machine buyout	The bill would authorize $325 million for one-time payments to states to replace punch card and lever voting machines with new equipment. A state could receive $4,000 for each of its polling precincts.
Election fraud	First-time voters would be required to produce a valid photo identification at some point during the registration process. If an individual did not have a driver's license, they could provide the last four digits of a Social Security number. Those with neither a license nor a Social Security number would be assigned a unique identifier. This goes into effect on Jan. 1, 2003.

tion requirements "may create a mess at the polls in 2004."

The changes will only work, voting rights advocates say, if poll workers are adequately trained in the new standards and rights for voters.

The NAACP and labor unions, which operate significant voter registration projects, expect to spend time and money updating their training procedures. But some groups may be able to avail themselves of federal grants in order to train their workers.

To help states, the measure also would establish an independent Election Assistance Commission (EAC) to provide advice and serve as a clearinghouse for information.

But Republicans argued that the EAC would not be a regulatory agency. "It's not going to be making rules and regulations every day from Washington, telling local officials how to run their elections," Ney said.

Instead, the onus would be on state and local officials to develop plans to comply with the new standards.

It took former Rhode Island Secretary of State Jim Langevin five years to completely overhaul the electoral system, beginning in 1994. Now a freshman Democratic congressman, Langevin said the most difficult part was persuading state lawmakers to put up the money.

"You need to do more than just buy voting machines," he said. "You need to have better poll-worker training and better qualified poll workers."

A main concern for Shelton and other voting rights advocates is that election officials will be slow in adopting the provisions of the bill, or not adopt them at all, which is why Shelton repeats the mantra of "enforcement, enforcement, enforcement."

Conferees on the bill debated whether to allow private individuals to bring lawsuits for violations of federal election law, with Democrats arguing for that right and Republicans opposing it.

Republicans won out, keeping

within the Justice Department the authority to investigate and file suit over violations. That rankled African-American Democrats and the NAACP, who profess little faith in Attorney General John Ashcroft's dedication to voting rights.

Shelton said he was "deeply concerned" about relying on the Justice Department.

Ashcroft lost a tight Missouri Senate race in 2000 to the late Gov. Mel Carnahan, a Democrat who was killed in a plane crash before the election. Carnahan's wife, Jean, was appointed to the seat and faces a challenge by former Republican Rep. James M. Talent on Nov. 5 for the remainder of the term.

In the aftermath of the 2000 election, in which Republicans claimed voter fraud cost their candidate, Missouri's senior senator, Christopher S. Bond, took up the fight against election irregularities and was instrumental in pressing for voter identification procedures and a statewide database of registered voters. "Things that are very important for honest elections," Bond said.

Fighting Fraud

The bill's identification provisions, which will take effect Jan. 1, 2003, will require first-time voters or those registering to vote to produce a valid picture identification, such as a driver's license, at some point in the process.

Those unable to produce a valid identification still would be permitted to cast a provisional ballot that would be set aside to be validated later.

Republicans said the requirements, coupled with the statewide voter database, would help curb fraud. "This was not a non-existent problem," said Mitch McConnell of Kentucky, the ranking Republican on the Senate Rules and Administration Committee.

But Democrats, especially African-Americans and Latinos, said it could have the effect of depressing voting in minority communities.

"I fear these provisions may lead to further disenfranchisement for Latino

voters," said Robert Menendez of New Jersey, vice chairman of the House Democratic Caucus.

Bond's insistence on the anti-fraud provisions and the backing he got on that issue from other Republicans were among the factors that delayed completion of the conference report. The House had passed its version of the legislation Dec. 12; the Senate acted April 11. (*2002 CQ Weekly, p. 957*)

As they shuttled back and forth between House and Senate offices this summer, the top negotiators, including Ney and Dodd, kept the talks mostly cordial, aides said. Dodd even brought his year-old daughter, Grace, to one conference meeting.

But Steny H. Hoyer of Maryland, the ranking Democrat on the House Administration panel, acknowledged that his party lacked the votes to pass a bill that did not contain the anti-fraud provisions.

Early the morning of Oct. 4, the top negotiators met in the conference room of House Speaker J. Dennis Hastert, R-Ill., to review a final list of major provisions. They agreed and left the last work for aides, who finished the conference report by 10 a.m.

The attention that the Nov. 5 elections will garner — aides from the House Administration Committee will be in attendance at polling places in South Florida, at the request of that state's GOP Rep. Mark Foley — may uncover further irregularities at polling places.

"Everyone is much more sensitive to both the strengths and weaknesses of the electoral process," said electionline.org's Chapin.

Indeed, in endorsing the conference report, the AFL-CIO said it would "closely monitor the progress of this new law — especially its voter identification requirements."

But supporters of the new election overhaul said they would like an improved system in place by the 2004 elections, hoping to avoid a repeat of 2000. ◆

Causes and Consequences

Lawmakers trying to take a farsighted view of pre-emption's repercussions

Seasoned commanders know that among the first casualties of war are their battle plans. Most acknowledge that such blueprints fly out the window once the fighting begins.

Likewise, lawmakers drafting legislation to authorize a war must cope with a diplomatic battleground whose terrain is historically as unpredictable as the fields of combat.

As members of Congress struggle to find acceptable wording for a resolution that sanctions the use of force against Iraq, a catalog of possible foreign policy repercussions hovers over the final vote. International reaction will depend on the precise language Congress spells out and whether the world community feels the United States has gone too far, too fast or too soon.

President Bush already has toned down his initial expectations for the resolution (S J Res 45), which called for what many critics interpreted as an imperial mandate not only to attack and overthrow Iraqi President Saddam Hussein but also to use American might elsewhere in the Middle East to shape a new regional order. On Sept. 26, he sent Congress a revised draft that is not as nearly as broad in scope as the original and that imposes conditions on any use of force. (*2002 CQ Weekly, p. 2497*)

But no matter what final language results from the jockeying between Congress and the White House over the resolution, some implications of congressional action already are clear, particularly in the short term.

Lawmakers know that while voting for such a resolution brings conflict one step closer, a strong vote in Congress will offer a clear sign of U.S. bipartisan determination to confront Iraq, presumably strengthening Bush's hand in winning United Nations Security Council approval of a tough new reso-

If Congress approves war with Iraq, Powell faces foreign policy unknowns.

lution that could sanction the use of force against Baghdad.

More important, they also know they effectively will have endorsed a historic shift in U.S. national security strategy that Bush has sought since the Sept. 11 terrorist attacks. This new strategy abandons the country's 50-year reliance on deterrence and arms control agreements, and operates on the premise that pre-emptive attack is the best way to deal with dangerous rogue states that seek to develop nuclear, chemical and biological weapons.

Breaking With the Past

"This is the beginning of a new military doctrine that justifies pre-emptive attacks," said Sen. Robert G. Torricelli, D-N.J., a member of the Foreign Relations Committee who favors such action. "We are unlikely to have a new doctrine and have it apply to only one case."

Other lawmakers and independent analysts agree that by voting for a use-of-force authorization, lawmakers will have added pre-emptive war to the set of foreign policy tools a president can turn to in dealing with threats to U.S. interests.

But when and where that doctrine will apply — and how it will fall into overall U.S. national security strategy — is likely to be a central focus of the debate in Congress, both on the Iraq resolution and in the months and years ahead.

"People are most concerned about what kind of precedent we may be setting for the next time we confront this kind of issue," said Ben Nelson, D-Neb., a member of the Senate Armed Services Committee.

The White House laid out a case for the potentially broad use of pre-emptive attacks in unveiling its new national security strategy Sept 20. Citing the failure to anticipate and prevent the Sept. 11 terrorist attacks, despite well-known fears about al Qaeda, the document said the United States can "no longer solely rely on a reactive posture."

The new strategy also states: "The greater the threat, the greater is the risk of inaction — and the more compelling the case for taking anticipatory action to defend ourselves, even if uncertainty remains as to the time and place of an enemy's attacks."

Some lawmakers, such as House Armed Services Committee member Lindsey Graham, R-S.C., support this broad approach, arguing that by acting pre-emptively, the United States not only will address immediate threats, but intimidate other potential enemies into bending to America's will.

"This is a notice to political leaders in these regimes that the United States is going to be more aggressive," Graham said.

But many lawmakers, both Demo-

Possible Global Repercussions of a U.S. Pre-Emptive Attack on Iraq

UNITED STATES
Increase in domestic terror attacks

EUROPE
Rising anti-Americanism

RUSSIA
Intensified pre-emptive assaults on rebels in Chechnya

SOUTH AMERICA
Deeper U.S. involvement in Colombian anti-rebel war

MIDDLE EAST
Destabilization of moderate Arab regimes; intensification of Israeli-Palestinian conflict

SUBCONTINENT
India could adopt pre-emptive doctrine in dealing with Pakistan

CHINA
May use pre-emptive doctrine to attack Taiwan

CQ GRAPHIC / MARILYN GATES-DAVIS

crats and Republicans, still have serious reservations that the Bush Doctrine of pre-emption will hurt U.S. foreign policy interests. They mention a rising resentment of the United States overseas or, even worse, countries that will emulate America's strategic example in managing their own threats and enemies.

"We always have had the right of pre-emption," said John Kerry, D-Mass., a member of the Senate Foreign Relations Committee. "And I want to make sure we preserve that right. But it's always something we've tried to keep on the back burner, under restraint."

Kerry said Bush erred by making the policy a centerpiece of his national security strategy. "What example does that set for China versus Taiwan, India versus Pakistan, and Russia versus Georgia and Chechnya?" he asked, referring to other countries that might be tempted to launch a pre-emptive attack.

Angering the World

Critics also warn that a congressional resolution will be particularly dangerous if it ultimately serves as the go-ahead for a war launched without Security Council endorsement. Such a move, these critics say, would renew longstanding tensions between the

United States and the United Nations, damaging the international organization's effectiveness. And they claim it also would spur resentment, particularly among U.S. allies, about American bullying of other nations. (2002 CQ Weekly, p. 2461)

"If we do it alone, it will only serve to emphasize the gap in power between the United States and other nations," said Leon Fuerth, the national security adviser for former Vice President Al Gore. "Finding a way to counter the United States will become the No. 1 priority in the world."

Fuerth's comments echo recent remarks by Gore and President Jimmy Carter. (2002 CQ Weekly, p. 2501)

Senate Foreign Relations Committee Chairman Joseph R. Biden Jr., D-Del., voiced similar sentiments at a Sept. 26 panel hearing with Secretary of State Colin L. Powell, saying Bush has not made "the case to the American people that the United States must solve the problem alone, if necessary.

"The degree to which we act alone correlates with the price we will have to pay in lives, dollars and influence around the world," Biden added.

Bush's revised draft resolution addresses some of these concerns by including a provision requiring the president to submit a determination that diplomatic efforts will not end the

threat to the United States from Iraq or force it to comply with existing Security Council resolutions.

Such procedural conditions may have come too late. The U.S. confrontation with Iraq already has stoked tensions between the United States and some of its European allies — particularly Germany.

German Chancellor Gerhard Schroeder narrowly won re-election Sept. 22 by appealing to the post-World War II pacifism and anti-Americanism of many left-wing Germans, insisting he would not support an attack on Iraq, even if it wins U.N. sanction.

His stance has soured German relations with the White House and with Congress. It also has raised the prospect that other European politicians may use an anti-American platform to win support. After Schroeder's victory, Bush broke with longstanding presidential tradition by not calling the chancellor to congratulate him. Jesse Helms of North Carolina, ranking Republican on the Senate Foreign Relations Committee, even suggested Bush might retaliate by pulling U.S. military bases out of Germany. This is not a realistic possibility, but it underscores the defiant mood in some congressional quarters.

Tensions with France, one of the

The Ghosts of Tonkin: Questions and Resolutions

"Resolved . . . That the Congress approves and supports the determination of the president . . . to take all necessary measures to repel any armed attack against the forces of the United States and to prevent further aggression. . . ."

Sound familiar?

Thirty-eight years ago, Congress chose these words for the Gulf of Tonkin resolution, authorizing President Lyndon B. Johnson's use of force in Vietnam.

Today, some critics and legal scholars say the scope of the president's war-making powers under his revised Iraq resolution may be just as broad as those in the notorious 1964 measure, only not as transparent.

The new Bush version, incorporating changes aimed at placating critics who had been comparing his initial draft to Tonkin, authorizes President Bush to "enforce" U.N. Security Council resolutions from the Gulf War period.

"No nation can unilaterally decide to enforce the U.N.'s resolutions," said Rep. Bob Filner, D-Calif. "Only the U.N. has that power." Filner, a former history professor, said he found this provision "incredibly disconcerting."

John Setear, professor of International Law at the University of Virginia, agrees. "There's a good case that the primary purpose of the U.N. was to make it the exclusive decision-maker about the use of force in international politics," he said.

The current Bush proposal effec-

Like Lyndon Johnson, President Bush is asking for broad authority to wage war.

tively would incorporate the requirements of the Gulf War resolutions into Congress' authorization. Among these would be U.N. Security Resolution 687, requiring weapons inspections, and the pre-war resolution 678, authorizing the use of "all necessary means" to evict Iraq from Kuwait.

But the pre-war resolution also includes a mandate to "restore international peace and security in the area" — almost the exact phrase stricken from the first Bush draft.

The White House Counsel's office declined to comment on whether this incorporation of past U.N. resolutions achieves the same result of granting Bush broad, Tonkin-like war powers.

But Senate GOP aides said such concerns are overblown. "Nothing like that would pass muster in the pub-

lic eye," one Republican staff member of the Foreign Relations Committee said. "The White House is not trying to be too clever by half."

Scope of Authority

In a Senate Foreign Relations Committee hearing Sept. 25 regarding Iraq, former National Security Adviser Robert McFarlane referred to the Tonkin episode as "fraud that was perpetrated on this body and our people" that "profoundly affected American attitudes toward launching war since that day."

Questions about the scope of authority that Congress should grant Bush in Iraq reflect the powerful legacy of Tonkin nearly four decades later.

The 1964 resolution authorized "the president, in his determination as Commander in Chief, to take all necessary measures." In the current draft, Bush requests authority to use "the Armed Forces . . . as he determines to be necessary and appropriate."

Rep. Dennis J. Kucinich, D-Ohio, said the new draft provides "an even more detailed statement of intent" than the first version, proving Bush is willing "to use every possible predicate for military action."

Gar Alperovitz, a former aide to Sen. Gaylord Nelson, D-Wis. (1963-81), said his boss considered offering a limiting amendment to the Tonkin resolution, which he withdrew upon assurances from the administration.

other four permanent members of the Security Council, have not been so sharp. But the French consistently have rebuffed U.S. efforts to win Security Council approval for a single resolution that would call on Hussein to admit U.N. weapons inspectors and authorize the use of force if he balks. The French prefer their own proposal to call first for the return of weapons inspectors, then consider a second resolution authorizing force only if those

efforts fail.

Britain is the only one of America's allies to back the U.S. proposal for a single resolution demanding that Iraq comply with U.N. demands or face a military attack. British Prime Minister Tony Blair outlined the case for action before Parliament on Sept. 24, disclosing more evidence of Iraq's efforts to develop and acquire weapons of mass destruction.

But even the British want the Unit-

ed States to act through the United Nations. They fear that failure to do so could damage the world body and the NATO alliance. And they do not want to be one of a handful of nations making up a "coalition of the willing" to invade Iraq. The United States formed such a coalition in 1998 when the United Nations failed to authorize the use of force to defend Kosovo.

"What really matters for our relations with Europe are whether we stick with our U.N. course or not," said Ivo Daalder of the Brookings Institution. "Having challenged the U.N. to take action, Bush will only aggravate the problem if he doesn't try to go through them."

But Daalder and lawmakers such as Doug Bereuter, R-Neb., a member of the House International Relations and Intelligence committees, also caution that winning U.N. approval for a tough anti-Iraq resolution will require the endorsement or acquiescence of Russia. And that will come with its own set of costs, both economic and political.

"The Russians can be bought both on foreign policy grounds and on economic grounds, " Daalder said. "At a minimum that will include the extension of the war in Chechnya into [neighboring] Georgia and a guarantee that a new government in Baghdad will honor Iraqi debts to Russia." Iraq owes Moscow an estimated $6 billion.

Russia also could demand other concessions, including a piece of Iraq's oil production, foreign policy specialists say.

Soothing the Arabs

Of the nations waiting to see how Security Council members come down on U.S. demands, none will be watching more anxiously than America's moderate Arab allies.

Nations such as Saudi Arabia have indicated they will support a U.S. attack — both politically and by providing vital military bases — only if the Security Council endorses military action.

Arab anger at the United States is running high, analysts note, because many believe that Bush, pushed by a pro-Israel Congress, essentially has sided with Israeli Prime Minister Ariel Sharon. Arab leaders cite Bush's call for the replacement of Palestinian Authority Chairman Yasser Arafat and the president's placing the onus for peace on the hard-pressed Palestinians.

Arab diplomats warn that an American attack on Iraq — another Arab country — would transform that anger into violent street protests, not only against the United States but also against the pro-American regimes of Jordan, Egypt, Morocco and the Persian Gulf.

These diplomats also warn that Hussein is likely to exploit these tensions by striking out at Israel as part of its response to an American attack. The Iraqis fired Scud missiles at Israel during the 1991 Persian Gulf War in an attempt to provoke an Israeli response and hopefully force fellow Arab states to withdraw from the coalition. Back then, Israeli did not retaliate. But Sharon has made it plain that Israel will retaliate against any Iraqi attack this time — a development that could complicate American efforts to soothe the Arab world.

"This escalation, spiraling out of control, could draw the Arab world into a regional war in which our Arab allies side with Iraq against the United States and against Israel," said Sen. Edward M. Kennedy, D-Mass., in a Sept. 27 speech. "And that would represent a fundamental threat to Israel, to the region, to the world economy, and to international order."

Recognizing these dangers, Defense Secretary Donald H. Rumsfeld has made clear in congressional hearings that he would push Israel to stay out of any conflict. In recent days, administration officials also have tried to appear more evenhanded in the conflict between Israel and the Palestinians.

In an unusual step, the United States abstained rather than veto a Security Council resolution Sept. 24 that called on Israel to end the siege of Arafat's headquarters in the West Bank and stop any further demolition in the compound. The U.N. resolution also called on the Palestinian Authority to bring to justice those responsible for attacks on Israelis.

A New Iraq

The buildup to war is testing U.S.-Arab relations, as will the aftermath of what will presumably be an American victory. While many Arab governments will be relieved to see Hussein toppled, they also will be concerned about the foreign policy pursued by a new Iraqi government.

The Saudis, for example, are worried that Iraq, with the world's second-largest oil reserves, will undermine its leadership of the OPEC oil cartel if it is freed from the artificial production constraints imposed by U.N. sanctions. Kuwait and Iran — both of which Iraq has invaded — want assurances that a post-Hussein government will not repeat the same aggressive behavior.

But first will come the challenge of building a democratic, market-based government in Baghdad on the ruins of Hussein's dictatorial rule. If an effort to form a new government fails, neighboring countries could end up fighting over the pieces of a dismembered Iraq. Turkey, for example, is worried Iraq's Kurds could join with Turkish Kurds to form a new and independent state. Meanwhile, Saudis fear that Iraq's Shiite Muslims could fall under the sway of fellow Shiites in neighboring Iran.

And while advocates of overthrowing Hussein champion a vision in which Iraq could serve as the cornerstone for a democratic transformation of the region, such a change would present a challenge to America's Arab allies — and to Congress.

Many anticipate a post-war U.S. occupation of Iraq that would last several decades. Congress would have to be prepared to expend considerable blood and treasure to maintain stability.

John Hulsman of the Heritage Foundation said he foresees a split among Republicans over how to handle a post-war Iraq. He anticipates the party's neoconservative call for large-scale nation-building activities will butt up against GOP realists who will demand a minimal U.S. presence.

All this, of course, is based on informed assumptions that the United States will go to war and make short work of Hussein. Other assumptions include one by Tom Lantos, the ranking Democrat on the House International Affairs Committee, that Iraq will emerge as a "jewel of democracy in the Arab world" — a prospect that cannot thrill the authoritarian regimes of the region.

But there is a lesson to be learned about assumptions — and the unforeseen consequences of war.

When Congress passed the 1991 Gulf War resolution (PL 102-1), which empowered President George Bush to oust Iraqi troops from Kuwait, the resolution also had a number of secondary effects that were not anticipated at the time. These ranged from Hussein's survival in power to the push by other nations and groups to develop nuclear, chemical and biological weapons to make up for the overwhelming superiority of U.S. forces.

Today, with no one able to predict the responses of Hussein, other Arab leaders and members of the U.N. Security Council, the main lesson is that some of the most important foreign policy concerns may be ones that neither the president nor lawmakers have yet envisioned. ◆

Personnel Issues Have Senate Stumbling on Homeland Security

Final vote remains a question mark

Many senators fretted this summer over the prospect of not finishing work on a homeland security bill by the first anniversary of the Sept. 11 terrorist attacks. Now, they are increasingly doubtful they will get done before the November elections.

The fourth week of debate on a measure (HR 5005) to create a new homeland security department ended in parliamentary gridlock Sept. 26, leading Majority Leader Tom Daschle, D-S.D., to threaten to pull the bill the week of Sept. 30 so the chamber could debate a resolution (S J Res 45) authorizing military action against Iraq. *(2002 CQ Weekly, p. 2496)*

The dispute continued to revolve around whether the president should have broader personnel authority over the new department than he has over most other government agencies, including the power to ban union representation.

Attempts to limit debate on a Democratic version of the bill by Joseph I. Lieberman, D-Conn., and a Republican substitute backed by the Bush administration failed Sept. 26, as the two sides accused each other of stalling

CQ Weekly Sept. 28, 2002

for political purposes.

White House Office of Homeland Security Director Tom Ridge, while publicly decrying the tactics of Democrats, held out hope for some sort of last-minute compromise. The administration and Senate Democrats continue to trade proposals that would allow the president to remove union protections from workers at the new department but would require some justification, such as an impending terrorist threat or changes in the workers' job classification.

"We want to keep the doors open. We want to keep talking. We still are talking," Ridge said during a visit to Capitol Hill on Sept. 26. "Maybe there will be an epiphany over the weekend."

However, some Democrats accused the White House of stalling debate in order to prevent a discussion of the sagging economy. They said a solution may not come until year's end.

"It's clearly the goal of the president's political operatives to keep us focused on anything but the economy," said Sen. Richard J. Durbin, D-Ill.

The Republican-controlled House, after a much briefer but no less partisan debate, passed a version of the homeland security bill July 26

Quick Contents

The dispute between the White House and Senate Democrats over personnel rules for the proposed homeland security department has come down to two competing floor amendments. If both sides dig in, the bill may not be resolved until after the elections.

Personnel Differences for Homeland Security Plan

One of the last major hurdles in legislation to create a department of homeland security is how personnel would be categorized and whether unions would be allowed. Two major plans came forward the week of Sept. 23. How they compare:

GRAMM-MILLER
Would allow the president to deny continued union representation to certain employees if their agency's mission "materially changed" and a majority of the workers would be involved primarily in intelligence, counterintelligence or investigating terrorism. It would require the White House to provide a written explanation of why it was removing workers from union participation.

BREAUX-CHAFEE-NELSON
Would allow the president to remove workers from their union contracts on national security grounds only if the workers' responsibilities changed significantly so that a majority of their duties involve intelligence, counterintelligence or investigative work directly related to terrorism. The administration would have to negotiate personnel changes with union representatives, subject to mediation by the Federal Services Impasses Panel.

that includes most of what Bush sought.

Each chamber is debating how to combine 22 federal agencies involved in counterterrorism into a new Cabinet-level department with at least 170,000 employees and a budget of $37.5 billion. Labor issues continually have been the major points of contention, as they were when the White House lost a showdown with unions over representation of airport screeners during last fall's consideration of an aviation security law (PL 107-71). (*2001 Almanac, p. 20-4*)

Republicans contend Democrats are intent on restricting presidential powers over personnel decisions that have been in place since John F. Kennedy asserted them by executive order in 1962.

GOP senators are intent on blocking Democrats from offering a compromise developed by John B. Breaux, D-La., Ben Nelson, D-Neb., and Lincoln Chafee, R-R.I., as an amendment to the Republican language. Democrats are trying to have the Senate vote first on the Breaux-Nelson-Chafee language, which would limit some of the president's powers.

"They want to have a vote on it their way; we want to have a vote on it our way. That suggests to me it's very close," said Phil Gramm, R-Texas, who cowrote the administration-backed language with Zell Miller, D-Ga.

The Gramm-Miller amendment would allow the administration to develop a new personnel system for the homeland security department outside existing civil service rules. It contains House-passed language on work rules giving the president authority to exclude workers from union representation in the new department if their individual agency's mission has "materially changed," and if their work is primarily with intelligence, counterintelligence or investigating terrorism.

The Breaux-Nelson-Chafee provision would allow the administration to change civil service protections in the new department, but only if the White House consults with union representatives. If the sides disagree, the matter would be put before the Federal Services Impasses Panel, a seven-member panel of presidential appointees that now functions in a similar arbitration role for workers at the Internal Revenue Service.

Compared to the Gramm-Miller amendment or the House version of the bill, the Breaux-Nelson-Chafee proposal also would make it more difficult for the president to exclude department workers from unions. It would allow the president to remove employees from unions only if their responsibilities change significantly so that a majority of their duties involve intelligence, counterintelligence or investigating terrorism. Virtually identical language drew a veto threat from the White House when it was offered in the House by Constance A. Morella, R-Md.

Maneuvering for Advantage

Daschle forced a showdown between the competing proposals Sept. 25 by employing a tactic Republicans frequently used when they controlled the chamber — and a tactic Daschle said in a July interview that he would never use. Daschle blocked amendments by the other party by filling all allowable amendment slots. That effectively prevented Republicans from getting a straight up-or-down vote on Gramm-Miller.

Democrats were emboldened by the belief that Chafee's decision to sign on with Breaux and Nelson — rumored for days and announced Sept. 24 — gave them a 51-vote majority on the personnel issue. However, as many as a dozen senators have yet to formally announced their positions.

The maneuvering culminated in back-to-back procedural votes Sept. 26 to limit further debate.

Senators rejected, 50-49, an attempt to invoke cloture on the Democratic version of the bill offered by Lieberman — 10 votes short of the necessary 60-vote majority. An attempt to limit debate on the Gramm-Miller GOP substitute also failed, 44-53. (*2002 CQ Weekly, p. 2543*)

The votes came as public employees unions lobbied undecided senators with phone calls and faxes from members. One fax from the American Federation of Government Employees reads: "Unions Are Not A Security Threat. So Why Is [President] Bush Treating Them Like One?" Unions believe they could pick up additional Republican support from George V. Voinovich of Ohio, John W. Warner of Virginia and Arlen Specter of Pennsylvania, all of whom have large union and public employee constituencies.

Before the showdown on personnel rules, the Senate approved, 90-8, an amendment to establish an independent commission to investigate the Sept. 11 terrorist attacks. (*2002 CQ Weekly, pp. 2517, 2542*)

The Senate also rejected, 28-70, an amendment by Robert C. Byrd, D-W.Va., that would have required creation of the new department subject to congressional approval in three stages over 13 months. (*2002 CQ Weekly, p. 2542*)

Republicans could add another wrinkle to the homeland security debate by trying to attach Bush's long-stalled faith-based initiative (HR 7) as an amendment to the bill. Rick Santorum, R-Pa., filed the amendment Sept. 24, but GOP leaders said they may only offer it as a last resort. Republicans would prefer an agreement to consider it separately. (*2002 CQ Weekly, p. 1662*)

If the amendment is offered, Democrats led by Jack Reed, D-R.I., and Richard J. Durbin, D-Ill., would try to slow it down by trying to add an employment discrimination ban similar to language in the 1993 national service law (PL 103-82), which created the AmeriCorps program. ◆

Democrats Embrace Homeland Security While Working on Separate Political Persona

With an eye on the midterm elections, Democrats walk a fine line between solidarity with a popular president's war on terror and their own domestic agenda

They could not have stood any closer. On June 12, Democratic icons Sen. Edward M. Kennedy of Massachusetts and Rep. John D. Dingell of Michigan joined Republican leaders in the White House Rose Garden as President Bush signed a new law to combat bio-terrorism. The lawmakers' message: When it comes to homeland security, there is no sunlight between us.

But this picture of wartime bipartisanship obscures a fierce struggle between Republicans and Democrats as they try to seize control of the political and legislative agenda before the November congressional elections. For now, Republicans feel that wartime politics have given them a slight edge with voters. But both parties recognize that voters are still focused on issues that affect their everyday lives. Much of the struggle involves how each party manages to juggle the two priorities.

Ever since Bush's June 6 announcement of his plan to create a new department of homeland security to fight domestic terrorism, Republicans strategists have applauded the president for shifting national attention away from strong Democratic issues, such as rising health care costs, and refocusing it squarely on national security — an issue that tends to favor Republicans.

"They're having trouble getting oxygen for their agenda," Rep. Thomas M. Davis III of Virginia, chairman of the National Republican Congressional Committee, said of the Democrats after Bush's announcement.

Indeed, a recent White House strategy paper instructed Republicans to use the war effort in their campaign to win full control of Congress.

But in Democratic circles, Bush's success in stealing the headlines does not mean the president has derailed the political debate on the traditional Democratic issues that rank high on voters' priority lists. "I have not seen anywhere that [national security] has changed how

Dingell and Kennedy, right, stand over Bush as he signs the bio-terrorism law in the Rose Garden on June 12. Democrats are embracing the idea of a homeland security department.

people will vote," said Michael P. Meehan, the Democratic National Committee's polling director.

Warning Signs

Recent public opinion polls seem to favor the Democrats on domestic issues: A May 24 survey conducted by Republican pollster Bill McInturff shows that six of 10 voters did not select terrorism as either the first or second issue that should be a priority for Congress and the president. The same study showed that the economy, jobs, social security, Medicare, health care and education all ranked higher than anti-terrorism as issues that will determine the electorate's votes for Congress.

Meanwhile, other polls contain additional warning signs for Republicans. A Gallup Poll of June 11 showed that the percentage of Americans who are "satisfied with the way things were going in the United States" dropped to 52 percent from 56 percent in early May and from 61 percent in mid-September.

Democratic Sen. Debbie Stabenow says she has observed this phenomenon

in her home state of Michigan. She flew to Detroit during the week of June 10 to meet with the big three automakers, about 40 small businesses and health care providers to discuss prescription drug costs. She said corporations were upset about the rising costs they must bear for employees and pensioners. Stabenow said those visits outside the Beltway prove that Bush's move to focus Congress' attention on homeland security "was not a master stroke."

At the same time, Bush still enjoys a 70 percent approval rating, according to a June 14 Gallup Poll, and Republicans believe his handling of the war on terror can provide them with political coattails in November. Even some Democrats such as Iowa Sen. Tom Harkin, who is locked in a tight race and targeted for defeat by the White House, are using Bush in their campaign ads.

Still, some Republicans are concerned that the president's war on terrorism also may detract from their own efforts to promote GOP approaches to domestic issues. House Republican Conference Chairman J.C. Watts Jr. of

Oklahoma, who helps guide the party's political message, notes that Republicans are slipping in the polls on education. In a June 12 memo to Republican House members, he exhorted his colleagues to focus on domestic issues such as education and prescription drugs.

And as voters fret about the economy, Watts said, Republicans can take advantage of the higher poll ranking they enjoy on this issue by stressing their job-creating policies.

"Republicans have to be careful," he warned. "We don't win elections on homeland security. It's a very dangerous strategy, in my opinion, to say we are going to win the election on the war. I think that's very short-sighted. "

Democratic Agenda Affected

Despite the polls that show the public favoring their domestic agenda, Democrats concede that Congress' need to deal with the creation of a homeland security department has affected their plans. House Minority Leader Richard A. Gephardt of Missouri acknowledged that his plans to introduce corporate responsibility reforms to prevent future Enron scandals are now on the back burner.

"There's no question that the whole war effort has made it much more difficult to get our message through in terms of Social Security, prescription drugs, Enron," said Rep. Robert T. Matsui D-Calif.

Democrats are trying to seize the agenda. And their first tactic appears to be an attempt to neutralize the traditional advantages that Republicans have on issues of security by eagerly embracing the president's homeland security plan.

"If there's no contrast on homeland security, people will go to the polls on other issues," said Erik Smith, Gephardt's spokesman.

Meanwhile, Gephardt has taken the Democratic embrace of the president's new homeland security department one step further, challenging Republicans to implement Bush's plan, not by year's end as the president requested, but by the first anniversary of the Sept. 11 attacks.

Outside Washington, some Republicans suspect Gephardt's deadline reflects his desire to return to the Democrats' domestic agenda by October, just before midterm elections. "I fully appreciate where Gephardt is coming from," said Karen Hanretty, spokes-

woman for the California State Republican Party. "They want this off their radar screen. But it's not going off the radar screen if you've got Arafat making threats over the weekend, Pakistan on the brink of nuclear war. Their timetables aren't the first Tuesday in November."

But some Republican strategists suspect Gephardt's deadline may have more to do with political positioning if Congress fails to create the homeland security department in the seven legislative weeks left until Sept. 11. "Gephardt knows internally in the House, there are big jurisdictional problems," said a top Republican strategist. "They're setting the date on the assumption that if the House doesn't pass it by then, whose fault is it?" Since Republicans control the House, this theory goes, it inoculates the Democrats from blame. (*2002 CQ Weekly*, p. 1583)

Democrats also are convinced that they can multitask this summer, passing the most significant government reorganization since World War II without losing sight of their legislative priorities, especially a bill on prescription drugs. "We have to do two things at once," Gephardt said. "We have to work hard and fast on homeland security, and we have to work on the domestic agenda that the American people feel very strongly about."

With the legislative clock ticking, Democrats also appear to recognize that there will be little time for floor debates and votes that would record party positions on key issues. So they are arranging public events where they can keep up their drumbeat on issues such as education, health care, corporate responsibility and the environment, while at the same time not allowing any differences to arise with Bush and the Republicans on homeland security and the war against terrorism.

During the week of June 10, Democrats organized a string of events to show they can juggle both agendas simultaneously. On Tuesday, party leaders from both chambers staged a rally to renew their call for an independent commission to investigate the events surrounding the Sept. 11 attacks. On Wednesday, Senate Majority Leader Tom Daschle, D-S.D., joined by "West Wing" television star Martin Sheen, attended a youth rally where he focused on education and the environment. At a later event, Daschle read a

letter he had written to Bush opposing cuts in Social Security benefits. On Thursday, House Democrats unveiled their prescription drug plan.

During the same week, Republicans tried to pack the schedule with their own political theater. On Wednesday, House Majority Whip Tom DeLay of Texas held a television event to renew his call for oil drilling in Alaska. But a Republican plan to roll out a prescription drug plan Thursday had to be postponed after a jurisdictional squabble between the House Ways and Means and Commerce committees. (*2002 CQ Weekly*, p. 1601)

Claiming Credit

Democrats also question whether Bush's high popularity ratings will translate into November votes. Party strategists note those ratings have not trickled down so far to individual GOP congressional candidates.

While Republicans feel secure in focusing on terrorism, "that's not going to start mattering much when the [political campaign] ads start flying," said Mark S. Mellman, strategist for the Democratic Senatorial Campaign Committee.

Another point Democrats are stressing is the credit they are due for coming up with the idea of a homeland security department in the first place. They note that against resistance from Bush and the GOP, Democrats had been calling for such a department, to be overseen by Congress, since October of last year. And on May 22, the Senate Governmental Affairs Committee even passed a bill to create the department. (*2002 CQ Weekly* p. 1387)

"This has been part of our agenda," Daschle said. "This is something we called for. This is something we reported out of the [Governmental] Affairs Committee on our side."

But with Bush and Republicans reclaiming homeland security, the Democratic strategy of taking credit could be risky if voters smell an attempt to question Bush's conduct of the war.

Earlier this year, Daschle had to back off when he questioned administrative plans for an invasion of Iraq while Osama bin Laden remained at large. Republicans pilloried Gephardt for asking what Bush knew and when he knew it after revelations that intelligence and FBI officials mishandled clues before Sept. 11.

"The Democrats' incessant attacks are not generating the response they want and are in fact hurting their message," Watts said.

Exploiting the War

Just as Democrats risk political damage by criticizing the president's stewardship of the war, Republicans run their own risks if they are seen to be exploiting the war for political gain.

The timing of Bush's announcement to create a new homeland security agency was viewed by some as political cover because it came on a day when an FBI whistleblower testified before a Senate panel on the bureau's sloppiness before Sept. 11.

"When all else fails, they fall back on the war on terrorism as a partisan political issue," said Democratic National Committee Chairman Terry McAuliffe at the Wisconsin Democratic Party Convention on June 7. "Everywhere the president goes, every political speech he gives, he tries to use the war as a wedge, claiming that we need to elect more Republicans in order to defeat the forces of terror."

McAuliffe added: "In a way, I feel sorry for the Republicans. What choice do they have? If not the war, what are they going to run on?"

But there is a war. And Republicans say Democrats cannot will it away.

David Winston, a Republican pollster who consults for Watts, says just as Republican candidates would be mistaken to overestimate the importance of the war on terrorism, it is a mistake to underestimate its political benefits.

"People are concerned there's going to be another attack," Winston said. "Personal safety and security are important values. They cut across all groups. . . . Point to me the district where a mother isn't concerned about a terrorist blowing up the shopping mall."

Those concerns may not be the decisive issue in an election, Winston said, but they "create a more favorable context for Republicans for whatever the political debate is."

For that reason, Republicans may be tempted to drag out the legislative process for establishing a homeland security department until a few days before midterm elections. "Certainly, these [security and terrorism] are issues that play to Republican's advantage," said a GOP Senate aide. "The longer we're talking about those, the better."

Cracks are appearing among Republican leaders. While House Speaker J. Dennis Hastert of Illinois and Majority Leader Dick Armey of Texas have accepted Gephardt's challenge to create the new department by Sept. 11, other Republican leaders, such as Watts and Senate Majority Leader Trent Lott of Mississippi, have begun hedging, saying such an important piece of legislation should not be rushed.

But there also are political risks to dragging out the legislative process. "Republicans will leave themselves open if they don't deliver by elections," said Hanretty of the California GOP. "Democrats can say, 'They've had the opportunity, they're the party in power — at least in the House — they've had the president behind them, and they still can't get the job done.'"

All this political strategizing presumes that the war on terror remains static. A major terrorist success against U.S. targets at home or abroad could drive security issues to the forefront — a development that could hurt Democrats.

"During a time of war, the president can control the political agenda," said Marshall Wittman, an analyst at the Hudson Institute. "Who knows what's going to intervene on the national security front?" he said. "That's out of the Democrats' hands. Ultimately, their fate is out of their hands." ◆

The High Cost of Might

A defense budget of almost $400 billion buys the U.S. a world of options

As the Pentagon prepares for a war against Iraq, one of the symbols of how far American military capabilities have come is a massive new military cargo vessel named after comedian Bob Hope.

But there is nothing funny about this ship. Longer than three football fields and 62,069 tons fully loaded, it has a cavernous bay that can accommodate as many as 1,000 combat vehicles, including heavy tanks, armored personnel carriers, artillery pieces and ammunition trailer trucks. With the ship's new ramp design, the vehicles can be loaded and unloaded in just a few days' time. And despite its size, this floating parking structure is not slow. Sailing from the East Coast fully loaded at a brisk 24 knots, the ship could reach the Persian Gulf in just three weeks.

The USNS *Bob Hope* is one of more than 40 ships the Navy has acquired in the past 20 years to reduce the time it would take to deliver heavily armed Army and Marine Corps units to trouble spots far from U.S. shores. As both Congress and the United Nations Security Council consider separate resolutions to approve the use of force against Iraq, it is this capability, coupled with the U.S. military's enormous firepower, that gives credence to President Bush's warning that he is prepared to act quickly and, if need be, unilaterally to disarm Iraq.

But in a broader sense, the ships underscore another fundamental truth about U.S. military power in the first decade of the 21st century: Because the United States spends so much more on defense than any other nation, it has a range of military capabilities that no other country or plausible alliance can match.

"Our nation's military forces are ready and able to do whatever the president asks of them," Gen. Richard Meyers, chairman of the Joint Chiefs of Staff, assured the Senate on Sept. 19.

In addition to improvements in intelligence gathering and firepower over

New Navy cargo ships, which can rapidly ferry tanks, artillery, and ammunition trailers to distant ports, have shortened the time needed to assemble an army to attack Iraq.

the last decade, Meyers specifically mentioned the military's enhanced capability to project its power overseas. He said strong congressional support for programs such as the "large medium-speed roll-on, roll-off ships has meant that we can deploy and sustain the force much better."

If Congress, as expected, votes to approve the use of force against Iraq, the Pentagon, using ships like the *Bob Hope,* will be able to assemble a large ground assault force near Iraq in a matter of weeks. By contrast, the build-up to the Persian Gulf War took more than five months. (*1990 Almanac, p. 726*)

Indeed, spending nearly $400 billion a year on defense buys a lot of options.

Historic Shift

This compression of the preparation time for battle is now possible because of a historic about-face by Congress on the issue of of overseas interventions. Deeply skeptical of such involvements in the immediate aftermath of the Vietnam War, members of Congress

have reversed themselves since the Iranian revolution of 1979 and promoted the shift, steadily providing the Pentagon with the funds to deploy forces as far as the Persian Gulf.

The hundreds of billions of dollars that Congress has given the Pentagon over the past two decades has bought not only fast new cargo ships but also paid for the construction of an archipelago of state-of-the-art military bases throughout the Persian Gulf that require only the insertion of U.S. forces and equipment to serve as the jumping-off points for war.

To this end, lawmakers also have generously funded exercises that have streamlined the complex mechanized ballet of flying in U.S. troops to marry up with the offloaded equipment and supplies already pre-positioned at bases and on cargo ships anchored in nearby countries.

Still, not even the U.S. defense establishment has the resources to wage a major war half a world away without breaking stride. Since the Sept. 11 attacks, the armed services have called up a total of 130,000 National Guard

U.S. Defense Spending Outstrips the World

War in Iraq easily could push U.S. military spending past the $400 billion mark — more than the next nine largest national defense budgets combined. Still, that level of

American defense spending represents just 3 percent of the American Gross Domestic Product. How U.S. budget compares to the top 10 and major Middle East powers.

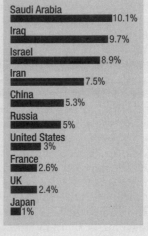

Defense spending as a percentage of Gross Domestic Product

Country	Percentage
Saudi Arabia	10.1%
Iraq	9.7%
Israel	8.9%
Iran	7.5%
China	5.3%
Russia	5%
United States	3%
France	2.6%
UK	2.4%
Japan	1%

(in billions of dollars)

Russia $58.8   Japan $44.4   China $41.2   France $34.3   UK $33.9   Germany $28.2   Italy $20.6   Saudi Arabia $18.3   Brazil $17.5

United States $294.7

Saudi Arabia $18.3   Israel $9.4   Iran $7.3   UAE $3.3   Iraq $1.5   Kuwait $3.2   Egypt $2.8

SOURCE: The International Institute for Strategic Studies (2000 numbers, latest available)

and reservists to guard airports, railways and other facilities at home and to serve overseas in the war against Afghanistan. In case of war with Iraq, military officials say a much larger number of reservists will be needed.

Nor is the Pentagon so flush with cash that it could absorb the cost of the war within the $378.6 billion budget Bush requested for fiscal 2003.

Based on the $61 billion price tag of the Persian Gulf War — costs that were borne largely by Japan, Germany and several Gulf states — a study by Democratic staff members of the House Budget Committee projects that an operation involving 250,000 U.S. troops would cost a similar amount. With only Britain willing to sign on to a war so far, those are costs the United States would have to bear largely alone.

Moreover, the study estimates that because the federal budget is no longer running a surplus, the increased borrowing needed to pay for the war could boost interest costs to the federal government by more than $30 billion over 10 years. (*Economy, p. 81*)

On Sept. 24, Mitchell E. Daniels Jr., chief of the Office of Management and Budget, said Bush would request supplemental appropriations bills to cover the incremental cost of fighting the war. That would cover such expenses as additional National Guard and reservist troops, fuel and maintenance, ammunition, and equipment replacement.

But the military operation would

not have to wait for Congress to advance the money to cover those expenses — especially if the United States launched its attack on Iraq before the end of the year.

The Pentagon could pay those bills by drawing from funds budgeted to cover routine training and maintenance scheduled for July through September, the last three months of the fiscal year. Funds provided by a supplemental to pay for unanticipated military operations are used, in fact, to replenish the accounts from which the money was borrowed to pay immediate costs.

If the supplemental is not enacted far enough in advance of the scheduled training and maintenance exercises, those activities must be canceled. Thus, it would be less disruptive to the Defense Department's routine operations if war against Iraq began early in a fiscal year, which starts Oct. 1. That would give Congress plenty of time to pass the supplemental needed to cover the incremental costs.

While additional funding would be needed to wage war against Iraq, however, the annual budgets routinely passed over the past two decades have provided the necessary up-front investment in forces, bases, transportation and communication links. Indeed, the kind of war that seems to be taking shape against Iraq is one the U.S. military has been anticipating for decades.

The most salient fact about the Pentagon budget is not that it is the

largest national military budget in the world, but that the country in second place — Russia — is so far behind.

According to the London-based International Institute for Strategic Studies (IISS), the U.S. Defense Department spent $294.7 billion in 2000 — five times the $58.8 billion that Russia spent. Moreover, U.S. spending accounted for about half the total of $591.9 billion spent by the 10 countries with the largest defense budgets — in other words, about as much as the next nine countries put together.

Moreover, of the $465 billion spent by all 19 members of NATO that year, the United States accounted for nearly two-thirds. It spent nearly nine times as much as either France or the United Kingdom and more than 10 times as much as Germany, the three members with the next-largest budgets.

Meanwhile, the 19 Arab countries stretching from Iran westward to Morocco spent $57.9 billion on defense — less than one-fifth as much as the U.S. outlay. And the five countries often branded by Washington as rogues — Iran, Iraq, Libya, Syria and North Korea — spent $13 billion, slightly more than the Pentagon spent on health care alone.

Power Gap Growing

As dramatic as these statistics are, they understate the current U.S. advantage. Congress will probably approve a Defense Department budget for 2003 that is very close to Bush's $378.6

billion request, which is more than 20 percent larger, allowing for inflation, than the 2000 budget covered by the IISS report. Thus, when the data is in for 2003, the Pentagon budget probably will account for more than half the total of the world's 10 largest military budgets.

Yet America's defense spending represents little more than a blip on the nation's economic radar screen. Because of the sheer size of the U.S. economy — last clocked at $10.3 trillion — defense spending represented only about 3 percent of the gross domestic product in 2000. Even with the hefty increases proposed by Bush, the Pentagon is expected to consume just 3.4 percent of the GDP in 2003.

To be sure, the U.S. defense budget is down markedly in inflation-adjusted terms compared with the heights reached during the Cold War. From a high point in fiscal 1985, when the Pentagon budget was $287 billion, the Defense Department's real purchasing power declined by more than one-third, bottoming out in fiscal 1998, when the budget was $295 billion.

But since then, the Pentagon budget has risen each year, in current dollars and in inflation-adjusted terms. Taking the 1985 budget as a baseline, Bush's $378.6 billion request for fiscal 2003 represents a reduction in purchasing power of about 18 percent.

The active-duty force rose from a post-Vietnam low of 2 million members to 2.2 million in 1985 and plateaued at that level until the Soviet empire began to disintegrate in 1989. From that point, the size of the active-duty force dropped by about one-third, to 1.4 million. (*2002 CQ Weekly, p. 2466*)

The administration of President George Bush insisted that the country still needed a robust military to defend against threats to its allies and interests around the world. Those threats began to emerge in late 1979, when a series of crises in the Persian Gulf convinced U.S. political leaders that the Pentagon would need to acquire the means to deploy a large force to the area to protect allies and critical oil supplies.

So at the same time the force was shrinking through the 1990s, it also was becoming more mobile. And a major impetus for the increased mobility was the potential need to field a force against Iraq quickly.

The military's obsession with mobility had its roots in the restrictions that

were imposed on the armed forces after the Vietnam War. Scarred by that conflict, Congress in 1967 took the extraordinary step of killing a major weapons program to make it harder for future presidents to dispatch U.S. forces to brush-fire wars.

At issue was a proposal by then-Defense Secretary Robert S. McNamara to build a fleet of 30 "fast-deployment logistics ships." Those vessels, which would have been nearly the size of the *Bob Hope*, were designed for the same purpose: to speed the deployment of a heavily armed Army unit to a hot spot by carrying tanks, trucks and supplies for troops that could be airlifted quickly to the scene. (*1967 Almanac, p. 220*)

What sealed the program's doom was the staunch opposition of Senate Armed Services Committee Chairman Richard B. Russell Jr., D-Ga. (1933-71), a Pentagon ally who had soured on the notion of military intervention in the Third World because of the Vietnam War.

"If it is easy for us to go anywhere and do anything, we will always be going somewhere and doing something," Russell said at the time, explaining his opposition to McNamara's project.

The anti-interventionism spawned by the Vietnam experience remained strong enough through the early 1970s to enable Congress to block for five years a proposal by Presidents Richard M. Nixon and Gerald R. Ford to build air and naval facilities in Diego Garcia, a British-controlled island 1,000 miles south of India. Critics warned that the project would provoke Russia to step up its naval deployments into the Indian Ocean. (*1975 Almanac, p. 383*)

But in 1975, the Ford administration finally prevailed, and construction began. At that point, the only U.S. force stationed anywhere near the Persian Gulf was the Navy's Middle East Force — a couple of destroyers and an unarmed flagship based in the emirate of Bahrain to show the flag.

A Real Mideast Presence

The shift to a much more robust presence that could quickly be reinforced came in two stages. The first big change came after an Islamic fundamentalist regime replaced Iran's pro-American Shah Mohammed Reza Pahlevi in early 1979 and the Soviet Union occupied Afghanistan at the end of that year. Seeing a threat to Per-

sian Gulf oil supplies, President Jimmy Carter deployed two aircraft carriers to the region and secured rights for U.S. forces to use air and naval bases in Oman, Somalia and Kenya. Quietly, construction of new base facilities also began in Saudi Arabia and other Persian Gulf states.

Meanwhile, two shipbuilding programs began that were reminiscent of McNamara's shelved cargo ship plan. Heavy combat gear and supplies for a Marine brigade were stored in a squadron of large cargo ships anchored at Diego Garcia, with two similar units in the Pacific and Mediterranean. And eight fast container ships were modified to carry the tanks and vehicles of a U.S.-based armored division to the Middle East within 30 days. In addition, the Pentagon resumed production of the C-5 long-range cargo plane.

When President George Bush dispatched U.S. forces to Saudi Arabia in 1990 after Iraq occupied neighboring Kuwait, the new rapid deployment systems performed largely as expected. But top Pentagon leaders acknowledged that, if Iraqi forces had continued their assault toward the Saudi oil fields rather than hunkering down in Kuwait, the U.S. forces on the scene in the first few months would have been hard-pressed.

So the 1990s saw a second round of initiatives to facilitate deployments to the Persian Gulf and elsewhere. First, 19 additional cargo ships were acquired, including the *Bob Hope*. Some of the new vessels, carrying the equipment for two Army tank brigades, joined the growing armada of supply ships at Diego Garcia; the rest of the new ships were docked in U.S. ports, earmarked to carry a second heavy division to wherever it might be needed.

In addition, agreements were negotiated with Kuwait to station a U.S. Army brigade in the emirate, along with a brigade's worth of equipment. A similar equipment pre-positioning agreement was reached with Qatar. With the deployment of forces for the war in Afghanistan, the overall number of Americans in the region surged late in 2001 .

All told, Brookings Institution military analyst Michael O'Hanlon estimates that the pre-positioned equipment and the high-speed U.S.-based ships would allow the Pentagon to assemble 50,000 troops in the region within 15 days, 100,000 within a month and 200,000 within two months. ◆

Guns and Butter, Again

Cost of war with Iraq would kill any chance of a quick return to balanced budgets

As U.S. forces were sweeping into Iraq in early 1991, George W. Bush's father — then the president — triumphantly declared, "By God, we've kicked the Vietnam syndrome once and for all."

Perhaps not entirely.

The elder President Bush was responding to the nation's newfound pride and confidence in the U.S. military's ability to achieve a clearly defined foreign policy objective. But history appears destined to repeat itself in at least one significant respect: The costly buildup for war has not dented Congress' desire to expand government programs at home. Nor is any sizable faction in Washington calling for tax increases.

In short, Washington is, by gridlocked default, falling squarely into a replay of Lyndon B. Johnson's Vietnam-era resistance to painful remedies on the revenue and the spending sides of the federal ledger to help underwrite the nation's expansive international expenses.

The result is likely to be persistent, large deficits for the foreseeable future. "Congress is currently engaged in a real feeding at the deficit trough, in both domestic and defense spending," said former Rep. Leon E. Panetta of California (1977-93), President Bill Clinton's first budget director and later his chief of staff. "It would be nice if somebody was talking about how the hell we're going to pay for it."

Low Inflation Helps

Even so, few economists are predicting a return to the kind of economic woes that followed a surge in Treasury borrowing related to the Vietnam buildup. For one thing, inflation as measured by the consumer price index is now running at only a 1.8 percent annual rate, a fraction of the 12.3 percent pace in 1974, when the Vietnam war was winding to a close.

In addition, productivity gains,

White House Budget Director Daniels says an Iraq war should be funded through supplemental bills to avoid increases in the baseline for yearly spending.

CQ PHOTO / SCOTT J. FERRELL

which totaled 4.8 percent in the last year — more than double the 2 percent average annual gain in the 1970s — reduce the pressure on companies to raise prices. So for now at least, deficit spending can finance the war on terrorism and any escalating conflict with Iraq without the government paying an immediate price through higher borrowing costs, economists say. (*Borrowing, p. 84*)

President Bush's budget director, Mitchell E. Daniels Jr., while warning against repeating what he considers the "guns and butter" mistakes in the past of allowing big increases in both defense and domestic spending during wartime, acknowledges that the nation is not ready to make the sacrifices necessary to tame the deficit.

"You have to decide what's most important," Daniels said. "If you were to conclude that a balanced budget is of primary importance, second only to national security, then to get there in

short order, you would have to go beyond this year's proposal for slow growth [in domestic spending]. These are the things we have to balance in a democracy."

Deficits do not cause inflation in the short run, according to David Wyss, chief economist at Standard & Poor's. But he said they can lead to price increases if deficits persist when the economy is strong and unemployment is low, because it causes the Federal Reserve to monetize the deficits by pumping extra cash into the economy at a time of strong consumer demand.

Wyss believes there is little danger of inflation over the next three years, although he warned that a war-related surge in oil prices to the $50-a-barrel level could spark another recession.

Allen Schick, a University of Maryland professor of public policy and an expert on the federal budget, said eventually the public might get worried enough about rising deficits to demand action. But if that happens, it will probably pressure Washington to raise taxes — rather than cut spending — if needed to fund a long, costly war.

"You're talking about the possibility, if the economy continues to be weak, of record [annual] budget deficits of $300 billion or more," Schick said.

Political Catch-22

Fiscally conservative House Democrat John Tanner of Tennessee said political courage will be required to save the nation from slipping into a long-term deficit abyss. "At some point leadership has to kick in and say, 'We can't keep going down this road,'" Tanner said.

In a sense, Washington is in a political Catch-22 in terms of dealing with the deficit as long as control of government remains divided. Democrats say the only way to reduce deficits is to consider every option, including halting the phase-in of some of the tax cuts enacted in last year's $1.35 trillion 10-year rev-

Potential Allies View Trade and Aid As Compensation for Cooperation

As the Bush administration tries to win the backing — or at least the quiet acquiescence — of Middle Eastern governments for a war against Iraq, diplomats and lobbyists are compiling wish lists of how the United States might provide compensation for their countries' cooperation.

Nations on the front lines — notably Turkey and Jordan, both close U.S. allies with populations wary of the war talk — will seek to offset the potentially devastating economic effects of such a conflict, according to diplomats and analysts.

"They're going to do everything they can to reduce the consequences and to cash in," said Shibley Telhami, a Middle East expert and Anwar Sadat Professor for Peace and Development at the University of Maryland.

Discussions so far have been carried out discreetly. But if a conflict looks imminent, ideas being floated now likely will become concrete requests, as they did during the 1991 Persian Gulf War. Ahead of that conflict, the United States forgave $6.7 billion in military aid loans to Egypt in return for that country's cooperation. (*1990 Almanac, p. 730*)

The United States paid only a small portion of the cost of that war, however, as Kuwait, Saudi Arabia, Japan, Germany and other countries paid about $54 billion of the $61 billion price tag. (*2002 CQ Weekly, p. 2506*)

Analysts, diplomats and lawmakers say the length of any war with Iraq, including how long the flow of Iraqi oil is disrupted, would affect the eventual price tag of American aid. Decisions about who controls the oil business in a post-Hussein Iraq are likely to be a part of these discussions, they say.

Low-Cost Oil

Jordan, which drew criticism for its perceived tilt toward Iraq in 1991, is now a close U.S. ally and beneficiary of U.S. aid. The United States has not publicly asked Jordan for permission to stage air or ground operations from its soil. Judith Kipper, an expert on the Middle East at the Center for Strategic and International Studies (CSIS) and the Council on Foreign Relations, predicts it will not. "Jordan is too vulnerable. They cannot afford to have American troops transit or use any of their facilities," Kipper said. If the United Nations approves military action, however, analysts predict Jordan will cooperate in some fashion.

Jordanian officials say that while they are doing all they can to avert war, they will seek help from the United States in persuading Saudi Arabia or another nation to provide a replacement for the low-cost oil they currently buy from Iraq under U.N. terms. If that does not happen, they likely will ask the United States for an emergency aid package before any conflict starts, to help them pay for the increased cost of energy.

Sources familiar with the Turkish government say that nation will not base its level of military cooperation on economic or political inducements. They stress, however, that Turkey already lost an estimated $40 billion to $80 billion in reduced trade. Turkey has been an important U.S. military ally, but is worried that a splintered Iraq could have internal political consequences, including greater unrest by its Kurdish minority. Given that, Turkey will not only look for increased U.S. backing for International Monetary Fund loans and some forgiveness on its $5 billion military debt to the United States, but also for longer-term measures.

Turkish businesses favor a renewed push for trade concessions, particularly for the textiles they want to sell to Americans.

The House Ways and Means Committee on Sept. 18 adopted an amendment to its miscellaneous trade legislation (HR 5385) that would expand trade relations with Turkey under the existing Qualified Industrial Zone (QIZ) program. This would allow Turkey to work with Israel to create areas where some products would be eligible for duty-free entry, provided Turkish and Israeli companies both were involved in producing the goods.

Turkish lobbyists and their allies in Congress' New Democrat coalition, however, say the QIZ program would not provide Turkish textile exporters with enough extra access to the U.S. market. "In order to really compensate some of the losses Turkey will face, trade is the single most important area the administration should focus on," said Abdullah Akyuz, president of the Washington

enue reduction package (PL 107-16). Republicans, including Daniels, believe the only way to tame deficits is through strong economic growth, which they say would be stunted if taxes were increased or scheduled future tax cuts aborted. (*2001 Almanac, p. 2-3*)

Sen. John Kerry, D-Mass., cited the growing budget deficit as a reason for Bush to get the world behind the efforts to oust Saddam Hussein. Yet Daniels — and many of Kerry's Democratic colleagues — expect that even if the United Nations can be persuaded to support another full-fledged war with Iraq, the United States probably cannot expect the kind of international financial support it had in the previous war. "There's no corner of the developed world that's in strong financial shape, and so that's probably another difficulty as other nations consider whether they will or won't contribute," Daniels said.

Norm Dicks, D-Wash., a member of the House Appropriations Defense and Military Construction subcommittees, added, "This time it's going to be the United States, it looks like, paying the lion's share of this."

Nor should the nation be expecting income from Iraq's oil fields to help offset the costs of a large-scale invasion, Daniels said. "There are multiple ques-

Allies May Seek U.S. Aid in Return for Help Against Iraq

TURKEY: A staunch U.S. ally in the region, it would like relief on its $5 billion military debt and could ask again for increased access to the U.S. textile market — a move sure to prompt resistance from Southern lawmakers.

BAHRAIN: Just designated a "major non-NATO ally," it now is eligible for training aid and other expanded ties.

PAKISTAN: In return for its continued help in capturing al Qaeda operatives, it wants to sell more inexpensive sheets, pillows and other products in the United States, an idea unpopular with U.S. textile manufacturers.

JORDAN: A major beneficiary of U.S. aid, it wants to ensure the flow of cheap oil and may ask for an emergency aid package.

QATAR: The government wants the U.S. military to remain in the country as a security insurance policy.

office of the Turkish Industrialists' and Businessmen's Association.

Allowing more textile imports, though, could be a tough sell. "My gut feeling is to oppose it, because I see [U.S.] textile workers losing their jobs," said Rep. Howard Coble, R-N.C., head of the congressional textile caucus.

Textile industry opposition whittled down the trade concessions sought by Pakistan, which overnight became a key U.S. ally in rooting out al Qaeda from Afghanistan. Pakistan did win a lifting of nuclear weapons sanctions and $100 million in aid. (*2001 Almanac, p. 11-8; 2002 CQ Weekly, pp. 1166, 491*)

Among the Gulf states, Bahrain already has secured U.S. government status as a "major non-NATO ally," clearing the way for training aid. Plus, the U.S. military is constructing a huge command post for U.S. air operations in the region at Qatar's Al Udeid Air Base, outside Doha. Ob-

servers say that tiny Qatar views Saudi Arabia's regional intentions warily and wants to make sure the United States sticks around after any war with Iraq as an insurance policy.

Human Rights Issues

Analysts say that Egypt could offer its cooperation, or at least its silence, to ensure that the administration and congressional appropriators do not cut off foreign assistance as punishment for human rights violations.

Under the fiscal 2003 foreign operations appropriations bill (HR 5410) approved Sept. 12 by the House Appropriations Committee, Egypt would receive $1.9 billion in aid, with about $1.3 billion earmarked for military assistance, and the rest for economic aid. (*2002 CQ Weekly, p. 2390*)

Some observers question how quick the United States should be to help out all askers. "We have a very

low standard for what constitutes 'helpful' in the Middle East," said Danielle Pletka, a former Senate Foreign Relations Committee aide who now works at the American Enterprise Institute. "With Jordan we're close to being maxed out. There is a limit."

Some observers simply think that congressional appropriators will not be able to stomach these nations' potential demands. Bulent Aliriza, director of the Turkey project at CSIS, noted that "[the Turks] want big bucks, and I don't think you can get big bucks through the Hill."

But for nations that go out on a limb — especially if it is against the will of their populations — U.S. lawmakers may find it hard to say no.

"We have to be prepared to help those countries," said Rep. Jim Kolbe, R-Ariz., chairman of the House Appropriations Committee's subcommittee on foreign operations, export financing and related programs.

tions involving prior claims on oil, and assumptions about what the oil markets would do in response to greater Iraqi production," Daniels said. "Potentially, [income from Iraqi oil] is a significant factor, but probably not one we should count on."

The first budget of Bush's presidency, submitted months before the terrorist attacks on New York and the Pentagon, proposed substantial annual in-

creases in defense spending. However, Republicans and the administration — and many hawkish Democrats — consider those funds catch-up pay for neglected routine needs. They say that any special costs to fight the war on terrorism and potentially resume hostilities with Iraq will come in addition to those baseline defense increases.

The White House expects that supplemental spending bills will continue

to be the primary vehicles for approving the cash needed to buy fuel, pay the costs of calling reservists to duty and maintain equipment. Meanwhile, Congress and the White House are busy sorting out the mechanics of how to get the Pentagon the cash it needs on a timely basis. (*2002 CQ Weekly, p. 2506*)

The White House has made efforts to deal at least partially with the unpredictability of war in the annual budget by creating a $10 billion defense contingency fund that could be allocated at the president's will. That proposal has been roundly rejected by legislators of both parties, who are quick to assert Congress' constitutional authority to direct all federal expenditures.

Appropriators from both parties said they agree that supplementals are the proper way to finance a war. "I don't know how you build a war into a baseline," said House Appropriations Committee Chairman C.W. Bill Young, R-Fla.

Dicks said that in addition to paying direct military costs, supplementals probably will be the vehicles for funding a host of civilian contracts related to the war efforts, including satellite time for telecommunications needs, transportation expenses for moving goods and troops, and purchases of supplies. "A lot of things have to be acquired from the private sector," Dicks said. "You've got to have these things available."

Pressure to Spend

In addition, Daniels said, using supplementals will make it easier to sort out permanent expenses from temporary ones after hostilities eventually subside. "There is a tendency always for surges in spending to be incorporated in the base, and then you never get them out," Daniels said. "Wars have sometimes left bigger governance and more spending than was really in the national interest, and it's also been true with surges in domestic spending."

However, advancing large "war" supplementals — perhaps multiple measures in some years — could conflict with the administration's goals of holding down spending on items unrelated to the war, because supplementals often become vehicles for members' special home-state projects.

In addition, supplementals can be time-consuming, slowing work on the 13 regular annual spending bills because the appropriators focus their attention largely on supplementals while they are in play. For example, the supplemental spending request Bush submitted to Congress earlier this year (PL 107-206) took four months to complete. (*2002 CQ Weekly, p. 1931*)

But so far, Congress has shown no sense of urgency while it awaits details of financing the nation's expanding military commitments, while also guarding domestic programs most members believe the public wants them to protect. ◆

War May Not Hurt Economy

A jump in Treasury Department borrowing to finance a war with Iraq is unlikely to cause an immediate spike in interest rates, economists say. But a war's long-term impact on the U.S. economy is more likely to depend on what happens to the price of oil and inflation in the years to come.

Lawrence Lindsey, the president's chief economic adviser, told the Wall Street Journal that even if the cost of a war equals 1 percent to 2 percent of the gross domestic product (GDP), the cost would be manageable. With the GDP now topping $10 trillion a year, that translates into $100 billion to $200 billion, an estimate the administration disavowed as too high.

Economists say even a $100 billion price tag would not roil the Treasury bond market. The thinking is that because economic growth already is so sluggish — and interest rates are at four-decade lows — additional Treasury borrowing would not immediately lead to a rise in the cost of buying a car, financing a home, or expanding a business. In practical terms, it is less costly to go to war with a weak economy.

"You almost never see countries in the midst of an economic boom engage in saber-rattling," said Barry P. Bosworth, an economist at the Brookings Institution.

Then, too, nervous investors have fled the stock market in droves in recent months in favor of safer investments, such as Treasury bonds. "In this environment, where stocks are weak, there is very little competition for money," said Tony J. Crescenzi, chief bond market strategist at Miller Tabak & Co.

Paying Down Debt

Because the federal budget moved into surplus during President Bill Clinton's second term, the Treasury was able to pay down $421.9 billion of the federal debt in the last four years, reducing the amount held by the public to $3.34 trillion.

Still, the government needs to sell new securities monthly to pay off existing issues with maturities ranging from four weeks to 30 years — and starting again this year, to finance deficit spending. A preliminary estimate shows Treasury public debt sales rose to $3.69 trillion in the fiscal year ending Sept. 30 from $2.47 trillion in fiscal 2001, in part because the fiscal 2002 deficit likely rose to $165 billion or more. (*2002 CQ Weekly, p. 2238*)

The Bush administration's Treasury Department ended the sale of 30-year bonds in October 2001 and essentially extended a bet first placed by the Clinton administration to save money by concentrating borrowing in debt with relatively short maturities. Two-year Treasury debt now yields 1.97 percent, for example, while 10-year notes yield 3.75 percent, and the last 30-year bonds were sold in August 2001 with a yield of 5.52 percent.

Inflation Risk

But that strategy could backfire if interest rates do go up, some on Wall Street warn. "That's the kind of thing professional investors do," Crescenzi said of the government's strategy. "That's not what a conservative government should do."

The risk is that if a war-related spike in oil prices were to persist, it could boost the U.S. inflation rate, which in the past usually has been a precursor to higher interest rates.

The most active crude oil futures now sell for $30.64 a barrel, up from a recent low of $17.72 a barrel in November 2001. Morgan Stanley economist Richard Berner says a $10 per barrel price increase would be "associated" with a 0.5 percent reduction, or $50 billion, in the GDP.

The administration is counting on Saudi Arabia and other countries to step up production if the flow of oil from Iraq, which possesses the world's second-largest proven reserves, is stopped even briefly.

But if the conflict were to spread throughout the Middle East, and disrupt the flow of oil from the entire region, all bets would be off.

Parties Use Judicial Standoff To Play to Core Constituents

Senate acrimony over nominations is at its worst in years, unlikely to improve

Under Hatch, left, then Leahy, the process of selecting and confirming federal judges has grown increasingly rancorous and political, with Democrats and Republicans using the fight to make polarizing appeals to their bases.

I t was exactly 15 years ago this month — Oct. 23, 1987 — that the Senate rejected the Supreme Court nomination of Robert H. Bork.

When it was over, after weeks of scorched-earth partisanship and 23 hours of floor debate over President Ronald Reagan's conservative nominee, West Virginia Democrat Robert C. Byrd counseled his colleagues that it was time to "start the healing, to lower our voices." (*1987 Almanac, p. 2600*)

And, for a time, there was relative peace. But it did not last. Today, near the end of the 107th Congress, the Senate is more bitterly divided over judicial nominees than at any time since Bork.

Increasingly, Democrats and Republicans have come to view the fight over federal judges as another powerful way to mobilize their base on Election Day — drawing a clear connection between the ideological balance of the courts and the balance of power on such hot-button issues as abortion and gun control.

Neither party wants to compromise, just as neither will give up closely held positions on such politically potent legislation as pension overhaul or a prescription drug benefit for seniors. Instead, they are taking the dispute to the voters.

The standoff has eroded the president's authority to shape the federal judiciary, leaving a sometimes understaffed bench where some vacancies have gone unfilled for years. At the same time, the concerted effort by parties to link judicial nominations to political ends threatens to undermine the public's confidence in the independence and integrity of the courts, say scholars who study judicial selection.

As the process for selecting and confirming judges becomes more political — and ideology plays a larger role — the judiciary could be tainted, said Sheldon Goldman, a political science professor at the University of Massachusetts at Amherst. Or, just as problematic, it could appear so.

"The problem is that it's been ratcheted up over the last 12 to 14 years," said Goldman, who has long studied the confirmation process. "It's spiraling out of control. It's in great danger, the judicial branch of the government."

The process began deteriorating when Republicans controlled the Senate during the Clinton administration, and with each election cycle it has grown more polarized and more political. Republicans, who accuse Democrats of stalling on President Bush's nominees in an effort to keep conservatives off the court, have retaliated by placing holds on almost all legislation coming out of the Senate Judiciary Committee. (*2002 CQ Weekly, p. 2665*)

Minority Leader Trent Lott, R-Miss., took to the floor Oct. 16 to complain loudly about Judiciary Chairman

How Bush Nominees Have Fared

In January 2001, just before President Bush was sworn in, there were 80 vacant seats on the U.S. District Court and Court of Appeals. The number now stands at 77. In July 1997, during the Clinton administration, the number of vacancies reached 102. A year and a half later, the number had been cut in half — to 50 vacancies, the lowest in recent years. Here is a look at the number of authorized seats (in parentheses), the current number of vacancies, nominees pending and Bush nominees confirmed for each of the 12 circuits. Seventeen District Court nominees still could be confirmed this year.

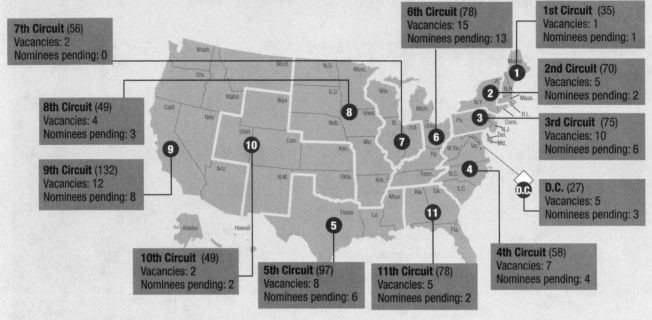

7th Circuit (56)
Vacancies: 2
Nominees pending: 0

8th Circuit (49)
Vacancies: 4
Nominees pending: 3

9th Circuit (132)
Vacancies: 12
Nominees pending: 8

10th Circuit (49)
Vacancies: 2
Nominees pending: 2

5th Circuit (97)
Vacancies: 8
Nominees pending: 6

11th Circuit (78)
Vacancies: 5
Nominees pending: 2

4th Circuit (58)
Vacancies: 7
Nominees pending: 4

6th Circuit (78)
Vacancies: 15
Nominees pending: 13

1st Circuit (35)
Vacancies: 1
Nominees pending: 1

2nd Circuit (70)
Vacancies: 5
Nominees pending: 2

3rd Circuit (75)
Vacancies: 10
Nominees pending: 6

D.C. (27)
Vacancies: 5
Nominees pending: 3

SOURCE: U.S. Senate Judiciary Committee/USCourts.gov

Patrick J. Leahy's handling of the process, accusing the Vermont Democrat of an "extraordinary and unprecedented violation of Senate rules and tradition."

Senate leaders are trying to come to an agreement that would allow them to vote this year on 17 District Court nominees that are pending in the Senate. But more than half of Bush's appeals court nominees — some of them nominated nearly 18 months ago — are still stuck in committee. The nominations almost certainly will die with the conclusion of this Congress.

And with the Senate expected to remain closely divided after Nov. 5, there will be ample motivation for both sides to keep fighting. Democrats and Republicans will be looking ahead to the 2004 elections, which will determine who controls both the White House and the Senate. They also will be positioning themselves for a battle over the next Supreme Court vacancy, the first since 1994.

No Going Back?

The process has become so acrimonious that it will be difficult to fix, said Elliot Slotnick, a political science professor at Ohio State University. Detente is still possible, if both sides agree to cool their rhetoric and work together, he said. But if things continue as they have in recent years, the process of vetting and confirming nominees could be changed irrevocably.

The Senate is at a crossroads, Slotnick said.

"The longer this stuff goes on, the more I think it becomes institutionalized, and that's the real danger," he said.

The power to make lifetime appointments to the federal bench is one of the president's most significant prerogatives. But under the Constitution, the Senate must give its "advice and consent." Over the past eight years, the Senate Judiciary Committee — first under Republican Orrin G. Hatch of Utah and now Leahy — has demanded a greater role. Leahy has said his committee will never be a "rubber stamp" for the White House, and he has used that position to justify the committee's rejection of two nominees.

At the same time, senators and interest groups have turned their focus to the lower courts, particularly the Court of Appeals. With the Supreme Court hearing a smaller share of the cases filed each term, the appeals courts more often have the final word on controversial issues. Consequently, the scrutiny of those nominees and the resulting partisan battles have grown more frequent and more intense. (2002 *CQ Weekly*, p. 531)

All eyes also are on the lower courts, because membership on the Supreme Court has been unusually stable. The court's makeup has not changed since Stephen G. Breyer was confirmed as a justice in 1994 — the longest stretch without change on the court since the early 19th century. Some advocates see the contest over the appellate courts as a warm-up for a battle over a spot on the Supreme Court.

A stable court, too, tends to take a more limited and predictable range of cases, leaving lower courts wide latitude in many areas, such as affirmative action, said Elliot Mincberg, legal director for the liberal advocacy group People for the American Way. That has caused groups such as Mincberg's to pay closer attention to lower-court nominees.

Interest groups, voters and lawmakers all have come to see a

Judiciary Chairman Leahy Shrugs Off GOP Barbs

Republicans often invoke the names of Sen. Edward M. Kennedy, D-Mass., and Senate Majority Leader Tom Daschle, D-S.D., to rally the troops.

Now, GOP fundraisers have added another Democrat — Patrick J. Leahy — to the list of liberals Republicans love to hate.

As chairman of the Senate Judiciary Committee, Leahy has become a lightning rod for his handling — Republicans say mistreatment — of President Bush's judicial nominees.

The Republican faithful "see Patrick Leahy says one thing and does another," said Dan Allen, spokesman for the National Republican Senatorial Committee.

The senior senator from Vermont shrugs off the criticism. "The last election up here I got 75 percent of the vote," he said, joking: "It's really hurting me."

Vermont prizes independent thinkers, he said. "I recall the last time the [GOP was] critical of a Vermonter it was Jim Jeffords," Leahy said. Jeffords, I-Vt., decided to leave the Republican Party in May 2001, ensuring the Senate would fall into Democratic hands.

Leahy, a former prosecutor, says he has tried to restore some efficiency to the judicial confirmation process. During his nearly two years at the head of the Judiciary Committee, Leahy has tried to speed through Bush's least controversial nominees — mostly those to U.S. District Court.

If the Senate ultimately confirms 17 District Court nominees that have been reported out of the Judiciary Committee, nearly 100 of Bush's judicial nominees will have been confirmed during the 107th.

"We will get through 100 judges in about 15 months," Leahy said. "And I think that's a success."

But some Republicans would argue with Leahy's assertion. Leahy's GOP critics have questioned the chairman's motivations, arguing he appears to be in the pocket of liberal advocacy organizations such as People for the American Way and the Alliance for Justice.

"It makes me wonder — as I have on many prior occasions — who is really running this committee," said Orrin G. Hatch of Utah, the ranking Republican on the Judiciary Committee. "Quite frankly, it seems that the answer is that the liberal special interest groups are the ones who call the shots around here. When they say, 'Jump,' some appear to say, 'How high?'"

Outside observers credit Leahy with bringing many of Bush's nominees to a vote. Democrats have accused Republicans of bottling up many of President Bill Clinton's nominees in committee.

Under Leahy, controversial nominees slowly are being brought to votes, said Elliot Slotnick, a political science professor at Ohio State University. Under Republicans, during the Clinton administration, the gridlock was near total, he said.

"It may be the case at this very moment, but I think the situation has been far from gridlock during the past year," Slotnick said. "The record of speed and confirmation is not anything like it was during the Clinton years."

One of Leahy's first acts as chairman was to shed sunlight on a procedural method that can be used to stall nominees — the blue slip process. Under the tradition, home-state senators must give their blessing — by returning blue slips — on a nominee before the Judiciary Committee will go forward.

Leahy still will not move forward on nominees who have not had blue slips returned, but he has made the blue slip information public. Now the opposition to Bush's nominees is more public than ever before.

If Democrats keep their majority in the Senate, Leahy says he has no plans to change his style.

clear connection between the federal judiciary and policy, said Goldman, the University of Massachusetts professor. They understand that the shape of the courts has a great deal to do with the shape of policy.

"There's a greater recognition that judges do make public policy," Goldman said. "It's the triumph of legal realism."

Goldman and others note that when the Supreme Court weighed in on recounts of Florida election ballots in the 2000 presidential election, the judiciary's perceived connection to public policy and politics was cemented.

"It made it so much more appar-ent," Goldman said. "It drove it all home: The contest over the courts is a contest over public policy."

On the Campaign Trail

Political parties — particularly Republicans — clearly see the issue's power to rally their base.

Although conventional wisdom holds that fights over nominations do not resonate with voters, Republican strategists say their core supporters are paying attention.

The GOP is talking about the confirmation process "more this cycle than we ever have," said a Senate GOP aide. "This gives us more evidence of why we need Republicans in control of the Senate."

Dan Allen, spokesman for the National Republican Senatorial Committee (NRSC) said the same: "For the base, you definitely see they have an understanding of who is in control of the judicial nomination process and who is obstructing the president's nominees," Allen said. "It's just one more example that our base is seeing: The Democrats are just holding up President Bush's agenda."

The issue does not play well every-

Success Rates for Judicial Nominations

How the past five presidents' nominations for federal (district and appeals court) judges have fared in the first two years of each term. Percentages in red indicate times when different parties controlled the White House and Senate.

PRESIDENT	NUMBER OF NOMINATIONS	PERCENT CONFIRMED
Jimmy Carter	69	93%
Ronald Reagan (1st term)	90	98%
Ronald Reagan (2nd term)	141	91%
George Bush	74	95%
Bill Clinton (1st term)	141	90%
Bill Clinton (2nd term)	105	70%
George W. Bush	130	62%

SOURCE: Congressional Research Service

where, but it has become important in some races. In the race for the Senate seat that South Carolina Republican Strom Thurmond is vacating, GOP Rep. Lindsey Graham repeatedly has invoked the name of Dennis Shedd, a nominee to the 4th U.S. Circuit Court of Appeals. Shedd has been waiting for a vote since May 2001.

In Texas, candidates vying for retiring Republican Phil Gramm's seat in the Senate have tangled over 5th Circuit nominee Priscilla Owen, a Texas Supreme Court justice. The Judiciary Committee rejected Owen's nomination in September. (2002 CQ *Weekly*, p. 2304)

The Democrat in that Senate race, former Dallas Mayor Ron Kirk, said he would have voted against Owen if he had been in the Senate.

In turn, the NRSC and the Texas GOP castigated Kirk in a radio ad, saying, "It's just plain wrong when politicians play politics with judicial appointments." The ad said Kirk is joining the "liberal crusade" of "special interests in Washington . . . out to stop Priscilla Owen and President Bush."

Bush has brought up the issue repeatedly on the campaign trail. "The Senate is doing a lousy job on my judge nominations," Bush said during an Oct. 14 campaign stop in Michigan.

He said there are numerous "reasons why we need to change the Senate [including making] sure that the federal bench represents the way you want them to serve."

In trying to drive home the importance of retaking control of the Senate, Republicans have highlighted the nominations process. A Senate GOP aide notes that the message is being delivered most in states with tossup Senate races.

"It is becoming a very effective message tool to reach out to new voters — Hispanics and women — and to motivate their base," the aide said.

The aide noted that the stalled nomination of Miguel Estrada, who would be the first Hispanic on the influential Court of Appeals for the D.C. Circuit, has begun to play well with some constituencies. "That is in fact becoming message material in states with Hispanic populations," the aide said.

Democrats and liberal groups have used the issue much less in their campaign messages, but they have raised it.

"The public is much more engaged in this issue than I think the White House has realized," said Nan Aron, president of the Alliance for Justice. "This issue has gained a great deal of visibility over the past two years."

People for the American Way, one of the groups that led the charge

against Owen and other Bush nominees, plans to begin airing a television spot touting the importance of maintaining a Democratic majority in the Senate in order to keep vetting Bush's nominees. As pictures of Hatch, Lott and conservative Supreme Court Justices Antonin Scalia and Clarence Thomas flash by, an announcer tells viewers that "unchecked" Republican power "would be devastating for a woman's right to choose, our environment, social security and corporate accountability — and could guarantee a Supreme Court controlled by the far right for decades."

The ad will air in states with tight Senate races.

Nominees Bottled Up

Tension over nominations has been building in the Senate all year, escalating in March when the Judiciary Committee rejected 5th Circuit nominee Charles W. Pickering Sr., and then again in September when it rejected Owen. (2002 CQ *Weekly*, p. 702)

Then, the week of Oct. 7, Leahy announced that he had indefinitely postponed a vote on Shedd. A week later, Republicans were still angry, in part because they saw it as a personal insult to the retiring Thurmond. Shedd, now a U.S. district judge in South Carolina, served as the Judiciary Committee's chief counsel when Thurmond was chairman.

Thurmond said Leahy had promised a vote on Shedd before the year was out. (2002 CQ *Weekly*, p. 2665)

In an Oct. 11 letter to Hatch, the ranking Republican on the Judiciary Committee, Leahy said he "would have liked to have been able to proceed," but "the debate on the Shedd nomination promised to be contentious and extended" and might not leave the committee enough time before the Senate adjourned to vote on a group of District Court nominees, as well as other items on the panel's agenda.

Judiciary Republicans, in an Oct. 16 reply to Leahy, said his explanation has "served only to exacerbate, rather than soothe, the wounds created by the unacceptable manner in which the committee has treated Sen. Thurmond and the nomination of Dennis Shedd."

Republicans also complain that Leahy has failed to consider all of Bush's judicial nominees. More than two dozen nominees — including some Bush announced May 9, 2001 — are pending before the Judiciary Committee and likely will have to be resubmitted by Bush next year.

But Democrats say the Judiciary Committee has sped through Bush's nominations at a rate far faster than Republicans considered former President Bill Clinton's, particularly during the final years of Clinton's second term.

"If I can do more in 15 months than they did in the previous 30, I'd say that this is a case of changing what I inherited," Leahy said. "I'm happy with the record we've had."

Democrats argue that Leahy has waded through a huge number of nominees, especially given everything he and the committee have had to contend with since Sept. 11, including anti-terrorism legislation (PL 107-56) and an anthrax-laced letter mailed to Leahy's office.

Democrats also point out they did not take control of the Senate until six months after the 107th Congress convened.

"If we go back, we would recognize there are a number of nominees who waited three and four years, and never even got a hearing," Majority Leader Tom Daschle, D-S.D., said Oct. 16. "Mr. Shedd was at least given a hearing. . . . That is far more than what a number of the nominees were given over the course of the Clinton administration."

In his first two years in office, Bush submitted 131 judicial nominations to the Senate — 32 to the U.S. Circuit Court of Appeals, 98 to the U.S. District Courts and one to the U.S. Court of International Trade.

The full Senate has confirmed 80 of those nominees — 14 to the Court of Appeals and 66 to District Court. Another 18 nominees have been approved by the Judiciary Committee and are pending before the Senate. Whether that group — one circuit court nominee endorsed by the Judiciary Committee in July and 17 District Court nominees approved by the panel Oct. 8 — will be confirmed this year is an open question.

Daschle and Lott are working to reach an agreement for moving those and Bush's executive nominees. Under Senate tradition, nominees on the Senate calendar generally are confirmed before a Congress adjourns.

Talks continued Oct. 17, but Daschle and Lott reached no final deal.

"The atmosphere is so poisoned by what we saw with Judge Shedd — and before that with Priscilla Owen, and before that with Charles Pickering —

High Court Rejections Shift Focus to Appeals Courts

Over the past nine sessions, the Supreme Court agreed to hear fewer than 2 percent of the cases filed. Last year, the court rejected more than 9,000 cases, letting the lower court rulings stand. As a result, appeals courts are playing a more important role in setting law. Meanwhile, the appellate court caseload has grown.

Appeals rejected by the Supreme Court

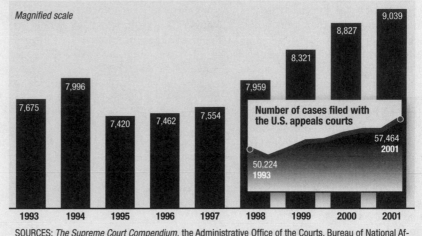

SOURCES: *The Supreme Court Compendium*, the Administrative Office of the Courts, Bureau of National Affairs U.S. Law Week, U.S. Supreme Court Clerk's Office

that I don't know if we're going to be able to move a thing," Lott said. "I'm going to try because I think there's some innocent people who are having their nominations delayed."

If the Senate remains in Democratic hands after the November elections, the process is not likely to change substantively. Leahy and other Judiciary Democrats, such as Charles E. Schumer of New York, have called repeatedly on the White House to consult more with home-state senators about Bush's choices for the judiciary, and they have promised to keep scrutinizing every nominee.

"If the Democrats continue to maintain control over the Senate, it is my sense they will continue to insist on meaningful participation in the process," Aron said. "If the Bush administration continues to nominate people without consultation, the Democrats will continue to put up a fight."

The fight could get even uglier if Republicans retake the Senate in November. Their margin of control is likely to be narrow, and there are a number of procedural tools Democrats could use to slow consideration of Bush nominees.

One of those tools is a filibuster, an extended debate to tie up the Senate and prevent a nominee from coming to

a vote on the floor. The GOP is certain to have less than the 60 seats that would be needed to guarantee they could block a filibuster.

Threat of Filibuster

Slotkin and Goldman said if Republicans do control the Senate, a controversial nominee who made it through the Judiciary Committee almost certainly would be met with an attempted filibuster in the Senate.

Democrats already have hinted at the possibility, especially if Republican leaders decide to push Pickering and Owen through the confirmation process again. Lott and administration officials have indicated they would revisit those nominees if the GOP retakes the majority.

Such a move "would be a mistake," Schumer said, adding if that happens, "We'll have to get in our caucus and determine [what to do]."

He did not rule out the possibility of a filibuster. "We'll cross that bridge when we come to it," he said. "I still think we'll keep the Senate."

Liberal groups say Democrats ought to consider a filibuster in some cases.

"We of course would always recommend that the Senate Democrats and

Republicans take their advice and consent responsibility seriously," said Ralph G. Neas, president of People for the American Way. "But if you have egregious nominees who really do want to not interpret the law but make the law — we're talking about the Owens and Pickerings — then the filibuster should be an option."

Another option for Democrats would be to force a vote to send nominees back to the Judiciary Committee — a tactic that has been employed with at least one Supreme Court nominee in the past.

No judicial nominee for a seat on the district or appeals courts has ever been rejected because of a filibuster, although senators have tried. Leaders have moved to cut off potentially lengthy debate on some nominations.

In the past 35 years, the Senate has tried to limit debate by invoking cloture on 13 judicial nominees. Only one — the 1968 nomination of Supreme Court Justice Abe Fortas to be chief justice — failed a cloture vote, 45-43. President Lyndon B. Johnson then withdrew the nomination at Fortas' request. (1968 Almanac, p. 2613)

In four other cases, a motion to limit debate failed or was withdrawn — but in all of those situations, the nominee ultimately was confirmed.

When the Senate in 1971 considered the Supreme Court nomination of William H. Rehnquist, a motion to invoke cloture failed 52-42, but Rehnquist later was confirmed. In the 106th Congress, a cloture vote on District Court nominee Ted Stewart also failed, but Stewart likewise was confirmed. (1971 Almanac, p. 111; 1999 Almanac, pp. 18-49, 18-54)

Setting New Ground Rules

Filibustering a lower court nominee would only deepen the rancor in the Senate, Republicans say. "They could do that, but it would break tradition," Lott said.

Jon Kyl, a Republican on the Judiciary Committee who frequently has rebuked panel Democrats for their handling of Bush's nominees, said employing a filibuster or other procedural moves to block a nominee could be dangerous in the long run.

"I've been in the majority and I've been in the minority, and the temptation is to take advantage of the situation in which you find yourself," Kyl said. "But you have to remember . . .

situations change."

Liberal advocates say Republicans who controlled the Senate during Clinton's last six years in office essentially filibustered his nominees by tying many up in committee.

"They prevented so many qualified nominees from getting hearings that their actions constituted a virtual filibuster," said Aron, president of the Alliance for Justice.

Democrats point to the 9th Circuit nominations of Richard A. Paez and Marcia L. Berzon, which were held up for years. Paez, nominated by Clinton in 1996, was confirmed in 2000. (2000 Almanac, p. 15-41)

But his long path to confirmation was rocky. The Judiciary Committee first endorsed Paez in March 1998, but Clinton had to resubmit the nomination in 1999 after the 105th Congress adjourned without confirming him.

The Judiciary Committee endorsed Paez again in July 1999, but his nomination was pending before the Senate until March 2000. Before the Senate voted March 8, 2000, to confirm both Paez and Berzon, members voted 85-14 to invoke cloture on Paez and 86-13 to invoke cloture on Berzon.

But even in 2000, the battle over Paez and Berzon was not nearly as acrimonious as now. And until Democrats and Republicans admit culpability, the situation is never going to improve, Goldman said.

The parties need to agree on a "new set of ground rules," such as promising every nominee a hearing and a vote in the Judiciary Committee, he said.

"The only way out of this imbroglio is for the Democrats and Republicans to say both sides have sinned: 'We've sinned equally and this is not functional for the judiciary,' " Goldman said. "The only way out of it is if the president and the senators, both Democrats and Republicans, look upon this as something that has to be worked out in a bipartisan way."

Liberal groups say it is vital for the White House to reach out to Senate Democrats.

"I hope that would change, but certainly, in light of the evidence, it doesn't seem like they want to change," Neas said. "If the president is going to continue to send Pickerings and Owens and those kind of nominees, I would hope the Senate Republicans will resist."

Senators and presidents have been able to come to an accord before. Gold-

man points to President Richard M. Nixon, who saw two Supreme Court nominees blocked by the Senate.

Fortas, the Supreme Court justice whose 1968 nomination to head the court had failed a cloture vote, continued for a time as an associate justice after Johnson withdrew his name. But he resigned early in the Nixon administration over evidence of financial misconduct.

Nixon first tried to fill the vacancy with Clement F. Haynsworth Jr., an appellate judge who was well respected but faced some of the same charges that forced Fortas to resign. Haynsworth also was accused of being hostile to civil rights groups, and ultimately, his nomination was rejected 45-55.

Stung by Haynsworth's rejection, Nixon in 1970 nominated G. Harrold Carswell, an undistinguished and relatively unknown appellate judge, for associate justice. Although it initially appeared Carswell would be confirmed, he ended up being rejected because of what senators perceived as his racial bias and less-than-stellar intellect. (1970 Almanac, p. 903)

"In 1969 and 1970, it was very bitter," Goldman said. "After Fortas was forced off the bench, it was acrimonious."

Seven days after Carswell's rejection, Nixon, who had abandoned his search for candidates in the South, nominated appellate judge Harry A. Blackmun for the Supreme Court post. (1970 Almanac, p. 1044)

Like Carswell and Haynsworth, Blackmun was perceived as a conservative, but after he was confirmed to the Supreme Court, Blackmun became one of its most liberal members.

"Only after Harry Blackmun was nominated" did the tenor of the confirmation process improve, Goldman said. "He was very conservative at that time, but his credentials were sterling; they heaved a great sigh of relief that here was somebody they could support. They saw it spiraling out of control. Nixon also saw it spiraling out of control."

A similar opportunity came after Reagan saw Supreme Court nominee Bork rejected by the Senate. Reagan turned to Anthony Kennedy to fill the open spot on the high court. Kennedy was perceived as far more moderate than Bork, Goldman said, and he breezed through. (1988 Almanac, p. 26)

"If he had another really hard-right clone of Bork," Goldman said, "who knows . . . what the outcome would have been?" ◆

Politics and Public Policy

The term *public policymaking* refers to action taken by the government to address issues on the public agenda; it also refers to the method by which a decision to act on policy is reached. The work of the president, Congress, the judiciary and the bureaucracy is to make, implement and rule on policy decisions. Articles in this section discuss major policy issues that came before the federal government in the second half of 2002.

The first two articles examine House and Senate committee agendas and leadership changes in the upcoming 108th Congress. Although the House will see few changes in leadership, the Senate will witness many of them as Republicans take control of the chamber and name new committee chairs. Committee and subcommittee chairs are powerful and influential, and their actions and decisions affect the policy making of Congress. The first article summarizes the membership changes and upcoming agendas for all of the House committees. The second article begins with a brief summary of changes in Senate committee chairs, followed by more detailed examinations of the Senate Appropriations, Armed Services, Finance and Judiciary Committees.

The other articles focus on the roles of Congress and the administration in making policies on energy, the environment and trade. The first article explores the need for a national energy policy, particularly one addressing oil production and consumption. The article examines the positions of Congress, the Bush administration and the American public on the issues of foreign oil, energy conservation and oil drilling in Alaska.

The next article examines the controversies surrounding environmental laws. Tensions between businesses and environmental activists have made compromise difficult for Congress. Indeed, Congress was unable to enact any significant environmental legislation in 2002.

The final article reveals how complicated foreign policy decisions can become. Twenty years ago, Congress passed the Jackson-Vanick trade law with the intent of helping Soviet Jews emigrate to Israel. Since the disintegration of the Soviet Union, the law has become an impediment to trade with Russia; each year the president must waive the trade restrictions against Russia and other former Soviet republics. Congress, however, is reluctant to repeal the law because of concerns related to U.S. chicken exportation and World Trade Organization issues. The matter is complicated by Russia's economic ties to Iran and Iraq as President George W. Bush seeks Russia's cooperation in the war on terrorism. How do these factors affect the future of U.S.–Russia relations?

GOP Victories Could Mean Less Mobility in 108th

Dan Burton the only committee chairman losing his seat to term limits

There will be much less shuffling of chairs when House committees organize for the 108th Congress than occurred two years ago. Then, Republican term limits for committee and subcommittee chairmen prompted changes on nearly every major committee.

With the GOP successfully protecting and expanding its House majority Nov. 5, only three House committees — Armed Services, Government Reform and Resources — are expected to be under the leadership of new chairmen in January.

The only committee chairman who will be forced out by the six-year limit is the Government Reform Committee's Dan Burton, R-Ind. Three other Republicans are interested in replacing him.

Western Republicans are eager to keep control of the Resources panel after the retirement of James V. Hansen, R-Utah. But next in line by virtue of seniority is moderate H. James Saxton of New Jersey.

Still to be determined are the ratios of Republican and Democratic seats on the following 20 House panels.

AGRICULTURE

With a farm law recently enacted, the Agriculture Committee is expecting a relatively light workload during the 108th Congress.

The panel's West Texas leadership team will be unchanged, as both Chairman Larry Combest, a Republican, and ranking Democrat Charles W. Stenholm return. The two lawmakers represent neighboring districts in the Texas panhandle.

The committee is likely to focus on the Agriculture Department's implementation of the farm law (PL 107-171). Several legislators have questioned the department's interpretation of several provisions of the complicated measure.

Management of national forests is another issue likely to come up. The farm law's authors largely dodged controversial forest issues in drafting the statute.

Western lawmakers have been pushing a bill (HR 5319) that would overhaul federal forest management and are expected to renew their efforts in the new Congress. Committee members also may be involved in efforts to overhaul the federal tobacco quota program.

A few senior members of the committee are retiring or were defeated in re-election bids. Saxby Chambliss, R-Ga., won election to the Senate. Senior Democrat Eva Clayton of North Carolina is retiring. Second-ranking committee

Democrat Gary A. Condit of California lost his primary election.

APPROPRIATIONS

After a shuffling of subcommittee chairmanships for the 107th Congress, the powerful committee expects much less change among its "cardinals" heading into the new Congress.

Chairman C.W. Bill Young, R-Fla., and ranking Democrat David R. Obey of Wisconsin remain in place. The two men have established a good working relationship even in the midst of partisan warfare.

Two cardinals with plum assignments — Joe Skeen, R-N.M., of the Interior panel and Sonny Callahan, R-Ala., at Energy and Water — are retiring. It will be up to Young to award the coveted chairmanships. While seniority is a guide, other factors including party and committee fealty could play a role.

Among those likely to be looking to trade in less powerful subcommittee posts for the Energy and Water and Interior jobs are District of Columbia Subcommittee Chairman Joe Knollenberg, R-Mich., Military Construction Subcommittee Chairman David L. Hobson, R-Ohio, and Legislative Branch Subcommittee Chairman Charles H. Taylor, R-N.C.

Knollenberg previously served on the Energy and Water panel and is interested in that chairmanship. Taylor, a forester, is a member of the Interior panel.

Once senior members are accommodated, two new cardinals will be ordained. Jack Kingston, R-Ga., is next in line in seniority. Three members of the House GOP's Class of 1994 — Rodney Frelinghuysen of New Jersey, Roger Wicker of Mississippi, and George Nethercutt of Washington — would be likely contenders for the final chairmanship.

No changes are expected in the Democratic roster of ranking minority members.

ARMED SERVICES

With Duncan Hunter, R-Calif., in line to become chairman, the Armed Services panel is likely to take on a more ambitious agenda reflecting his activist bent.

In general, the committee's long record of bipartisan support for the armed services is expected to continue. But Hunter's independence could make him a sometimes demanding ally for the Bush administration.

Hunter has objected to President Bush's past and projected defense budgets, calling them too small to fund military operations and new weaponry. He also has challenged the services on technical and organizational issues. In the early 1980s, he pressed the Navy to build submarines incorporating new technologies.

The most immediate question is whether Hunter will try to realign the subcommittees so that a single panel can oversee each weapons system through research and production. The Senate Armed Services Committee adopted such a procedure in the 1980s.

The 54-year-old Hunter will succeed 75-year-old Bob Stump, R-Ariz. The only subcommittee chairmanship falling vacant is Hunter's. Because House GOP rules allow each member only one committee or subcommittee chairmanship, Hunter will have to give up the gavel at Military Research and Development. The senior Republican on the committee who does not head a House subcommittee is William M. "Mac" Thornberry of Texas.

Ike Skelton of Missouri will continue to lead committee Democrats. All five subcommittee ranking minority members were re-elected on Nov. 5.

BUDGET

When President Bush sends his fiscal 2004 budget to Congress, he will again be able to count on a key ally in Budget Committee Chairman Jim Nussle, R-Iowa.

The committee's primary responsibility next year, writing an annual budget resolution that may include reconciliation instructions for additional tax cuts, is likely to once again be a partisan process. Nussle, who was re-elected to a seventh term on Nov. 5, is a Bush loyalist who endorsed the president's fiscal 2003 budget proposal even though it included a deficit. He can be expected to work to impose the Bush fiscal agenda on unenthusiastic appropriators who would prefer more spending.

The House adopted Nussle's fiscal 2003 budget resolution (H Con Res 353), but the Senate never voted on a budget. That scenario is unlikely to be repeated next year with the GOP in control of both chambers.

Committee Democrats will continue to balk at administration efforts to keep a rein on domestic spending. John M. Spratt Jr., S.C., will remain the committee's top Democrat, as the minority decides whether offering an alternate budget this year is worth the effort. In the House, budget resolution votes usually follow party lines.

The committee will lose its second-ranking Republican as John E. Sununu moves to the New Hampshire Senate seat he won on Nov. 5. Van Hilleary of Tennessee, an unsuccessful GOP gubernatorial candidate, also will be gone. Wes Watkins, R-Okla., is retiring.

Ken Bentsen, D-Texas, lost a Senate primary. Also departing are Democrats Bob Clement of Tennessee, who lost a Senate race, and the retiring Eva Clayton of North Carolina.

Each party had one vacant seat on the Budget Committee before the election.

EDUCATION AND THE WORKFORCE

The committee will find itself dealing with some of the same issues in the 108th Congress that have resulted in partisan deadlock the past two years.

At the top of that list are efforts to safeguard retirement savings plans, change work rules for welfare recipients and rewrite the authorization for special education programs (PL 105-17).

Chairman John A. Boehner, R-Ohio, and ranking Democrat George Miller of California will return. Boehner, a conservative GOP loyalist, and Miller, an ardent liberal, are on opposite sides of most issues. But they can compromise on occasion, as they did on last year's rewrite of the Elementary and Secondary Education Act (PL 107-110). The two likely will need to find common ground if any of the legislation on the committee's agenda is to become law.

The panel also will tackle new issues, including reauthorization of the Higher Education Act (PL 105-244). Democrats will seek a large increase in Pell Grant funding while Republicans want to streamline the financial aid process for students and colleges.

The committee also will try to reauthorize the Head Start program (PL 105-285). The White House wants more testing of children leaving Head Start.

Republicans will have to fill at least four vacancies. Marge Roukema of New Jersey, Lindsey Graham of South Carolina, Bob Schaffer of Colorado and Van Hilleary, R-Tenn., all are leaving the House.

Three Democrats will be gone, including the ranking minority members of two subcommittees. They include Tim Roemer, D-Ind., of the Select Education Subcommittee, the late Patsy T. Mink of Hawaii, of the 21st Century Competitiveness Subcommittee, and Lynn Rivers, D-Mich.

ENERGY AND COMMERCE

Chairman Billy Tauzin, R-La., is expected to move next year on proposals to protect consumer privacy and spur development of new technology including high-definition television and broadband Internet service.

John D. Dingell of Michigan will return as ranking Democrat. The minority wants to promote energy conservation measures and expand availability of generic prescription drugs.

In coming weeks, Tauzin hopes to continue work as chairman of a conference committee on the omnibus energy bill (HR 4). If that measure is not completed this year, it is certain to be at the top of his agenda next year.

Tauzin also is expected to move next year on legislation similar to a proposal (HR 1542) cosponsored by Dingell that would relax restrictions on the regional Bell telephone companies under the 1996 telecommunications overhaul (PL 104-104) to spur them to expand broadband Internet service. John McCain, R-Ariz., the incoming chairman of the Senate Commerce, Science and Transportation Committee, is expected to be more open to compromise on the measure than his predecessor, Ernest F. Hollings, D-S.C.

Tauzin is expected to work on legislation similar to a bill (HR 4678), sponsored by Cliff Stearns, R-Fla., that would require online vendors and other businesses to allow consumers to opt out of any sharing of their personal information with other companies. Tauzin also is working with Fred Upton, R-Mich., on a proposal to tighten a 1997 requirement (PL 105-33) that television broadcasters phase out analog signals and switch to digital by 2006.

Both parties are expected to promote measures to give patients additional rights when they deal with managed-care plans.

FINANCIAL SERVICES

Like its Senate counterpart, the Financial Services Committee will grapple next year with the issue of financial privacy.

That once-hot topic became an afterthought during the second session of the 107th Congress as committee members turned to bills related to homeland security and corporate accountability. But privacy will return to the agenda because a provision of the Fair Credit Reporting Act (PL 91-508) that pre-empts some privacy regulation by the states will expire at the end of 2003.

Chairman Michael G. Oxley, R-Ohio, favors a light touch when it comes to government regulation. A new ranking Democrat, Barney Frank of Massachusetts, will sit next to Oxley when the committee reconvenes in January. Frank replaces the retiring John J. LaFalce of New York. Oxley and Frank are expected to have a less contentious relationship than Oxley and LaFalce displayed.

The committee will oversee implementation of the new corporate fraud law (PL 107-204), particularly a new accounting industry oversight board. The panel also will continue its investigation of investment banking practices, including those involving initial public stock offerings, although Oxley favors industry self-regulation.

Oxley will continue to study whether to establish federal regulation of the insurance industry. He also is likely to revive legislation that would ease or eliminate dozens of regulations on banks, credit unions and thrifts, as well as a bill that would increase federal insurance coverage for bank deposits.

GOVERNMENT REFORM

Three Republicans will vie for the chairmanship of a committee that generally produces little-noticed legislation but grabs headlines with its investigations.

Term limits are ending Indiana Republican Dan Burton's tenure as chairman, a position he used to investigate the Clinton administration. Constance A. Morella of Maryland, the second-ranking Republican on the committee, lost her re-election fight, leaving Christopher Shays of Connecticut next in line to take the helm. But two members of the GOP leadership may have the inside track.

Thomas M. Davis III, who raised record sums for GOP House candidates in two terms as chairman of the National Republican Congressional Committee, would like the position. His Northern Virginia district is home to many federal workers and contractors. Davis was a government contract attorney in the private sector and has been active in remaking the government procurement process.

But Davis is outranked on the panel by Republican Policy Committee Chairman Christopher Cox, Calif., who has been on a leave of absence from the committee and wants to be considered for the chairmanship.

Neither Davis nor Cox has a longer tenure on the panel than Shays, who helped lead investigations into homeland security, the threat of biological, chemical and nuclear terrorism, Gulf War illness and hepatitis C in the nation's blood supply. He is chairman of the National Security, Veterans Affairs and International Relations Subcommittee.

Morella's loss also opens the chairmanship of the panel's District of Columbia subcommittee.

The committee's Democratic roster was changed very little by the election. Henry A. Waxman of California will continue as ranking Democrat. At least four Democrats now at the bottom of the panel's seniority list will be vying for membership on exclusive House committees and would have to leave Government Reform to take one of those slots.

Seats on the Government Reform Committee may be among the last filled when the House reorganizes in January.

HOUSE ADMINISTRATION

Bob Ney, R-Ohio, will begin his second term as chairman of the panel that oversees House safety, mail delivery and tours, as well as the Government Printing Office and the Smithsonian Institution.

The committee also is in charge of the construction of the $265 million Capitol visitors' center scheduled to open in 2005.

Ney said he expects no changes on the panel. While ranking Democrat Steny H. Hoyer of Maryland has not announced that he plans to give up that position in favor a party leadership position or a seat on another committee, Chaka Fattah of Pennsylvania is next in line if Hoyer departs.

The committee's role has changed considerably since the Sept. 11 terrorist attacks. Since then, the panel has focused on Capitol security rather than housekeeping. During the 108th Congress, the committee will consider whether House offices should receive only electronic mail to guard against exposure to hazardous substances.

While working to make the Capitol safer, Ney said he wants to make access easier for visitors, including lobbyists. The chairman said he will consider a proposal by lobbyists to grant them identification cards similar to those issued to congressional aides and journalists.

INTERNATIONAL RELATIONS

Although few major changes in policy or personnel are expected at the International Relations Committee in the 108th Congress, Chairman Henry J. Hyde, R-Ill. could find it easier to advance his agenda because of the Republican takeover of the Senate.

Hyde was repeatedly frustrated during the 107th Congress when bills he steered through the House died or languished in the Senate. Those efforts included legislation to authorize assistance to Afghanistan (HR 3994), combat HIV overseas (HR 2069), and restructure U.S. broadcasting and exchange programs (HR 3969).

Hyde is expected to make these items of unfinished business his first priorities in the 108th, along with hearings on relations with North Korea and Iraq. He is also likely to take another stab at rewriting the Export Administration Act (PL 96-72) governing exports of goods with both civilian and military purposes.

Hyde also expects to wade into the politically treacherous waters of foreign aid legislation. A foreign aid authorization bill has not been enacted since 1985. He would authorize a large increase in assistance to countries that support U.S. policies. And he hopes to unveil a "Marshall

Plan for the Middle East" to spur economic and political development.

The chairman is expected to work closely with ranking Democrat Tom Lantos. Hyde learned early in his tenure that it is difficult to move legislation without Lantos' backing and has taken care since to cut deals with the California Democrat.

The retirement of Benjamin A. Gilman, R-N.Y., creates an opening for a new chairman of the Middle East and South Asia Subcommittee — and a potential headache for Hyde. Dan Burton, R-Ind., a senior member of the panel, is eligible to take over the helm of the subcommittee. Burton is an outspoken critic of India at a time when Bush is seeking to contain dangerous tensions between India and neighboring Pakistan, both nuclear powers.

Democrats will have to find replacements for Earl F. Hilliard of Alabama and Cynthia A. McKinney of Georgia, two African-American lawmakers and ranking members of subcommittees who were defeated in primary elections. Brad Sherman of California and Robert Wexler of Florida are expected to take their place.

JUDICIARY

Chairman F. James Sensenbrenner Jr., R-Wis., and ranking Democrat John Conyers Jr. of Michigan will return to lead the Judiciary Committee, but subcommittee chairmanships will be shuffled.

The musical chairs were expected before the defeat Nov. 5 of George W. Gekas, R-Pa., who headed the influential Immigration, Border Security and Claims Subcommittee.

For months, two Judiciary Republicans — Lamar Smith of Texas and Robert W. Goodlatte of Virginia — have been jockeying for the helm of the Subcommittee on Courts, the Internet and Intellectual Property. Chairman Howard Coble, R-N.C., must give up the job because of term limits.

Smith appears likely to take over the top spot on the subcommittee, which has jurisdiction over technological issues from digital music to copyrights. Smith's district includes parts of Austin, Texas, which is home to Dell Computer Corp.

Goodlatte is the co-chairman of the Congressional Internet Caucus.

Smith now heads the Crime, Terrorism and Homeland Security Subcommittee. That chairmanship could go to Coble.

Gekas' defeat leaves open the Immigration Subcommittee chairmanship. Christopher B. Cannon of Utah is a likely candidate for the position, although Goodlatte and Bill Jenkins, R-Tenn., also may be considered.

RESOURCES

The Resources Committee will have a new chairman, but it remains uncertain who will wield the gavel.

Redistricting prompted the retirement of James V. Hansen, R-Utah, who took over as chairman for the 107th

Congress after Don Young, R-Alaska, gave up the position to head the Transportation and Infrastructure Committee.

Western conservatives want to retain control of the Resources panel, but the Republican next in line for the chairmanship based on seniority is New Jersey Republican James Saxton, a moderate.

Saxton has said that while he is interested in overseeing Resources, he also values his chairmanship of the Armed Services Military Installations and Facilities Subcommittee. His district includes three military facilities and the subcommittee's jurisdiction includes military construction, housing and base closures.

The conservatives would prefer almost any other committee member over Saxton, who has battled Western Republicans on several environmental issues including endangered species and property rights. He also has supported tougher clean water regulations.

A number of conservatives tout Elton Gallegly, R-Calif., for the chairmanship, although he is one step below Saxton in seniority. House Republicans do not rely solely on tenure in picking chairmen.

Gallegly would satisfy many conservatives and is a Westerner like Hansen. The Resources Committee has traditionally been led by lawmakers from the West, where the federal government has vast holdings. Gallegly said if he gets the job, protecting property rights would be at the top of his agenda.

Other Republicans interested in the Resources chairmanship include John J. "Jimmy" Duncan Jr. of Tennessee, Richard W. Pombo of California, and Barbara Cubin of Wyoming, among others.

Under Gallegly or another conservative chairman, the committee would be expected to continue its drive to reduce barriers to commercial development of public land.

Led by Pombo, the committee has been seeking support for a rewrite of the Endangered Species Act that would make it more difficult to designate an animal or plant as at risk of extinction.

The Resources Committee's ranking Democrat is likely to remain Nick J. Rahall II of West Virginia.

RULES

A change in one lawmaker's retirement plans and a primary victory should keep the Rules Committee's Republican roster intact.

Second-ranking Republican Porter J. Goss of Florida announced his intention to retire at the end of the 107th Congress but decided to seek re-election after the Sept. 11 attacks. The third-ranking GOP member of Rules, John Linder of Georgia, won a tough primary against Rep. Bob Barr.

The committee's 9-4 partisan ratio is expected to be maintained in the new Congress, so no GOP vacancies are likely. Chairman David Dreier, R-Calif., said he expects few changes in the committee's composition or procedures.

The Democratic lineup on the panel is uncertain as Democrats prepare to elect a new minority leader for the 108th Congress.

SCIENCE

No major shifts in personnel or policy are expected.

Chairman Sherwood L. Boehlert of New York, one of the most liberal Republicans in the House and a staunch environmentalist, has formed a close working relationship with ranking Democrat Ralph M. Hall of Texas, a conservative from the oil patch. That partnership is expected to continue as the committee considers legislation that would increase government investment in nanotechnology, which backers consider a potential trillion-dollar industry with implications for disease treatment, manufacturing and electronics.

The panel also will consider a reauthorization bill for NASA. Hall plans to question NASA's handling of the U.S.-led International Space Station, concerned that the agency has no plans to fully staff the facility and has decided to cancel a project aimed at extracting astronauts from the facility in the event of an emergency. Hall, an ardent supporter of the space station, began a probe in June of the decision by NASA Administrator Sean O'Keefe to cancel the Crew Return Vehicle project.

The only major shift in the panel's leadership is the departure of Space and Aeronautics Subcommittee Chairman Dana Rohrabacher, R-Calif., who has run up against his term limit.

SELECT INTELLIGENCE

An expected waiver to allow Florida Republican Porter J. Goss to continue his leadership of the panel should provide stability at what the Bush administration considers an important post in the war on terrorism.

Goss had planned to retire at the end of the 107th Congress, but GOP leaders convinced the former CIA agent that his expertise was needed. Now that he has been re-elected, House leaders are expected to grant a waiver to allow him to remain chairman.

Two other key players — Michael N. Castle, R-Del., and ranking Democrat Nancy Pelosi of California — are likely to be forced off the panel by term limits. Roemer is retiring and Gary A. Condit, D-Calif., lost his primary race. Those departures should ensure that all returning committee Democrats will be able to retain seats on the panel, even if the Republican gains in the House reduce the number of Democratic seats on House panels.

Sanford D. Bishop Jr. of Georgia is in line to become the committee's next ranking Democrat. Under an unofficial agreement reached two years ago, Bishop would complete his last two years on the select panel and then step aside at the end of the 109th Congress to let Jane Harman of California become the top Democrat.

The committee, which produces the annual intelligence authorization bill and oversees the intelligence community, is expected to continue on the path set after the Sept. 11 attacks. The current authorization (PL 107-108) includes a bipartisan agreement to embark on a five-year plan to strengthen intelligence capabilities.

If the fiscal 2003 intelligence authorization bill (HR 4628) does not result in the creation of a commission to investigate the Sept. 11 attacks, lawmakers almost certainly will have to revisit that issue in the 108th Congress.

SMALL BUSINESS

No major changes are expected at the low-profile Small Business Committee. With Donald Manzullo, R-Ill., returning as chairman, the business community can expect a continued focus on reducing tax and regulatory burdens.

One of Manzullo's top priorities is discouraging the government's practice of bundling together contracts to the disadvantage of small bidders. Ranking Democrat Nydia M. Velázquez, D-N.Y., also opposes bundling.

Last year, the committee approved a bipartisan bill (HR 2867) that would reduce bundling. House leaders declined to bring the measure to the floor. The Bush administration announced in October that it would encourage agencies to avoid bundling.

Manzullo emphasizes the importance to small business of free trade policies. He convened a hearing on how tariffs on imported steel are harming small companies in this country. But Manzullo also supports requiring the government to purchase U.S.-made products.

Velázquez, who in October criticized the performance of the Bush administration and House GOP leaders on small-business issues, would prefer the committee focus on modernizing the Small Business Administration and expanding its loan programs.

The departure of John Thune, R-S.D., an unsuccessful Senate candidate on Nov. 5, will leave at least one GOP committee seat vacant and could allow Maryland Republican Roscoe G. Bartlett to take Thune's position as chairman of the Rural Enterprises, Agriculture and Technology Subcommittee.

STANDARDS OF OFFICIAL CONDUCT

While House Democratic leaders will be scrambling to please members of their caucus seeking choice committee assignments, they may have just as much trouble finding members willing to fill at least two vacancies on the Committee on Standards of Official Conduct.

The ethics committee, perhaps the least popular assignment in the House, has the thankless task of enforcing House rules. Earlier this year, the panel recommended the expulsion of James A. Traficant Jr., D-Ohio (1985-2002), after his conviction on 10 federal felony counts of bribery and racketeering.

Ethics committee members can serve three two-year terms on the panel. Chairmen and ranking members have the option of serving a fourth term. The five Republicans now on the committee, including Chairman Joel Hefley of Colorado, have not reached the three-term limit and likely will be back for the 108th Congress.

Two Democrats, Ed Pastor of Arizona and Zoe Lofgren of California, have completed their three terms and must be replaced. Ranking Democrat Howard L. Berman of California is finishing his third term. It is not clear whether he will elect to serve a fourth.

TRANSPORTATION AND INFRASTRUCTURE

The committee will tackle a packed agenda with experienced hands at the wheel. Don Young, R-Alaska, will remain chairman and James L. Oberstar, D-Minn., will retain his position as ranking member.

But the fate of two senior committee members — Republican John J. "Jimmy" Duncan Jr. of Tennessee and Democrat Nick J. Rahall II of West Virginia — could have repercussions for the leadership of key subcommittees.

Duncan is a candidate for the Resources Committee chairmanship. His departure would open the chairmanship of the Transportation Committee's Water Resources and Environment Subcommittee. It is unclear who Duncan's successor would be, with one GOP committee aide saying those discussions will be put off until Duncan's future is clearer.

However, at least three other Transportation subcommittee chairmen appear content to stay in their current posts. John L. Mica of Florida, Tom Petri of Wisconsin, and Jack Quinn of New York are expected to retain their top posts on Aviation, Highways and Transit, and Railroads, respectively.

Rahall must decide whether he will relinquish his post as the ranking Democrat on the Resources Committee to become the ranking minority member on a Transportation subcommittee, perhaps the Highways and Transit panel. Should Rahall choose Resources, it would open the door for William O. Lipinski of Illinois to take over as the top Democrat on the prized Highways and Transit subcommittee.

That would probably set off a shuffle among ranking minority members, which likely would place Peter A. DeFazio of Oregon as the top Democrat on the Aviation Subcommittee.

During the 108th Congress, the committee will rewrite the 1998 highway authorization law TEA-21 (PL 105-178), and the 2000 Federal Aviation Administration authorization measure (PL 106-181). Those efforts likely will renew turf battles between authorizers and appropriators over funding priorities.

Committee members want to smooth fluctuations in highway spending that left them scrambling to find fiscal 2003 highway funding when Highway Trust Fund receipts dropped.

Outstanding aviation issues include whether to arm pilots, as well as whether to provide more financial relief to airlines. Also on the panel's plate is reauthorization of Amtrak.

VETERANS' AFFAIRS

No significant changes in leadership or focus are expected at the House Veterans' Affairs Committee.

Chairman Christopher H. Smith, R-N.J., and ranking Democrat Lane Evans of Illinois are expected to return to the posts where they have worked closely since Smith took over the committee's leadership two years ago.

Smith has taken an activist role on a relatively sleepy committee, attempting to consolidate its powers over veterans' issues and its control over funding at the Department of Veterans Affairs (VA).

With Evans' support, Smith probably will revisit two proposals that saw limited success in the 107th Congress. The first (HR 5250) would shift funding for veterans health programs from the discretionary to the mandatory budget, taking control from appropriators. Smith also is expected to continue pushing to expand programs that allow Pentagon and VA health care facilities to share resources and cut costs.

Other anticipated initiatives would seek more money for the national cemetery system and look for ways to force the Pentagon to more closely track information about exposure to chemical and biological hazards.

Work also has stalled in the 107th Congress on an omnibus veterans health care bill (S 2043). Lawmakers are expected to take up the bill again in the 108th Congress.

The subcommittee leadership lineup is difficult to predict. Health Subcommittee Chairman Jerry Moran, R-Kan. and ranking Democrat Bob Filner of California both have shown interest in their positions and could stay.

Benefits Subcommittee Chairman Mike Simpson, R-Idaho, also might keep his position. Ranking Democrat Silvestre Reyes of Texas might leave to take a subcommittee leadership slot on the Intelligence Committee.

It remains unclear if Oversight and Investigations Subcommittee Chairman Steve Buyer, R-Ind., or ranking Democrat Julia Carson of Indiana will seek positions on other panels.

WAYS AND MEANS

Proposals to make permanent the 2001 tax cuts, provide a Medicare prescription drug benefit and rewrite the 1996 welfare overhaul will be top priorities for returning Ways and Means Committee Chairman Bill Thomas, R-Calif.

Charles B. Rangel of New York will return as the ranking Democrat. The Democrats' top priorities will include more jobless benefits and tax breaks for working families.

Thomas is sure to champion Bush's top priority — making permanent provisions of the last year's tax cut (PL 107-16) that will expire in 2010. A tax cut extension could be moved as a stand-alone measure early next year.

A budget reconciliation bill also might include other tax measures aimed at spurring sluggish economic growth.

Thomas is under pressure to move quickly to head off a threat by the European Union to impose $4 billion in punitive tariffs if Congress does not eliminate tax breaks for U.S. exporters as required by a World Trade Organization ruling. Thomas' proposal (HR 5095) has been contentious because it would provide other tax breaks that benefit companies based on overseas operations, not overall sales or exports.

Still unclear is whether the administration will pursue a broader tax overhaul that could include eliminating the alternative minimum tax or cutting taxes on corporate dividends. Key Republicans also want to expand tax breaks for retirement saving.

Another possible priority for Thomas will be a rewrite of the 1996 welfare law (PL 104-193), most likely in a way that would be similar to a proposal (HR 4737) that was passed by the House and died in the Senate earlier this year.

Democrats want more aid for the poor to offset GOP proposals for tougher work requirements to move recipients off welfare.

Health care matters also fall under the committee's jurisdiction, and rival proposals for a prescription drug benefit under Medicare are likely to come up in the 108th Congress. But stock market losses are expected to delay efforts to promote Bush's plan to create private individual accounts for Social Security beneficiaries.

Jim McDermott of Washington is expected to replace the retiring William J. Coyne, D-Pa., as ranking Democrat on the Oversight Subcommittee. The defeat of Karen L. Thurman, D-Fla., may open a Democratic seat on the committee. ◆

New Rules for the 'A' Teams?

Kyl pushes for different criteria to allocate key committee slots

To the victors go the gavels, and Republicans who wrested control of the Senate from the Democrats will be chairing all 20 committees in the 108th Congress. This time, they have a somewhat firmer grip on the gavels.

In June 2001, James M. Jeffords of Vermont stunned the GOP by bolting to become an independent aligned with Democrats. Each Senate committee, then split 50-50 to reflect the even divide of the Senate as a whole, gained one Democratic slot.

Now, Republicans will hold at least a one-seat edge on every committee. Many incoming chairmen would like to shrink their panels by a seat or more, and the first members to go will be Democrats added after Jeffords' switch. Depending on the size of each panel and the party ratios, even more Democrats could be tossed off.

Decisions on the size of the committees and ratios will have to wait until after the Dec. 7 runoff election in Louisiana. That contest will determine the final party lineup in the Senate.

Although only 17 months have passed since control switched to Democrats, retirements and gavel-swapping mean Republicans in charge of up to 11 of the 20 Senate committees will be different from those who chaired the same panels at the start of the 107th.

Some changes are especially noteworthy. Susan Collins, R-Maine, will be only the third woman to chair a Senate committee as she takes over at Governmental Affairs. If Pete V. Domenici of New Mexico decides to chair the Energy and Natural Resources Committee instead of the Budget Committee, it would be the first time since the Budget panel was created in 1974 that any Republican other than Domenici would chair it. Fiscal conser-

CQ Weekly Nov. 9, 2002

Senate Committees	
Appropriations	p. 99
Armed Services	p. 101
Finance	p. 102
Judiciary	p. 103

vative Don Nickles, R-Okla., would take the gavel if Domenici gives it up. Otherwise, Nickles, outgoing GOP whip, will chair the Energy panel.

Patience has paid off for Richard G. Lugar, R-Ind., who has waited 16 years for a second chance to chair the Foreign Relations Committee.

While the committee chairmanships are largely settled, veterans and freshmen alike are vying for assignments to the most influential Senate committees — Appropriations, Armed Services and Finance. Seniority is the dominant factor in how both parties make committee assignments; returning senators get first crack at vacancies.

Senate rules prohibit members from serving on more than two major, or "A," committees: Agriculture, Appropriations, Armed Services, Banking, Commerce, Energy, Environment, Foreign Relations, Governmental Affairs, Judiciary, and Health, Education, Labor and Pensions. Senators also may serve on one "B" committee: Budget, Ethics, Indian Affairs, Rules and Administration, Select Aging, Select Intelligence, Small Business and Veterans' Affairs. A number of senators have received waivers to exceed these limits.

Currently, seniority controls the allotment of Republican seats on "A" panels. The list of such panels is circulated from senator to senator, in descending order of seniority, until all seats are filled.

That could change when Republicans meet Nov. 13 to choose their leaders and adopt rules for the 108th. Jon

Kyl, R-Ariz., chairman of the GOP Committee on Committees, will urge that Republican leaders be allowed to fill any "A" committee seats still open after two rounds of picks based on seniority. "B" committee assignments already are made by the leaders.

In determining seniority rankings within the GOP, past service in the Senate is paramount, followed by House service and governorships. No other government experience, either at the state or federal level, is considered. If two senators have equal experience, their names are placed in a hat and the first one drawn gets a seniority edge.

GOP Conference rules bar senators from serving on more than one of four "A" committees: Appropriations, Armed Services, Finance and Foreign Relations. Lugar, the top Republican on Foreign Relations for the 108th, will seek to remove the panel from that list.

Republicans have six-year term limits for committee chairmen and six-year limits for service as ranking Republican. Under a conference rules change in 2002, chairmen who were demoted to ranking member when Jeffords switched will not see any part of the 107th Congress count against their six-year term limit.

Democrats have no term limits for chairmen or ranking members. In making committee assignments, they treat seniority as the primary factor but not the sole determinant. They score seniority according to time spent as: senator, vice president, House member, Cabinet member or governor. Those who do not meet any of those criteria are ranked according to the population of their state.

In assigning seats on "A" committees, Democratic leaders also factor in how long a senator has waited for a seat on a particular panel and the regional and ideological balance of panel Democrats. ◆

Veteran Appropriator May Test Bush

TED STEVENS, R-Alaska

REPLACING: Robert C. Byrd, D-W.Va.

HOMETOWN: Girdwood

BORN: November 18, 1923; Indianapolis

RELIGION: Episcopalian

FAMILY: Wife, Catherine Chandler; six children

EDUCATION: U. of California, Los Angeles, B.A. 1947 Harvard U., LL.B. 1950

MILITARY SERVICE: Army Air Corps, 1943-46

APPOINTED: 1968 (Sixth elected full term begins 2003)

POLITICAL HIGHLIGHTS: U.S. attorney, 1953-56; Republican nominee for Senate, 1962; Alaska House, 1965-68 (majority leader and speaker pro tempore, 1967-68); sought Republican nomination for Senate, 1968

OTHER COMMITTEES: Appropriations; Commerce; Science & Transportation; Governmental Affairs; Rules & Administration

President Bush has spent almost two years vowing to break the congressional mind-set about spending. The chief targets of Bush's criticism have been the Appropriations committees, particularly the Senate panel, where Chairman Robert C. Byrd of West Virginia made for a convenient bogeyman when the Democrats were in the majority.

But Alaska's Ted Stevens, who will return to the chairmanship of one of the Senate's most influential committees as he begins his sixth full term in the Senate, is very much like Byrd — and not just because he shares the West Virginian's affinity for sending millions of dollars for federal projects back home each year.

Both take a bipartisan approach to moving appropriations legislation, and they are passionate defenders of congressional spending prerogatives. Stevens supported, along with every committee Republican, fiscal 2003 appropriations bills that would permit billions of dollars in spending that had not been requested by Bush.

And like Byrd, Stevens has had his share of scrapes with the White House — especially Mitchell E. Daniels Jr., the director of the Office of Management and Budget (OMB). When asked last year what Daniels could do to repair relations with Congress, Stevens replied: "Go home to Indiana."

When the 108th Congress convenes — soon after Stevens turns 79 this month and soon after he begins his 34th year as a senator in December — Stevens will become the longest-serving majority party senator. As a result he will assume the title of president pro tempore, another position Byrd will surrender to him.

In that largely symbolic role, Stevens will become third in the line of presidential succession behind the vice president and the Speaker of the House. More immediately, it will fall to Stevens to deal with 11 of the 13 fiscal 2003 appropriations bills that have yet to be enacted, and to tackle a whole new round of spending bills for fiscal 2004 — a process that may begin even before the current year's spending decisions are all made. Also looming is a huge springtime supplemental spending bill that may test the capacity of Stevens to add congressional priorities to Bush's requests. (*2002 CQ Weekly, p. 2859*)

Completing the current year's work will be a daunting task. Stevens believes that the $749 billion funding limit imposed by Bush and enforced by Daniels is woefully inadequate. And Stevens backed efforts to add more homeland security funding to the fiscal 2002 supplemental spending bills.

The Senate's fiscal 2003 spending bills exceed Bush's request by $20 billion, according to calculations by the Senate Budget Committee's GOP staff. With Bush and the more tight-fisted House Republicans riding high, however, Stevens will have to fight hard for any spending above the president's request.

In the end, though, Stevens is a party loyalist. He ran the committee from 1997 until the GOP lost its hold on the Senate in June 2001, after James M. Jeffords of Vermont quit the party and aligned with the Democrats. During his first four and a half years as chairman, he rarely if ever bucked orders from the leadership, and he produced spending bills at the tight levels imposed by Republican budget resolutions.

At the same time, however, Stevens grew accustomed to having President Bill Clinton use veto threats to leverage additional spending. Though he often grew testy during endgame negotiations with the Democratic White House, he invariably made the best of such opportunities to deliver for Alaska.

But Stevens has never before been called on to bring an appropriations cycle to completion in consort with a Republican in the White House. Given the current fiscal pinch, he may find the experience trying. The struggle within the GOP over spending could be particularly intense if Don Nickles of Oklahoma, one of the most fiscally conservative Republicans in the Senate, takes control of the Budget Committee as expected.

Although Byrd will now go back to being the ranking Democrat on both the full committee and its Interior Subcommittee, he will continue to wield considerable clout. Both Byrd and Stevens are legendary for their success in funneling federal dollars to their home states.

The committee should experience little change in its membership. If Mary L. Landrieu loses her Dec. 7 runoff election in Louisiana, it will not create a vacancy because the panel's 15 Democrats will have to thin their ranks to accommodate a 15-14 division in favor of Republicans. That could be bad news for Jack Reed of Rhode Island, who is the most junior Democrat.

Frank R. Lautenberg, D-N.J., who returns to the Senate after a two-year hiatus, probably will not reclaim his post on the panel.

It is likely that all ranking Republicans will reclaim the subcommittee chairmanships that they lost last year. The current Democratic chairmen will probably become the ranking members of their subcommittees.

Agriculture: Thad Cochran of Mississippi returns to the chair that he held for six and a half years of GOP rule. He has been a steady advocate of Southern interests, including rice, cotton, peanuts and sugar. Cochran also takes the helm of the Agriculture Committee, though that post could be somewhat less important in 2004 after the completion this year of a major reauthorization of farm programs (PL 107-171). Chairman Herb Kohl of Wisconsin, a strong defender of his state's dairy interests and a backer of federal food programs, will revert to ranking Democrat on the panel.

Commerce, Justice, State and Judiciary: This subcommittee has taken on greater importance as homeland security issues have moved to the forefront, and Judd Gregg of New Hampshire will regain the helm. Gregg is a confidant of Trent Lott of Mississippi, who is reclaiming the title of majority leader, and Gregg is among the more conservative members of the go-along, get-along Appropriations panel. Democrat Ernest F. Hollings of South Carolina, who has chaired or served as ranking member of the panel since 1983, returns to the ranking post.

Defense: Stevens will return to the chairmanship he held from 1995 to 2001, and his close friend Daniel K. Inouye of Hawaii again will become the ranking Democrat. The two have been their parties' senior representatives on this panel since 1989 and have worked well together. Stevens and Inouye have worked to focus more of the Pentagon's attention on the Pacific and Asia; Stevens' beloved Alaska probably will play a big role when a missile defense system is built.

Energy and Water Development: New Mexico Republican Pete V. Domenici retakes the gavel from Harry Reid of Nevada. Domenici, who has the option of also taking the chairmanship of the Energy and Natural Resources Committee, is a strong supporter of the Energy Department. The Sandia and Los Alamos national laboratories in his state stand to benefit from his return to the helm. Reid will continue to focus on protecting funding for renewable energy sources such as solar, wind and biomass.

Foreign Operations: Mitch McConnell of Kentucky, who is also expected to win the No. 2 GOP leadership post in the Senate, is another Lott loyalist on the committee. He is a steady conservative, but his work on Appropriations has reflected a pragmatic streak. Among the priorities McConnell has focused on in the past is increased U.S. aid to Ukraine, Georgia and Armenia, which he views as potential bulwarks against a resurgent Russia. Patrick J. Leahy of Vermont once again will become the ranking Democratic member.

Interior: Conrad Burns of Montana, whose initial term at the helm of Interior was interrupted by the switch in Senate control, will return to the post. Among the priorities he is likely to push is swift implementation of the Bush administration's "healthy forests initiative," which would permit greater clearing of trees in fire-prone areas without interference from environmentalists' lawsuits. The venerable Byrd returns to the ranking member post.

Labor, Health and Human Services, and Education: Arlen Specter of Pennsylvania, who is among the Senate's most moderate Republicans, is slated to return as chairman. Tom Harkin of Iowa returns as the ranking Democrat. In the past, Specter has been frustrated with the partisan gridlock that typically ensnares the subcommittee's bill, which is the largest domestic spending measure, and he has flirted with the idea of taking another gavel. But his spokesman said he is staying put. Among his priorities is keeping on track plans to double the budget of the National Institutes of Health.

Legislative Branch: Robert F. Bennett of Utah returns to the chairmanship of this panel, which invariably works on a bipartisan basis and focuses on the basic operations and services of Congress. He chaired the subcommittee from 1997 to 2001. Richard J. Durbin of Illinois will be ranking Democrat.

Transportation: Alabama Republican Richard C. Shelby retakes the gavel of this powerful subcommittee. Among the questions he will have to grapple with is whether to fund highway programs at levels above the White House request. The House version of the fiscal 2003 Transportation bill (HR 5559) would increase spending by $4.4 billion; the Senate version (S 2808) would raise spending by $8.6 billion. Patty Murray of Washington will become ranking Democrat.

Veterans, Housing, NASA and EPA: Christopher S. Bond, R-Mo., reclaims the chairmanship of this wide-ranging subcommittee. Bond has a well-deserved reputation for delivering federal dollars to Missouri. Bond has a long and close working relationship with top Democrat Barbara A. Mikulski of Maryland.

Treasury, Postal Service: Ben Nighthorse Campbell of Colorado again will chair this panel, which always seems to find its way into partisan scrapes. A central question is whether to use the bill as a vehicle to lift the ban on travel to Cuba by U.S. citizens. Byron L. Dorgan of North Dakota will become ranking Democrat.

Military Construction: Kay Bailey Hutchison of Texas returns to the helm of this low-profile subcommittee, which is nonetheless popular for the largess it bestows upon many lawmakers' states. The White House was critical of the panel's fiscal 2003 bill (PL 107-249), which administration officials considered too expensive. Bush signed it into law nonetheless. Dianne Feinstein of California becomes the top Democrat.

District of Columbia: Mike DeWine of Ohio, who briefly chaired the subcommittee in 2001, is expected to return. Landrieu will be the top Democrat on the panel if she wins; otherwise, the job likely would go to the junior returning Democrat left on the committee, probably Tim Johnson of South Dakota.

Armed Services Faces a Few Key Battles

JOHN W. WARNER, R-Va.

REPLACING: Carl Levin, D-Mich.

HOMETOWN: Alexandria

BORN: February 18, 1927; Washington, D.C.

RELIGION: Episcopalian

FAMILY: Divorced; three children

EDUCATION: Washington and Lee U., B.S. 1949 (engineering); U. of Virginia, LL.B. 1953

MILITARY SERVICE: Navy, 1944-46; Marine Corps, 1950-52; Marine Corps Reserve, 1952-64

ELECTED: 1978 (Beginning 5th term in 2003)

POLITICAL HIGHLIGHTS: Assistant U.S. attorney, 1956-60; undersecretary of the Navy, 1969-72; secretary of the Navy, 1972-74

OTHER COMMITTEES: Environment & Public Works; Health, Education, Labor & Pensions; Rules & Administration

Sen. John W. Warner, R-Va., returns to the chair of the Senate Armed Services Committee, where he established a reputation for innovative thinking during his last stint at the panel's helm (1999-2001).

Warner helped push the Air Force and Army to accelerate development and deployment of robot combat planes — weapons that have proven their worth in Afghanistan and the war against terrorism. He also created a new Armed Services subcommittee to oversee the Pentagon's plans to deal with unconventional threats.

With Warner in charge, the committee's longstanding bipartisan, pro-defense consensus remains intact, despite some recent contentious debates over President Bush's anti-missile defense program. This year, when the panel hammered out its version of the annual defense authorization bill (HR 4546), it split along party lines over the Democratic majority's insistence on slicing Bush's $7.8 billion missile defense request by more than 10 percent. (*2002 CQ Weekly, p. 1207*)

Given Bush's adamant support for the program, however, there was little chance the Senate would approve the proposed reduction. In the end, the Senate adopted an amendment by Warner and Chairman Carl Levin, D-Mich., allowing restoration of the missile defense funds.

A fundamental issue on which the two parties split for years — whether the United States should try to field a system that would violate the 1972 U.S.-Soviet treaty limiting anti-ballistic missiles (ABM) — is now moot after Bush's move in June to abrogate the landmark pact. Contrary to the predictions of liberal arms control advocates, the move sparked no apparent international reper-

cussions, and critics of the program have not rallied around any other fundamental policy as a basis for reining in the program.

Nevertheless, the missile defense program will remain controversial because of the size of its projected annual budgets. Democrats such as Levin and Armed Services member Jack Reed of Rhode Island, contend that Bush is pushing too much money at too many different anti-missile projects.

Aside from missile defense, battles may loom over the size of the defense budget, given the impact of the 2001 tax cut. Warner himself could start a lively debate over his insistence that the 1878 Posse Comitatus Act, which restricts domestic operations by military forces, be amended to give the Pentagon a freer hand in combating domestic terrorism. Defense Secretary Donald H. Rumsfeld insists that no such change is needed. (*2002 CQ Weekly, p. 2867*)

Meanwhile, the administration may drop some political hot potatoes in the committee's lap. Rumsfeld is expected to propose privatizing upward of 200,000 civilian jobs, a move sure to encounter vehement opposition from federal employees' unions. And he may propose changes in the weapons procurement process that would give the Pentagon more freedom to manage programs while reducing congressional control.

Because Warner chaired Armed Services for two and a half years, he would have to relinquish the job after the 109th under Senate GOP rules. Thus, with only four years to serve as chairman, Warner may be eager to place his personal stamp on the committee.

This should be good news for his state's largest private employer — the Northrop Grumman shipyard in Newport News that builds nuclear-powered aircraft carriers. But with Rumsfeld hinting that construction of the next carrier would remain on track, Warner also may be free to address a broader policy agenda.

Of the three Republicans leaving the committee, the only one in line to chair a subcommittee was Tim Hutchinson of Arkansas, who lost his bid for re-election. Three Republicans may be unable to serve as subcommittee chairs if they take full committee chairmanships: Pat Roberts of Kansas on the Intelligence Committee, Susan Collins of Maine on the Governmental Affairs Committee, and James M. Inhofe of Oklahoma on the Environment and Public Works Committee.

Among the newly elected Republicans, Saxby Chambliss of Georgia, John Cornyn of Texas, Elizabeth Dole of North Carolina and Lindsay Graham of South Carolina all represent states with a large defense presence and may be interested in joining the panel.

Georgia Democrat Max Cleland, who chaired the Personnel Subcommittee, lost his re-election bid. Mary L. Landrieu, D-La., whose political fate will be settled in a Dec. 7 runoff, chairs the subcommittee on new threats.

Full Plate for Finance Committee

CHARLES E. GRASSLEY, R-Iowa

REPLACING: Max Baucus, D-Mont.

HOMETOWN: New Hartford

BORN: September 17, 1933; New Hartford, Iowa

RELIGION: Baptist

FAMILY: Wife, Barbara Grassley; five children

EDUCATION: U. of Northern Iowa, B.A. 1955, M.A. 1956 (political science); U. of Iowa, attended 1957-58 (graduate studies)

MILITARY SERVICE: None

ELECTED: 1980 (4th term)

POLITICAL HIGHLIGHTS: Republican nominee for Iowa House, 1956; Iowa House, 1959-75; U.S. House, 1975-81

OTHER COMMITTEES: Budget; Judiciary; Joint Taxation

The Finance Committee may be the busiest panel in the Senate next year. Not only will it handle the new Republican majority's tax legislation, it has a stack of other major issues awaiting its attention.

Prescription drug coverage, a rewrite of the 1996 welfare overhaul law (PL 104-193), and a revision of the tax treatment of business income earned abroad will all demand attention. The most important legislation of 2003 may be the Finance Committee's slice of a budget reconciliation package that could carry a big portion of the GOP agenda.

The gavel will pass from Democrat Max Baucus of Montana to Republican Charles E. Grassley of Iowa, a centrist with populist leanings who does not hesitate to buck the White House. The two Midwestern, agrarian legislators get along well, but may be pushed into corners by their party leaders. Both Republican leader Trent Lott of Mississippi and Democratic leader Tom Daschle of South Dakota have seats on Finance, as does outgoing GOP Whip Don Nickles of Oklahoma, who may be the next chairman of the Budget Committee.

Four of the committee's 21 current members are leaving. Republicans Phil Gramm of Texas and Fred Thompson of Tennessee are retiring, as is Democrat Robert G. Torricelli of New Jersey. Frank H. Murkowski is Alaska's Republican governor-elect.

Rick Santorum, a conservative Pennsylvania Republican, is expected to join the Finance panel. Bill Frist, R-Tenn., and Kay Bailey Hutchison, R-Texas, also covet seats and would be next in line, although there will probably not be seats for both of them if the size of the committee is reduced. With Republicans now in the majority,

Torricelli will not be replaced. The most junior Democrat on the committee, Blanche Lincoln of Arkansas, could lose her seat as well.

High on the GOP agenda will be an effort to make permanent last-year's 10-year tax cut package (PL 107-16). But overcoming Democratic opposition will require 60 votes on the Senate floor. Grassley and GOP leaders are expected to begin by attempting to extend select portions of the tax package that are supported by conservative Democrats, including tax breaks for married couples, increased ceilings on contributions to retirement savings plans and repeal of the estate tax.

New tax breaks for small companies will probably be considered by the committee as an economic stimulus package. Grassley also is likely to back Bush's plan to allow taxpayers who do not itemize to take deductions for charitable contributions.

Rewriting the tax rules for foreign income is an urgent issue because the United States is facing $4 billion in European Union trade sanctions. A current tax break for U.S. exporters has been ruled an illegal subsidy by the World Trade Organization.

Republicans are eager to pass a prescription drug plan for seniors in 2003. Grassley joined Finance Committee members John B. Breaux, D-La., and James M. Jeffords I-Vt., to sponsor a bill (S 2) this year that would offer Medicare participants a drug benefit through private insurers.

Grassley's welfare agenda includes tougher work requirements.

Some corporate responsibility proposals left over from the 107th Congress are likely to reappear. Grassley strongly supports legislation to strengthen pension laws (S 1971) that was inspired by losses suffered by Enron Corp. employees. The new chairman also wants to restrict tax shelters and tax avoidance by companies that set up headquarters in offshore tax havens such as Bermuda.

Legislation to offer tax deductions for long-term care costs and provide more tax relief for farmers (S 312) is also high on Grassley's wish list.

When Grassley headed the committee for five months in 2001, he operated in a more inclusive manner than did successor Baucus when Democrats held the majority. Before moving a bill into markup, Grassley would approach each member of the panel to discuss priorities and review draft provisions. As a result, markups went more smoothly.

Grassley's avid attention to Congress' oversight function could provide a check on the Bush administration. He demonstrated his sharp eye in the 1980s, criticizing wasteful spending by the Pentagon. He irked the White House last month by asking the General Accounting Office to review whether personnel decisions by Janet Rehnquist, inspector general of the Health and Human Services Department, have undermined the policing of health care providers.

Accelerated Pace on Judicial Nominees

ORRIN G. HATCH, R-Utah

REPLACING: Patrick J. Leahy, D-Vt.

HOMETOWN: Salt Lake City

BORN: March 22, 1934; Pittsburgh, Pa.

RELIGION: Mormon

FAMILY: Wife, Elaine Hatch; six children

EDUCATION: Brigham Young U., B.S. 1959 (history); U. of Pittsburgh, J.D. 1962

MILITARY SERVICE: None

ELECTED: 1976 (5th term)

POLITICAL HIGHLIGHTS: Sought Republican nomination for president, 2000

OTHER COMMITTEES: Finance; Indian Affairs; Select Intelligence; Joint Taxation

The shift in Senate control returns the power of the judicial confirmation process to President Bush's allies, ensuring more of the administration's nominees will be endorsed by the Judiciary Committee.

Orrin G. Hatch, R-Utah, is poised to take over the committee and help usher more nominations to the floor. He and other Republicans have complained bitterly that current Chairman Patrick J. Leahy of Vermont and other Democrats have stalled action on Bush's nominees.

But Democrats likely will use all the delaying tactics available to them to fight the most controversial nominees in committee and on the floor.

The committee's new agenda also will reflect some of Hatch's personal priorities, including Internet security and privacy measures. And key Republican-supported proposals, such as revamping class action lawsuits, likely will move to the top of the committee's agenda.

But the issue of selecting and confirming federal judges is sure to dominate much of the panel's attention in the 108th Congress, just as it did in the 107th. (*2002 CQ Weekly, p. 2722*)

Tensions between panel Democrats and Republicans ratcheted up this year when the committee voted along party lines to reject two nominations: Charles W. Pickering Sr. and Priscilla Owen, both tapped for the 5th U.S. Circuit Court of Appeals. Sen. Trent Lott, R-Miss., has said he would move those nominees to the floor.

"We're going to confirm some judges that have been delayed, abused and really treated very unfairly," said Lott, who will be the majority leader in the 108th. "We'll have due diligence. But we're going to stop just abusing these people."

Liberal advocacy groups already are preparing to fight the confirmation of nominees they say are too conservative for the federal bench.

"If the president tries to pack the courts with conservative ideologues beholden to special interests and committed to turning back the clock on Americans' rights, fair-minded senators must invoke their constitutional 'advise and consent' power and stand firm," said Nan Aron, president of the liberal Alliance For Justice.

Under Hatch, the Judiciary Committee is likely to move quickly to consider the appellate nominations of Dennis Shedd and Miguel Estrada. The nomination of Shedd, a former GOP aide to the committee under retiring Sen. Strom Thurmond, R-S.C., to the 4th Circuit was expected to come to a committee vote in October. Estrada, picked for a spot on the influential District of Columbia Circuit Court of Appeals, had a hearing before the panel in September.

The panel also is expected to consider other GOP priorities early in the 108th. One broad target is what supporters call "tort reform," or limits on civil litigation and damage awards.

One such measure would rewrite the way class-action suits are handled and would shift into federal court most class actions involving plaintiffs and defendants from several states. The Senate Judiciary Committee approved similar legislation during the 106th Congress; another bill (S 1712) was the subject of a hearing in July.

"There's really no doubt in my mind the class action bill is positioned well for early consideration in the 108th," said Matt Webb, director of legal reform policy for the U.S. Chamber of Commerce.

"We think it's going to be a fairly good time in the committee as far as legal reform issues are concerned," Webb said, cautioning that "not everything is a slam dunk."

Other potential legislation to govern lawsuits would be related to asbestos and medical malpractice.

Hatch also is expected to bring up legislation that would bar people from creating, possessing or distributing sexual images that appear to be of minors but are produced without real children. Such legislation would be a second attempt to ban so-called virtual child pornography. The Supreme Court on April 16 struck down the first measure, the 1996 Child Pornography Prevention Act (PL 104-208). Lawmakers, including Hatch and Leahy, have been working on a rewrite of the law that would pass constitutional muster. (*2002 CQ Weekly, p. 1753*)

Judiciary also could become the testing ground for some of the administration's immigration initiatives. The panel has jurisdiction over immigration policy, and early in the 107th, it appeared Bush would fight strongly for some changes, including a proposal that would make it easier for thousands of illegal immigrants to apply for legal residency.

Not Even Rumblings of War Shake Loose an Energy Policy

Both parties are reluctant to push stringent changes in face of impending crisis

More than two years ago, when President Bush was running for office, a central theme of his campaign was the need for a national energy policy, primarily to reduce U.S. reliance on foreign oil.

The Clinton administration, Bush said, had allowed the country to drift without an energy plan. "We need an active exploration program in America," Bush said in an October 2000 debate. "The only way to become less dependent on foreign sources of crude oil is to explore at home."

But now, as the nation faces a potential war with Iraq and further turmoil in the oil regions of the Middle East, it is no closer to the kind of energy independence that Bush talked about.

The main reason is that members of Congress cannot agree on major steps, such as drilling for more oil in the Alaska wilderness or raising vehicle fuel economy standards, that would significantly reduce the nation's dependence on foreign oil.

Tauzin, left, is optimistic the conference will finish, but Barton, center, said it should be called off if senators do not compromise on ANWR drilling. At right is Sen. Jeff Bingaman, R-N.M.

The proposals the Bush administration has been implementing through federal agencies in the last year, together with the omnibus energy bill (HR 4) now in conference, would all have some effect, but mainly at the edges of the country's energy appetite. For instance, dozens of tax breaks in the bill designed to encourage energy production, efficiency and conservation will not make a big difference in imports but will help "on the margins," said Senate Finance Committee Chairman Max Baucus, D-Mont., who favors the provisions.

Bush's energy proposals are mainly geared to increase production, including opening Alaska's Arctic National Wildlife Refuge (ANWR) to oil and gas drilling, the keystone of his plan. Most Democrats balk at such a step, heeding environmental groups who say it could destroy one of the nation's natural treasures.

But many members of Congress are just as reluctant to require conservation measures that could slow the economy in a time of budget deficits, international instability and falling stock prices. Because there is no gasoline shortage comparable to the 1973 Arab oil embargo, lawmakers are loath to ask voters to make sacrifices, such as a significant increase in motor vehicle gas mileage. Plus, automakers and auto unions oppose such ideas.

As a result, even if Congress delivers on Bush's call for an energy bill, imports are likely to rise in the next decade. The Energy Department projects that U.S. energy consumption will increase by more than 35 percent in the next 20 years.

"The energy bill isn't going to change the dynamics at all in the short term," said Rep. Jim McCrery, a Republican on the energy conference from the oil-rich state of Louisiana.

Facing Up to Nature

A fundamental problem for all energy policymakers is that the United States holds only about 3 percent of the world's proven oil reserves. And as long as the country depends on oil to fuel its cars and planes and provide heating in cold regions, it is destined to import oil. The United States produced 5.8 million barrels of oil a day in 2002 and used 19.7 million, according to the American Petroleum Institute, an industry organization.

Energy industry experts say market forces will always influence the nation's reliance on foreign oil much more than any government policy. To entice oil and gas developers to produce more fuel, prices must rise enough to justify new investment. Similarly, new technologies that could cut drilling costs or produce sources of alternative energies will not be developed until there is a profit in using them.

Lawmakers say the main justification for the energy bill,

CQ Weekly Oct. 5, 2002

U.S. Oil Imports Come From Diverse Sources

In the first half of 2002, U.S. oil imports averaged slightly more than 11.2 thousand barrels per day, representing about 57.5 percent of total usage. About 21 percent of imports came from Persian Gulf countries.

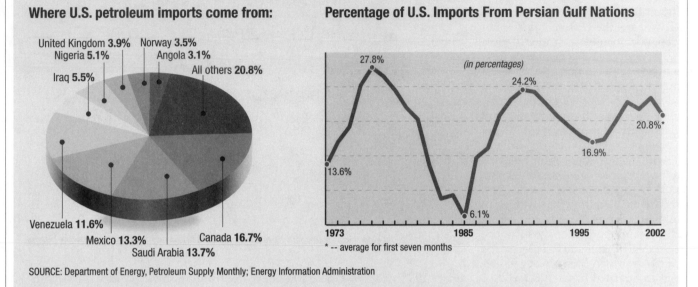

Where U.S. petroleum imports come from:

- United Kingdom **3.9%**
- Norway **3.5%**
- Nigeria **5.1%**
- Angola **3.1%**
- Iraq **5.5%**
- All others **20.8%**
- Venezuela **11.6%**
- Mexico **13.3%**
- Saudi Arabia **13.7%**
- Canada **16.7%**

Percentage of U.S. Imports From Persian Gulf Nations

(in percentages)

27.8% — 24.2% — 20.8%* — 16.9% — 13.6% — 6.1%

1973 — 1985 — 1995 — 2002

* -- average for first seven months

SOURCE: Department of Energy, Petroleum Supply Monthly; Energy Information Administration

Gas Prices Relatively Low When Adjusted for Inflation

U.S. average retail price of regular compared with those adjusted for inflation:

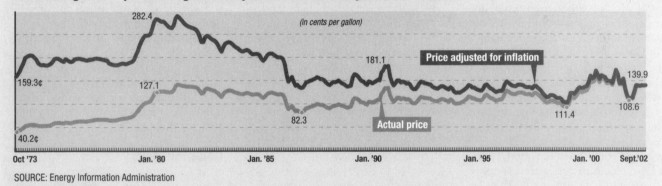

(in cents per gallon)

282.4 — 181.1 — Price adjusted for inflation — 139.9 — 159.3¢ — 127.1 — 82.3 — Actual price — 111.4 — 108.6 — 40.2¢

Oct '73 — Jan. '80 — Jan. '85 — Jan. '90 — Jan. '95 — Jan. '00 — Sept.'02

SOURCE: Energy Information Administration

which would cost taxpayers tens of billions of dollars, is that it would allow the United States to shift away from Middle East imports.

"We need a bill which encourages conservation, promotes new technologies, promotes renewables, but a bill which will encourage increase of supply here in America," Bush said Sept. 27 during a speech in Arizona. "We're too dependent on foreign sources of crude oil. And unfortunately, some of those people don't like us. For the sake of job security and national security, I need an energy bill, and I need it soon."

But some analysts disagree that Bush's proposals or the energy legislation would make much difference in freeing the nation from oil imports.

"This debate is a practical joke," said Anthony H. Cordesman, an expert on Middle Eastern oil at the Center for Strategic and International Studies (CSIS). "It is not a matter of coincidence that when Bush developed his energy policy, he didn't quantify in any meaningful way what the reduction in dependence would be. . . . All this is posturing and political bloviating."

Liberal Democrats such as Henry A. Waxman of California say the country would be better off without the bill. "This bill is an embarrassment," Waxman said Oct. 2. "If it fell by the wayside, that would be good for the country. We need to figure out a better energy policy. Especially in light of the fact that we're going to war with Iraq, we should be working on ways to become more self-sufficient, instead of just throwing more money at the oil, gas, coal and nuclear industries."

Sen. Frank H. Murkowski, R-Alaska, countered that Congress is on the right course with the legislation. "Our president has asked for our bill. Our constituents have asked that we pass an energy bill," he said. "We have an obligation to do what is right for America, and that is to come to grips with the reality that we are, at this time, clearly in a conflict, the nature of which we can only hope will not result in outright war with Iraq."

Difficult Choices

To be sure, the U.S. economy is not as dependent on oil as it was 20 years ago, nor does the oil come mostly from the Middle East. Canada is the largest supplier of petroleum and petroleum products. (*2002 CQ Weekly, p. 2574*)

The final bill will contain billions of dollars worth of incentives for oil and gas production in this country. It likely also will include support for research into new technologies, tax breaks for cars that use alternative fuels and a mandate to use more ethanol in gasoline, which advocates say could save fuel. It would permanently authorize the Strategic Petroleum Reserve on the Gulf Coast, which Bush already has ordered to be filled to its 700-million-barrel capacity.

Bush's energy proposals also go beyond the transportation sector, which consumes most of the nation's oil. Foreign oil is not needed for electricity, most of which is produced by coal, natural gas, nuclear plants and hydropower dams. (*2002 CQ Weekly, p. 2447*)

But critics say the incentives in the bill do more to help industry than to boost production or encourage conservation. If the nation was suffering from an energy crisis, analysts say, the government would have taken stronger steps to ease its reliance on oil from unstable and sometimes unfriendly Middle Eastern countries, which supplied 14 percent of U.S. imports in 2001. Instead, Congress rejected the most meaningful options because they required tough political choices.

The two most obvious examples of missed opportunities to cut imports are proposals to allow drilling in the coastal plain of ANWR and to force better fuel economy standards for motor vehicles, particularly for the popular but thirsty sport-utility vehicles (SUVs). (*2002 CQ Weekly, p. 643*)

One major way to reduce consumption would be to raise the Corporate Average Fuel Economy (CAFE) standards created in 1975 during the Ford administration. Those standards improved average fuel economy for cars from 14 to 27.5 miles per gallon — where they have remained ever since.

> **"**We're too dependent on foreign sources of crude oil. And unfortunately, some of those people don't like us. For the sake of job security and national security, I need an energy bill, and I need it soon.**"**
>
> —President
> George W. Bush

From 1995 to 1999, House Majority Whip Tom DeLay, R-Texas, led Republicans in adding language to annual transportation spending bills to prevent even a study of new standards.

During the energy bill debate, lawmakers did not pass tougher standards because they worried about public reaction and because they were lobbied by automakers and unions, who said that higher standards would cost jobs.

Conservatives trucked in "SUV soccer moms" to Capitol Hill to protest higher fuel economy standards — SUVs are governed by the light truck CAFE requirement that a manufacturer's fleet average 20.7 miles per gallon. Some are so heavy they are not governed by the standards at all.

Energy bill conferees have agreed to raise standards about one mile per gallon over six years by requiring savings of 5 billion gallons by 2014, which is two years later than the House would require in its bill.

The weak mileage standards are one reason environmental groups do not support the bill, even though it is unlikely to allow any drilling in ANWR. They also say Congress should do more to boost energy efficiency. The measure would allow tax credits for vehicles that use less oil, including gasoline-electric hybrid cars or future vehicles with fuel cells, but environmentalists say subsidies should be more generous.

Many economists and environmentalists say the most effective way to cut

consumption would be a fuel tax increase, which could be paired with tax cuts elsewhere. But for Republicans, tax increases are anathema. Democrats say such a tax would disproportionately affect low-income people. The issue is so politically volatile it was never seriously considered in the debate.

"Virtually no one supports this idea" politically, said Brookings Institution fellow Pietro S. Nivola, who said it would be more effective than high fuel standards because drivers would think twice about spending the extra money to drive their cars.

Cross Purposes

If policymakers are unwilling to force conservation on the public, they could encourage more production in the oil and gas fields the country has. But that poses other difficulties.

The Bush administration itself, which advocates more drilling on public lands, has not had uniform policies. Bush actually has banned drilling in some areas that developers had leased.

Earlier this year, Bush prevented development in the Gulf of Mexico near Florida waters because his brother, Florida Gov. Jeb Bush, who is campaigning for re-election, asked that the waters be protected. The government paid Collier Resources Co. to give up its drilling rights in south Florida and settled litigation with ChevronTexaco, Conoco and Murphy Oil to remove leases to drill for gas near Pensacola.

(2002 CQ Weekly, p. 1464)
Likewise, environmentalists have persuaded Congress to maintain drilling bans in waters on the East and West coasts, and last year it blocked drilling in national monument lands.

Of course, the biggest issue surrounding the entire energy bill is whether to drill in ANWR. (2002 CQ Weekly, p. 2047)

Republicans note that the amount of oil that could one day be drawn from the wilderness area on Alaska's Arctic coast would be the same as the United States imported from Iraq last year, according to government estimates.

"I can't think of a better way to tell Saddam Hussein, 'We don't need your oil,'" conference chairman Billy Tauzin, R-La., has said.

House members offered a potential ANWR compromise to the Senate on Oct. 1: In return for drilling, the House would agree to set aside an additional 10 million acres in the refuge as wilderness, the designation for public lands with high environmental protections where no development is allowed.

Republicans such as Rep. Joe L. Barton of Texas said the bill is not worth salvaging if Democrats will not compromise on the refuge. ANWR development also was the centerpiece of Bush's energy recommendations.

Barton added that provisions Democrats want, such as a plan to monitor climate change proposed by Robert C. Byrd, D-W.Va., and Ted Stevens, R-Alaska, would be "a non-starter until we start to see some movement on some other things," such as drilling in ANWR. House conferees rejected the climate change proposal Oct. 3.

Senate Democrats say they will not entertain any proposal to allow drilling in the refuge. Democrats disappointed environmentalists in the floor debate by compromising on a number of issues, including CAFE standards and a requirement for utility companies to use more renewable energy sources. But because it is such a high priority for environmentalists, most Democrats are holding firm against drilling in ANWR.

Sen. John B. Breaux of Louisiana is a conservative oil-state Democrat who has been unable to budge his party colleagues on the issue. He complains about doctrinaire positions.

"As long as we allow ourselves to be dictated to by outside groups, whether it's oil and gas groups or environmental groups who lock us into all-or-nothing positions, we'll end up not serving this country very well," Breaux said.

Searching for Sources

With the energy bill's most effective provisions essentially off the table, administration officials say they hope to use regulations and other means to allow more domestic production in areas such as the Rocky Mountain Front. (2002 CQ Weekly, p. 404)

But because development would take some time, officials are working to diversify the nation's sources of oil by encouraging increased production in Russia, Africa, Mexico and South America, where governments with strong ties to the United States are eager to capitalize on its energy needs.

"The solution isn't really in the U.S.," said Cynthia Quarterman, an energy attorney at Steptoe & Johnson who served as the director of the Minerals Management Service under the Clinton administration. "The answer is in other countries. . . . To its credit, the Bush administration has gone to Russia and West Africa to diversify its sources. Those pieces of policy are very important."

The administration sought to strengthen its ties with Russia during an energy summit the week of Sept. 30. Bush also has worked closely with Mexico President Vicente Fox in fostering cooperation on energy needs.

Trade pacts such as the North American Free Trade Agreement already have made it easier to work on energy needs with nations such as Canada and Mexico. Companies such as Marathon Oil Co., and Shell Oil Co., have projects in Mexico that allow the companies to pipe liquefied natural gas into the United States.

"It's still importing energy, but from a macro standpoint that's a more secure way of bringing imports into the U.S.," said Doug Glass, a senior attorney for the law firm Vinson & Elkins.

Breaks for Industry

Lawmakers still are sifting through various proposals to help the oil and gas industry, including a plan to allow owners of "marginal" wells that produce less than 30 barrels a day to get tax breaks and subsidies.

Companies such as El Paso Corp., ChevronTexaco, British Petroleum, and ExxonMobil could get funds to research deep-water drilling technology. The Senate bill would help states rehabilitate abandoned wells. The House bill would exempt deep-water wells from royalties for two years longer than current law allows.

Environmentalists oppose the House bill because it would do more to help the oil and gas industry than the Senate measure would. It would reimburse companies for conducting required environmental reviews, and would allow oil and gas producers to pay government royalties for drilling on public lands with in-kind transfers of oil, rather than with cash. The General Accounting Office has said such a system would be inefficient and could reduce company payments.

But the administration is concerned about the cost of the tax package and wants to limit it. The House package is $35 billion, while the Senate's is about $20 billion. Lobbyists and lawmakers said the White House would like to hold costs below $20 billion, though administration officials would not publicly comment on a specific price tag.

Short-Term Outlook

It is unclear whether the next few days of negotiations will produce a bill, but Tauzin insists he will get a deal or die trying.

"We're still making progress," he said Oct. 2. "Every day I sense that we're getting closer and closer."

A number of optimists were surprised by an outburst from Barton during the Oct. 2 conference session. If Senate Democrats continue to ignore Republican pleas for drilling in ANWR, he said, then "we ought to be up front about that and just call [the conference] off." He added that without a possible compromise, conferees "should tell the president we just can't do it and go about our business."

Both sides have been honing their political campaign attacks on the issues. Republicans say Democrats have stalled a bill the country desperately needs; Democrats say Republicans are only interested in helping the oil, gas and coal industries.

Optimists are counting on Tauzin to drive through a bill that would benefit industry interests in his state and in those of other House leaders. ◆

No Deals Reached This Year To Salvage Environmental Bills

Issues such as land use, oil drilling and global warming remain unresolved

Quick Contents

Congress this year has been unable to enact anything that would significantly affect the environment. Business groups and environmentalists are waging bitter campaigns that have left Congress even more deeply divided.

Congress never has an easy time enacting environmental laws, but this year it appears impossible.

Hostility between environmentalists and business interests in this election year has reached the point where there is almost no ground for compromise on such issues as automobile and industrial pollution, global warming, and logging or oil exploration on public lands. Congress also is focused more on foreign relations and security than on the environment.

As a result, legislation that would significantly affect the environment is almost invariably blocked in debate or left in committee. Congress has not been able to even pass appropriations bills to keep existing environmental programs running.

A $19.3 billion Interior spending bill (S 2708), for instance, has been stalled for weeks in the Senate because Republicans and Democrats disagree over whether to allow more logging in national forests to prevent wildfires. The House Resources Committee tried to move a separate measure (HR 5319) on forest-thinning, but a bipartisan deal fell apart and Republicans had to approve the bill on their own. Democrats thought it would allow too much logging.

The day before, legislation (HR 5428) to authorize about 400 Army Corps of Engineers water projects was pulled from the House suspension calendar after Democrats complained they were not being allowed to offer amendments that would have required outside reviews of Corps projects. The agency has been accused of using faulty economic data to justify some of its massive programs, many of which environmentalists say are harming rivers, streams and wildlife. (*2002 CQ Weekly, p. 2668*)

Lawmakers still may send President Bush an omnibus energy bill (HR 4) this year, but they may have to skip over contentious provisions that would affect the environment. Democrats refused to allow drilling for oil in Alaska's Arctic National Wildlife Refuge (ANWR) — the centerpiece of Bush's energy proposals — and Republicans, along with some Midwestern Democrats, would not permit any substantial increase in motor vehicle fuel economy standards.

Bush proposed more logging in public forests to help curb wildfires, which brought protesters to his Aug. 22 appearance in Central Point, Ore.

Energy conservation tax incentives likely to remain in the bill would have a marginal effect on energy consumption and pollution. The final bill also may require companies after five years to report their greenhouse gas emissions, which are linked to climate change. That provision could reduce the emissions, but the bill contains no explicit penalties to ensure healthier air.

Looking back over the 107th Congress, lawmakers say the most significant environmental legislation was a relatively modest law (PL 107-118) to help state and local governments clean up former industrial sites known as brownfields. It also shields some small businesses and landowners from superfund liability. (*2001 Almanac, p. 9-11*)

Even that legislation, which was scaled back from earlier efforts to overhaul the superfund program and came close to being killed several times, took most of the year to move through Congress and was finally cleared Dec. 20, 2001.

Modest Record

Environmental legislation has stalled in part the past year because lawmakers are focused on terrorism, homeland security and potential war with Iraq.

CQ Weekly Oct. 12, 2002

"Who cares about whales when people are dying?" said Larry J. Silverman, an environmental attorney and an adjunct professor of law for environmental science students at Johns Hopkins University.

Beyond that, the lack of action shows how little leeway there is for compromise on environmental issues. Neither side in Congress has been willing to give ground, or to be seen by supporters as giving ground.

Environmental organizations, business executives and lobbyists raise millions from their supporters to advocate polar-opposite positions, and the result is stalemate.

Particularly in an election year when control of both houses of Congress is at stake, lawmakers are wary of irritating their most loyal supporters. And neither environmentalists nor business groups want to compromise on issues such as drilling in ANWR or proposals to track greenhouse gas emissions. (*2002 CQ Weekly, p. 2570*)

In some states, local agencies and lawmakers have picked up the slack. Several states have enacted laws to control air pollutants such as mercury and carbon dioxide. Congress is still struggling with the issue, which is likely to come to a head before the 2004 presidential race. Both Democrats and Bush say they want to tighten air quality regulations, but they disagree over whether to regulate carbon dioxide, which many scientists say is a contributor to global warming.

But states can only control problems within their own borders, and many environmental issues are regional or national. Furthermore, the sluggish economy has caused budget problems for many states.

"Several members say that they're on the knife's edge of having to scale their programs back," said Steve Brown, executive director of the Environmental Council of the States, the trade association of state environmental regulators.

And the White House sometimes has stepped in to limit the ability of states to draw up their own rules. On Oct. 9, the administration announced that it would intervene on the side of automakers to block a California requirement that calls for 10 percent of the vehicles sold in the 2003-08 model years to be "zero-emission" or electric vehicles. The state revised its rules to grant automakers credit for selling hybrid vehicles, which run on electricity and gasoline, but car companies are challenging the rules. The case is pending before the U.S. 9th Circuit Court of Appeals in San Francisco.

Never an Easy Issue

Congress has always had difficulty enacting environmental laws, mainly because regulations can be expensive for business and landowners and are therefore seen by some lawmakers as a threat to the economy. Absent new or revised laws, federal regulators often are left to reinterpret old statutes.

During the 1990s, only three major environmental laws were enacted:

● The 1990 Clean Air Act (PL 101-549), which was pushed by President George Bush.

● The 1996 Safe Drinking Water Act (PL 104-182), which Republicans accepted as a way to shore up their environmental credentials.

● A 1996 rewrite of pesticide laws (PL 105-170). (*1990 Almanac, p. 229; 1996 Almanac, pp. 3-27; 4-4*)

"From 1997 forward, you've seen a lot of battles fought to a draw," said Phil Clapp, president of the National Environmental Trust and a former Democratic congressional aide. "That's largely because you had two administrations who were actively opposed to seeing major environmental legislation go forward."

The Clinton administration, Clapp said, worried that Republicans would accuse Vice President Al Gore of being an environmental extremist — "Ozone Man" as the elder George Bush called him in the 1988 campaign. The current Bush administration has closer ties to business, and particularly to the energy industry, than it does to environmentalists.

Clapp predicted that will change as the 2004 elections approach and Bush feels the need to burnish his environmental reputation. He angered environmentalists when, shortly after taking office, he reviewed and altered a number of Clinton administration regulations. Environmental lobbyists portray Bush as an extreme anti-environmentalist.

The president will need an environmental win, say Clapp and some other environmentalists, and the air quality legislation could provide that.

However, both sides would have to compromise in order to reach agreement, and some observers are skeptical.

"It's very difficult to do," said Ben Lieberman, a senior policy analyst with the Competitive Enterprise Institute, a conservative think tank. "It seems as if the Bush administration's better ideas are almost automatically attacked as anti-environmental, I think even unfairly."

"There's an element of the environmental community that's partisan, and strongly anti-Republican," Lieberman said. "So this becomes an issue that people are afraid to touch."

More Subtle Problems

Silverman, the environmental attorney, said the size and complexity of such issues are a major reason Congress cannot act.

"There are big global environmental issues, like energy and global warming, that are distracting because huge lobbying resources are being spent on them," he said. Also, "there's no appetite to spend a lot of money on these issues. Third, the problems are more complex than they were in the '70s. And the villains are less clear."

Thirty years ago, the United States was just beginning to enact major environmental statutes — the clean air and clean water laws. Environmental improvements were visible — this was an era when part of Lake Erie had caught fire — and the most dramatic problems of air and water pollution were reduced.

Today, the nation's remaining problems are just as serious but are more subtle. For instance, three decades ago communities were struggling with companies dumping pollution in water. Now, officials are trying to reduce runoff waste from harder-to-pinpoint sources, such as farms.

The outrage over these subtler problems is more muted than it was when the nation had few restrictions on polluting.

While Congress is focused on other issues, regulatory agencies continue to formulate environmental policy, some observers note.

"Agencies have the science, the staff and the ability to do massive rulemakings," said Bill Kovacs, vice president for environment and regulatory affairs at the U.S. Chamber of Commerce. "Compare that to the Hill, where you have sessions with five-minute rounds where you ask canned questions. . . . The processes are different, and it's becoming more difficult on the Hill to make the case on complex statutes that require scientific analysis. That's an inherent disadvantage that the Hill has that it can't overcome." ◆

White House and Kremlin Want End to Cold War Trade Law

Congress reluctant to repeal Jackson-Vanik due to poultry export, WTO issues

Quick Contents

The 1974 Jackson-Vanik trade law, intended to help Soviet Jews emigrate, has now become a vehicle for unrelated trade issues, ranging from Russia's membership in the World Trade Organization to U.S. chicken exports. And now it is affecting nuclear proliferation.

On the surface, it is hard to see why ending largely symbolic trade restrictions on Russia should be a big deal for either Congress or the Kremlin.

After all, the so-called Jackson-Vanik law, which bars normal trade with communist countries that forbid free emigration, has had little practical effect since the end of the Cold War. Indeed, President Bush promised Russian President Vladimir V. Putin last year that he would push Congress to repeal the law to reward the Kremlin for its support in the war on terrorism.

But Congress is not ready to roll over just yet. Its reluctance to repeal Jackson-Vanik stems from a dispute over U.S. exports of chicken to Russia and concerns over Russia's accession to the World Trade Organization (WTO). As a result, the issue has been left to fester as White House officials focus on more urgent foreign policy issues such as Iraq and North Korea.

Now, the fact that Congress and the administration have not followed through on Bush's pledge is becoming an increasing sore point in U.S.-Russian relations, convincing the Kremlin that the United States cannot be trusted to carry out its promises. And this

CQ Weekly Oct. 26, 2002

lack of faith has geopolitical consequences: It is hobbling administration efforts to persuade Russia to halt nuclear sales to Iran and to support a tough stance toward Iraq by the U.N. Security Council.

"The Russians know this is symbolic legislation, but to them it's symbolic of how we think about them," said Toby Gati, a former senior Clinton administration official who closely tracks Russian issues. "To them, it shows the priorities of the administration and how much political capital they are willing to expend on Russian issues."

Intended to Help Russian Jews

Named for the late Sen. Henry M. "Scoop" Jackson, D-Wash. (House 1941-53; Senate 1953-83), and former Rep. Charles A. Vanik, D-Ohio (1955-81), Jackson-Vanik became law as an amendment to the 1974 Trade Act (PL 93-618). It was designed to punish the Soviet Union for refusing to allow Soviet Jews to emigrate freely to Israel. (*1974 Almanac, p. 553, 514*)

The law requires the president to certify annually to Congress that a country meets certain emigration requirements before it can be eligible for normal trade ties. The disintegration of the Soviet Union and the resulting spike in Jewish emigration to Israel prompted U.S. presidents since 1990 to waive the restrictions for Russia and other former Soviet republics. Since 1994, Russia has met the U.S. mandate.

Many, including human rights advocates, now view Jackson-Vanik as an outdated impediment to trade. To Russia, it is as much an insult as an impediment.

"Russia wants to be treated like a significant power," said Jacqueline M. Miller, a Russia and Eurasia expert at the Center for Strategic and International Studies. "This is the kind of thing that significant powers shouldn't have to do."

Adding to this slight is the fact that former Soviet republics Kyrgyzstan and Georgia — not to mention communist giant China — were granted permanent normal trade relations (PNTR) status by Congress in 2000. (*2000 Almanac, p. 20-3*)

As Putin tries to move Russia into the WTO, normal trade ties with the United States are crucial.

Supporters of normalizing trade relations

AP PHOTO / MIKHAIL METZEL

Russia is limiting imports of American chicken to signal frustration with the 1974 Jackson-Vanik law.

with Russia point out that the economic impact of removing the Jackson-Vanik requirement would be minimal. U.S.-Russian trade is relatively insignificant in terms of each nation's total imports and exports. It is, however, more important to Moscow. While U.S. exports to Russia have hovered between $2 billion and $3 billion since 1992, Russian imports have grown in value from $500 million to nearly $7 billion in 2001.

For U.S. businesses, there is a sense that repealing Jackson-Vanik would improve the overall U.S.-Russian business and investment climate.

"The timing is right," said Jeffrey H. Jones, director of congressional affairs at the U.S.-Russia Business Council. "Jewish emigration is no longer an issue. We need to recognize the current reality." He said Jackson-Vanik's repeal would "lend a greater sense of stability to the commercial relationship."

Bush's Promise

Eliminating Jackson-Vanik requirements was a central focus of discussions between Putin and Bush when the two met at the president's Crawford, Texas, ranch in November 2001. With Russia's cooperation in the war on terrorism, Bush pledged to work with Congress to secure Russia's PNTR status.

House Ways and Means Committee Chairman Bill Thomas, R-Calif., who supports normal trade relations with Russia, has introduced legislation (HR 3553) that would eliminate roadblocks such as Jackson-Vanik. Human rights stalwart Tom Lantos of California, ranking Democrat on the House International Relations Committee, has indicated that he will now support PNTR status for Russia, provided that certain ongoing human rights safeguards are kept in place. (*2001 CQ Weekly, p. 2659*)

But as the State Department tried to fashion a deal that would send a Russia PNTR bill through Congress in time for the Bush-Putin summit in Moscow in May, the administration found how easily national security issues can get entangled in trade spats. (*2002 CQ Weekly, p. 1328*)

First, Senate Finance Committee Chairman Max Baucus, D-Mont., argued that the United States should make PNTR for Russia dependent on its acceptance in the WTO. That is the way Congress handled PNTR for China.

But even as administration and congressional negotiators worked on a deal that might lift the Jackson-Vanik restrictions on Russia while allowing Congress to weigh in later on Russia's joining the WTO, a more contentious issue arose: chickens.

In March, shortly after Bush's decision to put new tariffs on Russian and other foreign steel imports, Russia banned the American poultry imports for one month, citing the discovery of salmonella bacteria in U.S. chickens.

Russia was introduced to American chickens in the early 1990s when the first Bush administration sent food aid to the former Soviet states. Ordinary Russians came to love what became known then as nozhki Busha, or "Bush legs." But later Russian authorities restricted the U.S. imports, after Russian poultry producers accused the United States of trying to dominate the market.

Russia continued to restrict the chicken imports, prompting an outcry from the U.S. poultry industry, which views Russia as a major export market. Legislators from poultry industry states, including Senate Foreign Relations Committee Chairman Joseph R. Biden Jr., D-Del., and Rep. Nathan Deal, R-Ga., decided to hold the Jackson-Vanik issue hostage as long as Russia was blocking their chicken exports. (*2002 CQ Weekly, p. 1364*)

Poultry-state lawmakers and allies of labor who opposed Russia's admission to the WTO combined forces to torpedo an attempt to add a PNTR provision to the omnibus trade package (PL 107-210) before the Senate last spring. That dashed Bush's hopes of having a deal in hand when he met Putin on May 23. (*2002 CQ Weekly, p. 2021*)

Since then, the poultry dispute has been resolved — but only on the surface. In late August, U.S. negotiators reached an agreement with the Russians outlining new plant inspection guidelines and hygienic requirements.

But some in the U.S. poultry industry are not pleased with that deal and regard its implementation warily.

"The agreement was certainly not what we would have hoped for," said Toby Moore, a spokesman for the U.S. Poultry and Egg Export Council.

Moore said the terms of the agreement, which allows Russian officials to reinspect U.S. plants and cold storage facilities, are "very restrictive." In particular, Moore said, some tests demanded by the Russians to protect against animal diseases and track the use of antibiotics in feed appear to have questionable scientific merit.

Meanwhile, industry and congressional sources say that Baucus is not relenting on the WTO question either.

A Senate Democratic aide familiar with Baucus' thinking on the issue said the Senate Finance Committee chairman's stance has not changed: He is still firm in his belief that Congress should get to weigh in on WTO before normalizing trade relations with Russia.

Perhaps more significant is the fact that the administration has not approached Baucus or Senate Majority Leader Tom Daschle, D-S.D., about the Russia issue since last spring, although Democrats express a willingness to cut a deal, Senate aides say.

Paul V. Kelly, assistant secretary of State for legislative affairs, said that since their setback in May, top administration officials have decided to concentrate their lobbying on other, more pressing foreign policy issues, such as Iraq, once it became clear how tough it would be to win congressional support on repealing Jackson-Vanik.

"We were working other issues and just set it aside," Kelly said.

Profit or Proliferation

But that has allowed Russian officials to use Congress' unwillingness to repeal the law as an excuse for rebuffing U.S. demands to sever long-term and profitable economic ties with Iran and Iraq.

U.S. officials want the Kremlin to end those relationships as part of their broader efforts to foil Middle Eastern countries' attempt to acquire unconventional weapons and the missiles to deliver them.

"This has always been a talking point with the Kremlin, but now it's a generalized talking point that is cited and cited more often throughout the government," said Rose Gottemoeller, formerly a top Clinton administration non-proliferation official.

"The Russians don't want to be asked to give up something real when all they've been getting in return are promises," adds Gati.

Russian officials have amplified their complaints about Jackson-Vanik as U.S. diplomats have been working around the clock to win Moscow's support for a tough new U.N. resolution on Iraq that would provide for a rigorous weapons inspections regime and a credible threat of war if Baghdad fails to comply.

The Kremlin is concerned that if Iraqi President Saddam Hussein is ousted in a military invasion, a new Iraqi government will not repay billions of dollars that Iraq owes Russia. They also worry that a new government would void potentially lucrative oil concessions granted by Saddam.

Russia has been particularly outspoken in citing Jackson-Vanik as its rationale for continuing to fulfill a valuable contract to supply Iran with nuclear reactors. Russian scientists are nearing completion of an $800 million nuclear reactor at the Iranian coastal city of Bushehr. Moscow also signed agreements with Iran in July to provide as many as five more reactors. U.S. officials worry that the spent fuel, technology and scientific knowledge associated with the reactors could help Tehran build nuclear weapons.

Administration officials and lawmakers acknowledge that previous attempts to stop Russian cooperation with Iran by punishing Moscow have done little good. These sanctions have included cuts in U.S. foreign aid and withholding subsidies to Russia for the International Space Station. (2000 *Almanac, p. 11-10*)

In 1998, President Bill Clinton imposed sanctions on seven Russian companies and laboratories for aiding Iran's missile program after vetoing legislation that would have required sanctions against Moscow. (*1998 Almanac, p. 16-16*)

Recently, U.S. officials proposed easing some of Moscow's economic concerns by allowing Russia to store spent nuclear fuel from Asian nations such as South Korea and Taiwan if the Kremlin agrees to end its nuclear cooperation with Iran.

The Asian nations have no final depository for their high-level nuclear waste and have been intrigued by the idea of storing the fuel in Russia, which already has experience storing substantial quantities of its own spent fuel from weapons and civilian programs.

But under existing bilateral agreements with the United States, which provides the Asian nations with their

A Cold War Relic Lives On

To qualify for normal trading status under the Jackson-Vanik law, nations must either meet emigration requirements or win an annual presidential waiver of the restrictions, which Congress can block.

The countries that have met these requirements and therefore have "graduated" from the law's restrictions:	
Georgia, 2000	(PL 106-476)
China, 2000	(PL 106-286)
Kyrgyzstan, 2000	(PL 106-200)
Albania, 2000	(PL 106-200)
Bulgaria, 1996	(PL 104-162)
Romania, 1996	(PL 104-171)
Czechoslovakia, 1991	(PL 102-182)
Hungary, 1991	(PL 102-182)

The countries whose trade status still must be reviewed annually under the Jackson-Vanik restrictions:	
Vietnam	Ukraine
Armenia	Uzbekistan
Azerbaijan	Moldova
Belarus	
Kazakhstan	
Russia	
Tajikistan	
Turkmenistan	

reactor fuel, these countries are not allowed to export the spent fuel without Washington's permission, including a vote by Congress.

That gives U.S. officials leverage in talks with the Russians. A contract to store spent nuclear fuel could be worth between $10 billion and $30 billion to the Russians, said Robert E. Newman, the president of NPT International Ltd., a private organization that has been pushing Russian and U.S. officials to endorse such a deal.

"If the Russians end their sensitive cooperation with Iran, we have indicated we would be prepared to favorably consider such transfer arrangements potentially worth over $10 billion to Moscow," the State Department said in an Oct. 23 statement.

Trade Talks

Even though Russian officials are eager to conclude such an accord, they told the United States that congressional machinations over Jackson-Vanik have lessened their willingness to sacrifice immediate payoffs for long-term economic gains.

"Americans are being rather sly when they offer this kind of swap," Yuri Bespalko, a spokesman for the Russian Atomic Energy Ministry, told reporters in Moscow on Oct. 21. "It's better to have a bird in the hand than two in the bush."

Meanwhile, Russia's recalcitrance has encouraged the administration to think again about pushing the repeal

of Jackson-Vanik.

"It's something we should look and see if we can resurrect during the lame duck" Kelly said of the session of Congress that begins after next month's midterm elections.

But that could be tough if lawmakers succeed in linking Jackson-Vanik to the larger issue of Russia's entry into the WTO, as the administration tries to reconcile its foreign policy goals with the realities of international trade and those domestic special interests affected by it.

U.S. negotiators are making slow progress with Russia on WTO-relevant issues such as intellectual property rights, financial services, telecommunications and energy. But according to one U.S. trade official, discussions continue with Russia about normalizing the two nations' trade relationship.

"There's lots of dialogue going on," the official said, adding that the process of cementing strong trade ties, and Russia's inclusion in the WTO, could take a year or more. "There are lots of things that Russia is going to have to do," the official said.

With that in mind, companies that want to do business in Russia say prospects for a quick lifting of the Jackson-Vanik restrictions are not good.

Said one American industry source who asked not to be named: "Our understanding now is that it's not going anywhere." ◆

Appendix

The Legislative Process in Brief

Note: Parliamentary terms used below are defined in the glossary.

Introduction of Bills

A House member (including the resident commissioner of Puerto Rico and nonvoting delegates of the District of Columbia, Guam, the Virgin Islands and American Samoa) may introduce any one of several types of bills and resolutions by handing it to the clerk of the House or placing it in a box called the hopper. A senator first gains recognition of the presiding officer to announce the introduction of a bill.

As the usual next step in either the House or Senate, the bill is numbered, referred to the appropriate committee, labeled with the sponsor's name and sent to the Government Printing Office so that copies can be made for subsequent study and action. House and Senate bills may be jointly sponsored and carry several senators' names. A bill written in the executive branch and proposed as an administration measure usually is introduced by the chairman of the congressional committee that has jurisdiction, as a courtesy to the White House.

Bills—Prefixed with HR in the House, S in the Senate, followed by a number. Used as the form for most legislation, whether general or special, public or private.

Joint Resolutions—Designated H J Res or S J Res. Subject to the same procedure as bills, with the exception of a joint resolution proposing an amendment to the Constitution. The latter must be approved by two-thirds of both houses and is then sent directly to the administrator of general services for submission to the states for ratification instead of being presented to the president for his approval.

Concurrent Resolutions—Designated H Con Res or S Con Res. Used for matters affecting the operations of both houses. These resolutions do not become law.

Resolutions—Designated H Res or S Res. Used for a matter concerning the operation of either house alone and adopted only by the chamber in which it originates.

Committee Action

With few exceptions, bills are referred to the appropriate standing committees. The job of referral formally is the responsibility of the Speaker of the House and the presiding officer of the Senate, but this task usually is carried out on their behalf by the parliamentarians of the House and Senate. Precedent, statute and the jurisdictional mandates of the committees as set forth in the rules of the House and Senate determine which committees receive what kinds of bills. Bills are technically considered "read for the first time" when referred to House committees.

When a bill reaches a committee it is placed on the committee's calendar. Failure of a committee to act on a bill is equivalent to killing it and most fall by the legislative roadside. The measure can be withdrawn from the committee's purview only by a discharge petition signed by a majority of the House membership on House bills, or by adoption of a special resolution in the Senate. Discharge attempts rarely succeed and the Senate procedure has not been used for decades.

The first committee action taken on a bill usually is a request for comment on it by interested agencies of the government. The committee chairman may assign the bill to a subcommittee for study and hearings, or it may be considered by the full committee. Hearings may be public, closed (executive session) or both. A subcommittee, after considering a bill, reports to the full committee its recommendations for action and any proposed amendments.

The full committee then votes on its recommendation to the House or Senate. This procedure is called "ordering a bill reported." Occasionally a committee may order a bill reported unfavorably; most of the time a report, submitted by the chairman of the committee to the House or Senate, calls for favorable action on the measure since the committee can effectively "kill" a bill by simply failing to take any action.

After the bill is reported, the committee chairman instructs the staff to prepare a written report. The report describes the purposes and scope of the bill, explains the committee revisions, notes proposed changes in existing law and, usually, includes the views of the executive branch agencies consulted. Often committee members opposing a measure issue dissenting minority statements that are included in the report.

Usually, the committee "marks up" or proposes amendments to the bill. If the amendments are substantial and the measure is complicated, the committee may order a "clean bill" introduced, which will embody the proposed amendments. The original bill then is put aside and the clean bill, with a new number, is reported to the floor.

The chamber must approve, alter or reject the committee amendments before the bill itself can be put to a vote.

Floor Action

After a bill is reported back to the house where it originated, it is placed on the calendar.

There are five legislative calendars in the House, issued in one cumulative calendar titled *Calendars of the United States House of Representatives and History of Legislation*. The House calendars are:

The Union Calendar to which are referred bills raising revenues, general appropriations bills and any measures directly or indirectly appropriating money or property. It is the Calendar of the Committee of the Whole House on the State of the Union.

This graphic shows the most typical way in which proposed legislation is enacted into law. There are more complicated, as well as simpler, routes, and most bills never become law. The process is illustrated with two hypothetical bills, House bill No. 1 (HR 1) and

Senate bill No. 2 (S 2). Bills must be passed by both houses in identical form before they can be sent to the president. The path of HR 1 is traced by a gray line, that of S 2 by a black line. In practice, most bills begin as similar proposals in both houses.

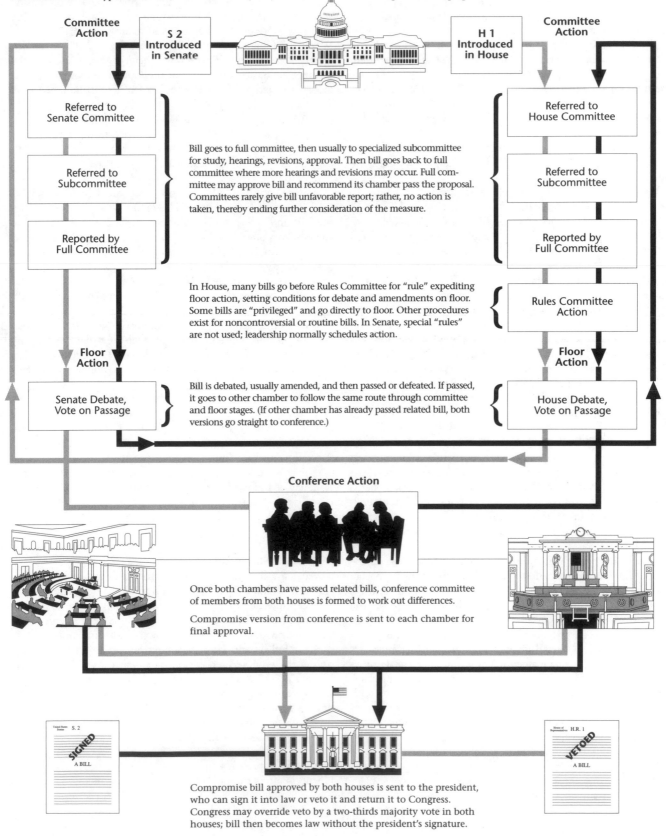

Committee Action

S 2 Introduced in Senate

H 1 Introduced in House

Committee Action

Referred to Senate Committee

Referred to Subcommittee

Reported by Full Committee

Bill goes to full committee, then usually to specialized subcommittee for study, hearings, revisions, approval. Then bill goes back to full committee where more hearings and revisions may occur. Full committee may approve bill and recommend its chamber pass the proposal. Committees rarely give bill unfavorable report; rather, no action is taken, thereby ending further consideration of the measure.

Referred to House Committee

Referred to Subcommittee

Reported by Full Committee

In House, many bills go before Rules Committee for "rule" expediting floor action, setting conditions for debate and amendments on floor. Some bills are "privileged" and go directly to floor. Other procedures exist for noncontroversial or routine bills. In Senate, special "rules" are not used; leadership normally schedules action.

Rules Committee Action

Floor Action

Senate Debate, Vote on Passage

Bill is debated, usually amended, and then passed or defeated. If passed, it goes to other chamber to follow the same route through committee and floor stages. (If other chamber has already passed related bill, both versions go straight to conference.)

Floor Action

House Debate, Vote on Passage

Conference Action

Once both chambers have passed related bills, conference committee of members from both houses is formed to work out differences.

Compromise version from conference is sent to each chamber for final approval.

S. 2 SIGNED A BILL

H.R. 1 VETOED A BILL

Compromise bill approved by both houses is sent to the president, who can sign it into law or veto it and return it to Congress. Congress may override veto by a two-thirds majority vote in both houses; bill then becomes law without the president's signature.

The House Calendar to which are referred bills of public character not raising revenue or appropriating money.

The Corrections Calendar to which are referred bills to repeal rules and regulations deemed excessive or unnecessary when the Corrections Calendar is called the second and fourth Tuesday of each month. (Instituted in the 104th Congress to replace the seldom-used Consent Calendar.) A three-fifths majority is required for passage.

The Private Calendar to which are referred bills for relief in the nature of claims against the United States or private immigration bills that are passed without debate when the Private Calendar is called the first and third Tuesdays of each month.

The Discharge Calendar to which are referred motions to discharge committees when the necessary signatures are signed to a discharge petition.

There is only one legislative calendar in the Senate and one "executive calendar" for treaties and nominations submitted to the Senate.

Debate. A bill is brought to debate by varying procedures. In the Senate the majority leader, in consultation with the minority leader and others, schedules the bills that will be taken up for debate. If it is urgent or important it can be taken up in the Senate either by unanimous consent or by a majority vote.

In the House, precedence is granted if a special rule is obtained from the Rules Committee. A request for a special rule usually is made by the chairman of the committee that favorably reported the bill. The request is considered by the Rules Committee in the same fashion that other committees consider legislative measures. The committee proposes a resolution providing for immediate consideration of the bill. The Rules Committee reports the resolution to the House where it is debated and voted on in the same fashion as regular bills.

The resolutions providing special rules are important because they specify how long the bill may be debated and whether it may be amended from the floor. If floor amendments are banned, the bill is considered under a "closed rule."

When a bill is debated under an "open rule," amendments may be offered from the floor. Committee amendments always are taken up first but may be changed, as may all amendments up to the second degree; that is, an amendment to an amendment to an amendment is not in order.

Duration of debate in the House depends on whether the bill is under discussion by the House proper or before the House when it is sitting as the Committee of the Whole House on the State of the Union. In the former, the amount of time for debate is allocated with an hour for each member if the measure is under consideration without a rule. In the Committee of the Whole the amount of time agreed on for general debate is equally divided between proponents and opponents. At the end of general discussion, the bill is often read section by section for amendment. Debate on an amendment is limited to five minutes for each side; this is called the "five-minute rule." In practice, amendments regularly are debated more than ten minutes, with members gaining the floor by offering pro forma amendments or obtaining unanimous consent to speak longer than five minutes.

Senate debate usually is unlimited. It can be halted only by unanimous consent or by "cloture," which requires a three-fifths majority of the entire Senate except for proposed changes in the Senate rules. The latter requires a two-thirds vote.

The House considers almost all important bills within a parliamentary framework known as the Committee of the Whole. It is not a committee as the word usually is understood; it is the full House meeting under another name for the purpose of speeding action on legislation. Technically, the House sits as the Committee of the Whole when it considers any tax measure or bill dealing with public appropriations. Upon adoption of a special rule, the Speaker declares the House resolved into the Committee of the Whole and appoints a member of the majority party to serve as the chairman. The rules of the House permit the Committee of the Whole to meet when a quorum of 100 members is present on the floor and to amend and act on bills. When the Committee of the Whole has acted, it "rises," the Speaker returns as the presiding officer of the House and the member appointed chairman of the Committee of the Whole reports the action of the committee and its recommendations. The Committee of the Whole cannot pass a bill; instead it reports the measure to the full House with whatever changes it has approved. The full House then may pass or reject the bill — or, on occasion, recommit the bill to committee. Amendments adopted in the Committee of the Whole may be put to a second vote in the full House.

Votes. Voting on bills may occur repeatedly before they are finally approved or rejected. The House votes on the rule for the bill and on various amendments to the bill. Voting on amendments often is a more illuminating test of a bill's support than is the final tally. Sometimes members approve final passage of bills after vigorously supporting amendments that, if adopted, would have scuttled the legislation.

The Senate has three different methods of voting: an untabulated voice vote, a standing vote (called a division) and a recorded roll call to which members answer "yea" or "nay" when their names are called. The House also employs voice and standing votes, but since January 1973 yeas and nays have been recorded by an electronic voting device, eliminating the need for time-consuming roll calls.

After amendments to a bill have been voted upon, a vote may be taken on a motion to recommit the bill to committee. If carried, this vote is usually a death blow to the bill. If the motion is unsuccessful, the bill then is "read for the third time." After the third reading a vote on passage is taken. The final vote may be followed by a motion to reconsider, and this motion may be followed by a move to lay the motion on the table. Usually, those voting for the bill's passage vote for the tabling motion, thus safeguarding the final passage action. With that, the bill has been formally passed by the chamber.

Action in Second Chamber

After a bill is passed it is sent to the other chamber. This body may then take one of several steps. It may pass the bill as is — accepting the other chamber's language. It may send the bill to committee for scrutiny or alteration, or reject the entire bill, advising the other chamber of its actions. Or it simply may ignore the bill submitted while it continues work on its own version of the proposed legislation. Frequently, one chamber may approve a version of a bill that is greatly at variance with the version already passed by the other chamber, and then substitute its contents for the language of the other, retaining only the latter's bill number.

Often the second chamber makes only minor changes. If these are readily agreed to by the other chamber, the bill then is routed to the president. However, if the opposite chamber significantly alters the bill submitted to it, the measure usually is "sent to conference." The chamber that has possession of the "papers" (engrossed bill, engrossed amendments, messages of transmittal) requests a conference and the other chamber may agree to it. If the second chamber does not agree, the bill dies.

Examples of Legislative Documents

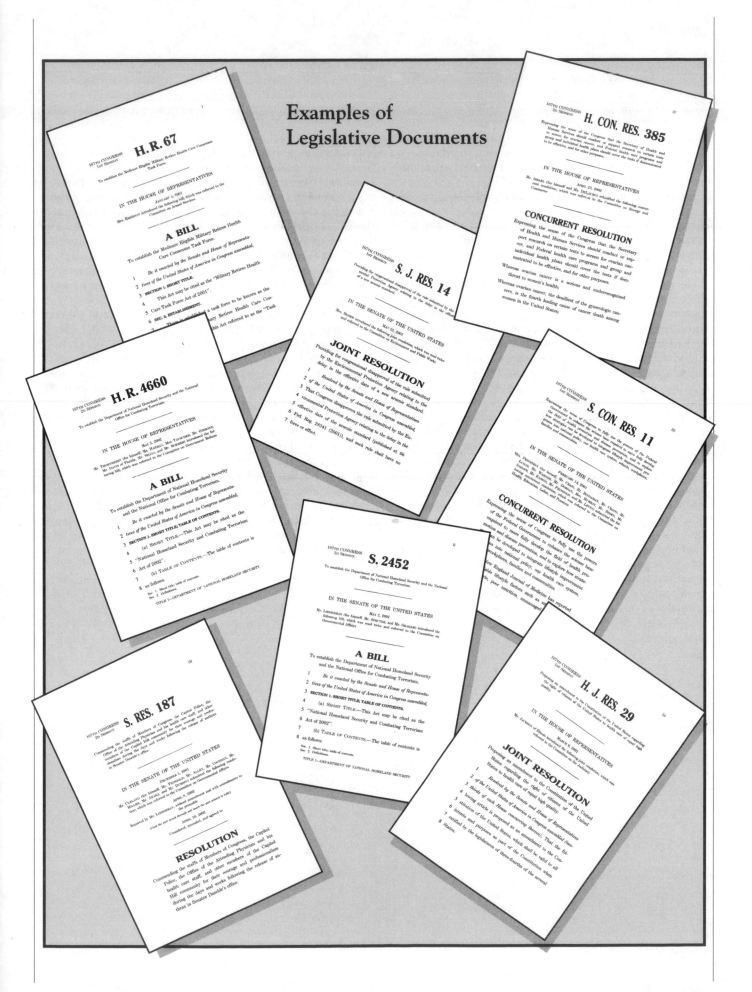

Conference Action

A conference works out conflicting House and Senate versions of a legislative bill. The conferees usually are senior members from the committees that managed the legislation who are appointed by the presiding officers of the two houses. Under this arrangement the conferees of one house have the duty of trying to maintain their chamber's position in the face of amending actions by the conferees (also referred to as "managers") of the other house.

The number of conferees from each chamber may vary, the range usually being from seven to nine members in each group, depending on the length or complexity of the bill involved. But a majority vote controls the action of each group so that a large representation does not give one chamber a voting advantage over the other chamber's conferees.

Theoretically, conferees are not allowed to write new legislation in reconciling the two versions before them, but this curb sometimes is bypassed. Many bills have been put into acceptable compromise form only after new language was provided by the conferees. Frequently the ironing out of difficulties takes days or even weeks. Conferences on involved, complex and controversial bills sometimes are particularly drawn out.

As a conference proceeds, conferees reconcile differences between the versions, but generally they grant concessions only insofar as they remain sure that the chamber they represent will accept the compromises. Occasionally, uncertainty over how either house will react, or the positive refusal of a chamber to back down on a disputed amendment, results in an impasse, and the bills die in conference even though each was approved by its sponsoring chamber.

When the conferees have reached agreement, they prepare a conference report embodying their recommendations (compromises) and a joint explanatory statement. The report, in document form, must be submitted to each house. The conference report must be approved by each house. Consequently, approval of the report is approval of the compromise bill. In the order of voting on conference reports, the chamber that asked for a conference yields to the other chamber the opportunity to vote first.

Final Action

After a bill has been passed by both the House and Senate in identical form, all of the original papers are sent to the enrolling clerk of the chamber in which the bill originated. The clerk then prepares an enrolled bill, which is printed on parchment paper.

When this bill has been certified as correct by the secretary of the Senate or the clerk of the House, depending on which chamber originated the bill, it is signed first (no matter whether it originated in the Senate or House) by the Speaker of the House and then by the president of the Senate. It is next sent to the White House to await action.

If the president approves the bill, he signs it, dates it and usually writes the word "approved" on the document. If the president does not sign it within 10 days (Sundays excepted) and Congress is in session, the bill becomes law without his signature.

If Congress adjourns *sine die* at the end of the second session the president can pocket veto a bill and it dies without Congress having the opportunity to override.

A president vetoes a bill by refusing to sign it and, before the ten-day period expires, returning it to Congress with a message stating his reasons. The message is sent to the chamber that originated the bill. If no action is taken on the message, the bill dies. Congress, however, can attempt to override the president's veto and enact the bill, "the objections of the president to the contrary notwithstanding." Overriding a veto requires a two-thirds vote of those present in each chamber, who must number a quorum and vote by roll call.

If the president's veto is overridden by a two-thirds vote in both houses, the bill becomes law. Otherwise it is dead.

When bills are passed finally and signed, or passed over a veto, they are given law numbers in numerical order as they become law. There are two series of numbers, one for public and one for private laws, starting at the number "1" for each two-year term of Congress. They are then identified by law number and by Congress — for example, Private Law 10, 105th Congress; Public Law 33, 106th Congress (or PL 106-33).

The Budget Process in Brief

Through the budget process, the president and Congress decide how much to spend and tax during the upcoming fiscal year. More specifically, they decide how much to spend on each activity, ensure that the government spends no more than that and spends it only for that activity and report on that spending at the end of each budget cycle.

The President's Budget

The law requires that, by the first Monday in February, the president submit to Congress his proposed federal budget for the next fiscal year, which begins on October 1. To accomplish this the president establishes general budget and fiscal policy guidelines. Based on these guidelines, executive branch agencies make requests for funds and submit them to the White House's Office of Management and Budget (OMB) nearly a year before the start of a new fiscal year. The OMB, receiving direction from the president and administration officials, reviews the agencies' requests and develops a detailed budget by December. From December to January the OMB prepares the budget documents, so that the president can deliver it to Congress in February.

The president's budget is the executive branch's plan for the next year — but it is just a proposal. After receiving it, Congress has its own budget process to follow from February to October. Only after Congress passes the required spending bills — and the president signs them — has the government created its actual budget.

Action in Congress

Congress first must pass a "budget resolution" — a framework within which the members of Congress will make their decisions about spending and taxes. It includes targets for total spending, total revenues and the deficit, and allocations within the spending target for the two types of spending — discretionary and mandatory.

Discretionary spending, which currently accounts for about 33 percent of all federal spending, is what the president and Congress must decide to spend for the next year through the thirteen annual appropriations bills. It includes money for such activities as the FBI and the Coast Guard, for housing and education, for NASA and highway and bridge construction and for defense and foreign aid.

Mandatory spending, which currently accounts for 67 percent of all spending, is authorized by laws that have already been passed. It includes entitlement spending — such as for Social Security, Medicare, veterans' benefits and food stamps — through which individuals receive benefits because they are eligible based on their age, income or other criteria. It also includes interest on the national debt, which the government pays to individuals and institutions that hold Treasury bonds and other government securities. The only way the president and Congress can change the spending on entitlement and other mandatory programs is if they change the laws that authorized the programs.

Currently, the law requires that legislation that would raise mandatory spending or lower revenues — compared to existing law — be offset by spending cuts or revenue increases. This requirement, called "pay-as-you-go" is designed to prevent new legislation from increasing the deficit.

Once Congress passes the budget resolution, legislators turn their attention to passing the 13 annual appropriations bills and, if they choose, "authorizing" bills to change the laws governing mandatory spending and revenues.

Congress begins by examining the president's budget in detail. Scores of committees and subcommittees hold hearings on proposals under their jurisdiction. The House and Senate Armed Services Authorizing Committees, and the Defense and Military Construction Subcommittees of the Appropriations Committees, for instance, hold hearings on the president's defense budget. The White House budget director, cabinet officers and other administration officials work with Congress as it accepts some of the president's proposals, rejects others and changes still others. Congress can change funding levels, eliminate programs or add programs not requested by the president. It can add or eliminate taxes and other sources of revenue, or make other changes that affect the amount of revenue collected. Congressional rules require that these committees and subcommittees take actions that reflect the congressional budget resolution.

The president's budget, the budget resolution and the appropriations or authorizing bills measure spending in two ways — "budget authority" and "outlays." Budget authority is what the law authorizes the federal government to spend for certain programs, projects or activities. What the government actually spends in a particular year, however, is an outlay. For example, when the government decides to build a space exploration system, the president and Congress may agree to appropriate $1 billion in budget authority. But the space system may take ten years to build. Thus, the government may spend $100 million in outlays in the first year to begin construction and the remaining $900 million during the next nine years as the construction continues.

Congress must provide budget authority before the federal agencies can obligate the government to make outlays. When Congress fails to complete action on one or more of the regular annual appropriations bills before the fiscal year begins on October 1, budget authority may be made on a temporary basis through continuing resolutions. Continuing resolutions make budget authority available for limited periods of time, generally at rates related through some formula to the rate provided in the previous year's appropriation.

Monitoring the Budget

Once Congress passes and the president signs the federal appropriations bills or authorizing laws for the fiscal year, the government monitors the budget through (1) agency program managers and budget officials, including the Inspectors General, who report only to the agency head; (2) the Office of Management and Budget; (3) congressional committees; and (4) the General Accounting Office, an auditing arm of Congress.

This oversight is designed to (1) ensure that agencies comply with legal limits on spending and that agencies use budget authority only for the purposes intended; (2) see that programs are operating consistently with legal requirements and existing policy; and (3) ensure that programs are well managed and achieving the intended results.

The president may withhold appropriated amounts from obligation only under certain limited circumstances — to provide for contingencies, to achieve savings made possible through changes in requirements or greater efficiency of operations or as otherwise provided by law. The Impoundment Control Act of 1974 specifies the procedures that must be followed if funds are withheld. Congress can also cancel previous authorized budget authority by passing a rescissions bill — but it also must be signed by the president.

Bigger Bite Amendment—An amendment that substantively changes a portion of a text including language that had previously been amended. Normally, language that has been amended may not be amended again. However, a part of a sentence that has been changed by amendment, for example, may be changed again by an amendment that amends a "bigger bite" of the text — that is, by an amendment that also substantively changes the unamended parts of the sentence or the entire section or title in which the previously amended language appears. The biggest possible bite is an amendment in the nature of a substitute that amends the entire text of a measure. Once adopted, therefore, such an amendment ends the amending process.

Bill—The term for the chief vehicle Congress uses for enacting laws. Bills that originate in the House of Representatives are designated as HR, those in the Senate as S, followed by a number assigned in the order in which they are introduced during a two-year Congress. A bill becomes a law if passed in identical language by both houses and signed by the president, or passed over the president's veto, or if the president fails to sign it within ten days after receiving it while Congress is in session.

Bill of Attainder—An act of a legislature finding a person guilty of treason or a felony. The Constitution prohibits the passage of such a bill by the U.S. Congress or any state legislature.

Bills and Resolutions Introduced—Members formally present measures to their respective houses by delivering them to a clerk in the chamber when their house is in session. Both houses permit any number of members to join in introducing a bill or resolution. The first member listed on the measure is the sponsor; the other members listed are its cosponsors.

Bills and Resolutions Referred—After a bill or resolution is introduced, it is normally sent to one or more committees that have jurisdiction over its subject, as defined by House and Senate rules and precedents. A Senate measure is usually referred to the committee with jurisdiction over the predominant subject of its text, but it may be sent to two or more committees by unanimous consent or on a motion offered jointly by the majority and minority leaders. In the House, a rule requires the Speaker to refer a measure to the committee that has primary jurisdiction. The Speaker is also authorized to refer measures sequentially to additional committees and to impose time limits on such referrals.

Bipartisan Committee—A committee with an equal number of members from each political party. The House Committee on Standards of Official Conduct and the Senate Select Committee on Ethics are the only bipartisan, permanent full committees.

Borrowing Authority—Statutory authority permitting a federal agency, such as the Export-Import Bank, to borrow money from the public or the Treasury to finance its operations. It is a form of backdoor spending. To bring such spending under the control of the congressional appropriation process, the Congressional Budget Act requires that new borrowing authority shall be effective only to the extent and in such amounts as are provided in appropriations acts.

Budget—A detailed statement of actual or anticipated revenues and expenditures during an accounting period. For the national government, the period is the federal fiscal year (Oct. 1 to Sept. 30). The budget usually refers to the president's budget submission to Congress early each calendar year. The president's budget estimates federal government income and spending for the upcoming fiscal year and contains detailed recommendations for appropriation, revenue and other legislation. Congress is not required to accept or even vote directly on the president's proposals, and it often revises the president's budget extensively. (See Fiscal Year.)

Budget Act—Common name for the Congressional Budget and Impoundment Control Act of 1974, which established the basic procedures of the current congressional budget process; created the House and Senate Budget Committees; and enacted procedures for reconciliation, deferrals and rescissions. (See Budget Process; Deferral; Impoundment; Reconciliation; Rescission. See also Gramm-Rudman-Hollings Act of 1985.)

Budget and Accounting Act of 1921—The law that, for the first time, authorized the president to submit to Congress an annual budget for the entire federal government. Before passage of the act, most federal agencies sent their budget requests to the appropriate congressional committees without review by the president.

Budget Authority—Generally, the amount of money that may be spent or obligated by a government agency or for a government program or activity. Technically, it is statutory authority to enter into obligations that normally result in outlays. The main forms of budget authority are appropriations, borrowing authority and contract authority. It also includes authority to obligate and expend the proceeds of offsetting receipts and collections. Congress may make budget authority available for only one year, several years or an indefinite period, and it may specify definite or indefinite amounts.

Budget Enforcement Act of 1990—An act that revised the sequestration process established by the Gramm-Rudman-Hollings Act of 1985, replaced the earlier act's fixed deficit targets with adjustable ones, established discretionary spending limits for fiscal years 1991 through 1995, instituted pay-as-you-go rules to enforce deficit neutrality on revenue and mandatory spending legislation and reformed the budget and accounting rules for federal credit activities. Unlike the Gramm-Rudman-Hollings Act, the 1990 act emphasized restraints on legislated changes in taxes and spending instead of fixed deficit limits.

Budget Enforcement Act of 1997—An act that revised and updated the provisions of the Budget Enforcement Act of 1990, including by extending the discretionary spending caps and pay-as-you-go rules through 2002.

Budget Process—(1) In Congress, the procedural system it uses (a) to approve an annual concurrent resolution on the budget that sets goals for aggregate and functional categories of federal expenditures, revenues and the surplus or deficit for an upcoming fiscal year; and (b) to implement those goals in spending, revenue and, if necessary, reconciliation and debt-limit legislation. (2) In the executive branch, the process of formulating the president's annual budget, submitting it to Congress, defending it before congressional committees, implementing subsequent budget-related legislation, impounding or sequestering expenditures as permitted by law, auditing and evaluating programs and compiling final budget data. The Budget and Accounting Act of 1921 and the Congressional Budget and Impoundment Control Act of 1974 established the basic elements of the current budget process. Major revisions were enacted in the Gramm-Rudman-Hollings Act of 1985 and the Budget Enforcement Act of 1990.

Budget Resolution—A concurrent resolution in which Congress establishes or revises its version of the federal budget's broad financial features for the upcoming fiscal year and several additional fiscal years. Like other concurrent resolutions, it does not have the force of law, but it provides the framework within which Congress subsequently considers revenue, spending and other budget-implementing legislation. The framework consists of two basic elements: (1) aggregate budget amounts (total revenues, new budget authority, outlays, loan obligations and loan guarantee commitments, deficit or surplus and debt limit); and (2) subdivisions of the relevant aggregate amounts among the functional categories of the budget. Although it does not allocate funds to specific programs or accounts, the budget committees' reports accompanying the resolution often discuss the major program assumptions underlying its functional amounts. Unlike those amounts, however, the assumptions are not binding on Congress.

By Request—A designation indicating that a member has introduced a measure on behalf of the president, an executive agency or a private individual or organization. Members often introduce such measures as a courtesy because neither the president nor any person other than a member of Congress can do so. The term, which appears next to the sponsor's name, implies that the member who introduced the measure does not necessarily endorse it. A House rule dealing with by-request introductions dates from 1888, but the practice goes back to the earliest history of Congress.

Byrd Rule—The popular name of an amendment to the Congressional Budget Act that bars the inclusion of extraneous matter in any reconciliation legislation considered in the Senate. The ban is enforced by points of order that the presiding officer sustains. The provision defines different categories of extraneous matter, but it also permits certain exceptions. Its chief sponsor was Sen. Robert C. Byrd, D-W.Va.

Calendar—A list of measures or other matters (most of them favorably reported by committees) that are eligible for floor consideration. The House has five calendars; the Senate has two. A place on a calendar does not guarantee consideration. Each house decides which measures and matters it will take up, when and in what order, in accordance with its rules and practices.

Calendar Wednesday—A House procedure that on Wednesdays permits its committees to bring up for floor consideration nonprivileged measures they have reported. The procedure is so cumbersome and susceptible to dilatory tactics, however, that it is rarely used.

Call Up—To bring a measure or report to the floor for immediate consideration.

Casework—Assistance to constituents who seek assistance in dealing with federal and local government agencies. Constituent service is a high priority in most members' offices.

Caucus—(1) A common term for the official organization of each party in each house. (2) The official title of the organization of House Democrats. House and Senate Republicans and Senate Democrats call their organizations "conferences." (3) A term for an informal group of members who share legislative interests, such as the Black Caucus, Hispanic Caucus and Children's Caucus.

Censure—The strongest formal condemnation of a member for misconduct short of expulsion. A house usually adopts a resolution of censure to express its condemnation, after which the presiding officer reads its rebuke aloud to the member in the presence of his or her colleagues.

Chairman—The presiding officer of a committee, a subcommittee or a task force. At meetings, the chairman preserves order, enforces the rules, recognizes members to speak or offer motions and puts questions to a vote. The chairman of a committee or subcommittee usually appoints its staff and sets its agenda, subject to the panel's veto.

Chamber—The Capitol room in which a house of Congress normally holds its sessions. The chamber of the House of Representatives, officially called the Hall of the House, is considerably larger than that of the Senate because it must accommodate 435 representatives, four delegates and one resident commissioner. Unlike the Senate chamber, members have no desks or assigned seats. In both chambers, the floor slopes downward to the well in front of the presiding officer's raised desk. A chamber is often referred to as "the floor," as when members are said to be on or going to the floor. Those expressions usually imply that the member's house is in session.

Christmas Tree Bill—Jargon for a bill adorned with amendments, many of them unrelated to the bill's subject, that provide benefits for interest groups, specific states, congressional districts, companies and individuals.

Classes of Senators—A class consists of the thirty-three or thirty-four senators elected to a six-year term in the same general election. Because the terms of approximately one-third of the senators expire every two years, there are three classes.

Clean Bill—After a House committee extensively amends a bill, it often assembles its amendments and what is left of the bill into a new measure that one or more of its members introduces as a "clean bill." The revised measure is assigned a new number.

Clerk of the House—An officer of the House of Representatives responsible principally for administrative support of the legislative process in the House. The clerk is invariably the candidate of the majority party.

Cloakrooms—Two rooms with access to the rear of each chamber's floor, one for each party's members, where members may confer privately, sit quietly or have a snack. The presiding officer sometimes urges members who are conversing too loudly on the floor to retire to their cloakrooms.

Closed Hearing—A hearing closed to the public and the media. A House committee may close a hearing only if it determines that disclosure of the testimony to be taken would endanger national security, violate any law or tend to defame, degrade or incriminate any person. The Senate has a similar rule. Both houses require roll-call votes in open session to close a hearing.

Closed Rule—A special rule reported from the House Rules Committee that prohibits amendments to a measure or that only permits amendments offered by the reporting committee.

Cloture—A Senate procedure that limits further consideration of a pending proposal to thirty hours in order to end a filibuster. Sixteen senators must first sign and submit a cloture motion to the presiding officer. One hour after the Senate meets on the second calendar day thereafter, the chair puts the motion to a yea-and-nay vote following a live quorum call. If three-fifths of all senators (sixty if there are no vacancies) vote for the motion, the Senate must take final action on the cloture proposal by the end of the thirty hours of consideration and may consider no other business until it takes that action. Cloture on a proposal to amend the Senate's standing rules requires approval by two-thirds of the senators present and voting.

Code of Official Conduct—A House rule that bans certain actions by House members, officers and employees; requires them to conduct themselves in ways that "reflect creditably" on the House; and orders them to adhere to the spirit and the letter of House rules and those of its committees. The code's provisions govern the receipt of outside compensation, gifts and honoraria and the use of campaign funds; prohibit members from using their clerk-hire allowance to pay anyone who does not perform duties commensurate with that pay; forbids discrimination in members' hiring or treatment of employees on the grounds of race, color, religion, sex, handicap, age or national origin; orders members convicted of a crime who might be punished by imprisonment of two or more years not to participate in committee business or vote on the floor until exonerated or reelected; and restricts employees' contact with federal agencies on matters in which they have a significant financial interest. The Senate's rules contain some similar prohibitions.

College of Cardinals—A popular term for the subcommittee chairmen of the appropriations committees, reflecting their influence over appropriation measures. The chairmen of the full appropriations committees are sometimes referred to as popes.

Comity—The practice of maintaining mutual courtesy and civility between the two houses in their dealings with each other and in members' speeches on the floor. Although the practice is largely governed by long-established customs, a House rule explicitly cautions its members not to characterize any Senate action or inaction, refer to individual senators except under certain circumstances, or quote from Senate proceedings except to make legislative history on a measure. The Senate has no rule on the subject but references to the House have been held out of order on several occasions. Generally the houses do not interfere with each other's appropriations although minor conflicts sometimes occur. A refusal to receive a message from the other house has also been held to violate the practice of comity.

Committee—A panel of members elected or appointed to perform some service or function for its parent body. Congress has four types of committees: standing, special or select, joint, and, in the House, a Committee of the Whole. Committees conduct investigations, make studies, issue reports and recommendations and, in the case of standing committees, review and prepare measures on their assigned subjects for action by their respective houses. Most committees divide their work among several subcommittees. With rare exceptions, the majority party in a house holds a majority of the seats on its committees, and their chairmen are also from that party.

Committee Jurisdiction—The legislative subjects and other functions assigned to a committee by rule, precedent, resolution or statute. A committee's title usually indicates the general scope of its jurisdiction but often fails to mention other significant subjects assigned to it.

Committee of the Whole—Common name of the Committee of the Whole House on the State of the Union, a committee consisting of all members of the House of Representatives. Measures from the union calendar must be considered in the Committee of the Whole before the House officially completes action on them; the committee often considers other major bills as well. A quorum of the committee is 100, and it meets in the House chamber under a chairman appointed by the Speaker. Procedures in the Committee of the Whole expedite consideration of legislation because of its smaller quorum requirement, its ban on certain motions and its five-minute rule for debate on amendments. Those procedures usually permit more members to offer amendments and participate in the debate on a measure than is normally possible. The Senate no longer uses a Committee of the Whole.

Committee Ratios—The ratios of majority to minority party members on committees. By custom, the ratios of most committees reflect party strength in their respective houses as closely as possible.

Committee Report on a Measure—A document submitted by a committee to report a measure to its parent chamber. Customarily, the report explains the measure's purpose, describes provisions and any amendments recommended by the committee and presents arguments for its approval.

Committee Veto—A procedure that requires an executive department or agency to submit certain proposed policies, programs or action to designated committees for review before implementing them. Before 1983, when the Supreme Court declared that a legislative veto was unconstitutional, these provisions permitted committees to veto the proposals. Committees no longer conduct this type of policy review, and the term is now something of a misnomer. Nevertheless, agencies usually take the pragmatic approach of trying to reach a consensus with the committees before carrying out their proposals, especially when an appropriations committee is involved.

Concur—To agree to an amendment of the other house, either by adopting a motion to concur in that amendment or a motion to concur with an amendment to that amendment. After both houses have agreed to the same version of an amendment, neither house may amend it further, nor may any subsequent conference change it or delete it from the measure. Concurrence by one house in all amendments of the other house completes action on the measure; no vote is then necessary on the measure as a whole because both houses previously passed it.

Concurrent Resolution—A resolution that requires approval by both houses but does not need the president's signature and therefore cannot have the force of law. Concurrent resolutions deal with the prerogatives or internal affairs of Congress as a whole. Designated H. Con. Res. in the House and S. Con. Res. in the Senate, they are numbered consecutively in each house in their order of introduction during a two-year Congress.

Conferees—A common title for managers, the members from each house appointed to a conference committee. The Senate usually authorizes its presiding officer to appoint its conferees. The Speaker appoints House conferees, and under a rule adopted in 1993, can remove conferees "at any time after an original appointment" and also appoint additional conferees at any time. Conferees are expected to support the positions of their houses despite their personal views, but in practice this is not always the case. The party ratios of conferees generally reflect the ratios in their houses. Each house may appoint as many conferees as it pleases. House conferees often outnumber their Senate colleagues; however, each house has only one vote in a conference, so the size of its delegation is immaterial.

Conference—(1) A formal meeting or series of meetings between members representing each house to reconcile House and Senate differences on a measure (occasionally several measures). Because one house cannot require the other to agree to its proposals, the conference usually reaches agreement by compromise. When a conference completes action on a measure, or as much action as appears possible, it sends its recommendations to both houses in the form of a conference report, accompanied by an explanatory statement. (2) The official title of the organization of all Democrats or Republicans in the Senate and of all Republicans in the House of Representatives. (See Party Caucus.)

Conference Committee—A temporary joint committee formed for the purpose of resolving differences between the houses on a measure. Major and controversial legislation usually requires conference committee action. Voting in a conference committee is not by individuals but within the House and Senate delegations. Consequently, a conference committee report requires the support of a majority of the conferees from each house. Both houses require that conference committees open their meetings to the public. The Senate's rule permits the committee to close its meetings if a majority of conferees in each delegation agree by a roll-call vote. The House rule permits closed meetings only if the House authorizes them to do so on a roll-call vote. Otherwise, there are no congressional rules governing the organization of, or procedure in, a conference committee. The committee chooses its chairman, but on measures that go to conference annually, such as general appropriation bills, the chairmanship traditionally rotates between the houses.

Conference Report—A document submitted to both houses that contains a conference committee's agreements for resolving their differences on a measure. It must be signed by a majority of the conferees from each house separately and must be accompanied by an explanatory statement. Both houses prohibit amendments to a conference report and require it to be accepted or rejected in its entirety.

Congress—(1) The national legislature of the United States, consisting of the House of Representatives and the Senate. (2) The national legislature in office during a two-year period. Congresses are numbered sequentially; thus, the 1st Congress of 1789–1791 and the 106th Congress of 1999–2001. Before 1935, the two-year period began on the first Monday in December of odd-numbered years. Since then it has extended from January of an odd-numbered year through noon on Jan. 3 of the next odd-numbered year. A Congress usually holds two annual sessions, but some have had three sessions and the 67th Congress had four. When a Congress expires, measures die if they have not yet been enacted.

Congressional Accountability Act of 1995 (CAA)—An act applying eleven labor, workplace and civil rights laws to the legislative branch and establishing procedures and remedies for legislative branch employees with grievances in violation of these laws. The following laws are covered by the CAA: the Fair Labor Standards Act of 1938; Title VII of the Civil Rights Act of 1964; Americans with Disabilities Act of 1990; Age Discrimination in Employment Act of 1967; Family and Medical Leave Act of 1993; Occupational Safety and Health Act of 1970; Chapter 71 of Title 5, U.S. Code (relating to federal service labor-management relations); Employee Polygraph Protection Act of 1988; Worker Adjustment and Retraining Notification Act; Rehabilitation Act of 1973; and Chapter 43 of Title 38, U.S. Code (relating to veterans' employment and reemployment).

Congressional Budget and Impoundment Control Act of 1974—The law that established the basic elements of the congressional budget process, the House and Senate Budget Committees, the Congressional Budget Office and the procedures for congressional review of impoundments in the form of rescissions and deferrals proposed by the president. The budget process consists of procedures for coordinating congressional revenue and spending decisions made in separate tax, appropriations and legislative measures. The impoundment provisions were intended to give Congress greater control over executive branch actions that delay or prevent the spending of funds provided by Congress.

Congressional Budget Office (CBO)—A congressional support agency created by the Congressional Budget and Impoundment Control Act of 1974 to provide nonpartisan budgetary information and analysis to Congress and its committees. CBO acts as a scorekeeper when Congress is voting on the federal budget, tracking bills to ensure they comply with overall budget goals. The agency also estimates what proposed legislation would cost over a five-year period. CBO works most closely with the House and Senate Budget Committees.

Congressional Directory—The official who's who of Congress, usually published during the first session of a two-year Congress.

Congressional District—The geographical area represented by a single member of the House of Representatives. For states with only one representative, the entire state is a congressional district. As of 2001 seven states had only one representative each: Alaska, Delaware, Montana, North Dakota, South Dakota, Vermont and Wyoming.

Congressional Record—The daily, printed and substantially verbatim account of proceedings in both the House and Senate chambers. Extraneous materials submitted by members appear in a section titled "Extensions of Remarks." A "Daily Digest" appendix contains highlights of the day's floor and committee action plus a list of committee meetings and floor agendas for the next day's session.

Although the official reporters of each house take down every word spoken during the proceedings, members are permitted to edit and "revise and extend" their remarks before they are printed. In the Senate section, all speeches, articles and other material submitted by senators but not actually spoken or read on the floor are set off by large black dots, called bullets. However, bullets do not appear when a senator reads part of a speech and inserts the rest. In the House section, undelivered speeches and materials are printed in a distinctive typeface. The term "permanent Record" refers to the bound volumes of the daily Records of an entire session of Congress.

Congressional Research Service (CRS)—Established in 1917, a department of the Library of Congress whose staff provide nonpartisan, objective analysis and information on virtually any subject to committees, members and staff of Congress. Originally the Legislative Reference Service, it is the oldest congressional support agency.

Congressional Support Agencies—A term often applied to three agencies in the legislative branch that provide nonpartisan information and analysis to committees and members of Congress: the Congressional Budget Office, the Congressional Research Service of the Library of Congress and the General Accounting Office. A fourth support agency, the Office of Technology Assessment, formerly provided such support but was abolished in the 104th Congress.

Congressional Terms of Office—A term normally begins on Jan. 3 of the year following a general election and runs two years for representatives and six years for senators. A representative chosen in a special election to fill a vacancy is sworn in for the remainder of the predecessor's term. An individual appointed to fill a Senate vacancy usually serves until the next general election or until the end of the predecessor's term, whichever comes first. Some states, however, require their governors to call a special election to fill a Senate vacancy shortly after an appointment has been made.

Constitutional Rules—Constitutional provisions that prescribe procedures for Congress. In addition to certain types of votes required in particular situations, these provisions include the following: (1) the House chooses its Speaker, the Senate its president pro tempore and both houses their officers; (2) each house requires a majority quorum to conduct business; (3) less than a majority may adjourn from day to day and compel the attendance of absent members; (4) neither house may adjourn for more than three days without the consent of the other; (5) each house must keep a journal; (6) the yeas and nays are ordered when supported by one-fifth of the members present; (7) all revenue-raising bills must originate in the House, but the Senate may propose amendments to them. The Constitution also sets out the procedure in the House for electing a president, the procedure in the Senate for electing a vice president, the procedure for filling a vacancy in the office of vice president and the procedure for overriding a presidential veto.

Constitutional Votes—Constitutional provisions that require certain votes or voting methods in specific situations. They include (1) the yeas and nays at the desire of one-fifth of the members present; (2) a two-thirds vote by the yeas and nays to override a veto; (3) a two-thirds vote by one house to expel one of its members and by both houses to propose a constitutional amendment; (4) a two-thirds vote of senators present to convict someone whom the House has impeached and to consent to ratification of treaties; (5) a two-thirds vote in each house to remove political disabilities from persons who have engaged in insurrection or rebellion or given aid or comfort to the enemies of the United States; (6) a majority vote in each house to fill a vacancy in the office of vice president; (7) a majority vote of all states to elect a president in the House of Representatives when no candidate receives a majority of the electoral votes; (8) a majority vote of all senators when the Senate elects a vice president under the same circumstances; and (9) the casting vote of the vice president in case of tie votes in the Senate.

Contempt of Congress—Willful obstruction of the proper functions of Congress. Most frequently, it is a refusal to obey a subpoena to appear and testify before a committee or to produce documents demanded by it. Such obstruction is a misdemeanor and persons cited for contempt are subject to prosecution in federal courts. A house cites an individual for contempt by agreeing to a privileged resolution to that effect reported by a committee. The presiding officer then refers the matter to a U.S. attorney for prosecution.

Continuing Body—A characterization of the Senate on the theory that it continues from Congress to Congress and has existed continuously since it first convened in 1789. The rationale for the theory is that under the system of staggered six-year terms for senators, the terms of only about one-third of them expire after each Congress and, therefore, a quorum of the Senate is always in office. Consequently, under this theory, the Senate, unlike the House, does not have to adopt its rules at the beginning of each Congress because those rules continue from one Congress to the next. This makes it extremely difficult for the Senate to change its rules against the opposition of a determined minority because those rules require a two-thirds vote of the senators present and voting to invoke cloture on a proposed rules change.

Continuing Resolution (CR)—A joint resolution that provides funds to continue the operation of federal agencies and programs at the beginning of a new fiscal year if their annual appropriation bills have not yet been enacted; also called continuing appropriations. Continuing resolutions are enacted shortly before or after the new fiscal year begins and usually make funds available for a specified period. Additional resolutions are often needed after the first expires. Some continuing resolutions have provided appropriations for an entire fiscal year. Continuing resolutions for specific periods customarily fix a rate at which agencies may incur obligations based either on the previous year's appropriations, the president's budget request, or the amount as specified in the agency's regular annual appropriation bill if that bill has already been passed by one or both houses. In the House, continuing resolutions are privileged after Sept. 15.

Contract Authority—Statutory authority permitting an agency to enter into contracts or incur other obligations even though it has not received an appropriation to pay for them. Congress must eventually fund them because the government is legally liable for such payments. The Congressional Budget Act of 1974 requires that new contract authority may not be used

unless provided for in advance by an appropriation act, but it permits a few exceptions.

Correcting Recorded Votes—The rules of both houses prohibit members from changing their votes after a vote result has been announced. Nevertheless, the Senate permits its members to withdraw or change their votes, by unanimous consent, immediately after the announcement. In rare instances, senators have been granted unanimous consent to change their votes several days or weeks after the announcement. Votes tallied by the electronic voting system in the House may not be changed. But when a vote actually given is not recorded during an oral call of the roll, a member may demand a correction as a matter of right. On all other alleged errors in a recorded vote, the Speaker determines whether the circumstances justify a change. Occasionally, members merely announce that they were incorrectly recorded; announcements can occur hours, days or even months after the vote and appear in the Congressional Record.

Cosponsor—A member who has joined one or more other members to sponsor a measure.

Credit Authority—Authority granted to an agency to incur direct loan obligations or to make loan guarantee commitments. The Congressional Budget Act of 1974 bans congressional consideration of credit authority legislation unless the extent of that authority is made subject to provisions in appropriation acts.

C-SPAN—Cable-Satellite Public Affairs Network, which provides live, gavel-to-gavel coverage of Senate floor proceedings on one cable television channel and coverage of House floor proceedings on another channel. C-SPAN also televises important committee hearings in both houses. Each house also transmits its televised proceedings directly to congressional offices.

Current Services Estimates—Executive branch estimates of the anticipated costs of federal programs and operations for the next and future fiscal years at existing levels of service and assuming no new initiatives or changes in existing law. The president submits these estimates to Congress with the annual budget and includes an explanation of the underlying economic and policy assumptions on which they are based, such as anticipated rates of inflation, real economic growth and unemployment, plus program caseloads and pay increases.

Custody of the Papers—Possession of an engrossed measure and certain related basic documents that the two houses produce as they try to resolve their differences over the measure.

Dance of the Swans and the Ducks—A whimsical description of the gestures some members use in connection with a request for a recorded vote, especially in the House. When members want their colleagues to stand in support of the request, they move their hands and arms in a gentle upward motion resembling the beginning flight of a graceful swan. When they want their colleagues to remain seated to avoid such a vote, they move their hands and arms in a vigorous downward motion resembling a diving duck.

Dean—Within a state's delegation in the House of Representatives, the member with the longest continuous service.

Debate—In congressional parlance, speeches delivered during consideration of a measure, motion or other matter, as distinguished from speeches in other parliamentary situations, such as one-minute and special order speeches when no business is pending. Virtually all debate in the House of Representatives is under some kind of time limitation. Most debate in the Senate is unlimited; that is, a senator, once recognized, may speak for as long as he or she chooses, unless the Senate invokes cloture.

Debt Limit—The maximum amount of outstanding federal public debt permitted by law. The limit (or ceiling) covers virtually all debt incurred by the government except agency debt. Each congressional budget resolution sets forth the new debt limit that may be required under its provisions.

Deferral—An impoundment of funds for a specific period of time that may not extend beyond the fiscal year in which it is proposed. Under the Impoundment Control Act of 1974, the president must notify Congress that he is deferring the spending or obligation of funds provided by law for a project or activity. Congress can disapprove the deferral by legislation.

Deficit—The amount by which the government's outlays exceed its budget receipts for a given fiscal year. Both the president's budget and the annual congressional budget resolution provide estimates of the deficit or surplus for the upcoming and several future fiscal years.

Degrees of Amendment—Designations that indicate the relationships of amendments to the text of a measure and to each other. In general, an amendment offered directly to the text of a measure is an amendment in the first degree, and an amendment to that amendment is an amendment in the second degree. Both houses normally prohibit amendments in the third degree — that is, an amendment to an amendment to an amendment.

Delegate—A nonvoting member of the House of Representatives elected to a two-year term from the District of Columbia, the territory of Guam, the territory of the Virgin Islands or the territory of American Samoa. By law, delegates may not vote in the full House but they may participate in debate, offer motions (except to reconsider) and serve and vote on standing and select committees. On their committees, delegates possess the same powers and privileges as other members and the Speaker may appoint them to appropriate conference committees and select committees.

Denounce—A formal action that condemns a member for misbehavior; considered by some experts to be equivalent to censure. (See Censure.)

Dilatory Tactics—Procedural actions intended to delay or prevent action by a house or a committee. They include, among others, offering numerous motions, demanding quorum calls and recorded votes at every opportunity, making numerous points of order and parliamentary inquiries and speaking as long as the applicable rules permit. The Senate rules permit a battery of dilatory tactics, especially lengthy speeches, except under cloture. In the House, possible dilatory tactics are more limited. Speeches are always subject to time limits and debate-ending motions. Moreover, a House rule instructs the Speaker not to entertain dilatory motions and lets the Speaker decide whether a motion is dilatory. However, the Speaker may not override the constitutional right of a member to demand the yeas and nays, and in practice usually waits for a point of order before exercising that authority. (See Cloture.)

Discharge a Committee—Remove a measure from a committee to which it has been referred in order to make it available for floor consideration. Noncontroversial measures are often discharged by unanimous consent. However, because congressional committees have no obligation to report measures referred to them, each house has procedures to extract controversial measures from recalcitrant committees. Six discharge procedures are available in the House of Representatives. The Senate uses a motion to discharge, which is usually converted into a discharge resolution.

District Office—Representatives maintain one or more offices in their districts for the purpose of assisting and communicating with constituents. The costs of maintaining these offices are paid from members' official allowances. Senators can use the official expense allowance to rent offices in their home state, subject to a funding formula based on their state's population and other factors.

District Work Period—The House term for a scheduled congressional recess during which members may visit their districts and conduct constituency business.

Division Vote—A vote in which the chair first counts those in favor of a proposition and then those opposed to it, with no record made of how each member votes. In the Senate, the chair may count raised hands or ask senators to stand, whereas the House requires members to stand; hence, often called a standing vote. Committees in both houses ordinarily use a show of hands. A division usually occurs after a voice vote and may be demanded by any member or ordered by the chair if there is any doubt about the outcome of the voice vote. The demand for a division can also come before a voice vote. In the Senate, the demand must come before the result of a voice vote is announced. It may be made after a voice vote announcement in the House, but only if no intervening business has transpired and only if the member was standing and seeking recognition at the time of the announcement. A demand for the yeas and nays or, in the House, for a recorded vote, takes precedence over a division vote.

Doorkeeper of the House—A former officer of the House of Representatives who was responsible for enforcing the rules prohibiting unauthorized persons from entering the chamber when the House is in session. The doorkeeper was usually the candidate of the majority party. In 1995 the office was abolished and its functions transferred to the sergeant at arms.

Effective Dates—Provisions of an act that specify when the entire act or individual provisions in it become effective as law. Most acts become effective on the date of enactment, but it is sometimes necessary or prudent to delay the effective dates of some provisions.

Electronic Voting—Since 1973 the House has used an electronic voting system to record the yeas and nays and to conduct recorded votes. Members vote by inserting their voting cards in one of the boxes at several locations in the chamber. They are given at least fifteen minutes to vote. When several votes occur immediately after each other, the Speaker may reduce the voting time to five minutes on the second and subsequent votes. The Speaker may allow additional time on each vote but may also close a vote at any time after the minimum time has expired. Members can change their votes at any time before the Speaker announces the result. The House also uses the electronic system for quorum calls. While a vote is in progress, a large panel above the Speaker's desk displays how each member has voted. Smaller panels on either side of the chamber display running totals of the votes and the time remaining. The Senate does not have electronic voting.

Enacting Clause—The opening language of each bill, beginning "Be it enacted by the Senate and House of Representatives of the United States of America in Congress assembled..." This language gives legal force to measures approved by Congress and signed by the president or enacted over the president's veto. A successful motion to strike it from a bill kills the entire measure.

Engrossed Bill—The official copy of a bill or joint resolution as passed by one chamber, including the text as amended by floor action and certified by the clerk of the House or the secretary of the Senate (as appropriate). Amendments by one house to a measure or amendments of the other also are engrossed. House engrossed documents are printed on blue paper; the Senate's are printed on white paper.

Enrolled Bill—The final official copy of a bill or joint resolution passed in identical form by both houses. An enrolled bill is printed on parchment. After it is certified by the chief officer of the house in which it originated and signed by the House Speaker and the Senate president pro tempore, the measure is sent to the White House for the president's signature.

Entitlement Program—A federal program under which individuals, businesses or units of government that meet the requirements or qualifications established by law are entitled to receive certain payments if they seek such payments. Major examples include Social Security, Medicare, Medicaid, unemployment insurance and military and federal civilian pensions. Congress cannot control their expenditures by refusing to appropriate the sums necessary to fund them because the government is legally obligated to pay eligible recipients the amounts to which the law entitles them.

Equality of the Houses—A component of the Constitution's emphasis on checks and balances under which each house is given essentially equal status in the enactment of legislation and in the relations and negotiations between the two houses. Although the House of Representatives initiates revenue and appropriation measures, the Senate has the right to amend them. Either house may initiate any other type of legislation, and neither can force the other to agree to, or even act on, its measures. Moreover, each house has a potential veto over the other because legislation requires agreement by both. Similarly, in a conference to resolve their differences on a measure, each house casts one vote, as determined by a majority of its conferees. In most other national bicameral legislatures, the powers of one house are markedly greater than those of the other.

Ethics Rules—Several rules or standing orders in each house that mandate certain standards of conduct for members and congressional employees in finance, employment, franking and other areas. The Senate Permanent Select Committee on Ethics and the House Committee on Standards of Official Conduct investigate alleged violations of conduct and recommend appropriate actions to their respective houses.

Exclusive Committee—(1) Under the rules of the Republican Conference and House Democratic Caucus, a standing committee whose members usually cannot serve on any other standing committee. As of 2000 the Appropriations, Energy and Commerce (beginning in the 105th Congress), Ways and Means and Rules Committees were designated as exclusive committees. (2) Under the rules of the two party conferences in the Senate, a standing committee whose members may not simultaneously serve on any other exclusive committee.

Executive Calendar—The Senate's calendar for committee reports on its executive business, namely treaties and nominations. The calendar numbers indicate the order in which items were referred to the calendar but have no bearing on when or if the Senate will consider them. The Senate, by motion or unanimous consent, resolves itself into executive session to consider them.

Executive Document—A document, usually a treaty, sent by the president to the Senate for approval. It is referred to a committee in the same manner as other measures. Resolutions to ratify treaties have their own "treaty document" numbers. For example, the first treaty submitted in the 106th Congress would be "Treaty Doc 106-1."

Executive Order—A unilateral proclamation by the president that has a policy-making or legislative impact. Members of Congress have challenged some executive orders on the grounds that they usurped the authority of the legislative branch. Although the Supreme Court has ruled that a particular order exceeded the president's authority, it has upheld others as falling within the president's general constitutional powers.

Executive Privilege—The assertion that presidents have the right to withhold certain information from Congress. Presidents have based their claim on (1) the constitutional separation of powers; (2) the need for secrecy in military and diplomatic affairs; (3) the need to protect individuals from unfavorable publicity; (4) the need to safeguard the confidential exchange of ideas in the executive branch; and (5) the need to protect individuals who provide confidential advice to the president.

Executive Session—(1) A Senate meeting devoted to the consideration of treaties or nominations. Normally, the Senate meets in legislative session; it resolves itself into executive session, by motion or by unanimous consent, to deal with its executive business. It also keeps a separate Journal for executive sessions. Executive sessions are usually open to the public, but the Senate may choose to close them.

Expulsion—A member's removal from office by a two-thirds vote of his or her house; the supermajority is required by the Constitution. It is the most severe and most rarely used sanction a house can invoke against a member. Although the Constitution provides no explicit grounds for expulsion, the courts have ruled that it may be applied only for misconduct during a member's term of office, not for conduct before the member's election. Generally, neither house will consider expulsion of a member convicted of a crime until the judicial processes have been exhausted. At that stage, members sometimes resign rather than face expulsion. In 1977 the House adopted a rule urging members convicted of certain crimes to voluntarily abstain from voting or participating in other legislative business.

Extensions of Remarks—An appendix to the daily Congressional Record that consists primarily of miscellaneous extraneous material submitted by members. It often includes members' statements not delivered on the floor, newspaper articles and editorials, praise for a member's constituents and noteworthy letters received by a member, among other material. Representatives supply the bulk of this material; senators submit very little. "Extensions of Remarks" pages are separately numbered, and each number is preceded by the letter "E." Materials may be placed in the Extensions of Remarks section only by unanimous consent. Usually, one member of each party makes the request each day on behalf of his or her party colleagues after the House has completed its legislative business of the day.

Federal Debt—The total amount of monies borrowed and not yet repaid by the federal government. Federal debt consists of public debt and agency debt. Public debt is the portion of the federal debt borrowed by the Treasury or the Federal Financing Bank directly from the public or from another federal fund or account. For example, the Treasury regularly borrows money from the Social Security trust fund. Public debt accounts for about 99 percent of the federal debt. Agency debt refers to the debt incurred by federal agencies such as the Export-Import Bank but excluding the Treasury and the Federal Financing Bank, which are authorized by law to borrow funds from the public or from another government fund or account.

Filibuster—The use of obstructive and time-consuming parliamentary tactics by one member or a minority of members to delay, modify or defeat proposed legislation or rules changes. Filibusters are also sometimes used to delay urgently needed measures to force the body to accept other legislation. The Senate's rules permitting unlimited debate and the extraordinary majority it requires to impose cloture make filibustering particularly effective in that chamber. Under the stricter rules of the House, filibusters in that body are short-lived and therefore ineffective and rarely attempted.

Fiscal Year—The federal government's annual accounting period. It begins Oct. 1 and ends on the following Sept. 30. A fiscal year is designated by the calendar year in which it ends and is often referred to as FY. Thus, fiscal year 1998 began Oct. 1, 1997, ended Sept. 30, 1998, and is called FY98. In theory, Congress is supposed to complete action on all budgetary measures applying to a fiscal year before that year begins. It rarely does so.

Five-Minute Rule—A House rule that limits debate on an amendment offered in Committee of the Whole to five minutes for its sponsor and five minutes for an opponent. In practice, the committee routinely permits longer debate by two devices: the offering of pro forma amendments, each debatable for five minutes, and unanimous consent for a member to speak longer than five minutes. Consequently, debate on an amendment sometimes continues for hours. At any time after the first ten minutes, however, the committee may shut off debate immediately or by a specified time, either by unanimous consent or by majority vote on a nondebatable motion. The motion, which dates from 1847, is also used in the House as in Committee of the Whole, where debate also may be shut off by a motion for the previous question.

Floor—The ground level of the House or Senate chamber where members sit and the houses conduct their business. When members are attending a meeting of their house they are said to be on the floor. Floor action refers to the procedural actions taken during floor consideration such as deciding on motions, taking up measures, amending them and voting.

Floor Manager—A majority party member responsible for guiding a measure through its floor consideration in a house and for devising the political and procedural strategies that might be required to get it passed. The presiding officer gives the floor manager priority recognition to debate, offer amendments, oppose amendments and make crucial procedural motions.

Frank—Informally, members' legal right to send official mail postage free under their signatures; often called the franking privilege. Technically, it is the autographic or facsimile signature used on envelopes instead of stamps that permits members and certain congressional officers to send their official mail free of charge. The franking privilege has been authorized by law since the first Congress, except for a few months in 1873. Congress reimburses the U.S. Postal Service for the franked mail it handles.

Function or Functional Category—A broad category of national need and spending of budgetary significance. A category provides an accounting method for allocating and keeping track of budgetary resources and expenditures for that function because it includes all budget accounts related to the function's subject or purpose such as agriculture, administration of justice, commerce and housing and energy. Functions do not necessarily correspond with appropriations acts or with the budgets of individual agencies. As of 2000 there were twenty functional categories, each divided into a number of subfunctions.

Gag Rule—A pejorative term for any type of special rule reported by the House Rules Committee that proposes to prohibit amendments to a measure or only permits amendments offered by the reporting committee.

Galleries—The balconies overlooking each chamber from which the public, news media, staff and others may observe floor proceedings.

General Accounting Office (GAO)—A congressional support agency, often referred to as the investigative arm of Congress. It evaluates and audits federal agencies and programs in the United States and abroad on its initiative or at the request of congressional committees or members.

General Appropriation Bill—A term applied to each of the thirteen annual bills that provide funds for most federal agencies and programs and also to the supplemental appropriation bills that contain appropriations for more than one agency or program.

Germaneness—The requirement that an amendment be closely related — in terms of subject or purpose, for example — to the text it proposes to amend. A House rule requires that all amendments be germane. In the Senate, only amendments offered to general appropriation bills and budget measures or proposed under cloture must be germane. Germaneness rules can be waived by suspension of the rules in both houses, by unanimous consent agreements in the Senate and by special rules from the Rules Committee in the House. Moreover, presiding officers usually do not enforce germaneness rules on their own initiative; therefore, a nongermane amendment can be adopted if no member raises a point of order against it. Under cloture in the Senate, however, the chair may take the initiative to rule amendments out of order as not being germane, without a point of order being made. All House debate must be germane except during general debate in the Committee of the Whole, but special rules invariably require that such debate be "confined to the bill." The Senate requires germane debate only during the first three hours of each daily session. Under the precedents of both houses, an amendment can be relevant but not necessarily germane. A crucial factor in determining germaneness in the House is how the subject of a measure or matter is defined. For example, the subject of a measure authorizing construction of a naval vessel is defined as being the construction of a single vessel; therefore, an amendment to authorize an additional vessel is not germane.

Gerrymandering—The manipulation of legislative district boundaries to benefit a particular party, politician or minority group. The term originated in 1812 when the Massachusetts legislature redrew the lines of state legislative districts to favor the party of Gov. Elbridge Gerry, and some critics said one district looked like a salamander. (See also Congressional District; Redistricting.)

Gramm-Rudman-Hollings Act of 1985—Common name for the Balanced Budget and Emergency Deficit Control Act of 1985, which established new budget procedures intended to balance the federal budget by fiscal year 1991. (The timetable subsequently was extended and then deleted.) The act's chief sponsors were senators Phil Gramm (R-Texas), Warren Rudman (R-N.H.) Ernest Hollings (D-S.C.).

Grandfather Clause—A provision in a measure, law or rule that exempts an individual, entity or a defined category of individuals or entities from complying with a new policy or restriction. For example, a bill that would raise taxes on persons who reach the age of sixty-five after a certain date inherently grandfathers out those who are sixty-five before that date. Similarly, a Senate rule limiting senators to two major committee assignments also grandfathers some senators who were sitting on a third major committee before a specified date.

Grants-in-Aid—Payments by the federal government to state and local governments to help provide for assistance programs or public services.

Hearing—Committee or subcommittee meetings to receive testimony on proposed legislation during investigations or for oversight purposes. Relatively few bills are important enough to justify formal hearings. Witnesses often include experts, government officials, spokespersons for interested groups, officials of the General Accounting Office and members of Congress.

Hold—A senator's request that his or her party leaders delay floor consideration of certain legislation or presidential nominations. The majority leader usually honors a hold for a reasonable period of time, especially if its purpose is to assure the senator that the matter will not be called up during his or her absence or to give the senator time to gather necessary information.

Hold (or Have) the Floor—A member's right to speak without interruption, unless he or she violates a rule, after recognition by the presiding officer. At the member's discretion, he or she may yield to another member for a question in the Senate or for a question or statement in the House, but may reclaim the floor at any time.

Hold-Harmless Clause—In legislation providing a new formula for allocating federal funds, a clause to ensure that recipients of those funds do not receive less in a future year than they did in the current year if the new formula would result in a reduction for them. Similar to a grandfather clause, it has been used most frequently to soften the impact of sudden reductions in federal grants. (See Grandfather Clause.)

Hopper—A box on the clerk's desk in the House chamber into which members deposit bills and resolutions to introduce them. In House jargon, to drop a bill in the hopper is to introduce it.

Hour Rule—A House rule that permits members, when recognized, to hold the floor in debate for no more than one hour each. The majority party member customarily yields one-half the time to a minority member. Although the hour rule applies to general debate in Committee of the Whole as well as in the House, special rules routinely vary the length of time for such debate and its control to fit the circumstances of particular measures.

House As In Committee of the Whole—A hybrid combination of procedures from the general rules of the House and from the rules of the Committee of the Whole, sometimes used to expedite consideration of a measure on the floor.

House Calendar—The calendar reserved for all public bills and resolutions that do not raise revenue or directly or indirectly appropriate money or property when they are favorably reported by House committees.

House Manual—A commonly used title for the handbook of the rules of the House of Representatives, published in each Congress. Its official title is Constitution, Jefferson's Manual and Rules of the House of Representatives.

House of Representatives—The house of Congress in which states are represented roughly in proportion to their populations, but every state is guaranteed at least one representative. By law, the number of voting representatives is fixed at 435. Four delegates and one resident commissioner also serve in the House; they may vote in their committees but not on the House floor. Although the House and Senate have equal legislative power, the Constitution gives the House sole authority to originate revenue measures. The House also claims the right to originate appropriation measures, a claim the Senate disputes in theory but concedes in practice. The House has the sole power to impeach, and it elects the president when no candidate has received a majority of the electoral votes. It is sometimes referred to as the lower body.

Immunity—(1) Members' constitutional protection from lawsuits and arrest in connection with their legislative duties. They may not be tried for libel or slander for anything they say on the floor of a house or in committee. Nor may they be arrested while attending sessions of their houses or when traveling to or from sessions of Congress, except when charged with treason, a felony or a breach of the peace. (2) In the case of a witness before a committee, a grant of protection from prosecution based on that person's testimony to the committee. It is used to compel witnesses to testify who would otherwise refuse to do so on the constitutional ground of possible selfincrimination. Under such a grant, none of a witness's testimony may be used against him or her in a court proceeding except in a prosecution for perjury or for giving a false statement to Congress. (See also Contempt of Congress.)

Impeachment—The first step to remove the president, vice president or other federal civil officers from office and to disqualify them from any future federal office "of honor, Trust or Profit." An impeachment is a formal charge of treason, bribery or "other high Crimes and Misdemeanors." The House has the sole power of impeachment and the Senate the sole power of trying the charges and convicting. The House impeaches by a simple majority vote; conviction requires a two-thirds vote of all senators present.

Impeachment Trial, Removal and Disqualification—The Senate conducts an impeachment trial under a separate set of twenty-six rules that appears in the Senate Manual. Under the Constitution, the chief justice of the United States presides over trials of the president, but the vice president, the president pro tempore or any other senator may preside over the impeachment trial of another official.

The Constitution requires senators to take an oath for an impeachment trial. During the trial, senators may not engage in colloquies or participate in arguments, but they may submit questions in writing to House managers or defense counsel. After the trial concludes, the Senate votes separately on each article of impeachment without debate unless the Senate orders the doors closed for private discussions. During deliberations senators may speak no more than once on a question, not for more than ten minutes on an interlocutory question and not more than fifteen minutes on the final question. These rules may be set aside by unanimous consent or suspended on motion by a two-thirds vote.

The Senate's impeachment trial of President Clinton in 1999 was only the second such trial involving a president. It continued for five weeks, with the Senate voting not to convict on the two impeachment articles.

Senate impeachment rules allow the Senate, at its own discretion, to name a committee to hear evidence and conduct the trial, with all senators thereafter voting on the charges. The impeachment trials of three federal judges were conducted this way, and the Supreme Court upheld the validity of these rules in Nixon v. United States, 506 U.S. 224, 1993.

An official convicted on impeachment charges is removed from office immediately. However, the convicted official is not barred from holding a federal office in the future unless the Senate, after its conviction vote, also approves a resolution disqualifying the convicted official from future office. For example, federal judge Alcee L. Hastings was impeached and convicted in 1989, but the Senate did not vote to bar him from office in the future. In 1992 Hastings was elected to the House of Representatives, and no challenge was raised against seating him when he took the oath of office in 1993.

Impoundment—An executive branch action or inaction that delays or withholds the expenditure or obligation of budget authority provided by law. The Impoundment Control Act of 1974 classifies impoundments as either deferrals or rescissions, requires the president to notify Congress about all such actions and gives Congress authority to approve or reject them.

Inspector General (IG) In the House of Representatives—A position established with the passage of the House Administrative Reform Resolution of 1992. The duties of the office have been revised several times and are now contained in House Rule II. The inspector general (IG), who is subject to the policy direction and oversight of the Committee on House Administration, is appointed for a Congress jointly by the Speaker and the majority and minority leaders of the House. The IG communicates the results of audits to the House officers or officials who were the subjects of the audits and suggests appropriate corrective measures. The IG submits a report of each audit to the Speaker, the majority and minority leaders and the chairman and ranking minority member of the House Administration Committee; notifies these five members in the case of any financial irregularity discovered; and reports to the Committee on Standards of Official Conduct on possible violations of House rules or any applicable law by any House member, officer or employee. The IG's office also has certain duties to audit various financial operations of the House that had previously been performed by the General Accounting Office.

Instruct Conferees—A formal action by a house urging its conferees to uphold a particular position on a measure in conference. The instruction may be to insist on certain provisions in the measure as passed by that house or to accept a provision in the version passed by the other house. Instructions to conferees are not binding because the primary responsibility of conferees is to reach agreement on a measure and neither House can compel the other to accept particular provisions or positions.

Investigative Power—The authority of Congress and its committees to pursue investigations, upheld by the Supreme Court but limited to matters related to, and in furtherance of, a legitimate task of the Congress. Standing committees in both houses are permanently authorized to investigate matters within their jurisdictions. Major investigations are sometimes conducted by temporary select, special or joint committees established by resolutions for that purpose.

Some rules of the House provide certain safeguards for witnesses and others during investigative hearings. These permit counsel to accompany witnesses, require that each witness receive a copy of the committee's rules and order the committee to go into closed session if it believes the testimony to be heard might defame, degrade or incriminate any person. The committee may subsequently decide to hear such testimony in open session. The Senate has no rules of this kind.

Item Veto—Item veto authority, which is available to most state governors, allows governors to eliminate or reduce items in legislative measures presented for their signature without vetoing the entire measure and sign the rest into law. A similar authority was briefly granted to the U.S. president under the Line Item Veto Act of 1996. According to the majority opinion of the Supreme Court in its 1998 decision overturning that law, a constitutional amendment would be necessary to give the president such item veto authority.

Jefferson's Manual—Short title of Jefferson's Manual of Parliamentary Practice, prepared by Thomas Jefferson for his guidance when he was president of the Senate from 1797 to 1801. Although it reflects English parliamentary practice in his day, many procedures in both houses of Congress are still rooted in its basic precepts. Under a House rule adopted in 1837, the manual's provisions govern House procedures when applicable

and when they are not inconsistent with its standing rules and orders. The Senate, however, has never officially acknowledged it as a direct authority for its legislative procedure.

Johnson Rule—A policy instituted in 1953 under which all Democratic senators are assigned to one major committee before any Democrat is assigned to two. The Johnson Rule is named after its author, Sen. Lyndon B. Johnson, D-Texas, then the Senate's Democratic leader. Senate Republicans adopted a similar policy soon thereafter.

Joint Committee—A committee composed of members selected from each house. The functions of most joint committees involve investigation, research or oversight of agencies closely related to Congress. Permanent joint committees, created by statute, are sometimes called standing joint committees. Once quite numerous, only four joint committees remained as of 2002: Joint Economic, Joint Taxation, Joint Library and Joint Printing. None has authority to report legislation.

Joint Resolution—A legislative measure that Congress uses for purposes other than general legislation. Similar to a bill, it has the force of law when passed by both houses and either approved by the president or passed over the president's veto. Unlike a bill, a joint resolution enacted into law is not called an act; it retains its original title. Most often, joint resolutions deal with such relatively limited matters as the correction of errors in existing law, continuing appropriations, a single appropriation or the establishment of permanent joint committees. Unlike bills, however, joint resolutions also are used to propose constitutional amendments; these do not require the president's signature and become effective only when ratified by three-fourths of the states. The House designates joint resolutions as H.J. Res., the Senate as S.J. Res. Each house numbers its joint resolutions consecutively in the order of introduction during a two-year Congress.

Joint Session—Informally, any combined meeting of the Senate and the House. Technically, a joint session is a combined meeting to count the electoral votes for president and vice president or to hear a presidential address, such as the State of the Union message; any other formal combined gathering of both houses is a joint meeting. Joint sessions are authorized by concurrent resolutions and are held in the House chamber, because of its larger seating capacity. Although the president of the Senate and the Speaker sit side by side at the Speaker's desk during combined meetings, the former presides over the electoral count and the latter presides on all other occasions and introduces the president or other guest speaker. The president and other guests may address a joint session or meeting only by invitation.

Joint Sponsorship—Two or more members sponsoring the same measure.

Journal—The official record of House or Senate actions, including every motion offered, every vote cast, amendments agreed to, quorum calls and so forth. Unlike the Congressional Record, it does not provide reports of speeches, debates, statements and the like. The Constitution requires each house to maintain a Journal and to publish it periodically.

Junket—A member's trip at government expense, especially abroad, ostensibly on official business but, it is often alleged, for pleasure.

Killer Amendment—An amendment that, if agreed to, might lead to the defeat of the measure it amends, either in the house in which the amendment is offered or at some later stage of the legislative process. Members sometimes deliberately offer or vote for such an amendment in the expectation that it will undermine support for the measure in Congress or increase the likelihood that the president will veto it.

King of the Mountain (or Hill) Rule—(See Queen of the Hill Rule.)

LA—(See Legislative Assistant.)

Lame Duck—Jargon for a member who has not been reelected, or did not seek reelection, and is serving the balance of his or her term.

Lame Duck Session—A session of a Congress held after the election for the succeeding Congress, so called after the lame duck members still serving.

Last Train Out—Colloquial name for last must-pass bill of a session of Congress.

Law—An act of Congress that has been signed by the president, passed over the president's veto or allowed to become law without the president's signature.

Lay on the Table—A motion to dispose of a pending proposition immediately, finally and adversely; that is, to kill it without a direct vote on its substance. Often simply called a motion to table, it is not debatable and is adopted by majority vote or without objection. It is a highly privileged motion, taking precedence over all others except the motion to adjourn in the House and all but three additional motions in the Senate. It can kill a bill or resolution, an amendment, another motion, an appeal or virtually any other matter.

Tabling an amendment also tables the measure to which the amendment is pending in the House, but not in the Senate. The House does not allow the motion against the motion to recommit, in Committee of the Whole, and in some other situations. In the Senate it is the only permissible motion that immediately ends debate on a proposition, but only to kill it.

(The) Leadership—Usually, a reference to the majority and minority leaders of the Senate or to the Speaker and minority leader of the House. The term sometimes includes the majority leader in the House and the majority and minority whips in each house and, at other times, other party officials as well.

Legislation—(1) A synonym for legislative measures: bills and joint resolutions. (2) Provisions in such measures or in substantive amendments offered to them. (3) In some contexts, provisions that change existing substantive or authorizing law, rather than provisions that make appropriations.

Legislation on an Appropriation Bill—A common reference to provisions changing existing law that appear in, or are offered as amendments to, a general appropriation bill. A House rule prohibits the inclusion of such provisions in general appropriation bills unless they retrench expenditures. An analogous Senate rule permits points of order against amendments to a general appropriation bill that propose general legislation.

Legislative Assistant (LA)—A member's staff person responsible for monitoring and preparing legislation on particular subjects and for advising the member on them; commonly referred to as an LA.

Legislative Day—The day that begins when a house meets after an adjournment and ends when it next adjourns. Because the House of Representatives normally adjourns at the end of a daily session, its legislative and calendar days usually coincide. The Senate, however, frequently recesses at the end of a daily session, and its legislative day may extend over several calendar days, weeks or months. Among other uses, this technicality permits the Senate to save time by circumventing its morning hour, a procedure required at the beginning of every legislative day.

Legislative History—(1) A chronological list of actions taken on a measure during its progress through the legislative process. (2) The official documents relating to a measure, the entries in the Journals of the two houses on that measure and the Congressional Record text of its consideration in both houses. The documents include all committee reports and the conference report and joint explanatory statement, if any. Courts and affected federal agencies study a measure's legislative history for congressional intent about its purpose and interpretation.

Legislative Process—(1) Narrowly, the stages in the enactment of a law from introduction to final disposition. An introduced measure that becomes law typically travels through reference to committee; committee and subcommittee consideration; report to the chamber; floor consideration; amendment; passage; engrossment; messaging to the other house; similar steps in that house, including floor amendment of the measure; return of the measure to the first house; consideration of amendments between the houses or a conference to resolve their differences; approval of the conference report by both houses; enrollment; approval by the president or override of the president's veto; and deposit with the Archivist of the United States. (2) Broadly, the political, lobbying and other factors that affect or influence the process of enacting laws.

Legislative Veto—A procedure, declared unconstitutional in 1983, that allowed Congress or one of its houses to nullify certain actions of the president, executive branch agencies or independent agencies. Sometimes called congressional vetoes or congressional disapprovals. Following the Supreme Court's 1983 decision, Congress amended several legislative veto statutes to require enactment of joint resolutions, which are subject to presidential veto, for nullifying executive branch actions.

Limitation on a General Appropriation Bill—Language that prohibits expenditures for part of an authorized purpose from funds provided in a general appropriation bill. Precedents require that the language be phrased in the negative: that none of the funds provided in a pending appropriation bill shall be used for a specified authorized activity. Limitations in general appropriation bills are permitted on the grounds that Congress can refuse to fund authorized programs and, therefore, can refuse to fund any part of them as long as the prohibition does not change existing law. House precedents have established that a limitation does not change existing law if it does not impose additional duties or burdens on executive branch officials, interfere with their discretionary authority or require them to make judgments or determinations not required by existing law. The proliferation of limitation amendments in the 1970s and early 1980s prompted the House to adopt a rule in 1983 making it more difficult for members to offer them. The rule bans such amendments during the reading of an appropriation bill for amendments, unless they are specifically authorized in existing law. Other limitations may be offered after the reading, but the Committee of the Whole can foreclose them by adopting a motion to rise and report the bill back to the House. In 1995 the rule was amended to allow the motion to rise and report to be made only by the majority leader or his or her designee. The House Appropriations Committee, however, can include limitation provisions in the bills it reports.

Line Item—An amount in an appropriation measure. It can refer to a single appropriation account or to separate amounts within the account. In the congressional budget process, the term usually refers to assumptions about the funding of particular programs or accounts that underlie the broad functional amounts in a budget resolution. These assumptions are discussed in the reports accompanying each resolution and are not binding.

Line-Item Veto—(See Item Veto.)

Line Item Veto Act of 1996—A law, in effect only from January 1997 until June 1998, that granted the president authority intended to be functionally equivalent to an item veto, by amending the Impoundment Control Act of 1974 to incorporate an approach known as enhanced rescission. Key provisions established a new procedure that permitted the president to cancel amounts of new discretionary appropriations (budget authority), new items of direct spending (entitlements) or certain limited tax benefits. It also required the president to notify Congress of the cancellation in a special message within five calendar days after signing the measure. The cancellation would become permanent unless legislation disapproving it was enacted within thirty days. On June 25, 1998, in Clinton v. City of New York the Supreme Court held the Line Item Veto Act unconstitutional, on the grounds that its cancellation provisions violated the presentment clause in Article I, clause 7, of the Constitution.

Live Pair—A voluntary and informal agreement between two members on opposite sides of an issue, one of whom is absent for a recorded vote, under which the member who is present withholds or withdraws his or her vote to offset the failure to vote by the member who is absent. Usually the member in attendance announces that he or she has a live pair, states how each would have voted and votes "present." In the House, under a rules change enacted in the 106th Congress, a live pair is only permitted on the rare occasions when electronic voting is not used.

Live Quorum—In the Senate, a quorum call to which senators are expected to respond. Senators usually suggest the absence of a quorum, not to force a quorum to appear, but to provide a pause in the proceedings during which senators can engage in private discussions or wait for a senator to come to the floor. A senator desiring a live quorum usually announces his or her intention, giving fair warning that there will be an objection to any unanimous consent request that the quorum call be dispensed with before it is completed.

Loan Guarantee—A statutory commitment by the federal government to pay part or all of a loan's principal and interest to a lender or the holder of a security in case the borrower defaults.

Lobby—To try to persuade members of Congress to propose, pass, modify or defeat proposed legislation or to change or repeal existing laws. Lobbyists attempt to promote their preferences or those of a group, organization or industry. Originally the term referred to persons frequenting the lobbies or corridors of legislative chambers in order to speak to lawmakers. In a general sense, lobbying includes not only direct contact with members but also indirect attempts to influence them, such as writing to them or persuading others to write or visit them, attempting to mold public opinion toward a desired legislative goal by various means and contributing or arranging for contributions to members' election campaigns. The right to lobby stems from the First Amendment to the Constitution, which bans laws that abridge the right of the people to petition the government for a redress of grievances.

Lobbying Disclosure Act of 1995—The principal statute requiring disclosure of — and also, to a degree, circumscribing — the activities of lobbyists. In general, it requires lobbyists who spend more than 20 percent of their time on lobbying activities to register and make semiannual reports of their activities to the clerk of the House and the secretary of the Senate, al-though the law provides for a number of exemptions. Among the statute's prohibitions, lobbyists are not allowed to make contributions to the legal defense fund of a member or high government official or to reimburse for official travel. Civil penalties for failure to comply may include fines of up to $50,000. The act does not include grassroots lobbying in its definition of lobbying activities.

The act amends several other lobby laws, notably the Foreign Agents Registration Act (FARA), so that lobbyists can submit a single filing. Since the measure was enacted, the number of lobby registrations has risen from about 12,000 to more than 20,000. In 1998 expenditures on federal lobbying, as disclosed under the Lobbying Disclosure Act, totaled $1.42 billion. The 1995 act supersedes the 1946 Federal Regulation of Lobbying Act, which was repealed in Section 11 of the 1995 Act.

Logrolling—Jargon for a legislative tactic or bargaining strategy in which members try to build support for their legislation by promising to support legislation desired by other members or by accepting amendments they hope will induce their colleagues to vote for their bill.

Lower Body—A way to refer to the House of Representatives, which is considered pejorative by House members.

Mace—The symbol of the office of the House sergeant at arms. Under the direction of the Speaker, the sergeant at arms is responsible for preserving order on the House floor by holding up the mace in front of an unruly member, or by carrying the mace up and down the aisles to quell boisterous behavior. When the House is in session, the mace sits on a pedestal at the Speaker's right; when the House is in Committee of the Whole, it is moved to a lower pedestal. The mace is forty-six inches high and consists of thirteen ebony rods bound in silver and topped by a silver globe with a silver eagle, wings outstretched, perched on it.

Majority Leader—The majority party's chief floor spokesperson, elected by that party's caucus — sometimes called floor leader. In the Senate, the majority leader also develops the party's political and procedural strategy, usually in collaboration with other party officials and committee chairmen. The majority leader negotiates the Senate's agenda and committee ratios with the minority leader and usually calls up measures for floor action. The chamber traditionally concedes to the majority leader the right to determine the days on which it will meet and the hours at which it will convene and adjourn. In the House, the majority leader is the Speaker's deputy and heir apparent and helps plan the floor agenda and the party's legislative strategy and often speaks for the party leadership in debate.

Managers—(1) The official title of members appointed to a conference committee, commonly called conferees. The ranking majority and minority managers for each house also manage floor consideration of the committee's conference report. (2) The members who manage the initial floor consideration of a measure. (3) The official title of House members appointed to present impeachment articles to the Senate and to act as prosecutors on behalf of the House during the Senate trial of the impeached person.

Mandatory Appropriations—Amounts that Congress must appropriate annually because it has no discretion over them unless it first amends existing substantive law. Certain entitlement programs, for example, require annual appropriations.

Markup—A meeting or series of meetings by a committee or subcommittee during which members mark up a measure by offering, debating and voting on amendments to it.

Means-Tested Programs—Programs that provide benefits or services to low-income individuals who meet a test of need. Most are entitlement programs, such as Medicaid, food stamps and Supplementary Security Income. A few—for example, subsidized housing and various social services—are funded through discretionary appropriations.

Members' Allowances—Official expenses that are paid for or for which members are reimbursed by their houses. Among these are the costs of office space in congressional buildings and in their home states or districts; office equipment and supplies; postage-free mailings (the franking privilege); a set number of trips to and from home states or districts, as well as travel elsewhere on official business; telephone and other telecommunications services; and staff salaries.

Member's Staff—The personal staff to which a member is entitled. The House sets a maximum number of staff and a monetary allowance for each member. The Senate does not set a maximum staff level, but it does set a monetary allowance for each member. In each house, the staff allowance is included with office expenses allowances and official mail allowances in a consolidated allowance. Representatives and senators can spend as much money in their consolidated allowances for staff, office expenses or official mail, as long as they do not exceed the monetary value of the three allowances combined. This provides members with flexibility in operating their offices.

Method of Equal Proportions—The mathematical formula used since 1950 to determine how the 435 seats in the House of Representatives should be distributed among the fifty states in the apportionment following each decennial census. It minimizes as much as possible the proportional difference between the average district population in any two states. Because the Constitution guarantees each state at least one representative, fifty seats are automatically apportioned. The formula calculates priority numbers for each state, assigns the first of the 385 remaining seats to the state with the highest priority number, the second to the state with the next highest number and so on until all seats are distributed. (See Apportionment.)

Midterm Election—The general election for members of Congress that occurs in November of the second year in a presidential term.

Minority Leader—The minority party's leader and chief floor spokesman, elected by the party caucus; sometimes called minority floor leader. With the assistance of other party officials and the ranking minority members of committees, the minority leader devises the party's political and procedural strategy.

Minority Staff—Employees who assist the minority party members of a committee. Most committees hire separate majority and minority party staffs but they also may hire nonpartisan staff. Senate rules state that a committee's staff must reflect the relative number of its majority and minority party committee members, and the rules guarantee the minority at least one-third of the funds available for hiring partisan staff. In the House, each committee is authorized thirty professional staff, and the minority members of most committees may select up to ten of these staff (subject to full committee approval). Under House rules, the minority party is to be "treated fairly" in the apportionment of additional staff resources. Each House committee determines the portion of its additional staff it allocates to the minority; some committees allocate one-third; and others allot less.

Modified Rule—A special rule from the House Rules Committee that permits only certain amendments to be offered to a measure during its floor consideration or that bans certain specified amendments or amendments on certain subjects.

Morning Business—In the Senate, routine business that is to be transacted at the beginning of the morning hour. The business consists, first, of laying before the Senate, and referring to committees, matters such as messages from the president and the House, federal agency reports and unreferred petitions, memorials, bills and joint resolutions. Next, senators may present additional petitions and memorials. Then committees may present their reports, after which senators may introduce bills and resolutions. Finally, resolutions coming over from a previous day are taken up for consideration. In practice, the Senate adopts standing orders that permit senators to introduce measures and file reports at any time, but only if there has been a morning business period on that day. Because the Senate often remains in the same legislative day for several days, weeks or months at a time, it orders a morning business period almost every calendar day for the convenience of senators who wish to introduce measures or make reports.

Morning Hour—A two-hour period at the beginning of a new legislative day during which the Senate is supposed to conduct routine business, call the calendar on Mondays and deal with other matters described in a Senate rule. In practice, the morning hour very rarely, if ever, occurs, in part because the Senate frequently recesses, rather than adjourns, at the end of a daily session. Therefore the rule does not apply when the senate next meets. The Senate's rules reserve the first hour of the morning for morning business. After the completion of morning business, or at the end of the first hour, the rules permit a motion to proceed to the consideration of a measure on the calendar out of its regular order (except on Mondays). Because that normally debatable motion is not debatable if offered during the morning hour, the majority leader may, but rarely does, use this procedure in anticipating a filibuster on the motion to proceed. If the Senate agrees to the motion, it can consider the measure until the end of the morning hour, and if there is no unfinished business from the previous day it can continue considering it after the morning hour. But if there is unfinished business, a motion to continue consideration is necessary, and that motion is debatable.

Motion—A formal proposal for a procedural action, such as to consider, to amend, to lay on the table, to reconsider, to recess or to adjourn. It has been estimated that at least eighty-five motions are possible under various circumstances in the House of Representatives, somewhat fewer in the Senate. Not all motions are created equal; some are privileged or preferential and enjoy priority over others. Some motions are debatable, amendable or divisible, while others are not.

Multiple and Sequential Referrals—The practice of referring a measure to two or more committees for concurrent consideration (multiple referral) or successively to several committees in sequence (sequential referral). A measure may also be divided into several parts, with each referred to a different committee or to several committees sequentially (split referral). In theory this gives all committees that have jurisdiction over parts of a measure the opportunity to consider and report on them.

Before 1975, House precedents banned such referrals. A 1975 rule required the Speaker to make concurrent and sequential referrals "to the maximum extent feasible." On sequential referrals, the Speaker could set deadlines for reporting the measure. The Speaker ruled that this provision authorized him to discharge a committee from further consideration of a measure and place it on the appropriate calendar of the House if the committee fails to meet the Speaker's deadline. The Speaker also used combinations of concurrent and sequential referrals. In 1995 joint referrals were prohibited. Now each measure is referred to a primary committee and also may be referred, either concurrently or sequentially, to one or more other committees, but usually only for consideration of portions of the measure that fall within the jurisdiction of each of those other committees.

In the Senate, before 1977 concurrent and sequential referrals were permitted only by unanimous consent. In that year, a rule authorized a privileged motion for such a referral if offered jointly by the majority and minority leaders. Debate on the motion and all amendments to it is limited to two hours. The motion may set deadlines for reporting and provide for discharging the committees involved if they fail to meet the deadlines. To date, this procedure has never been invoked; multiple referrals in the Senate continue to be made by unanimous consent.

Multiyear Appropriation—An appropriation that remains available for spending or obligation for more than one fiscal year; the exact period of time is specified in the act making the appropriation.

Multiyear Authorization—(1) Legislation that authorizes the existence or continuation of an agency, program or activity for more than one fiscal year. (2) Legislation that authorizes appropriations for an agency, program or activity for more than one fiscal year.

Nomination—A proposed presidential appointment to a federal office submitted to the Senate for confirmation. Approval is by majority vote. The Constitution explicitly requires confirmation for ambassadors, consuls, "public Ministers" (department heads) and Supreme Court justices. By law, other federal judges, all military promotions of officers and many high-level civilian officials must be confirmed.

Oath of Office—Upon taking office, members of Congress must swear or affirm that they will "support and defend the Constitution...against all enemies, foreign and domestic," that they will "bear true faith and allegiance" to the Constitution, that they take the obligation "freely, without any mental reservation or purpose of evasion," and that they will "well and faithfully discharge the duties" of their office. The oath is required by the Constitution, and the wording is prescribed by a statute. All House members must take the oath at the beginning of each new Congress. Usually, the member with the longest continuous service in the House swears in the Speaker, who then swears in the other members. The president of the Senate or a surrogate administers the oath to newly elected or reelected senators.

Obligation—A binding agreement by a government agency to pay for goods, products, services, studies and the like, either immediately or in the future. When an agency enters into such an agreement, it incurs an obligation. As the agency makes the required payments, it liquidates the obligation. Appropriation laws usually make funds available for obligation for one or more fiscal years but do not require agencies to spend their funds during those specific years. The actual outlays can occur years after the appropriation is obligated, as with a contract for construction of a submarine that may provide for payment to be made when it is delivered in the future. Such obligated funds are often said to be "in the pipeline." Under these circumstances, an agency's outlays in a particular year can come from appropriations obligated in previous years as well as from its current-year appropriation. Consequently, the money Congress appropriates for a fiscal year does not equal the total amount of appropriated money the government will actually spend in that year.

Off-Budget Entities—Specific federal entities whose budget authority, outlays and receipts are excluded by law from the calculation of budget totals, although they are part of government spending and income. As of early 2001, these included the

Social Security trust funds (Federal Old-Age and Survivors Insurance Fund and the Federal Disability Insurance Trust Fund) and the Postal Service. Government-sponsored enterprises are also excluded from the budget because they are considered private rather than public organizations.

Office of Management and Budget (OMB)—A unit in the Executive Office of the President, reconstituted in 1970 from the former Bureau of the Budget. The Office of Management and Budget (OMB) assists the president in preparing the budget and in formulating the government's fiscal program. The OMB also plays a central role in supervising and controlling implementation of the budget, pursuant to provisions in appropriations laws, the Budget Enforcement Act and other statutes. In addition to these budgetary functions, the OMB has various management duties, including those performed through its three statutory offices: Federal Financial Management, Federal Procurement Policy and Information and Regulatory Affairs.

Officers of Congress—The Constitution refers to the Speaker of the House and the president of the Senate as officers and declares that each house "shall chuse" its "other Officers," but it does not name them or indicate how they should be selected. A House rule refers to its clerk, sergeant at arms and chaplain as officers. Officers are not named in the Senate's rules, but Riddick's Senate Procedure lists the president pro tempore, secretary of the Senate, sergeant at arms, chaplain and the secretaries for the majority and minority parties as officers. A few appointed officials are sometimes referred to as officers, including the parliamentarians and the legislative counsels. The House elects its officers by resolution at the beginning of each Congress. The Senate also elects its officers, but once elected Senate officers serve from Congress to Congress until their successors are chosen.

Omnibus Bill—A measure that combines the provisions of several disparate subjects into a single and often lengthy bill.

One-Minute Speeches—Addresses by House members that can be on any subject but are limited to one minute. They are usually permitted at the beginning of a daily session after the chaplain's prayer, the pledge of allegiance and approval of the Journal. They are a customary practice, not a right granted by rule. Consequently, recognition for one-minute speeches requires unanimous consent and is entirely within the Speaker's discretion. The Speaker sometimes refuses to permit them when the House has a heavy legislative schedule or limits or postpones them until a later time of the day.

Open Rule—A special rule from the House Rules Committee that permits members to offer as many floor amendments as they wish as long as the amendments are germane and do not violate other House rules.

Order of Business (House)—The sequence of events prescribed by a House rule during the meeting of the House on a new legislative day that is supposed to take place, also called the general order of business. The sequence consists of (1) the chaplain's prayer; (2) reading and approval of the Journal; (3) the pledge of allegiance; (4) correction of the reference of public bills to committee; (5) disposal of business on the Speaker's table; (6) unfinished business; (7) the morning hour call of committees and consideration of their bills; (8) motions to go into Committee of the Whole; and (9) orders of the day. In practice, the House never fully complies with this rule. Instead, the items of business that follow the pledge of allegiance are supplanted by any special orders of business that are in order on that day (for example, conference reports; the corrections, discharge or private calendars; or motions to suspend the rules) and by other privileged business (for example, general appropriation bills and special rules) or measures made in order by special rules or unanimous consent. The regular order of business is also modified by unanimous consent practices and orders that govern recognition for one-minute speeches (which date from 1937) and for morning-hour debates, begun in 1994. By this combination of an order of business with privileged interruptions, the House gives precedence to certain categories of important legislation, brings to the floor other major legislation from its calendars in any order it chooses and provides expeditious processing for minor and noncontroversial measures.

Order of Business (Senate)—The sequence of events at the beginning of a new legislative day, as prescribed by Senate rules and standing orders. The sequence consists of (1) the chaplain's prayer; (2) the pledge of allegiance; (3) the designation of a temporary presiding officer if any; (4) Journal reading and approval; (5) recognition of the majority and minority leaders or their designees under the standing order; (6) morning business in the morning hour; (7) call of the calendar during the morning hour (largely obsolete); and (8) unfinished business from the previous session day.

Organization of Congress—The actions each house takes at the beginning of a Congress that are necessary to its operations. These include swearing in newly elected members, notifying the president that a quorum of each house is present, making committee assignments and fixing the hour for daily meetings. Because the House of Representatives is not a continuing body, it must also elect its Speaker and other officers and adopt its rules.

Original Bill—(1) A measure drafted by a committee and introduced by its chairman or another designated member when the committee reports the measure to its house. Unlike a clean bill, it is not referred back to the committee after introduction. The Senate permits all its legislative committees to report original bills. In the House, this authority is referred to in the rules as the "right to report at any time," and five committees (Appropriations, Budget, House Administration, Rules and Standards of Official Conduct) have such authority under circumstances specified in House Rule XIII, clause 5.

(2) In the House, special rules reported by the Rules Committee often propose that an amendment in the nature of a substitute be considered as an original bill for purposes of amendment, meaning that the substitute, as with a bill, may be amended in two degrees. Without that requirement, the substitute may only be amended in one further degree. In the Senate, an amendment in the nature of a substitute automatically is open to two degrees of amendment, as is the original text of the bill, if the substitute is offered when no other amendment is pending.

Original Jurisdiction—The authority of certain committees to originate a measure and report it to the chamber. For example, general appropriation bills reported by the House Appropriations Committee are original bills, and special rules reported by the House Rules Committee are original resolutions.

Other Body—A commonly used reference to a house by a member of the other house. Congressional comity discourages members from directly naming the other house during debate.

Outlays—Amounts of government spending. They consist of payments, usually by check or in cash, to liquidate obligations incurred in prior fiscal years as well as in the current year, including the net lending of funds under budget authority. In federal budget accounting, net outlays are calculated by subtracting the amounts of refunds and various kinds of reimbursements to the government from actual spending.

Override a Veto—Congressional enactment of a measure over the president's veto. A veto override requires a recorded two-thirds vote of those voting in each house, a quorum being present. Because the president must return the vetoed measure to its house of origin, that house votes first, but neither house is required to attempt an override, whether immediately or at all. If an override attempt fails in the house of origin, the veto stands and the measure dies.

Oversight—Congressional review of the way in which federal agencies implement laws to ensure that they are carrying out the intent of Congress and to inquire into the efficiency of the implementation and the effectiveness of the law. The Legislative Reorganization Act of 1946 defined oversight as the function of exercising continuous watchfulness over the execution of the laws by the executive branch.

Oxford-Style Debate—The House held three Oxford-style debates in 1994, modeled after the famous debating format favored by the Oxford Union in Great Britain. Neither chamber has held Oxford-style debates since then. The Oxford-style debates aired nationally over C-SPAN television and National Public Radio. The organized event featured eight participants divided evenly into two teams, one team representing the Democrats (then holding the majority in the chamber) and the other the Republicans. Both teams argued a single question chosen well ahead of the event. A moderator regulated the debate, and began it by stating the resolution at issue. The order of the speakers alternated by team, with a debater for the affirmative speaking first and a debater for the opposing team offering a rebuttal. The rest of the speakers alternated in kind until all gained the chance to speak.

Parliamentarian—The official advisor to the presiding officer in each house on questions of procedure. The parliamentarian and his or her assistants also answer procedural questions from members and congressional staff, refer measures to committees on behalf of the presiding officer and maintain compilations of the precedents. The House parliamentarian revises the House Manual at the beginning of every Congress and usually reviews special rules before the Rules Committee reports them to the House. Either a parliamentarian or an assistant is always present and near the podium during sessions of each house.

Party Caucus—Generic term for each party's official organization in each house. Only House Democrats officially call their organization a caucus. House and Senate Republicans and Senate Democrats call their organizations conferences. The party caucuses elect their leaders, approve committee assignments and chairmanships (or ranking minority members, if the party is in the minority), establish party committees and study groups and discuss party and legislative policies. On rare occasions, they have stripped members of committee seniority or expelled them from the caucus for party disloyalty.

Pay-as-You-Go (PAYGO)—A provision first instituted under the Budget Enforcement Act of 1990 that applies to legislation enacted before Oct. 1, 2002. It requires that the cumulative effect of legislation concerning either revenues or direct spending should not result in a net negative impact on the budget. If legislation does provide for an increase in spending or decrease in revenues, that effect is supposed to be offset by legislated spending reductions or revenue increases. If Congress fails to enact the appropriate offsets, the act requires presidential sequestration of sufficient offsetting amounts in specific direct spending accounts. Congress and the president can circumvent this requirement if both agree that an emergency requires a particular action or if a law is enacted declaring that deteriorated economic circumstances make it necessary to suspend the requirement.

Appendix

Permanent Appropriation—An appropriation that remains continuously available, without current action or renewal by Congress, under the terms of a previously enacted authorization or appropriation law. One such appropriation provides for payment of interest on the public debt and another the salaries of members of Congress.

Permanent Authorization—An authorization without a time limit. It usually does not specify any limit on the funds that may be appropriated for the agency, program or activity that it authorizes, leaving such amounts to the discretion of the appropriations committees and the two houses.

Permanent Staff—Term used formerly for committee staff authorized by law, who were funded through a permanent authorization and also called statutory staff. Most committees were authorized thirty permanent staff members. Most committees also were permitted additional staff, often called investigative staff, who were authorized by annual or biennial funding resolutions. The Senate eliminated the primary distinction between statutory and investigative staff in 1981. The House eliminated the distinction in 1995 by requiring that funding resolutions authorize money to hire both types of staff.

Personally Obnoxious (or Objectionable)—A characterization a senator sometimes applies to a president's nominee for a federal office in that senator's state to justify his or her opposition to the nomination.

Pocket Veto—The indirect veto of a bill as a result of the president withholding approval of it until after Congress has adjourned sine die. A bill the president does not sign but does not formally veto while Congress is in session automatically becomes a law ten days (excluding Sundays) after it is received. But if Congress adjourns its annual session during that ten-day period the measure dies even if the president does not formally veto it.

Point of Order—A parliamentary term used in committee and on the floor to object to an alleged violation of a rule and to demand that the chair enforce the rule. The point of order immediately halts the proceedings until the chair decides whether the contention is valid.

Pork or Pork Barrel Legislation—Pejorative terms for federal appropriations, bills or policies that provide funds to benefit a legislator's district or state, with the implication that the legislator presses for enactment of such benefits to ingratiate himself or herself with constituents rather than on the basis of an impartial, objective assessment of need or merit. The terms are often applied to such benefits as new parks, post offices, dams, canals, bridges, roads, water projects, sewage treatment plants and public works of any kind, as well as demonstration projects, research grants and relocation of government facilities. Funds released by the president for various kinds of benefits or government contracts approved by him allegedly for political purposes are also sometimes referred to as pork.

Postcloture Filibuster—A filibuster conducted after the Senate invokes cloture. It employs an array of procedural tactics rather than lengthy speeches to delay final action. The Senate curtailed the postcloture filibuster's effectiveness by closing a variety of loopholes in the cloture rule in 1979 and 1986.

Power of the Purse—A reference to the constitutional power Congress has over legislation to raise revenue and appropriate monies from the Treasury. Article I, Section 8 states that Congress "shall have Power To lay and collect Taxes, Duties, Imposts and Excises, [and] to pay the Debts." Section 9 declares: "No Money shall be drawn from the Treasury, but in Consequence of Appropriations made by Law."

Preamble—Introductory language describing the reasons for and intent of a measure, sometimes called a whereas clause. It occasionally appears in joint, concurrent and simple resolutions but rarely in bills.

Precedent—A previous ruling on a parliamentary matter or a long-standing practice or custom of a house. Precedents serve to control arbitrary rulings and serve as the common law of a house.

President of the Senate—One constitutional role of the vice president is serving as the presiding officer of the Senate, or president of the Senate. The Constitution permits the vice president to cast a vote in the Senate only to break a tie, but the vice president is not required to do so.

President Pro Tempore—Under the Constitution, an officer elected by the Senate to preside over it during the absence of the vice president of the United States. Often referred to as the "pro tem," this senator is usually a member of the majority party with the longest continuous service in the chamber and also, by virtue of seniority, a committee chairman. When attending to committee and other duties the president pro tempore appoints other senators to preside.

Presiding Officer—In a formal meeting, the individual authorized to maintain order and decorum, recognize members to speak or offer motions and apply and interpret the chamber's rules, precedents and practices. The Speaker of the House and the president of the Senate are the chief presiding officers in their respective houses.

Previous Question—A nondebatable motion which, when agreed to by majority vote, usually cuts off further debate, prevents the offering of additional amendments and brings the pending matter to an immediate vote. It is a major debate-limiting device in the House; it is not permitted in Committee of the Whole in the House or in the Senate.

Private Bill—A bill that applies to one or more specified persons, corporations, institutions or other entities, usually to grant relief when no other legal remedy is available to them. Many private bills deal with claims against the federal government, immigration and naturalization cases and land titles.

Private Calendar—Commonly used title for a calendar in the House reserved for private bills and resolutions favorably reported by committees. The private calendar is officially called the Calendar of the Committee of the Whole House.

Private Law—A private bill enacted into law. Private laws are numbered in the same fashion as public laws.

Privilege—An attribute of a motion, measure, report, question or proposition that gives it priority status for consideration. Privileged motions and motions to bring up privileged questions are not debatable.

Privilege of the Floor—In addition to the members of a house, certain individuals are admitted to its floor while it is in session. The rules of the two houses differ somewhat but both extend the privilege to the president and vice president, Supreme Court justices, cabinet members, state governors, former members of that house, members of the other house, certain officers and officials of Congress, certain staff of that house in the discharge of official duties and the chamber's former parliamentarians. They also allow access to a limited number of committee and members' staff when their presence is necessary.

Pro Forma Amendment—In the House, an amendment that ostensibly proposes to change a measure or another amendment by moving "to strike the last word" or "to strike the requisite number of words." A member offers it not to make any actual change in the measure or amendment but only to obtain time for debate.

Pro Tem—A common reference to the president pro tempore of the Senate or, occasionally, to a Speaker pro tempore. (See President Pro Tempore; Speaker Pro Tempore.)

Procedures—The methods of conducting business in a deliberative body. The procedures of each house are governed first by applicable provisions of the Constitution, and then by its standing rules and orders, precedents, traditional practices and any statutory rules that apply to it. The authority of the houses to adopt rules in addition to those specified in the Constitution is derived from Article I, Section 5, clause 2, of the Constitution, which states: "Each House may determine the Rules of its Proceedings...." By rule, the House of Representatives also follows the procedures in Jefferson's Manual that are not inconsistent with its standing rules and orders. Many Senate procedures also conform with Jefferson's provisions, but by practice rather than by rule. At the beginning of each Congress, the House uses procedures in general parliamentary law until it adopts its standing rules.

Proxy Voting—The practice of permitting a member to cast the vote of an absent colleague in addition to his or her own vote. Proxy voting is prohibited on the floors of the House and Senate, but the Senate permits its committees to authorize proxy voting, and most do. In 1995, House rules were changed to prohibit proxy voting in committee.

Public Bill—A bill dealing with general legislative matters having national applicability or applying to the federal government or to a class of persons, groups or organizations.

Public Debt—Federal government debt incurred by the Treasury or the Federal Financing Bank by the sale of securities to the public or borrowings from a federal fund or account.

Public Law—A public bill or joint resolution enacted into law. It is cited by the letters "PL" followed by a hyphenated number. The digits before the hyphen indicate the number of the Congress in which it was enacted; the digits after the hyphen indicate its position in the numerical sequence of public measures that became law during that Congress. For example, the Budget Enforcement Act of 1990 became PL 101-508 because it was the 508th measure in that sequence for the 101st Congress. (See also Private Law.)

Qualification (of Members)—The Constitution requires members of the House of Representatives to be twenty-five years of age at the time their terms begin. They must have been citizens of the United States for seven years before that date and, when elected, must be "Inhabitant[s]" of the state from which they were elected. There is no constitutional requirement that they reside in the districts they represent. Senators are required to be thirty years of age at the time their terms begin. They must have been citizens of the United States for nine years before that date and, when elected, must be "Inhabitant[s]" of the states in which they were elected. The "Inhabitant" qualification is broadly interpreted, and in modern times a candidate's declaration of state residence has generally been accepted as meeting the constitutional requirement.

Queen of the Hill Rule—A special rule from the House Rules Committee that permits votes on a series of amendments, especially complete substitutes for a measure, in a specified order, but directs that the amendment receiving the greatest number of votes shall be the winning one. This kind of rule permits the House to vote directly on a variety of alternatives to a measure. In doing so, it sets aside the precedent that once an amendment has been adopted, no further amendments may be offered to the text it has amended. Under an earlier practice, the Rules Committee reported "king of the hill" rules under which there also could be votes on a series of amendments,

again in a specified order. If more than one of the amendments was adopted under this kind of rule, it was the last amendment to receive a majority vote that was considered as having been finally adopted, whether or not it had received the greatest number of votes.

Quorum—The minimum number of members required to be present for the transaction of business. Under the Constitution, a quorum in each house is a majority of its members: 218 in the House and 51 in the Senate when there are no vacancies. By House rule, a quorum in Committee of the Whole is 100. In practice, both houses usually assume a quorum is present even if it is not, unless a member makes a point of no quorum in the House or suggests the absence of a quorum in the Senate. Consequently, each house transacts much of its business, and even passes bills, when only a few members are present. For House and Senate committees, chamber rules allow a minimum quorum of one-third of a committee's members to conduct most types of business.

Quorum Call—A procedure for determining whether a quorum is present in a chamber. In the Senate, a clerk calls the roll (roster) of senators. The House usually employs its electronic voting system.

Ramseyer Rule—A House rule that requires a committee's report on a bill or joint resolution to show the changes the measure, and any committee amendments to it, would make in existing law. The rule requires the report to present the text of any statutory provision that would be repealed and a comparative print showing, through typographical devices such as stricken-through type or italics, other changes that would be made in existing law. The rule, adopted in 1929, is named after its sponsor, Rep. Christian W. Ramseyer, R-Iowa. The Senate's analogous rule is called the Cordon Rule.

Rank or Ranking—A member's position on the list of his or her party's members on a committee or subcommittee. When first assigned to a committee, a member is usually placed at the bottom of the list, then moves up as those above leave the committee. On subcommittees, however, a member's rank may not have anything to do with the length of his or her service on it.

Ranking Member—(1) Most often a reference to the minority member with the highest ranking on a committee or subcommittee. (2) A reference to the majority member next in rank to the chairman or to the highest ranking majority member present at a committee or subcommittee meeting.

Ratification—(1) The president's formal act of promulgating a treaty after the Senate has approved it. The resolution of ratification agreed to by the Senate is the procedural vehicle by which the Senate gives its consent to ratification. (2) A state legislature's act in approving a proposed constitutional amendment. Such an amendment becomes effective when ratified by three-fourths of the states.

Reapportionment—(See Apportionment.)

Recess—(1) A temporary interruption or suspension of a meeting of a chamber or committee. Unlike an adjournment, a recess does not end a legislative day. Because the Senate often recesses from one calendar day to another, its legislative day may extend over several calendar days, weeks or even months. (2) A period of adjournment for more than three days to a day certain, especially over a holiday or in August during odd-numbered years.

Recess Appointment—A presidential appointment to a vacant federal position made after the Senate has adjourned sine die or has adjourned or recessed for more than thirty days. If the president submits the recess appointee's nomination during the next session of the Senate, that individual can continue to serve until the end of the session even though the Senate might have rejected the nomination. When appointed to a vacancy that existed thirty days before the end of the last Senate session, a recess appointee is not paid until confirmed.

Recommit—To send a measure back to the committee that reported it; sometimes called a straight motion to recommit to distinguish it from a motion to recommit with instructions. A successful motion to recommit kills the measure unless it is accompanied by instructions.

Recommit a Conference Report—To return a conference report to the conference committee for renegotiation of some or all of its agreements. A motion to recommit may be offered with or without instructions.

Recommit with Instructions—To send a measure back to a committee with instructions to take some action on it. Invariably in the House and often in the Senate, when the motion recommits to a standing committee, the instructions require the committee to report the measure "forthwith" with specified amendments.

Reconciliation—A procedure for changing existing revenue and spending laws to bring total federal revenues and spending within the limits established in a budget resolution. Congress has applied reconciliation chiefly to revenues and mandatory spending programs, especially entitlements. Discretionary spending is controlled through annual appropriation bills.

Recorded Vote—(1) Generally, any vote in which members are recorded by name for or against a measure; also called a record vote or roll-call vote. The only recorded vote in the Senate is a vote by the yeas and nays and is commonly called a roll-call vote. (2) Technically, a recorded vote is one demanded in the House of Representatives and supported by at least one-fifth of a quorum (forty-four members) in the House sitting as the House or at least twenty-five members in Committee of the Whole.

Recorded Vote by Clerks—A voting procedure in the House where members pass through the appropriate "aye" or "no" aisle in the chamber and cast their votes by depositing a signed green (yea) or red (no) card in a ballot box. These votes are tabulated by clerks and reported to the chair. The electronic voting system is much more convenient and has largely supplanted this procedure. (See Committee of the Whole; Recorded Vote; Teller Vote.)

Redistricting—The redrawing of congressional district boundaries within a state after a decennial census. Redistricting may be required to equalize district populations or to accommodate an increase or decrease in the number of a state's House seats that might have resulted from the decennial apportionment. The state governments determine the district lines. (See Apportionment; Congressional District; Gerrymandering.)

Referral—The assignment of a measure to committee for consideration. Under a House rule, the Speaker can refuse to refer a measure if the Speaker believes it is "of an obscene or insulting character."

Report—(1) As a verb, a committee is said to report when it submits a measure or other document to its parent chamber. (2) A clerk is said to report when he or she reads a measure's title, text or the text of an amendment to the body at the direction of the chair. (3) As a noun, a committee document that accompanies a reported measure. It describes the measure, the committee's views on it, its costs and the changes it proposes to make in existing law; it also includes certain impact statements. (4) A committee document submitted to its parent chamber that describes the results of an investigation or other study or provides information it is required to provide by rule or law.

Representative—An elected and duly sworn member of the House of Representatives who is entitled to vote in the chamber. The Constitution requires that a representative be at least twenty-five years old, a citizen of the United States for at least seven years and an inhabitant of the state from which he or she is elected. Customarily, the member resides in the district he or she represents. Representatives are elected in even-numbered years to two-year terms that begin the following January.

Reprimand—A formal condemnation of a member for misbehavior, considered a milder reproof than censure. The House of Representatives first used it in 1976. The Senate first used it in 1991. (See also Censure; Code of Official Conduct; Denounce; Ethics Rules; Expulsion; Seniority Loss.)

Rescission—A provision of law that repeals previously enacted budget authority in whole or in part. Under the Impoundment Control Act of 1974, the president can impound such funds by sending a message to Congress requesting one or more rescissions and the reasons for doing so. If Congress does not pass a rescission bill for the programs requested by the president within forty-five days of continuous session after receiving the message, the president must make the funds available for obligation and expenditure. If the president does not, the comptroller general of the United States is authorized to bring suit to compel the release of those funds. A rescission bill may rescind all, part or none of an amount proposed by the president, and may rescind funds the president has not impounded.

Reserving the Right To Object—Members' declaration that at some indefinite future time they may object to a unanimous consent request. It is an attempt to circumvent the requirement that members may prevent such an action only by objecting immediately after it is proposed.

Resident Commissioner from Puerto Rico—A nonvoting member of the House of Representatives, elected to a four-year term. The resident commissioner has the same status and privileges as delegates. Like the delegates, the resident commissioner may not vote in the House or Committee of the Whole.

Resolution—(1) A simple resolution; that is, a nonlegislative measure effective only in the house in which it is proposed and not requiring concurrence by the other chamber or approval by the president. Simple resolutions are designated H. Res. in the House and S. Res. in the Senate. Simple resolutions express nonbinding opinions on policies or issues or deal with the internal affairs or prerogatives of a house. (2) Any type of resolution: simple, concurrent or joint. (See Concurrent Resolution; Joint Resolution.)

Resolution of Inquiry—A resolution usually simple rather than concurrent calling on the president or the head of an executive agency to provide specific information or papers to one or both houses.

Resolution of Ratification—The Senate vehicle for agreeing to a treaty. The constitutionally mandated vote of two-thirds of the senators present and voting applies to the adoption of this resolution. However, it may also contain amendments, reservations, declarations or understandings that the Senate had previously added to it by majority vote.

Revenue Legislation—Measures that levy new taxes or tariffs or change existing ones. Under Article I, Section 7, clause 1 of the Constitution, the House of Representatives originates federal revenue measures, but the Senate can propose amendments to them. The House Ways and Means Committee and the Senate Finance Committee have jurisdiction over such measures, with a few minor exceptions.

Revise and Extend One's Remarks—A unanimous consent request to publish in the Congressional Record a statement a member did not deliver on the floor, a longer statement than the one made on the floor or miscellaneous extraneous material.

Revolving Fund—A trust fund or account whose income remains available to finance its continuing operations without any fiscal year limitation.

Rider—Congressional slang for an amendment unrelated or extraneous to the subject matter of the measure to which it is attached. Riders often contain proposals that are less likely to become law on their own merits as separate bills, either because of opposition in the committee of jurisdiction, resistance in the other house or the probability of a presidential veto. Riders are more common in the Senate.

Roll Call—A call of the roll to determine whether a quorum is present, to establish a quorum or to vote on a question. Usually, the House uses its electronic voting system for a roll call. The Senate does not have an electronic voting system; its roll is always called by a clerk.

Rule—(1) A permanent regulation that a house adopts to govern its conduct of business, its procedures, its internal organization, behavior of its members, regulation of its facilities, duties of an officer or some other subject it chooses to govern in that form. (2) In the House, a privileged simple resolution reported by the Rules Committee that provides methods and conditions for floor consideration of a measure or, rarely, several measures.

Rule Twenty-Two—A common reference to the Senate's cloture rule. (See Cloture)

Second-Degree Amendment—An amendment to an amendment in the first degree. It is usually a perfecting amendment.

Secretary of the Senate—The chief financial, administrative and legislative officer of the Senate. Elected by resolution or order of the Senate, the secretary is invariably the candidate of the majority party and usually chosen by the majority leader. In the absence of the vice president and pending the election of a president pro tempore, the secretary presides over the Senate. The secretary is subject to policy direction and oversight by the Senate Committee on Rules and Administration. The secretary manages a wide range of functions that support the administrative operations of the Senate as an organization as well as those functions necessary to its legislative process, including record keeping, document management, certifications, housekeeping services, administration of oaths and lobbyist registrations. The secretary is responsible for accounting for all funds appropriated to the Senate and conducts audits of Senate financial activities. On a semiannual basis the secretary issues the Report of the Secretary of the Senate, a compilation of Senate expenditures.

Section—A subdivision of a bill or statute. By law, a section must be numbered and, as nearly as possible, contain "a single proposition of enactment."

Select or Special Committee—A committee established by a resolution in either house for a special purpose and, usually, for a limited time. Most select and special committees are assigned specific investigations or studies but are not authorized to report measures to their chambers. However, both houses have created several permanent select and special committees and have given legislative reporting authority to a few of them: the Ethics Committee in the Senate and the Intelligence Committees in both houses. There is no substantive difference be-

tween a select and a special committee; they are so called depending simply on whether the resolution creating the committee calls it one or the other.

Senate—The house of Congress in which each state is represented by two senators; each senator has one vote. Article V of the Constitution declares that "No State, without its Consent, shall be deprived of its equal Suffrage in the Senate." The Constitution also gives the Senate equal legislative power with the House of Representatives. Although the Senate is prohibited from originating revenue measures, and as a matter of practice it does not originate appropriation measures, it can amend both. Only the Senate can give or withhold consent to treaties and nominations from the president. It also acts as a court to try impeachments by the House and elects the vice president when no candidate receives a majority of the electoral votes. It is often referred to as "the upper body," but not by members of the House.

Senate Manual—The handbook of the Senate's standing rules and orders and the laws and other regulations that apply to the Senate, usually published once each Congress.

Senator—A duly sworn elected or appointed member of the Senate. The Constitution requires that a senator be at least thirty years old, a citizen of the United States for at least nine years and an inhabitant of the state from which he or she is elected. Senators are usually elected in even-numbered years to six-year terms that begin the following January. When a vacancy occurs before the end of a term, the state governor can appoint a replacement to fill the position until a successor is chosen at the state's next general election or, if specified under state law, the next feasible date for such an election, to serve the remainder of the term. Until the Seventeenth Amendment was ratified in 1913, senators were chosen by their state legislatures.

Senatorial Courtesy—The Senate's practice of declining to confirm a presidential nominee for an office in the state of a senator of the president's party unless that senator approves.

Seniority—The priority, precedence or status accorded members according to the length of their continuous service in a house or on a committee.

Seniority Loss—A type of punishment that reduces a member's seniority on his or her committees, including the loss of chairmanships. Party caucuses in both houses have occasionally imposed such punishment on their members, for example, for publicly supporting candidates of the other party.

Seniority Rule—The customary practice, rather than a rule, of assigning the chairmanship of a committee to the majority party member who has served on the committee for the longest continuous period of time.

Seniority System—A collection of long-standing customary practices under which members with longer continuous service than their colleagues in their house or on their committees receive various kinds of preferential treatment. Although some of the practices are no longer as rigidly observed as in the past, they still pervade the organization and procedures of Congress.

Sequestration—A procedure for canceling budgetary resources — that is, money available for obligation or spending — to enforce budget limitations established in law. Sequestered funds are no longer available for obligation or expenditure.

Sergeant at Arms—The officer in each house responsible for maintaining order, security and decorum in its wing of the Capitol, including the chamber and its galleries. Although elected by their respective houses, both sergeants at arms are invariably the candidates of the majority party.

Session—(1) The annual series of meetings of a Congress.

Under the Constitution, Congress must assemble at least once a year at noon on Jan. 3 unless it appoints a different day by law. (2) The special meetings of Congress or of one house convened by the president, called a special session. (3) A house is said to be in session during the period of a day when it is meeting.

Severability (or Separability) Clause—Language stating that if any particular provisions of a measure are declared invalid by the courts the remaining provisions shall remain in effect.

Sine Die—Without fixing a day for a future meeting. An adjournment sine die signifies the end of an annual or special session of Congress.

Slip Law—The first official publication of a measure that has become law. It is published separately in unbound, single-sheet form or pamphlet form. A slip law usually is available two or three days after the date of the law's enactment.

Speaker—The presiding officer of the House of Representatives and the leader of its majority party. The Speaker is selected by the majority party and formally elected by the House at the beginning of each Congress. Although the Constitution does not require the Speaker to be a member of the House, in fact, all Speakers have been members.

Speaker Pro Tempore—A member of the House who is designated as the temporary presiding officer by the Speaker or elected by the House to that position during the Speaker's absence.

Speaker's Vote—The Speaker is not required to vote, and the Speaker's name is not called on a roll-call vote unless so requested. Usually, the Speaker votes either to create a tie vote, and thereby defeat a proposal or to break a tie in favor of a proposal. Occasionally, the Speaker also votes to emphasize the importance of a matter.

Special Session—A session of Congress convened by the president, under his constitutional authority, after Congress has adjourned sine die at the end of a regular session. (See Adjournment Sine Die; Session.)

Spending Authority—The technical term for backdoor spending. The Congressional Budget Act of 1974 defines it as borrowing authority, contract authority and entitlement authority for which appropriation acts do not provide budget authority in advance. Under the Budget Act, legislation that provides new spending authority may not be considered unless it provides that the authority shall be effective only to the extent or in such amounts as provided in an appropriation act.

Spending Cap—The statutory limit for a fiscal year on the amount of new budget authority and outlays allowed for discretionary spending. The Budget Enforcement Act of 1997 requires a sequester if the cap is exceeded.

Split Referral—A measure divided into two or more parts, with each part referred to a different committee.

Sponsor—The principal proponent and introducer of a measure or an amendment.

Staff Director—The most frequently used title for the head of staff of a committee or subcommittee. On some committees, that person is called chief of staff, clerk, chief clerk, chief counsel, general counsel or executive director. The head of a committee's minority staff is usually called minority staff director.

Standing Committee—A permanent committee established by a House or Senate standing rule or standing order. The rule also describes the subject areas on which the committee may report bills and resolutions and conduct oversight. Most introduced measures must be referred to one or more standing committees according to their jurisdictions.

Standing Order—A continuing regulation or directive that has the force and effect of a rule, but is not incorporated into the standing rules. The Senate's numerous standing orders, like its standing rules, continue from Congress to Congress unless changed or the order states otherwise. The House uses relatively few standing orders, and those it adopts expire at the end of a session of Congress.

Standing Rules—The rules of the Senate that continue from one Congress to the next and the rules of the House of Representatives that it adopts at the beginning of each new Congress.

Standing Vote—An alternative and informal term for a division vote, during which members in favor of a proposal and then members opposed stand and are counted by the chair.

Star Print—A reprint of a bill, resolution, amendment or committee report correcting technical or substantive errors in a previous printing; so called because of the small black star that appears on the front page or cover.

State of the Union Message—A presidential message to Congress under the constitutional directive that the president shall "from time to time give to the Congress Information of the State of the Union, and recommend to their Consideration such Measures as he shall judge necessary and expedient." Customarily, the president sends an annual State of the Union message to Congress, usually late in January.

Statutes at Large—A chronological arrangement of the laws enacted in each session of Congress. Though indexed, the laws are not arranged by subject matter nor is there an indication of how they affect or change previously enacted laws. The volumes are numbered by Congress, and the laws are cited by their volume and page number. The Gramm-Rudman-Hollings Act, for example, appears as 99 Stat. 1037.

Straw Vote Prohibition—Under a House precedent, a member who has the floor during debate may not conduct a straw vote or otherwise ask for a show of support for a proposition. Only the chair may put a question to a vote.

Strike From the *Record*—Expunge objectionable remarks from the Congressional Record, after a member's words have been taken down on a point of order.

Subcommittee—A panel of committee members assigned a portion of the committee's jurisdiction or other functions. On legislative committees, subcommittees hold hearings, mark up legislation and report measures to their full committee for further action; they cannot report directly to the chamber. A subcommittee's party composition usually reflects the ratio on its parent committee.

Subpoena Power—The authority granted to committees by the rules of their respective houses to issue legal orders requiring individuals to appear and testify, or to produce documents pertinent to the committee's functions, or both. Persons who do not comply with subpoenas can be cited for contempt of Congress and prosecuted.

Subsidy—Generally, a payment or benefit made by the federal government for which no current repayment is required. Subsidy payments may be designed to support the conduct of an economic enterprise or activity, such as ship operations, or to support certain market prices, as in the case of farm subsidies.

Sunset Legislation—A term sometimes applied to laws authorizing the existence of agencies or programs that expire annually or at the end of some other specified period of time. One of the purposes of setting specific expiration dates for agencies and programs is to encourage the committees with jurisdiction over them to determine whether they should be continued or terminated.

Sunshine Rules—Rules requiring open committee hearings and business meetings, including markup sessions, in both houses, and also open conference committee meetings. However, all may be closed under certain circumstances and using certain procedures required by the rules.

Supermajority—A term sometimes used for a vote on a matter that requires approval by more than a simple majority of those members present and voting; also referred to as extraordinary majority.

Supplemental Appropriation Bill—A measure providing appropriations for use in the current fiscal year, in addition to those already provided in annual general appropriation bills. Supplemental appropriations are often for unforeseen emergencies.

Suspension of the Rules (House)—An expeditious procedure for passing relatively noncontroversial or emergency measures by a two-thirds vote of those members voting, a quorum being present.

Suspension of the Rules (Senate)—A procedure to set aside one or more of the Senate's rules; it is used infrequently, and then most often to suspend the rule banning legislative amendments to appropriation bills.

Task Force—A title sometimes given to a panel of members assigned to a special project, study or investigation. Ordinarily, these groups do not have authority to report measures to their respective houses.

Tax Expenditure—Loosely, a tax exemption or advantage, sometimes called an incentive or loophole; technically, a loss of governmental tax revenue attributable to some provision of federal tax laws that allows a special exclusion, exemption or deduction from gross income or that provides a special credit, preferential tax rate or deferral of tax liability.

Televised Proceedings—Television and radio coverage of the floor proceedings of the House of Representatives has been available since 1979 and of the Senate since 1986. They are broadcast over a coaxial cable system to all congressional offices and to some congressional agencies on channels reserved for that purpose. Coverage is also available free of charge to commercial and public television and radio broadcasters. The Cable-Satellite Public Affairs Network (C-SPAN) carries gavel-to-gavel coverage of both houses.

Teller Vote—A voting procedure, formerly used in the House, in which members cast their votes by passing through the center aisle to be counted, but not recorded by name, by a member from each party appointed by the chair. The House deleted the procedure from its rules in 1993, but during floor discussion of the deletion a leading member stated that a teller vote would still be available in the event of a breakdown of the electronic voting system.

Third-Degree Amendment—An amendment to a second-degree amendment. Both houses prohibit such amendments.

Third Reading—A required reading to a chamber of a bill or joint resolution by title only before the vote on passage. In modern practice, it has merely become a pro forma step.

Three-Day Rule—(1) In the House, a measure cannot be considered until the third calendar day on which the committee report has been available. (2) In the House, a conference report cannot be considered until the third calendar day on which its text has been available in the Congressional Record. (3) In the House, a general appropriation bill cannot be considered until the third calendar day on which printed hearings on the bill have been available. (4) In the Senate, when a committee votes to report a measure, a committee member is entitled to three calendar days within which to submit separate views for inclusion in the committee report. (In House committees, a member is entitled to two calendar days for this purpose, after the day on which the committee votes to report.) (5) In both houses, a majority of a committee's members may call a special meeting of the committee if its chairman fails to do so within three calendar days after three or more of the members, acting jointly, formally request such a meeting.

In calculating such periods, the House omits holiday and weekend days on which it does not meet. The Senate makes no such exclusion.

Tie Vote—When the votes for and against a proposition are equal, it loses. The president of the Senate may cast a vote only to break a tie. Because the Speaker is invariably a member of the House, the Speaker is entitled to vote but usually does not. The Speaker may choose to do so to break, or create, a tie vote.

Title—(1) A major subdivision of a bill or act, designated by a roman numeral and usually containing legislative provisions on the same general subject. Titles are sometimes divided into subtitles as well as sections. (2) The official name of a bill or act, also called a caption or long title. (3) Some bills also have short titles that appear in the sentence immediately following the enacting clause. (4) Popular titles are the unofficial names given to some bills or acts by common usage. For example, the Balanced Budget and Emergency Deficit Control Act of 1985 (short title) is almost invariably referred to as Gramm-Rudman (popular title). In other cases, significant legislation is popularly referred to by its title number (see definition (1) above). For example, the federal legislation that requires equality of funding for women's and men's sports in educational institutions that receive federal funds is popularly called Title IX.

Track System—An occasional Senate practice that expedites legislation by dividing a day's session into two or more specific time periods, commonly called tracks, each reserved for consideration of a different measure.

Transfer Payment—A federal government payment to which individuals or organizations are entitled under law and for which no goods or services are required in return. Payments include welfare and Social Security benefits, unemployment insurance, government pensions and veterans benefits.

Treaty—A formal document containing an agreement between two or more sovereign nations. The Constitution authorizes the president to make treaties, but the president must submit them to the Senate for its approval by a two-thirds vote of the senators present. Under the Senate's rules, that vote actually occurs on a resolution of ratification. Although the Constitution does not give the House a direct role in approving treaties, that body has sometimes insisted that a revenue treaty is an invasion of its prerogatives. In any case, the House may significantly affect the application of a treaty by its equal role in enacting legislation to implement the treaty.

Trust Funds—Special accounts in the Treasury that receive earmarked taxes or other kinds of revenue collections, such as user fees, and from which payments are made for special purposes or to recipients who meet the requirements of the trust funds as established by law. Of the more than 150 federal government trust funds, several finance major entitlement programs, such as Social Security, Medicare and retired federal employees' pensions. Others fund infrastructure construction and improvements, such as highways and airports.

Unanimous Consent—Without an objection by any member. A unanimous consent request asks permission, explicitly or implicitly, to set aside one or more rules. Both houses and their committees frequently use such requests to expedite their proceedings.

Uncontrollable Expenditures—A frequently used term for federal expenditures that are mandatory under existing law and therefore cannot be controlled by the president or Congress without a change in the existing law. Uncontrollable expenditures include spending required under entitlement programs and also fixed costs, such as interest on the public debt and outlays to pay for prior-year obligations. In recent years, uncontrollables have accounted for approximately three-quarters of federal spending in each fiscal year.

Unfunded Mandate—Generally, any provision in federal law or regulation that imposes a duty or obligation on a state or local government or private sector entity without providing the necessary funds to comply. The Unfunded Mandates Reform Act of 1995 amended the Congressional Budget Act of 1974 to provide a mechanism for the control of new unfunded mandates.

Union Calendar—A calendar of the House of Representatives for bills and resolutions favorably reported by committees that raise revenue or directly or indirectly appropriate money or property. In addition to appropriation bills, measures that authorize expenditures are also placed on this calendar. The calendar's full title is the Calendar of the Committee of the Whole House on the State of the Union.

Upper Body—A common reference to the Senate, but not used by members of the House.

U.S. Code—Popular title for the United States Code: Containing the General and Permanent Laws of the United States in Force on…. It is a consolidation and partial codification of the general and permanent laws of the United States arranged by subject under 50 titles. The first six titles deal with general or political subjects, the other forty-four with subjects ranging from agriculture to war, alphabetically arranged. A supplement is published after each session of Congress, and the entire Code is revised every six years.

User Fee—A fee charged to users of goods or services provided by the federal government. When Congress levies or authorizes such fees, it determines whether the revenues should go into the general collections of the Treasury or be available for expenditure by the agency that provides the goods or services.

Veto—The president's disapproval of a legislative measure passed by Congress. The president returns the measure to the house in which it originated without his signature but with a veto message stating his objections to it. When Congress is in session, the president must veto a bill within ten days, excluding Sundays, after the president has received it; otherwise it becomes law without his signature. The ten-day clock begins to run at midnight following his receipt of the bill. (See also Committee Veto; Item Veto; Line Item Veto Act of 1996; Override a Veto; Pocket Veto.)

Voice Vote—A method of voting in which members who favor a question answer aye in chorus, after which those opposed answer no in chorus, and the chair decides which position prevails.

Voting—Members vote in three ways on the floor: (1) by shouting "aye" or "no" on voice votes; (2) by standing for or against on division votes; and (3) on recorded votes (including the yeas and nays), by answering "aye" or "no" when their names are called or, in the House, by recording their votes through the electronic voting system.

War Powers Resolution of 1973—An act that requires the president "in every possible instance" to consult Congress before committing U.S. forces to ongoing or imminent hostilities. If the president commits them to a combat situation without congressional consultation, the president must notify Congress within forty-eight hours. Unless Congress declares war or otherwise authorizes the operation to continue, the forces must be withdrawn within sixty or ninety days, depending on certain conditions. No president has ever acknowledged the constitutionality of the resolution.

Well—The sunken, level, open space between members' seats and the podium at the front of each chamber. House members usually address their chamber from their party's lectern in the well on its side of the aisle. Senators usually speak at their assigned desks.

Whip—The majority or minority party member in each house who acts as assistant leader, helps plan and marshal support for party strategies, encourages party discipline and advises his or her leader on how colleagues intend to vote on the floor. In the Senate, the Republican whip's official title is assistant leader.

Yeas and Nays—A vote in which members usually respond "aye" or "no" (despite the official title of the vote) on a question when their names are called in alphabetical order. The Constitution requires the yeas and nays when a demand for it is supported by one-fifth of the members present, and it also requires an automatic yea-and-nay vote on overriding a veto. Senate precedents require the support of at least one-fifth of a quorum, a minimum of eleven members with the present membership of 100.

Congressional Information on the Internet

A huge array of congressional information is available for free at Internet sites operated by the federal government, colleges and universities and commercial firms. The sites offer the full text of bills introduced in the House and Senate, voting records, campaign finance information, transcripts of selected congressional hearings, investigative reports and much more.

THOMAS

The most important site for congressional information is THOMAS (*http://thomas.loc.gov*), which is named for Thomas Jefferson and operated by the Library of Congress. THOMAS' highlight is its databases containing the full text of all bills introduced in Congress since 1989, the full text of the *Congressional Record* since 1989 and the status and summary information for all bills introduced since 1973.

THOMAS also offers special links to bills that have received or are expected to receive floor action during the current week and newsworthy bills that are pending or that have recently been approved. Finally, THOMAS has selected committee reports, answers to frequently asked questions about accessing congressional information, publications titled *How Our Laws Are Made* and *Enactment of a Law* and links to lots of other congressional Web sites.

House of Representatives

The U.S. House of Representatives site (*http://www.house.gov*) offers the schedule of bills, resolutions and other legislative issues the House will consider in the current week. It also has updates about current proceedings on the House floor and a list of the next day's meeting of House committees. Other highlights include a database that helps users identify their representative, a directory of House members and committees, the House ethics manual, links to Web pages maintained by House members and committees, a calendar of congressional primary dates and candidate-filing deadlines for ballot access, the full text of all amendments to the Constitution that have been ratified and those that have been proposed but not ratified and lots of information about Washington, D.C., for visitors.

Another key House site is The Office of the Clerk On-line Information Center (*http://clerkweb.house.gov*), which has records of all roll-call votes taken since 1990. The votes are recorded by bill, so it is a lengthy process to compile a particular representative's voting record. The site also has lists of committee assignments, a telephone directory for members and committees, mailing label templates for members and committees, rules of the current Congress, election statistics from 1920 to the present, biographies of Speakers of the House, biographies of women who have served since 1917 and a virtual tour of the House Chamber.

One of the more interesting House sites is operated by the Subcommittee on Rules and Organization of the House Committee on Rules (*http://www.house.gov/rules/crs_reports. htm*). Its highlight is dozens of Congressional Research Service reports about the legislative process. Some of the available titles include *Legislative Research in Congressional Offices: A Primer, How to Follow Current Federal Legislation and Regulations; Investigative Oversight: An Introduction to the Law, Practice and Procedure of Congressional Inquiry;* and *Presidential Vetoes 1789 – Present: A Summary Overview.*

Senate

At least in the Internet world, the Senate is not as active as the House. Its main Web site (*http://www.senate.gov*) has records of all roll-call votes taken since 1989 (arranged by bill), brief descriptions of all bills and joint resolutions introduced in the Senate during the past week and a calendar of upcoming committee hearings. The site also provides the standing rules of the Senate, a directory of senators and their committee assignments, lists of nominations that the president has submitted to the Senate for approval, links to Web pages operated by senators and committees and a virtual tour of the Senate.

Information about the membership, jurisdiction and rules of each congressional committee is available at the U.S. Government Printing Office site (*http://www.access.gpo.gov/congress/index.html*). It also has transcripts of selected congressional hearings, the full text of selected House and Senate reports and the House and Senate rules manuals.

General Reference

The U.S. General Accounting Office, the investigative arm of Congress, operates a site (*http://www.gao.gov*) that provides the full text of its reports from 1975 to the present. The reports cover a wide range of topics: aviation safety, combating terrorism, counternarcotics efforts in Mexico, defense contracting, electronic warfare, food assistance programs, Gulf War illness, health insurance, illegal aliens, information technology, long-term care, mass transit, Medicare, military readiness, money laundering, national parks, nuclear waste, organ donation and student loan defaults, among others.

The GAO Daybook is an excellent current awareness tool. This electronic mailing list distributes a daily list of reports and testimony released by the GAO. Subscriptions are available by sending an e-mail message to *majordomo@www.gao.gov*, and in the message area typing "subscribe daybook" (without the quotation marks).

Current budget and economic projections are provided at the Congressional Budget Office Web site (*http://www.cbo.gov*). The site also has reports about the economic and budget outlook for the next decade, the president's budget proposals, federal civilian employment, Social Security privatization, tax reform, water use conflicts in the West, marriage and the federal income tax and the role of foreign aid in development, among other topics. Other highlights include monthly budget updates, historical budget data, cost estimates for bills reported by congressional committees and transcripts of congressional testimony by CBO officials.

Campaign Finance

Several Internet sites provide detailed campaign finance data for congressional elections. The official site is operated by the Federal Election Commission (*http://www.fec.gov*), which regulates political spending. The site's highlight is its database of campaign reports filed from May 1996 to the present by House and presidential candidates, political action committees and political party committees. Senate reports are not included because they are filed with the Secretary of the Senate. The reports in the FEC's database are scanned images of paper reports filed with the commission.

The FEC site also has summary financial data for House and Senate candidates in the current election cycle, abstracts of court decisions pertaining to federal election law from 1976 to 1997, a graph showing the number of political action committees in existence each year from 1974 to the present and a directory of national and state agencies that are responsible for releasing information about campaign financing, candidates on the ballot, election results, lobbying and other issues. Another useful feature is a collection of brochures about federal election law, public funding of presidential elections, the ban on contributions by foreign nationals, independent expenditures supporting or opposing a candidate for federal office, contribution limits, filing a complaint, researching public records at the FEC and other topics. Finally, the site provides the FEC's legislative recommendations, its annual report, a report about its first twenty years in existence, the FEC's monthly newsletter, several reports about voter registration, election results for the most recent presidential and congressional elections and campaign guides for corporations and labor organizations, congressional candidates and committees, political party committees and nonconnected committees.

The best online source for campaign finance data is Political Money Line (*http://www.tray.com*). The site's searchable databases provide extensive itemized information about receipts and expenditures by federal candidates and political action committees from 1980 to the present. The data, which are obtained from the FEC, are quite detailed. For example, for candidates contributions can be searched by Zip Code. The site also has lists of the top political action committees in various categories, lists of the top contributors from each state and much more.

Another interesting site is the American University Campaign Finance Website (*http://www1.soc.american.edu/campfin*), which is operated by the American University School of Communication. It provides electronic files from the FEC that have been reformatted in .dbf format so they can be used in database programs such as Paradox, Access and FoxPro. The files contain data on PAC, committee and individual contributions to individual congressional candidates.

More campaign finance data is available from the Center for Responsive Politics (*http://www.opensecrets.org*), a public interest organization. The center provides a list of all "soft money" donations to political parties of $100,000 or more in the current election cycle and data about "leadership" political action committees associated with individual politicians. Other databases at the site provide information about travel expenses that House members received from private sources for attending meetings and other events, activities of registered federal lobbyists and activities of foreign agents who are registered in the United States.

Index